TEXAS GOVERNMENT TODAY

Structures, functions,
political processes

The Dorsey Series in Political Science

Consulting Editor **Samuel C. Patterson** The University of Iowa

TEXAS GOVERNMENT TODAY
Structures, functions, political processes

BERYL E. PETTUS
Sam Houston State University

RANDALL W. BLAND
Southwest Texas State University

Revised Edition 1979

THE DORSEY PRESS
Homewood, Illinois
60430

Irwin-Dorsey Limited
Georgetown, Ontario
L7G 4B3

ISBN 0-256-02199-6
Library of Congress Catalog Card No. 78-70956
Printed in the United States of America

1 2 3 4 5 6 7 8 9 0 ML 6 5 4 3 2 1 0 9

To our professors who most profoundly
shaped our lives:

Clarence A. Berdahl
Paul C. Bartholomew
Lynwood M. Holland
Wilbourn E. Benton
and
Benjamin H. Newcomb

Preface

The revisions in this edition are extensive, although we have been careful not to disturb the basic structure of the book. We are more certain than ever of the need for such a study. Instead of simply a descriptive analysis in a current context, we have tried to discover what is permanent and characteristic of Texas politics, political institutions, and political processes. We have attempted to demonstrate the functional distinctions and consequences of the Texas political system as an entity.

We have strengthened and made more explicit the various themes which run the course of the book: the impact of political culture, consequences of constitutional restrictions, politics of Sunbelt economic development policies, public policy performance in a comparative context, "no party" politics, consequences of aggregation of inputs by interest groups, direct interest group access to political institutions, underdevelopment of the political system, importance of integration of sizable ethnic minorities into the social and economic fabric of Texas, federal government as the chief instrument of change, and, finally, the remarkable stability of the Texas regime structure.

Of primary importance are changes designed to make the text more interesting and readable. We believe that the end product is a superior teaching and learning instrument. In this Revised Edition, the language has been simplified, the format of the book has been made more attractive, summary points have been added at the end of each chapter, and major conclusions and headings stand out more clearly. More than twice as many illustrations, graphs, charts, figures, and maps are included. Also, new or additional information has been added on the systems model, political culture, interest groups, illegal aliens, the migrant farmworker force, major state programs (education, welfare, highways), school district governments, local finance, major state administrative officials, public policy performance, local property taxation, the urban condition today, and the economic development strategies of Texas' dominant social and economic elites.

Several persons have made substantial contributions to this study. We wish to express our gratitude and appreciation, in particular, to our contributing authors, Preston Lee Lawrence (Chapter Two) and Alfred Burke Sullivan (Chapter Five and the "interest group" section of Chapter Three). Special thanks go also to colleagues whose contributions carry over in this Revised Edition: John W. Holcombe, Edwin S. Davis, Dan Farlow, Jim Chapman, Richard D. Feld, Sam W. Hawkins, and James Hugh Broussard. Most of these individuals contributed also to our revision efforts. In addition, we would like to thank the people who helped us with this edition, especially Robert Biles and Richard Copeland; and our reviewers, Wendell Bedichek, Marijo Coleman, R. Michael Stevens, and the Dorsey Press's consulting editor in political science, Samuel C. Patterson.

In the main, responsibility for this edition of *Texas Government Today* rests with the authors, including any errors of fact or judgment. We would like to state our appreciation for use of library facilities at our academic institutions and for the generous assistance of many librarians, including Grace Standley and Brenda Shelton Olds.

Special thanks go to our wives, Joan Howard Pettus and Barbara Baca Bland, for the special quality of our relationships which helped to compensate for loss of time spent with them.

March 1979   **Beryl E. Pettus**
                                                                Randall W. Bland

Contents

List of tables and figures

CHAPTER ONE
Environments of the political system

CHAPTER TWO
Politics of ethnic minorities

CHAPTER THREE
Parties, elections, and interest groups

CHAPTER FOUR
The legislature at work

CHAPTER SIX
State administration

CHAPTER SEVEN
The courts, criminal justice, and civil liberties

CHAPTER EIGHT
Metropolitan and rural problems: The intergovernmental context

CHAPTER NINE
Local governments

CHAPTER TEN
Public finance, public programs, and politics of the budgetary process

CHAPTER ONE

Environments of the political system

Should we venture out beyond the narrow confines of habitual behavior, we will carry with us our traditional values—for what else will guide us?

SAM BASS WARNER, JR.*

In this textbook we attempt to capture the tone and spirit, as well as the patterns and policies, of Texas government and politics today. Certainly, we draw from the rich tradition and culture to explain institutions, attitudes, and political behavior. Our historic Constitution of 1876, in every article and phrase, reflects the glorious, if troubled, history of Texas from earliest times, but especially the reaction of contemporary Texans to the Civil War, Reconstruction, and wrenching social change. And many of the amendments to that document bear testimony to great social, economic, and political change since 1876.

If Texas and Texans strike wonder, and even bewilderment, in the minds of many Americans, it is for our legendary flamboyance as much in politics as in business. For the two go together as if they were made for each other. Texas is in a period of great economic development, and politics and government dance to the tune of big money and big deals.

Flamboyance in business and politics is, of course, part of a larger distinctive quality of Texans, a deeply felt pride and chauvinism which seem very strange to many Americans. Texans perceive themselves as strong, independent, and right, and they resent criticism, particularly from outsiders. "I'm a plain old 'pore' Texan but a thoroughbred, and I resent any damyankee coming in and telling us what is right or wrong with Texas!" exclaimed one letter writer in reaction to a book which was felt to be too heavy-handed in its treatment of Texas' Sharpstown scandals.[1]

Attitudes also commonly manifest themselves as "antifederal, antisocial welfare, antitax radicalism," all tied in with the dominant business values.[2] Large and populous, booming, sharply prideful of a rich heritage,

* *The Urban Wilderness* (New York: Harper & Row, Pubs., 1972), pp. 267–68.

and narrowly parochial in outlook, Texas seems incessantly in love with its myths and images of gushers, Cadillacs, and invincible football teams.

Dominant attitudes find expression in other institutions besides government. But government seems particularly vulnerable to their appeal, from our tenacious attachment to our outdated, restrictive Constitution to the fewer than 170 days every two years that the legislature is privileged to meet and legislate. Not only in the Constitution and political structures but in processes and policies do the historic, dominant values find expression.

But there are other, modernizing influences at work as well. And we will see the parts as well as the whole of political and governmental life in Texas. To give a sufficiently meaningful and useful introduction to Texas government and politics today is our prime desire.

THE POLITICAL SYSTEM

Government and politics do not exist alone, and they do not, of course, operate in a vacuum. For government itself is a subsystem, that is, one part of a larger system of interconnected and interdependent parts. Government cannot be disconnected from the whole. Its strengths and virtues, its weaknesses and defects, are a reflection of the whole of society, and its actions and spirit infect us all.

In political science today, we commonly use the systems model to:

1. Convey the idea of government as part of a larger system.
2. Show in a simplistic, abstract way the linkages or connections which exist among the various parts.
3. See governmental processes and actions in a larger, meaningful context.
4. Examine all essential elements in order to develop explanations about why government operates and performs the way it does.
5. Study policy results in relation to resources, structures, and operations of the political system.

The interconnected components of the larger system of which Texas government is a part we label the physical, social, cultural, economic, and demographic *environments* of government and politics. These elements we can briefly, if somewhat simplistically, identify and describe as follows:

Physical environment: topographical, physical characteristics (rivers, harbors, plains, mountains, land area, space), climate, and resources (water, oil, gas, coal, timber, soil, minerals, and others).

Social environment: social groups and institutions, such as families, associations, groups, movements, churches, corporations, universities, tradition, and culture.

Political cultural environment: that part of culture which is political—a web of deep-seated traditional attitudes, beliefs, ideals, myths, and symbols about the place, role, and efficacy of government and politics in our lives.

Economic environment: "private enterprise" institutions and activities, as in banking, insurance, oil exploration, manufacturing, retailing, services, transportation, mining, and agriculture.

Demographic environment: the distribution and density of Texans in the land area and local jurisdictions subject to the authority of the government of Texas.

These environmental components in their existence, influence, and functions generate short-term and long-term effects. They affect each other. For example, technology in the economic system supplies the knowledge and wherewithal to develop physical resources and overcome physical barriers. And they affect government. Although persons inside government and politics affect each other, the principal effects on government come from *environmental influences* generated by the activities and interests of people in the various families, associations, groups, and institutions which form the "external," larger environment of government and politics. See Figure 1–1.

These environmental influences come to bear directly on legislators, judges, and executives through what they have learned about society and its values and norms. We can conceptualize this effect and other effects as *inputs* into the political system. These inputs are transmitted by and through major groups and institutions which, on occasion or more frequently, operate politically, that is, to influence selection of government personnel and/or content of public policy decisions. Expectations, explicit demands, supports (both for measures and for the political system),

FIGURE 1–1

The systems model

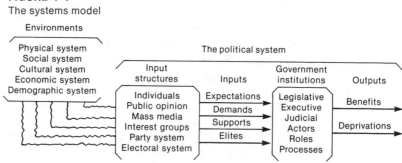

and political elites, who make political decisions, are the classes of inputs.

These elites are government offcials and other political actors, such as lobbyists, party officials, and others, who are intimately connected, usually day-to-day, with political decision making. The elites preside over the governmental institutions and process demands and supports. Decisions made or ratified in the governing process are viewed as the *outputs* of the political system. They form the basis of various governmental programs to regulate, allocate resources, extract resources, and dispense symbolic rewards of government. These government decisions and programs themselves evoke reactions, or they alter conditions, which evoke responses. These responses and reactions, as well as influences from the altered conditions, may generate information and demands which are fed back into the political system for adjustments or new decisions and government programs. These actions and influences are called *feedback effect* (not shown in Figure 1–1).

Using the systems model, we turn now to an examination of some of the significant ways in which various environments affect the inputs, structures, and processes of government and help to determine the primary characteristics, functional aspects (consequences), and policy performance of the political system. By *policy performance* we mean (1) how well the system represents people to process their demands and (2) the adequacy of government programs in terms of needs of people as revealed by basic environmental conditions, resources, and problems in Texas.

The first objective is to judge the quality of input structures and of the inputs themselves and the ability of the political system to receive and process demands from all population groups and segments. The second objective is to judge the adequacy of government regulations, services, and programs against their ostensible purposes and apparent needs. The total resources used and the equitable allocation of services and programs are further considerations in government's performance. As an example, if we find that demands of some Texans are not transmitted to government, for one reason or another, then we would expect low, rather inadequate levels of services to those groups or segments of the population as compared with government benefits enjoyed by other Texans.[3] In this example, also, we see the useful aspects of the systems model which were stated earlier.

In the following sections, we deal with the *impacts* of each environment on the Texas political system. Because of space restrictions, what we have to say is necessarily brief, sketchy, and only suggestive. It should be remembered that each component environment is intermingled with every other component so that the complexity of this great environmental system almost defies description.

POLITICAL CULTURE AND THE SOCIAL ENVIRONMENT

Political culture

By political culture, we mean a set of common, deep-seated traditional attitudes, beliefs, and ideals—along with a bundle of sentiments, myths, and symbols—about government and politics. Political culture, because it involves mental images, beliefs, and emotional commitments about the place and efficacy of governments in our lives, colors our perceptions and views of political happenings and our expectations about government actions. What we believe about government and what we expect from political activity tend to determine our own participation in politics. If we believe that government is an important agency, that political activity is proper, that participation does make an important difference, and that we will be gratified in some way, we will probably set aside time and other resources and develop our political skills. Thus, these factors govern the types and quality of interactions between us and our political leaders. They also shape the performance of government. A chain connects our beliefs and perceptions to what government actually does.

What of the politically unskilled, apathetic, inactive persons? Their rationalizations about their inability and unwillingness to participate also spring from political culture. Unable to cope with the real world of politics and government, they must substitute myths and symbols for an adequate understanding of the political system and a realistic appraisal of its actors. So *whatever the quality* of our images, perceptions, beliefs, and emotional attachments, the political culture imparts meaning and gives substantial structure to the political system for everyone.[4]

Texas political culture

Professor Daniel J. Elazar has found that the American political culture is a synthesis of different historic influences, with various regional variations which stamp each of the American states with a politics of distinctive styles and tones. The Texas subculture Elazar labels as *traditionalistic-individualistic* (TI) in its orientations.[5] We need not be concerned here with the other classifications found in the American states.

The Texas subculture flowed historically by emigration from the Old South. As it was carried across this vast state, it was progressively diluted by distance, time, social change, physical and economic environments, and by individualistic values stemming from European immigration. This process of diffusion of the traditionalistic elements of the Old South culture and the melding of different individualistic values produced our TI cultural pattern. See Table 1–1, which lists the basic political assumptions

TABLE 1–1
Assumptions of traditionalistic and individualistic subcultures

Political elements	As viewed in the traditionalistic subculture	As viewed in the individualistic subculture
Government	The realm of the well-born and socially prominent to maintain existing hierarchical social order—a social purpose	A marketplace for distribution of favors and rewards to private groups—a utilitarian, economic purpose
Politics	The realm of the few who expect to gain personally but not necessarily monitarily; personalistic politics by a small, self-perpetuating elite who inherit their "right" and responsibility to politics and government	The province of professionals; a dirty, if necessary, business run for competition for talent and rewards; access to marketplace is encouraged by parties, which are organizations that facilitate competition for winning office and tangible, economic rewards
Corruption	Violation of a "trust" of the right to rule because it strikes at the root of the political system	A little corruption is expected as a "surcharge" for services rendered by government to economic groups
Innovation	Conservative and custodial except for policies which serve the social group; reluctance to initiate or open up the system to others	Unwillingness to initiate new programs unless connected with economic development goals

Source: Prepared from pp. 93–102 in *American Federalism: A View From the States* by Daniel Elazar (TYC). Copyright © 1972 by Harper & Row, Publishers, Inc. Reprinted by permission of the publisher.

of the traditionalistic subculture and the individualistic subculture out of which the Texas TI amalgam emerged. Although some contradictions were created, in the main, however, *a new cultural synthesis* developed. From our distinctive historical experience, the size of our territory, our peculiar economic conditions, and other determinants was created a high degree of cultural unity, much insularity, and an extremely stable political system.

This cultural milieu has affected the nature of our governmental structures, processes, and policies, and it has set distinctive styles of politics and political activity. In time, we have fashioned a complex system of distinctive political-system characteristics which reflect both Old South traditional and newer individualistic values and experiences.[6] They are also, in some respects, distinctively Texan.

Texas political system characteristics

Elitism Traditionalistic and individualistic subcultures have both worked in Texas to produce strong elitist tendencies. The traditionalistic strain emphasizes an elite based upon social ties and family connections, while the individualistic tends to promote an elitism based on economic activity and gain. Thus, governments are viewed as having limited purposes and are arranged to process a small range of demands (principally those of elites.) Social and economic developments, including concentrating great wealth in the hands of a few, work along with cultural values to place and keep effective political power in the hands of a social and economic establishment.

The dominant elite is characterized more in terms of an *institutionalized set of values* than as a closed, self-perpetuating elite. The Texas establishment, as James Conaway states, is a loose but effective "*subrosa* accord established among like-minded men, the effects of which are felt with some financial encouragement here, some legal or political expertise there, until the society reflects the values of its unseen plutocracy."[7] This dominant economic elitism values the distribution of government goods, services, grants, and incentives but not the burden of regulations or the concerns and burdens of social welfare and social service programs. The establishment is a "corporate welfare community" which "grew out of the New Deal, preserving the reliance of business upon government, but dispensing with the [New Deal's] social concern."[8]

Personalism, factionalism, and class Personalistic, elitist, and factional politics always appear in a political system in the absence of a viable competitive party system. Handed down to Texas in the historic baggage of the traditionalistic subculture is one-partyism, a relatively non-competitive electoral and legislative arrangement, which tends to produce "an issueless politics," focusing on cults of personality and other extraneous "nonissues."[9]

But Texas politics is more than a throwback to an earlier cultural period.[10] To the ingredients of (1) individualistic values and (2) traditional structures, including one-partyism, is added a third, volatile element (3) a measure of class conflict, involving a relatively high level of strife between "haves" and "have-nots."[11] In Texas, the traditionalistic pattern of noncompetitive, issueless politics, combined with the babble of personalistic and demagogic appeals, is broken frequently by candidate conflict on public issues drawn solidly on class and ideological lines. A liberal tradition, which traces back through a strong Populist movement,[12] serves to challenge, on occasion, the dominant individualistic assumptions of conservative elites. Since the New Deal era, the liberals have coalesced around *national* standards, leadership, and issues of the Democratic party. Texas' dominant conservatives, defenders of traditionalism, emphasize, on the other hand, an *insular* political system, which continues to serve their individualistic, elitist, and conservative approaches to government and economics.

See Figure 1–2 for an expression of class politics in voting patterns. We see that in the Democratic primary, liberal Democratic Senator Ralph W. Yarborough received the votes disproportionately of low socioeconomic status (SES) persons, as judged by their low income, education, and vocational status. On the other hand, Lloyd Bentsen, Yarborough's successful conservative Democratic challenger, drew disproportionately from high SES persons. Note that the loyal Democratic low SES Yarborough voters switched to Bentsen in the November general election, while Republican George Bush drew disproportionately from the erstwhile Bentsen supporters, the high SES groups. "Bentsen once again demonstrated the classic and ironical ability of conservative Texas Democrats to appeal to the affluent whites in the primary and then to rally the New Deal coalition against a Republican in the general election."[13]

Party competition has been shunned in traditionalistic fashion, and most voters, to 1978, at least, worked to keep the state and local governments in Texas in conservative Democratic officeholders. The governmental system, far from being benevolent in the southern tradition, often appears crudely self-serving and corrupt because of the play of dominant economic interests in noncompetitive elections and governmental processes. In the Texas TI subculture, competition is valued in business and in a scramble for government favors, but competitive parties and processes pose a danger to establishment dominance.

Conservative cohesion   A high degree of unity of purpose of conservatives, based on their individualistic values, maintains control of state government in conservative hands. Politically effective measures, such as:

Building strong conservative political leadership.

Restraining political participation of the masses.[14]

Encouraging voting of all conservatives (regardless of party) in the Democratic primaries.

Keeping up a drumfire of propaganda against party, particularly of the national Democratic party.

Isolating a large and active liberal Democratic party faction.

have strengthened control of the Texas political system. Conservative political leadership plays custodial and noninnovative roles in government, while extolling growth, competition, innovation, initiative, and strength in the largely privately run economy.

Economic development goals   In only one policy area, economic development, does Texas government claim strong, innovative policies. In a

10

FIGURE 1–2

Class and voting in Texas Democratic primaries and general elections*

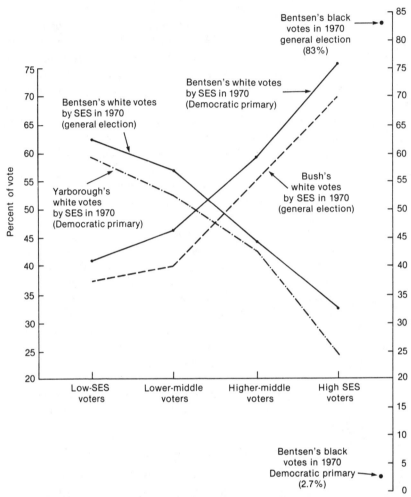

* Voter preferences by SES for Lloyd M. Bentsen, Jr., conservative Democrat, over Ralph W. Yarborough, liberal Democratic incumbent, and voter preferences by SES for Lloyd M. Bentsen, Jr., conservative Democrat, over George Bush, Republican, in the 1970 Democratic primary and the 1970 general election—voters in Houston, Fort Worth, and Waco, Texas.

Source: Prepared from data in Numan V. Bartley and Hugh D. Graham, *Southern Politics and the Second Reconstruction* (Baltimore: Johns Hopkins University Press, 1975), p. 161.

study done on behalf of the Illinois Manufacturers' Association, Texas obtained the "best composite score" among the 50 states on factors which included no income taxes, low existent tax burden, low public debt, antilabor legislation, low welfare outlays, low government payrolls, and low number of government units per 1,000 population.[15] "Texas spends its available revenues on programs which benefit the state and its people through business and economic stimulation," trumpets Bob Bullock, Comptroller of Public Accounts.[16]

Amidst enormous resources and opportunities for private wealth, the value is promoted that community intervention in private activities should be limited to economic development objectives. This cultural attitude favors, of course, business corporations and other private institutions and associational groups supportive of the political orthodoxy. As examples, state utilities, which are granted public franchises and monopolies, were totally exempted until 1975 from a policy of state regulation, and an extreme set of antiunion and antilabor statutes constrain organized labor. Business enterprises are looked upon as benevolent activities run by the "best people," while countervailing efforts of individuals to organize themselves for greater economic protection are hailed as destructive of a "right to work."[17] "The absence of a corporation income tax shows businesses that the people and the Legislature of Texas are supportive of business development," affirms Texas' chief tax collector.[18]

Interplay of race and social and political conservatism Traditionalistic and individualistic subcultures in Texas find an affinity of sentiments and merge also on race and social and political conservatism.[19] Traditional elements in East Texas still raise racial issues when they think the social system is threatened. And they make common cause with extreme individualists who also see dangers lurking in breaks with tradition. In the 1968 presidential election, for example, the major strength of southern third party presidential candidate George C. Wallace was in East Texas, as expected, and among lower-middle class neighborhoods and highly affluent subdivisions in West Texas.[20]

Explosive racial issues, such as busing of students, provoke emotional responses from many whites regardless of socioeconomic station. These and other emotionally divisive *social issues,* such as "law and order," "right to work," "socialism," "gun control," "women's lib," and "abortion," while legitimate bases for discussion, are often raised cynically by individualistic candidates against opponents who are perceived as "soft" on newer, modernizing issues and on governmental intervention in the economy. Candidates suspected of being for regulation of business, protection of union labor, higher taxes, larger spending, and public welfare are particularly vulnerable. Thus, in all of Texas a "more dominant social conservatism" now thrives over a "game but historically outweighted populism."[21] Even in rural East Texas, where populism only recently thrived, the play on conservative social sentiments has eroded this section as a source of progressive candidates and policies.[22]

Absence of mass linkages In practice, the values and attitudes which count in the marketplace in any society are those of an interested, attentive, resourceful, and skilled population. Dominant sentiments may emanate from the top of the social system. Usually, however, mass communications linkages to the people offer opportunities for popular acquiescence in public policies, if not also serving as conduits for representation and demands in the political system. But some of Texas' traditional *input structures* are defective, and all are not utilized by very many people. Texas' parties are noncompetitive, most contests are decided in the issueless politics of the primaries, and most people are unskilled or unconcerned. Issues are raised and demands processed by a very small portion of the population.

Several interlocking factors in the Texas political system discourage political participation as an end in itself:[23]

An historic pattern of restricted access points to decision-making arenas, strengthened by force of habit and political culture.

The political culture, with negative attitudes toward the appropriateness and utility of political participation.

Inequitable distribution among the population of resources for participation, such as money, social status, free time, and influence in institutions of socialization (such as schools, churches, clubs, and the like).

A pattern of complex externalities which discourage participation, including relatively underdeveloped electoral and party systems and a huge, powerful array of economic interests in all economic sectors.

Interest group politics   In the presence of the above factors, it is probable that the chief agents of inputs and of conversion of political demands to public policy in the Texas political system are the dominant economic interest groups.[24] Politics abhors a vacuum. The true role of the dominant interests in relation to the masses of people may be the use of the public media (mass communications) and the more basic socialization agents (schools, churches, civic clubs, chambers of commerce) to establish and reinforce cultural values more harmonious with the political attitudes and myths of the elites who join and manage the pressure groups. Certainly, these elitist organizational linkages to socialization processes exist, and they can be sensitive receptors of the dominant political, social, and economic philosophy. By generating from the top a mass base of values and myths supportive of the regime and its operations, interest group politics can seem to dance to the tune of democratic values.[25]

Strength of cultural impact?

The above characteristics are the hallmarks of a firmly traditionalistic political system in a more modern social and economic setting. The cumulative policy impact of this relatively "closed" political system run by conservative, noninnovative[26] elites, is extremely poor performance in most public service areas.

As seen in Table 1–2, Texas spends *below the average of the 50 states* in all of six basic policy areas, except in higher education where Texas ranks 28th among the states. The ranking of Texas in all six major areas combined is 34th among the states. The most poorly supported area, true to Texas' TI political culture, is public welfare. About 70 percent of what Texas spends annually in welfare is federal money through grants in aid. Thus, it can be said that Texas would not have a viable program of public welfare without federal governmental aid and requirements.

Texas supports only *basic services,* and these poorly. Overall support of the six areas (which account for more than 80 percent of state-local spending annually) is only 81.2 percent of the U.S. average. If this figure is low, Texas' support of all other public policy areas is only 64.6 percent of the average spent by the American states, giving Texas a rank of 46 among the states! The concept of political culture helps to account for a level of government services in Texas which is much lower than one would expect from viewing the base of economic resources and the level of economic development. In fact, the American regions (and the states which comprise them) are drawing together in economic resources. See Figure 1–3.

Most Texans are ill served by both political and economic systems. Poverty is rampant among the aged, blacks, children, Hispanics, and families headed by women. Even among all 12.4 million Texans, one of six is below the poverty level, with Texas having 10 percent of all the country's poor![27] Economic deprivation, of course, is associated with social problems, such as breakup of the nuclear family, poor health, unemployment, and poor housing. Poverty is also a *political* problem, reflecting

TABLE 1–2
Per capita spending in Texas by state and local governments in major policy areas, as percent of average among the 50 states, and Texas' rank among the American states

Policy area	Percent of U.S. average	Texas' rank
Higher education	100.1	28
Highways and streets	94.3	37
Local schools	86.5	37
Health and hospitals	78.4	28
Police protection	71.8	29
Public welfare	56.3	42
Average	81.2	34
All other areas	64.6	46

Source: Prepared from data in Texas Research League, *Texas State and Local Government: A Financial Handbook* (Austin: Texas Research League, February 1977), p. 6.

FIGURE 1–3

Closing the regional income gap, 1929–1974

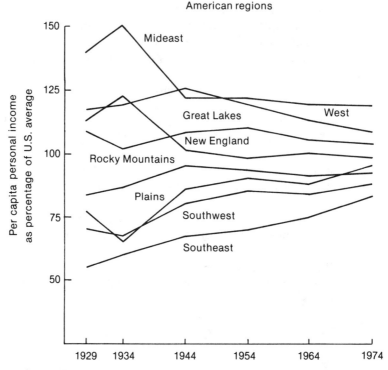

American regions

Source: *Intergovernmental Perspective,* 1, no. 1 (Fall 1975): 18.

lack of political skills, political resources, and status in the political community. Until very recently, these conditions were reflected in elitist constitutional and statutory bars to acquiring political skills.[28] In the area of voting rights, "Historically, Texas election laws have been barriers to public access to the political system."[29] Texas inequities have been at issue in most landmark election law cases before the United States Supreme Court. Texas ranks 44th on a composite index of state program innovation, an average of 46th in voting in the last several presidential elections, and 40th in income distributional equality.

Besides the aspect of deprivations placed upon political participation through the input structure, another facet of poor policy performance is the placement of constraints upon the institutions of government. These serious limitations, which hamper if not cripple government, are discussed later in this chapter (in the section on the Texas Constitution) and throughout this textbook. This policy of restraints on government seem by now to jibe perfectly well with what we know to be dominant values and sentiments of the poltical culture—about what Texans believe government should be permitted to do, what government is capable of doing for people, who should participate in government, how important participation is in public affairs as compared with private enterprise, the "dirty" and "corrupt" nature of politics, and suspicion of the legislature.

The concept of political culture is not intended to be a fine honed tool for predicting behavior in particular individuals or in social classes of persons. "Political culture is related to the *frequency* and *probability* of various kinds of political behavior and not to their rigid determination."[30] The concept is valuable in that it allows us to see and understand the basic congruence of our current public institutions and institutional and individual political behavior with our underlying historic attitudes, habits of thought, beliefs, and myths. Institutional and policy consequences flow easily and congruently from the common values of the political culture. If, as Kenneth Newton says, "a strong sentiment . . . holds that private institutions are both more efficient and somehow morally superior to public ones, . . . there is greater reliance on private bodies to supply services."[31] Further, the public policy domain is much smaller than in political systems in which public institutions and public policy solutions are valued and sought. This inevitable connection among (1) cultural beliefs, values, and sentiments; (2) the institutional arrangements of society; and (3) public policy outcomes is portrayed in Figure 1–4.

The political culture of a state is not static. Urbanization, among other dynamic forces, seems to be having a particularly strong impact on social values and lifestyles. But so far, these changes have not been reflected

FIGURE 1–4
Illustrating linkages among cultural values, the public and private institutional framework, and public policy outcomes, with feedback results

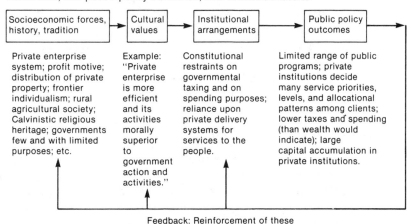

Socioeconomic forces, history, tradition	Cultural values	Institutional arrangements	Public policy outcomes
Private enterprise system; profit motive; distribution of private property; frontier individualism; rural agricultural society; Calvinistic religious heritage; governments few and with limited purposes; etc.	Example: "Private enterprise is more efficient and its activities morally superior to government action and activities."	Constitutional restraints on governmental taxing and on spending purposes; reliance upon private delivery systems for services to the people.	Limited range of public programs; private institutions decide many service priorities, levels, and allocational patterns among clients; lower taxes and spending (than wealth would indicate); large capital accumulation in private institutions.

Feedback: Reinforcement of these patterns as long as the political culture remains essentially the same.

greatly in the public structures, processes, and policies in Texas. For some reason, liberal lifestyles, mass communications, and other forces produce conservatism and social unconcern.

"... Long live the establishment"

Recent events have had an unusually unsettling effect on the marriage of convenience between the Texas establishment and the Democratic party. In 1968 and 1972 the governorship went to second choices. Both Preston Smith and Dolph Briscoe were "weak" governors, and neither kicked over party traces, even with Senator George McGovern on the ticket. Further, loyalist liberals and moderates captured the state Democratic committee.

When Attorney General John Hill upset Governor Briscoe in the 1978 primary, establishment figures apparently viewed Hill as "too liberal" and "unreliable." No doubt the most progressive Democratic nominee in 30 years, Hill was not loath to work with liberals and moderates in the party. Significantly, "almost 100 influential business and professional leaders in the Houston establishment" only reluctantly endorsed Hill four days before the general election.[32]

Republican ranks have been greatly augmented, and Briscoe barely nosed out the Republican in 1972. Emigration of thousands of Republicans to Texas' large metropolitan areas, plus low turnout and popular disorientation in 1978, permitted money, organization, media blitz, and dedicated, zealous Republican activism to work an upset.

Bill Clements is governor and the establishment likes his conservatism. Conservatives have worked together for years in Democratic primaries, gubernatorial patronage, and policy priorities. If Clements' conservatism does not prove too shrill and extreme, the establishment may take on a permanently Republican coloration in state politics, as it has for decades in presidential politics. The greatest unknown—and risk for them—is competition in Democratic primaries and perhaps subsequently in general elections. Certainly, conservatives will maintain their great hold on Texas institutions for the immediate future and claim credit in economic payoffs. But their manipulative tasks will become much more difficult.

PHYSICAL AND ECONOMIC ENVIRONMENTS

The policies of government which are generated by physical and economic characteristics of Texas include highway building programs, airport construction, air traffic regulations, weather forecasting, water acquisition facilities, harbor dredging, agricultural services, oil and gas proration, and taxation policies. While the physical environment presents barriers—distance, depth, elevation, temperature, and shortages, it also offers natural resources which are utilized by the economic system—arable land, water, petroleum, natural gas, metals, fisheries, timber, and water transportation. Since World War II, Texas has been undergoing a rapid process of industrialization, business growth, urbanization, and technological development which together have greatly changed the economic system and altered the social interactions and lifestyles of millions of Texans. The goals of economic development have been preeminently the goals of society. Governments, state and local, have been called upon to serve in positive ways the extensive economic objectives.

By all business indicators, marked success has been achieved. Forty-four percent of insurance corporations are home-based in Texas. Fifty-seven percent of the nation's petrochemical industry is found on our Gulf Coast. With 1,238 banking corporations, Texas ranks first among the states in the number of commercial banks. In agriculture, Texas abounds in cattle companies, timber enterprises, cotton production businesses, and other agribusiness, ranking second or third among the states in cash receipts from livestock and crops. Oil refining is still Texas' greatest industry, as measured by value of products, but consumer goods and machinery industries are growing more rapidly as Texas enters a higher technological stage.[33]

Positive government in economic development

Government in the traditionalistic-individualistic subculture ordinarily occupies a largely secondary and nonpositive role. But it has not been hesitant to lend in Texas, in a highly positive fashion, its authority and other resources to overcome limitations of the physical environment and build the infrastructure of a modernized, highly technological private enterprise system. As is true in other societies undergoing economic development, economic development has had the highest priority. Timber, oil, gas, land, and metals, all mainly in private hands, have been utilized and exploited under government subsidies, protection, nonregulation, transportation facilities, taxation policies, and other benefits.

We are called farsighted if we acquiesce in highly expensive public and private plans to alter radically the physical environment of rivers, harbors, streams, and reservoirs and overcome mountains, distance, and depth. In 1968, when the annual budget of Texas state government was $2.3 billions, the state's establishment attempted to obtain voter approval of a $3.5 billions bond issue amendment to the Constitution for a Texas Water Plan to benefit principally agribusiness on the High Plains.[34] The latest plan involves an astronomically expensive project of canals, rivers, ditches, reservoirs, and pump stations to import and transport water from Northeast Arkansas to West Texas.[35] On the other hand, social programs are called visionary and labeled as "wild spending schemes" too expensive for the economic system to bear. Federal grants-in-aid heavily support most of the state's social programs, except in education. Thus, a policy bias exists in Texas about what programs are worthy of large state and local support.

A development politics biases state programs in another way. Development policies emphasize physical aspects—buildings, bridges, streets, highways, coal slurry pipelines, communications links, and the like, all of which are quite necessary in a modern economic system. In physical matters, the efficiency, expertise, business, banking, managerial, and engineering skills of private economic elites can be brought to bear. Underlying social problems of illiteracy, racial discrimination, health and medical problems, crime, and poverty are much less susceptible to solutions from these skills.[36]

Results of this programmatic bias include noninnovation in social programs, a lagging behind front-running states by decades, and a lack of many services found in other states. "Texas state government has yet to assume some important functions . . . such as housing, urban renewal, and mass transportation."[37] To this list can be added land-use controls, minimum wage enforcement, occupational health and safety standards, and others. Recently enacted farsighted legislation includes energy resources policies, regulation of public utilities, and strip-mining standards.

Resource starvation of governments

State government and local governments, particularly in metropolitan areas, exist in the midst of evidence of near boundless private wealth, while being literally starved for financial and other resources to meet minimal needs (for water, police protection, sewers, garbage pickup, clean air, mass transportation) of their people and the ever enlarging demands of business and industry. With an abundance of corporations, an index of income inequality which places Texas in the front rank, and grinding poverty of one-sixth of its people, Texas has neither a corporate income tax nor a tax on individual incomes. Besides money, governments also suffer from a lack of formal legal and constitutional authority, a shortage of leadership, and a difficulty of building political input structures for establishing broad-based inputs and supports for leadership, innovation, and services.

Political underdevelopment in the midst of modernization

Economic indicators, technology, educational levels, social changes, and demographic indicators all describe a modern society. But certain political changes which usually accompany economic and social development have not kept pace. Lack of party competition, unskilled and unconcerned potential electorates, low rates of political participation, and extremely low governmental outlays for social programs and education all characterize the political system. Myths, habit, political strategy, and feelings generated by conflict and tradition serve to retard political modernization.

Economic development, conservatives believe, is a direct result of public policies which fall under two headings:

Expansionary fiscal policies—low tax rates, no income taxes, "self-regulation" of financial institutions, dependence upon "broad-based" taxes, unequal property tax rates at local levels which produce intrastate tax havens for light industry, no stamp tax on real property transactions, low governmental budgets, and "pay-as-you-go" appropriations.

Exploitation, rather than conservation, of natural and human resources —little regulation of industry, structuring state administration under "citizen boards" and commissions, "right to work" and other policies designed to keep wages low and inhibit union strength in collective bargaining, absence of land-use controls, lack of policies designed to change radically the abundance of cheap labor sources found in ethnic minorities and poor whites, and policies lending the help and support of government to general development goals.

Although the strength of the causal effect of these fiscal policies and exploitive programs on economic growth rates in Texas has not been established empirically, an article of *faith* among conservatives, both Democratic and Republican, is that conservative unity and solidarity is good for Texas. Strategies are regularly devised to keep all conservatives, regardless of their national party preferences, voting in the Democratic primaries in order that conservatives will continue in office. Evidence points to habit as powerful as strategy.

If internal conservative solidarity in state politics has been unbroken since the advent of the New Deal, the conservative establishment feels threatened from the outside by Washington. Policies of the national government, whether under Republicans or Democrats, are neither so inflationary nor exploitive as those established over generations by conservative Democratic regimes in Texas. This difference in policy orientation of national and state regimes accounts for much of the solidarity among Texas conservatives, as well as national-state conflict, along with the strident battle cry of "states' rights."

Additional elements of the conservative strategem to reduce political risks is to keep a strong conservative Democratic congressional delegation and to practice, or threaten to practice, "presidential Republicanism" by voting for Republican presidential candidates. Although habit underlies the voting of many Texans in Democratic primaries, among conservative establishmentarians the felt necessity of protecting "Texas' peculiar institutions" and values may account, more than habit, for the incomplete tickets of Republican candidates for public office at state and local levels. Stresses are increasing so that the political juggling act is becoming more difficult under the impact of social changes which have accompanied economic development in Texas.

DEMOGRAPHIC ENVIRONMENT

The distribution of Texas' 12.4 million people over the land area of Texas and the resulting densities of population are important dimensions of the demographic environment. These aspects affect the total number of governments, growth in size of governments, political behavior and demands, availability of public services, and political socialization patterns, not to mention social and economic patterns.

Texas is a geographic area larger than New England and the Middle Atlantic states combined. While its population once was rural, sparse, and fairly evenly distributed, massive population shifts and growth have been experienced, particularly during the past two generations. In 1940 Texas was 54.6 percent rural. Today, Texas is less than 20 percent rural (see Table 1–3), and the population has doubled.

Census Bureau terms

The Census Bureau uses and defines several terms to distinguish the extent of population concentration and density, as follows:

An *urbanized area*—contains a city (or twin cities) of at least 50,000 persons, plus surrounding territory, whether incorporated into cities or not, of certain population density (persons per square mile).

Urban population—all persons who live in urbanized areas and in places (usually incorporated towns, cities, or villages) having 2,500 or more inhabitants.

TABLE 1–3
Changing rural-urban balance: Texas and the nation

	Rural population		Urban population	
Year	Texas	Nation	Texas	Nation
1940	54.6%	37.0%	45.4%	63.0%
1950	37.3	36.0	62.7	64.0
1960	25.0	30.1	75.0	69.9
1970	20.3	26.5	79.7	73.5

Source: U.S. Bureau of the Census, *Census of Population: 1970,* Vol. 1, *Characteristics of the Population,* Part 1, *United States Summary,* Sections 1 and 2 (Washington, D.C.: U.S. Government Printing Office, 1973).

Rural population—all other persons not classified as urban population. (Rural population is divided into two subclasses: farm and nonfarm population.)

Standard metropolitan statistical area (SMSA)—an area consisting of one or more counties containing at least one central city (or contiguous twin cities, such as Bryan and College Station) of 50,000 or more population. (SMSAs are named for their core city or cities.)

Standard consolidated statistical area (SCSA)—two or more SMSAs. (The Houston-Galveston SCSA, one of only 13 nationally, is the only SCSA in Texas.)

Table 1–4 gives the breakdown of Texas population in 1970 in the various census classifications with percentages. Note that urban population and rural population encompass the total population, the other designations being subclasses of urban population and rural population.

Metropolitan areas in Texas

Texas has more metropolitan areas than any other state. And even more striking than the urban percentage of Texas population (79.7 percent) is the proportion of Texans who live in the state's 25 metropolitan areas (76.9 percent). The world in which most Texans live is not made up of a thousand small towns, villages, and cities of Texas, or even of Texas' mid-sized municipalities! And for most Texans today, the images of Grandmother's farm as presented in the Coke ads, are far removed from reality. Most young Texans today are born and will grow up in Texas' teeming metropolitan areas, or they will move there for employment. That is why, among the young, as well as many older persons, songs about Luckenbach, Texas are met with such nostalgic enthusiasm. About 10 million persons today live in only 25 Texas areas of highly concentrated population which constitute less than 8 percent of the total land area. See Figure 1–5.

TABLE 1–4
Population distribution in Texas, 1970

Classification	Population		Percentage	
Urban population		8,920,946		79.7
All 25 SMSAs	8,605,387		76.9	
Three largest SMSAs	5,624,765		50.2	
Rural population		2,275,784		20.3
Nonfarm population	1,803,742		16.1	
Farm population	472,042		4.2	
Total Texas population		11,196,730		100.0

Source: U.S. Department of Commerce, Bureau of the Census, *1970 Census of Population*, vol. 1: *Characteristics of Population*, part 45: *Texas*, section 1 (Washington, D.C.: U.S. Government Printing Office, 1973), Tables 9, 134, and 136.

FIGURE 1-5

Boundaries of SMSAs in Texas, 1979

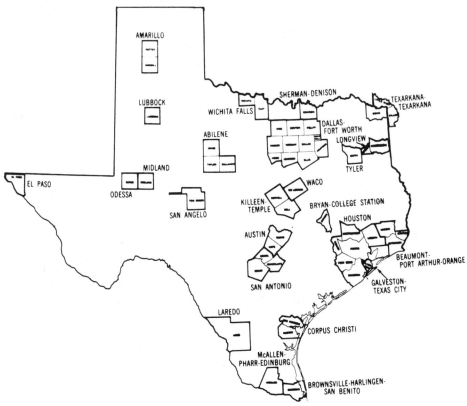

Source: Office of Management and Budget, Executive Office of the President, *Standard Metropolitan Statistical Areas,* rev. ed. (Washington, D.C.: U.S. Government Printing Office, 1975).

Standard metropolitan statistical areas (SMSAs) are not governmental units. Within the 25 SMSAs lie only 52 of 254 Texas counties. But these same counties contain one third of the school districts, two fifths of the municipalities, and two fifths of other special districts in Texas. The utility of Census Bureau units lies in the use by both government and private enterprise of the considerable amount of statistics collected and reported for each area. For example, aside from the symbolic benefits, the enlarged, combined census data of all kinds for the Houston-Galveston SCSA brought additional governmental and private economic benefits, such as larger federal grants for planning, additional airline routes, and new industries impressed by the size of potential markets. Thus, the SMSAs and SCSAs are treated as economic and social regions, with trade, commerce, services, manufacturing, communications facilities, recreation, and cultural affairs and activities dominated in large measure by the affairs, life, and influences of the central cities. The largest Texas SMSA, Dallas-Fort Worth, comprises 11 counties, has more than 2.5 million people, and is dominated by the cities of Dallas and Fort Worth and their numerous suburban places and municipalities.[38]

Rural Texas

Although the percentage of rural Texans is small, nearly 2.5 million persons live in the farm and nonfarm sectors. This fact plus a peculiar set of problems, political distinctives, and a lower level of public services justify separate and extensive treatment.[39] Migration of the young to the cities, political conservatism, deterioration of public services, denial of the existence of poverty, and inability of many rural Texans to countenance public solutions to "private" problems—all these give the age-old problems of low educational attainment, poor health, unemployment, protection from crime, low salaries, and transportation a much graver cast and a larger impact than even in Texas' teeming cities.[40] Newer concerns, such as mass transportation, pollution, land use, drug abuse, noise, mental health, and quality of life, generally affect the cities more than they affect rural people.

Texas' new "dual regionalism"

Demarcations between rural and urban Texas point to a new regionalism in Texas. The traditional study of substate regionalism is based upon divisions imposed by physical and natural features—climate, river systems, terrain, vegetation, and resources—which produced social, political, and economic distinctions among people of East Texas, the Panhandle, Gulf Coast, South Texas, Central Texas, and other traditional substate regions. In the final years of the 20th century, differences between metropolitan Texas and rural Texas may separate Texans more than distance, climate, and terrain.

The large metropolitan areas, whether El Paso, Austin, Houston, or Dallas, tend to be very much alike in the basic environmental forces and government policies which affect life styles and quality of existence. The most obvious remaining reminder of the old traditional substate regionalism is an ethnic difference—blacks in East Texas and Hispanics in South Texas—which separates these two regions from each other and tends to set both of them apart from the remainder of the state.[41] Both minorities formerly resided predominantly in rural areas. But migration of the two groups to the metropolitan areas serves to demonstrate the heavy erosion of the old regional patterns by the newer, dominant demographic trends.

LEGAL-CONSTITUTIONAL CONTEXT

The federal structure

Federal and state constitutions fix legal and political boundaries of governmental jurisdictions and establish an interlocking federal structure of 50 states and the national government. The Texas political system is circumscribed by two constitutions, the Texas Constitution of 1876 and the United States Constitution of 1789.

The United States Constitution, an instrument of the people, divides governmental authority and tasks functionally between the national government and the 50 American states. Although bestowed with expressly mentioned functions, the national political regime has authority to carry out its enumerated powers, and it is supreme in the exercise of its own constitutionally limited authority. National legal provisions may place restraints upon state governments or award the initiative to the national government for many programs and policies.

Under the United States Constitution, state governments are reserved the remainder of the totality of powers which the people delegate to organized governments. Although this reservation is an authorization to the states to establish a vast array of programs and services affecting the daily lives of the people, Texans, in establishing their own state constitutions, have traditionally placed many legal restraints upon state and local governments which are neither anticipated nor required by the United States Constitution.

Under the federal system, the people of Texas established, through their own constitution, their own separate political structure in Austin and, for their convenience, in the localities. Because 49 other state governments exist, Texas' authority is limited also *territorially*. The power of Texas stops at the state boundaries. But Texas governments interact constantly with many other units, including the national government, working out patterns of legal and political responsibilities and interdependence, which are labeled *intergovernmental relations*. Dynamic patterns of independence and interdependence, cooperation and conflict, centralization and decentralization, expansion and contraction have been established largely in the political process, not in our written constitutions.

Functions of American constitutions

American constitutions (1) establish *structures of public authority* (legislative, executive, administrative, and judicial); (2) authorize *processes of selection* of governmental authorities (legislators, executives, administrators, and judges); (3) list formal *resources of power and authority* (such as in executive appointments); and (4) set *limitations on regime authority* (for example, by listing individual civil liberties and by providing limited terms of public officials).

Thus, constitutions (5) help establish the *legitimacy of public authority* by making provisions for a regime (the structures of governments and powers) grounded in the people, with channels of representation from the people. Therefore, constitutions (6) accommodate *resolution of conflict* and (7) authorize the *outputs of the political system* in the form of public policies. Constitutions also (8) establish a *basis of certainty in the law* and (9) help provide *continuity and stability of basic institutions.* Finally, legitimate procedures or mechanisms provided in constitutions (10) contemplate *change and adaptation of law and institutions* to dynamic environmental conditions (such as industrialization, urbanization, population growth, and technological development).

Organization of constitutions

American constitutions have common organizational arrangements and components. A *preamble* may state the ends or purposes of government, as in the federal Constitution:

> We the people of the United States, in order to form a more perfect Union, establish justice, insure domestic tranquility, provide for the common defense, promote the general welfare, and secure the blessings of liberty to ourselves and our posterity, do ordain and establish this Constitution for the United States of America.

Or the preamble may be a simple salutation, as in the Texas Constitution: "Humbly invoking the blessings of Almighty God, the people of the State of Texas, do ordain and establish this Constitution."

The main body of a constitution is composed of *articles,* which establish the framework and powers of the government and the method of formal amendment. Articles are divided into *sections* and *clauses.* This structural arrangement facilitates ready reference to any portion of the fundamental law. For example, Article I, Section 8 of the United States Constitution contains the enumerated powers of the Congress.

The final component part of written constitutions consists of *amendments.* A list of formal amendments may follow the main body, or the formal changes may be incorporated, as they are adopted, into the related articles, as is the practice with respect to the Texas Constitution.

Philosophical foundations

Common functions and organization of American constitutions point to common philosophical foundations. These underpinnings consist, however, more of brief *theoretical assumptions* than complete philosophical treatises. Unlike constitutions in many other countries, the brief provisions of American constitutions are limited largely to governmental structures and powers.

Based upon the writings of John Locke, as reflected particularly in Jefferson's *Declaration of Independence,* the normative theoretical foundations of American constitutions include *origin* of government in compact between the people and their rulers, government policies based upon *consent* of the governed, *rights* of the people to alter or abolish their governments, existence of natural rights before the creation of governments, and *liberties* of the people against their governments.

Most of these philosophical assumptions underlie the ideal of *limited government.* Therefore, a written constitution, most of all, is an expression or institutionalization of the principle of limitations placed upon the exercise of governmental authority. American governments are constitutionally limited in several ways: (1) by structural mechanisms, such as bicameralism, separation of powers, and federalism; (2) by specific statements of authority of the officials in power; (3) by electoral processes of selection and rejection of candidates for public office; and (4) by lists of individual liberties found in our Bills of Rights.

Texas and national constitutions compared

From functional, structural, and philosophical standpoints, the Texas Constitution is very similar to the United States Constitution. A source of structure, organization, selection, and powers of their respective governments, subject to popular and organizational limitations, these constitutions are organizationally the same and are relatively easy to amend formally. Table 1–5 compares the two basic documents in their organization, subject headings, and parts.

In length, number of amendments, flexibility, and provisions for positive government, the Texas Constitution of 1876 is quite in contrast with the national fundamental law of 1789. Rather accurately reflecting the concerns of the people and their social, economic, and political environment in the postbellum conditions of Radical Reconstruction, the Texas document is very long, specifying numerous detailed restrictions upon governments, particularly in finance and in certain policy areas. Containing an estimated 63,000 words, one of the longest state constitutions, it has been characterized as more a "code of statute laws" than a basic or fundamental law. In contrast, the United States Constitution contains scarcely 10,000 words, and it is general, nonspecific, and brief—a genuine fundamental law.

As a product of its great length and detail, the Texas Constitution is highly *inflexible.* Having been permitted to grow and change virtually only by the formal amending process, by 1979 the Texas Constitution had been amended 233 times. The number of amendments a constitution has is a

TABLE 1-5
The United States and Texas Constitutions compared: Organization, subject matter, parts

United States Constitution	Subject or part	Texas Constitution
Preamble	Preamble	Preamble
Amendments I–X (1791)	Bill of Rights	Article I (29 sections)
	Separation of Powers	Article II (1 section)
Article I (10 sections)	Legislative	Article III (62 sections)
Article II (4 sections)	Executive	Article IV (26 sections)
Article III (3 sections)	Judicial	Article V (30 sections)
Amendments XV, XIX, XXIV and XXVI	Suffrage	Article VI (5 sections)
	Education	Article VII (17 sections)
	Taxation and Revenue	Article VIII (19 sections)
	Counties	Article IX (12 sections)
	Railroads	Article X (1 section)
	Municipal Corporations	Article XI (10 sections)
	Private Corporations	Article XII (2 sections)
	Land Titles	Article XIII (0 sections)
	Public Lands	Article XIV (1 section)
	Impeachment	Article XV (8 sections)
Article IV (4 sections)	Federal Relations	
Article V (1 section)	Mode of Amending	Article XVII (2 sections)
Article VI (1 section)	General Provisions	Article XVI (50 sections)
Article VII (1 section)	Ratification	
16 (since 1791)	Amendments	226 to 1978
7 articles, 24 sections		17 articles, 227 sections

function of *length* of that constitution (holding age constant). The longer the constitution, the greater the number of amendments. Great length originally, plus additional detail by formal amendments, may also be a function of the activities of interest groups. Further contributing to change by the formal amending procedure are the attitudes of judges and the attorney general in Texas. As stated by Professor Janice C. May:

> The entire amendment process is significantly affected by the traditionally cautious view taken by the judiciary and the Attorney General on the meaning of constitutional provisions, which has the effect of increasing the burden on the amendment process.[42]

The United States Constitution, in contrast, has been amended only 16 times since the Bill of Rights (Amendments I–X) was added nearly

200 years ago. All commentators point to the great flexibility and growth of the national constitution by methods other than by formal amendment: (1) by custom and usage, (2) by congressional elaboration, (3) by court interpretation, and (4) by executive action. In contrast, the Texas Constitution changes virtually only by formal amendments.

The Texas Constitution

Social mandates, benefits, and deprivations Besides establishing structures of governments based upon implicit philosophic foundations, most state constitutions, in lengthy sections, also mandate some traditional social concerns and provide a distribution of economic benefits and deprivations. Prominent social considerations in Texas include protection of the elite status of the University of Texas and of Texas A&M University, conservation and development of water and other natural resources, and maintenance of a system of public free schools. Written into recently adopted state constitutions are the goals of protection of the environment and provision of adequate health care.

The struggle of groups for retention of long-range benefits and deprivations is a prominent feature of all constitutional conventions. The basic document becomes, in effect, a ratification of the division of political rewards which have been guaranteed over a lengthy period of time—some of them since the beginning of the Anglo poiitical community before 1836. Among the rewards and limitations in the present constitution— some of which have mainly symbolic effect—are separate and community property for husbands and wives, a usury provision, regulation of alcoholic beverages, prohibition against lotteries, prohibition against branch banking, protection of homesteads and personal property against forced sale, prohibition against wage garnishment, guarantee of mechanics' liens for work performed, limitation on state spending for welfare, property tax benefits for lands in agricultural production, local tax limitations, debt limitations, and pension benefits for school teachers and other public employees. Many of these provisions reflect such deep-seated attitudes in the political culture of Texas that they are called "sacred cows" of the constitutional system. So basic are these benefits and deprivations that they can be expected to continue in any "new" or revised constitution. Largely impervious to change, they help lend continuity, stability, and predictability to Texas public law and policies.

Amending process Amending the Texas Constitution is a relatively simple two-step procedure—*proposal* and *ratification*. Amendments may be proposed at any session of the legislature, but to be proposed at special sessions they must be included within the call of the governor. *Proposal* is by a two-thirds vote of the total membership in each of the two branches of the legislature. *Ratification* is by a majority vote of the electorate participating in voting on the proposed amendments at a regular or special election designated by the legislature. To enable voters to understand proposed amendments, explanatory statements prepared by the secretary of state and approved by the attorney general are published twice in the state's newspapers within 60 days of a ratifying election. After canvass of election returns by the secretary of state, proclamations of the adoption of amendments are made by the governor.

Although the amending process is more complex than statute-making, the amending procedure need take no longer than statute-making. Bills, unless passed by a two-thirds majority, do not become in force as statutes until 90 days after the close of a session. The legislature, which has the power to provide for the calling of a special ratifying election at any time, could just as quickly bring about a vote of the electorate on proposed constitutional amendments. Of course, not all constitutional amendments are self-enacting, and state legislative enactments may be needed to carry them into effect.

Tempo of change by amendment   Captive of an earlier, simpler time (which conditions continued to prevail in Texas well into the 20th century), the Texas Constitution of 1876 experienced only 44 amendments in its first 50 years. See Table 1–6. In the next 25 years, 1927–1951 (which contained the nationalizing events of the Great Depression and World War II, accompanied by vast social and economic change), the tempo of formal amendment tripled, to 2.6 formal changes per year, while the adoption by the electorate jumped to 62.9 percent.

The past quarter century has witnessed far-reaching social and economic changes. As a result, since 1951, the rate of formal amendment has doubled, while the voters have increased the adoption rate to 74.4 percent of amendments proposed. More than one half of all amendments to our Constitution have been adopted in the past 25 years!

This tempo of change by constitutional amendments is a commentary upon

The great length and detail of the document as written in 1876,

Success of the constitutional framers in forging nonenduring constitutional provisions, and

TABLE 1–6
Tempo of constitutional amendments in Texas

Time period	Amendments		Amendment rate per year	Adoption rate (proposed/ ratified)
	Proposed	Ratified		
1876–1926	97	44	0.9	45.4%
1927–1951	105	66	2.6	62.9
1952–1977	156	116	4.5	74.4
Totals	358	226	2.2	62.1%

Source: Prepared from data in Texas Legislative Council, *Proposed Constitutional Amendments Analyzed* (Austin: Texas Legislative Council, 1973), p. 5 (updated).

A strategy since 1876 of adding additional detail by amendments.

If plans for comprehensive revision continue to be unsuccessful and if the "strategy of detail" prevails, we shall see an additional 120 amendments in the next two decades.[43]

A bundle of constraints on popular government The Constitution of 1876 is notorious for its restraints on popular rule. By constraints, or restraints, is *not* meant, of course, the democratic ideal of placing constitutional limitations on the political regime in order to preserve individual liberties against the state. Instead, these constraints are restraints placed to limit the people's ability to use government to enhance their economic and social quality of life or even to protect themselves against other individuals or groups. "Because of the resentment of the Reconstruction Government of 1869, many delegates voted for detailed constraints on future governments."[44] Governments, state and local, are unable to react effectively to demands for services, programs, and regulations. While all U.S. governments are hemmed in by constitutional limitations, they are ordinarily endowed with sufficient power and authority to secure the blessings of liberty and other advantages stemming from the creation and maintenance of an ordered society.

Stateways versus folkways: Federal action as instrument of constitutional change A system of constraints, then, operates to negate liberties and means by which individuals may secure their basic rights to effective citizenship and other civil liberties. Only recently, the Texas Constitution was so restrictive of the right to vote that both the size of the electorate and the characteristics of registered voters were altered. Persons screened away from the input structures by legal and constitutional provisions were lower status persons of all races, groups, and areas of Texas.[45] The Texas Constitution effectively restrained *its own citizens,* so that constraints which barred access to voting, quality education, equal employment opportunity, and other privileges have had to be eliminated by civil rights actions brought under the United States Constitution. Few initiatives for change came from within the Texas political system. Nowhere has the force of federal law in recent years been stronger in changing the folkways of human behavior than in the area of civil rights, particularly in voting rights, school desegregation, and campaign rhetoric.[46] But traditional habits, lack of participatory skills and resources, little political party machinery, and the negative impact of poor social and economic environments cut deeply into the levels of voting and other forms of public participation in Texas.

A chief explanation of continued restrictive constitutional amendments is found in the stability of the structure of the dominant coalition of economic groups in Texas. Groups vie for privilege by struggling to place provisions in the basic law. The benefits provided by these amendments, of course, assume greater *legitimacy* than those offered in mere statute law. The stronger the interest groups, as in Texas, the easier is the amending process, the greater are the number of proposed amendments, and the larger the adoption rate.[47] Indicating a dominant historic alliance of interests, the amendments retain the restrictive nature of the *original* subject matter. The framers of the Constitution of 1876 fixed the details and rules by which privilege continues to pay off.

Analysis of recent amendments

An assessment of recent constitutional amendments, based upon data from a study of Professor May of 105 amendments adopted 1951–72,[48] will serve to

Illuminate basic characteristics of the Texas fundamental law,

Illustrate types of constitutional restraints,

Give instances of institutional privilege,

Distinguish levels of participation in ratifying elections,

Note patterns of defeat and victory of the several classes of proposed constitutional amendments,

Characterize voter behavior in choosing among constitutional proposals

Raise questions about the types of persons who take the trouble to vote on constitutional amendments, and

Distinguish certain attitudes of these voters about the various policy subjects which they are called upon to approve or reject.

The legislative article was the subject of 40 percent of the changes during the period, while four other articles—general provisions, counties, taxation and revenue, and education (refer to Table 1–5)—accounted for two thirds of the remainder. The judiciary article, on the other hand, was subject to only five proposed changes, all of which were ratified.

Excessive detail Illustrating the strategy of adding detailed provisions is the legislative article, which contains 62 sections and comprises one fourth of the entire Constitution. This article, in addition to basic outline of structures, procedures, selection and powers of the legislature, contains numerous substantive provisions on such subjects as lotteries, teacher retirement, rural fire-prevention districts, state debt, veterans' land program, Texas Water Development Board, state medical education, student loans, county roads, toll roads, coverage of state and local employees by Social Security, prohibitions against local and special legislation, seat of state government, workers' compensation insurance program, public assistance programs, state building fund, compensation of persons improperly fined or imprisoned, assistance to survivors of law enforcement officers, and municipal and state retirement systems.

Financial restraints   Nearly 60 percent of amendments related to evading or overcoming financial and other limitations on state and local governments, for example:

Prohibition against state debt except to a maximum of $200,000 for defense and related matters and casual deficiencies—evaded by amendments which authorize debt for specific purposes, for example, for water development, Art. III, Sec. 49c.

Prohibition of grants of public money to private individuals and purposes except to indigent and disabled Confederate soldiers and sailors—amended often because grants of public money are essential to modern government.

Limitation of total amount of state spending for welfare programs— amended several times since 1933 to continue to match federal contributions and programs.

Restrictions on authority of local governments to incur indebtedness for road-building and water conservation programs—amended numerous times to create financial flexibility, but resulting in confusing and contradictory provisions.

Earmarked tax receipts for specific spending programs—29 amendments, 1951–1972, created five new funds, earmarked other moneys, and affected eight other constitutional funds, resulting in even fewer options of the state legislature in appropriations.

Negative government   In addition to these financial restrictions are embedded, restrictive, detailed provisions which limit specific services and programs. Nearly one half of the proposed amendments contained provisions designed to expand services in some specific manner, as by raising financial limitations or increasing eligibility. Most of these changes established new limitations, however broader than the former. Restrictions were piled upon restrictions.

To illustrate the cycle, workers' compensation, first provided to state employees by a 1936 amendment, was extended by amendments to county workers in 1948, to municipal employees in 1952, and to all personnel of all political subdivisions in 1962. The same cycle was followed in public retirement systems.

The legislature ties its own hands   But the legislature itself, by a two-thirds vote, proposed the original amendments above. The legislature has not chosen to attempt to break the cycle of constitutional restraints, even with respect to its own policymaking authority! Reasons for this limited, cautious, conservative, and legalistic approach to public policy and constitutional change must be found in the Texas political culture.

Levels of voter paritcipation   The highest levels of voter participation in 19 ratifying elections, 1951–1971, occurred in general elections in presidential years. The largest turnout came in 1956, when 57.5 percent of registered voters voted on several amendments, while the average voting rate for five presidential election years during the period was 51 percent. See Table 1–7. Note the differential of 30 percentage points between the rate of voting for candidates for president and the rate of voting on proposed constitutional amendments which appeared at the bottom of the same ballots. "A candidate's race pulls the voter into the ballot booth; while there he may or may not vote on the amendments."[49]

In nine special elections (with no candidates on the ballots), the average participation rate was only 16 percent. The lowest rate (6.7 percent) came in the special election of 1956, when only one amendment, on welfare, was voted on and approved. An average participation level in all 19 ratifying elections of only 17 percent is realized if the number of voters as a percentage of voting age population is used![50]

While controversial amendments drew more voters in all types of elections, a correlation between participation rates and the proportion of amendments rejected or ratified was found only in special elections, where the percentage of rejections increased as participation increased.

Controversial and unpopular issues Of the 17 proposed amendments which drew the most votes, six pertained to welfare issues. Other controversial changes, as measured by turnout, margin of votes, and rejection rates, dealt with service of women on juries, higher interest rates, four-year terms for governor and other high elective executives, liquor by the drink, veterans' land program enlargements, retirement programs of public personnel, and municipal employees' workers' compensation.

Least popular of all issues were proposals relating to local government programs of limited application across the state. Success or failure of proposed amendments is more closely related, however, to type of election than to subject matter.[51] Knowing this, the legislature, which

TABLE 1–7
Average participation of registered voters in ratifying elections, percent of total amendments submitted and approved: By type of election, 1951–1971

Elections		Average percent voting on		Percent amendments	
Type	*Number*	*Candidates*	*Amendments*	*Submitted*	*Approved*
General elections (presidential years)	5	81	51	24	77
General elections (nonpresidential years)	5	52	39	44	84
Special elections (no candidates on ballot)	9	—	16	33	51

Source: Prepared from data in Janice C. May, *Amending the Texas Constitution* (Austin: Texas Advisory Commission on Intergovernmental Relations, 1972), pp. 20, 47.

designates the type of election for ratification amendments, sometimes seems to follow a strategy for rejection or approval of certain amendments.

The rational voter: "Search and destroy" Among persons who vote on amendments, particularly in special elections where voters are not distracted by euphoria of support of favorite candidates, the average voter performs in a highly discriminating fashion. He or she sifts through the list of proposed changes in a negative strategy of "search and destroy" to record his or her dislikes. Little evidence exists that one or a few unpopular amendments tend to bring down all the proposals. Further, ballot position seemingly makes little difference. And Texans have never performed in the manner of the "Louisiana syndrome" of voting down all proposals.

Who is this minority (17 percent, on the average, of all possible qualified voters) which sifts through proposed amendments and the even smaller group who holds ratification or defeat in its hands? These voters may not be typical of all voting-age population, or even of all habitual voters. All persons who vote for a candidate in general elections do not bother to vote on amendments. No one knows who these elites are who hold in their hands constitutional change in Texas. Although improbable, it is statistically possible that an entirely different group of ratifers and rejecters goes into each of the different types of ratifying elections.

Attitudinal patterns Persons taking the trouble to vote tend to support structural changes in the judiciary, expanded programs in education, and creation of hospital districts, even though the last is a local matter. They also commonly favor the highly restrictive amendments on public welfare. Tax exemptions, however, are disfavored unless they are on homesteads or involve veterans. About 70 percent of rejected proposals concern government finance, the area most restricted in the Constitution. And unlike acceptance of proposed changes in judicial structure, voters are suspicious of changes in organization of executive and legislative branches. Positive evidence of antipathy toward the democratic branch of state government is rejection in 1959, 1968, 1969, and 1972 of a proposed pay raise (in varying amounts) for state legislators.

Constitutional revision

An irony stands out. Numerous amendments submitted piecemeal have not altered the characteristics of the Constitution since it was written in 1876. Constitutional amendments do not necessarily constitute constitutional revision! On the contrary, in Texas "progressive deterioration" has resulted.[52]

Three abortive attempts at comprehensive revision have been made since the 1950s. The latest effort fizzled miserably November 4, 1975, when voters crushed by more than two to one a revised, shortened, and modernized document (17,000 words) which would have set Texas on the road to positive government. This latest attempt had its origin in a strong reform spirit produced in 1971 by the Sharpstown scandals. In retrospect, it appears, however, that not reform spirit but long-run tendencies of distrust and lack of confidence in popular government sparked the constitutional revision effort and other changes, including a new governor, new legislative leadership, and numerous reform measures. Surveys demonstrate that Watergate on the national level served to establish higher and higher levels of cynicism and popular suspicion, directed, oddly enough, more at U.S. legislatures than offending executives. Under these circumstances, empowering the Texas legislature to act as a constitutional convention has to be a major strategic blunder. By autumn, 1975, the short-run reform impetus in Texas apparently had spent itself. The old order was reasserted. Governor Dolph Briscoe, who had never really joined the revision effort, celebrated the end of the "new leadership" by articulating the old fear and praising the soundness of the old verities. He spoke of higher taxes as a result of proposed annual sessions of the legislature, of the need only of "citizen legislators" who take time from their private endeavors to journey to Austin once every two years, and of a state Constitution which has "served Texas well for a hundred years."[53]

Perhaps the urge for constitutional reform never ran very deep. As stated by one observer:

> The sparkplug for the antirevision movement was the old Houston business establishment. . . . Perhaps they just changed their mind like Dolph Briscoe, the governor they elected that year and a man whose rural, business-oriented conservatism perfectly symbolizes the old order.[54]

But there was leadership for the revised Constitution by Attorney General John Hill, Lieutenant Governor William P. Hobby, Land Commissioner Bob Armstrong, and others.

Perhaps symbolic tactical errors and "goofs" were committed in the revision process and campaign for revision. Members of the legislature, rather than a specially elected body, served as the constitutional convention. The legislature failed to produce a document[55] amidst 33 separate votes to put together a draft constitution. The image projected was self-serving pressure-group politics as usual.

A third set of problems exist which go to the heart of the democratic process. Visibility of constitutional issues is commonly extremely low, few people seem to pay much attention, issues raised in connection with revision are very complex and difficult to simplify, voting turnout is commonly low, and a problem of "cumulating objections" to a revised constitution (based on different objections to a thousand different provisions by a majority of voters) can be generated. These conditions when they exist together and reinforce one another make any popular effort and any affirmative referendum difficult to achieve.

A good guess about the future is that an essential base, described as a "chronic feeling of uneasiness about the present Texas Constitution,"[56] does exist for constitutional reform. But a successful revision effort would most probably necessitate strong, unified leadership, a specially elected convention, a membership which projects an aura of dedication to the public interest, issues which appear rather simple, and a united, extensive, broad-based campaign for ratification.[57]

CONCLUSIONS

No U.S. state exists in a vacuum. Texas is no exception. Its politics and government are mightily influenced by the state's physical, social, politico-cultural, economic and demographic environments, and by external forces such as the other states and the national government. Our analysis in this chapter has concentrated on the internal environments of Texas itself, and we have pinpointed the following major conclusions about the setting of Texas government and politics:

1. The shape and form which is taken by the various environments that make up Texas have a pronounced effect upon the characteristics of Texas government and politics. The nature of these environments have an important bearing upon the capacity of the Texas political system to make public policies. More generally, we may speak of the effects of the principal elements of the environment of Texas in relation to the "policy performance" of our political system. The notion of policy performance embraces more than merely making policies; it includes how well the political system represents the interests of Texans, how adequately government programs address Texas problems, environmental conditions, and resource availability, and how equitably governmental services are allocated among Texans.

2. The political culture of a state—that set of common and deep-seated attitudes, beliefs, and ideals about the role of government and politics in our lives and in society—molds and shapes the way a political system works. Texas has a distinctive political culture, melding both traditional and individualistic elements. Personalism, factionalism, non-competitive politics, political conservatism, persistent patterns of constitutional restraints, and the absence of substantial political party organization give Texas politics a traditionalistic, 19th century cast. The elitism, centrality of interest-group conflict, overt racism, and emphasis upon economic development illustrate Texas' individualistic cultural features. As a relatively closed system, dedicated to private economic

development and small government, Texas government has not been characterized by particularly impressive policy performance.

3. Texas politics has been dominated by powerful economic interest groups with strong enough allies among noneconomic groups and in government so that we may speak of a "Texas establishment." This establishment, or elite, consists of persons who share beliefs and values, especially the value of keeping government small but using it to foster economic development, and the value of accumulating capital in a few hands, expressed in low and regressive taxation and minimal governmental services.

4. Traditionalistic government in Texas has lent its resources and authority to developing the state's natural resources, and building a modernized, industrialized, urbanized, technological, business-oriented society. As a modernizing society, economic development has the highest priority among Texas governmental functions. Thus programs for highways, correctional institutions, and higher education have been pursued fairly aggressively, but social welfare programs have received pallid state support and would not be viable without massive assistance from the federal government. The modernization of Texas is indicated by its development as an urbanized state, but its 2.5 million rural inhabitants, with their special problems, cultural influence, agricultural production, and sheer land area, contribute much to the quality of Texas.

5. A state's constitution is a reflection of its politico-cultural bases. Unlike the Constitution of the United States, the Texas Constitution is long, detailed, restrictive, inflexible, and subject to change mainly by formal constitutional amendment. The restraints embedded in the Texas Constitution persist because of the stability of the dominant coalition of interest groups in Texas, who most notably have managed to maintain stringent limitations on the power of the legislature. Although one might wonder why the state's Constitution is regarded as legitimate, especially when amendments to it have so often been approved by a small minority of the electorate, it appears that most Texans agree with former Governor Dolph Briscoe, who in 1975 insisted that the document had served Texas well for a hundred years.

CHAPTER TWO

Politics of ethnic minorities

I've been to the mountain-top. . . . And I've looked over, and I've seen the Promised Land.

MARTIN LUTHER KING, JR.*

To a very large extent, the patterns of political action in the Texas system are shaped by the population size and the distribution of the population in terms of geography, age, education, occupational characteristics, living standards, and other similar social, economic, and demographic characteristics. In Chapter One the general patterns of this environment of Texas politics were sketched.

This chapter deals specifically with the racial minorities in the state. A separate discussion of this topic is justified because of the substantial size of the minority population, the serious, politically relevant distinctions between the Anglo and the non-Anglo populations of the state,[1] and the longstanding sociocultural and political discrimination directed toward the minority population.

A continuing theme of this volume is that the politics of Texas illustrates many traits of an underdeveloped political system. The treatment and role of the state's racial minorities presents further evidence in support of this theme. Blacks and Mexican-Americans in Texas have been accorded treatment very similar to that given to social and political outgroups in the underdeveloped countries. Patterns of social and economic discrimination and segregation, political disenfranchisement, and continued lack of access to the resources of the system have continued to be the salient characteristics of the political situation for non-Anglo minorities.

However, while Texas' racial minorities share characteristics such as relative and absolute poverty, lack of education, poor housing, low-paying and low-status jobs, and exclusion from the political processes,

* Quoted in Don McKee, *Martin Luther King, Jr.* (New York: G. P. Putnam's Sons, 1969), pp. 179–180.

Mexican-Americans and blacks form two very distinct groups in Texas. Each has a separate background, identity, goals, special interests and needs. Even in urban areas, where economic pressures have forced the two groups into the same residential areas, strong efforts have been made to preserve black and chicano neighborhoods.

There is little evidence to suggest that the shared conditions of deprivation and discrimination have resulted in any substantial cooperation among the racial minorities in the political arena. Whether the competition stems from the psychological need for a subordinate group to satisfy status insecurities or is simply the product of the struggle of each group to obtain as much as possible of the scarce resources, it is evident that conflict, as much as if not more than cooperation, has characterized relations between chicanos and blacks in Texas.

DEMOGRAPHIC BACKGROUND

Historical development

Blacks   The first blacks came to Texas as slaves in the first half of the 19th century. Apparently the bulk of the present black population component in Texas is descended from those slaves or came in the immediate post-Civil War period to establish a new life as freedmen, away from the scene of their enslavement. The insignificant 20th century immigration, largely from neighboring southern states, has brought a black population with attitudes and behavioral patterns only marginally different from the prevailing mold. Substantial increases in the Anglo and Mexican-American populations, due to both immigration from other states and abroad as well as high birthrates, especially for Mexican-Americans, in conjunction with some emigration of blacks from Texas, has cut the percentage of black population from nearly 25 percent in the latter 1800s to about 12.5 percent in 1970.[2] The percentage is now again increasingly slightly, due largely to high birthrates.

During the Reconstruction era blacks were quite active in Texas politics. Registration and voting turnouts were high, and the first Reconstruction legislature contained two Negro senators and nine representatives. Forty-six blacks held legislative and constitutional convention seats in the period from the Civil War to 1896. By the turn of the century, however, not only were there no black legislators, but blacks had been effectively disenfranchised statewide.

After Reconstruction, Texas blacks were forced into conditions that amounted to little more than the servitude that prevailed before the Civil War. Blacks became tenant farmers, day laborers, janitors, and entered other undesired (by Anglos) and extremely low-paying jobs. Education and other public services were closed or virtually closed to the black population. The re-established white majority regarded black political activism as particularly dangerous. Lynchings and other physical violence were employed when other means of discouragement failed. The Democratic primary, where the actual political choices were made, was legally closed to blacks from the turn of the century until the late 1940s and unofficially closed in some areas until even later. Significant improvement in the socioeconomic and political conditions of the black minority in Texas is largely a post-World War II phenomenon.

Spanish/Mexican The history of the Spanish/Mexican element of the Texas population is considerably longer and more complex. The Indians which dominate the Indian-Spanish (mestizo) racial mixture of Mexcian-Americans in Texas were permanent residents of the area of what is now Mexico and Texas 10 to 15 millenia before Columbus and maybe longer. The accomplishments of the relatively advanced ancient civilizations of Central Mexico, including developed systems of education, complex urban centers, advanced road networks, and a calendar more accurate than the one we use today, provide a continuing source of pride for those of Mexican ancestry. Teotihuacán (about the time of Christ) was a city of 60,000–100,000 and the Aztec capital, Tenochtitlán, on the current site of Mexico City, was a settlement of 60,000 people.

The Spanish conquest beginning in the 1500s only very slowly made its way northward, and even by the early 19th century probably no more than 10,000 people of Spanish or mixed Spanish-Indian background were settled in the area of what is now Texas. One census report for 1830 gave figures of about 6,000 Spanish-Mexican population, compared to 30,000 Anglos and black slaves. Whatever the exact figures might be, clearly the Spanish-speaking were already a minority in their own country by 1835 and became much more so after Texas separated from Mexico.

Until 1890, there were only small increments to the existing Mexican-American population in Texas; according to one writer only about 30,000 came into all the Southwest during this period.[3] The vigorous efforts of Texas law enforcement agencies, especially the Texas Rangers, and the discrimination accorded all non-Anglos further served to discourage potential immigration to the former Mexican province. However, in the period 1890–1925, especially during and immediately after the Mexican Revolution (1910–20), a very large Immigration occurred, as indicated in Table 2–1. Between 1910 and 1930 nearly 700,000 Mexicans legally migrated to the U.S., most of them coming to Texas. Since World War II the relatively attractive economic conditions in the U.S. Southwest have enticed a continuing stream of both legal and illegal immigration. The size of the 20th century flow is evidenced by the fact that as late as 1960 over 45 percent of the Mexican-American population of Texas was either born in Mexico or had at least one parent born in Mexico. By 1970 that percentage had dropped to 36 percent, but this still translates into over

TABLE 2–1
Mexican-born in Texas and the Southwest

	1880	1890	1900	1910
New Mexico	5,173	4,504	6,649	11,918
Arizona	9,330	11,534	14,172	29,987
California	8,648	7,164	8,068	32,694
Texas	43,161	51,559	71,062	125,016

Source: U.S. Department of Commerce, *Census of Population, General Social and Economic Characteristics* (Washington, D.C.: U.S. Government Printing Office) for the respective years.

700,000 individuals with at least one foreign-born parent. Two other figures are interesting in this same context. An incredibly high 1.8 million Texans in the 1970 census said their mother tongue was Spanish; the total number of Spanish-surnamed or Spanish-speaking was just over 2 million. Another indication that the enticement of Texas is still strong to Mexicans is the fact that there are over 300,000 legal aliens in the state, and no one knows and few care to guess the number of illegal aliens. (One interesting guess came from a U.S. immigration official who said that about one million illegal aliens were in Texas as of early 1975.)

The 1960 census reports that the Spanish-surnamed in Texas constituted 14.8 percent of the population; by 1970 this figure had increased to 18.4 percent. This marked increase is partially due to a change in census procedures and definitions, but the percentage of Mexican-Americans in Texas is undoubtedly rising and probably increasing sharply due to high birthrates and immigration. While no detailed data are available since the 1970 census, census bureau estimates for 1976 show that the predominantly Mexican-American areas, especially the larger urban complexes, have grown more rapidly than even the significant growth experienced statewide. Of the five predominantly Mexican-American countries of over 100,000 population, only Nueces county grew less than ten percent. Bexar increased by 11 percent, El Paso by 18 percent, Hidalgo by 27 percent, and Cameron by 28 percent, while the statewide growth was 11.5 percent. Furthermore, these census counts undoubtedly significantly underestimate the chicano population totals, particularly given the hazy legal status of many of this population and the enormous number of illegal aliens. Not surprisingly, many Mexican-American political leaders see the political salvation of their people in these increasing numbers.

Urbanization The black population in Texas in the 19th century was concentrated almost exclusively in the rural and small town areas in the eastern half of the state, basically in the area east and north of a line from Sherman-Denison in the north through Dallas to San Antonio east to Houston. In the 20th century two great migrations have occurred.

During the first half of the century blacks in Texas, like their brothers in other southern states, moved in massive numbers to Midwestern and Northern cities. This movement has slowed sharply since 1950. More significant for contemporary Texas politics, the second migration of blacks in Texas has been a tidal wave movement into the big cities of the state. Three of every five black Texans live in the three metropolitan areas of Houston, Dallas-Fort Worth, and Beaumont-Port Arthur.

The Mexican-American pattern is somewhat different. The 19th century pattern was overwhelmingly rural, and a major movement from rural to urban settings has occurred in recent decades and continues. The major migration in recent decades, however, has been across the border into Texas cities. About two of every three Mexican-Americans in Texas live in the seven metropolitan areas of San Antonio, Houston, El Paso, McAllen-Pharr-Edinburg, Corpus Christi, Brownsville, and Dallas, in that order. Bexar (San Antonio), El Paso, and Nueces (Corpus Christi) counties have non-Anglo (primarily Mexican-American) majorities. Of the eight counties of over 200,000 population, only Tarrant (Fort Worth) has a non-Anglo population of less than 25 percent. One of the most revealing pieces of information regarding what has happened in the past few years (and continues even now) in the cities of Texas is the composition of public school enrollment. A combination of black and chicano movement to the cities, high birth rates among minorities, and substantial "white flight" to the suburbs has brought non-Anglo majorities to five of the six state school districts with more than 50,000 students in the fall of 1977. Table 2–2 provides figures for the major urban districts and several

TABLE 2–2
Public school enrollments, selected districts, by ethnic group, 1970 and 1977

Districts	Number of Students		Percent Anglo		Percent Black		Percent Hispanic		Percent Non-Anglo	
	1970	1977	1970	1977	1970	1977	1970	1977	1970	1977
Houston	241,138	206,998	49.4	32.1	35.6	44.0	14.4	22.8	50.0	66.8
Dallas	164,005	136,546	57.2	35.4	33.9	48.2	8.5	15.3	42.4	63.5
Fort Worth	88,144	69,977	63.7	49.0	26.7	35.6	9.2	14.8	35.9	50.4
San Antonio	77,253	64,277	22.9	13.9	15.3	15.8	61.5	70.0	76.8	85.8
El Paso	62,545	63,040	40.5	32.7	3.0	3.5	55.8	63.0	58.8	66.5
Ysleta-El Paso	33,263	42,645	35.7	25.7	2.7	2.6	60.9	70.8	63.6	73.4
Austin	54,974	58,991	64.4	58.3	15.1	16.7	20.4	24.1	35.5	40.8
Corpus Christi	45,914	39,509	42.6	32.1	5.7	5.9	51.6	61.7	57.3	67.6
Lubbock	33,585	32,292	65.3	59.4	11.6	12.7	23.0	27.3	34.6	40.0
Waco	18,360	15,251	65.5	50.3	20.7	33.6	13.6	15.8	34.3	49.4
Port Arthur	16,111	12,611	51.0	39.6	44.3	53.6	4.6	4.9	48.9	58.5
Beaumont	14,877	11,566	53.5	40.5	44.0	54.8	2.4	3.7	46.4	58.5
Spring Branch	39,771	38,545	98.4	92.0	0.1	1.5	1.4	4.7	1.5	6.2
Pasadena	35,691	36,570	92.2	82.0	0.0	0.8	7.5	16.3	7.5	17.1
Richardson	30,111	36,554	95.7	93.7	3.3	3.7	0.6	1.3	3.9	5.0
Garland	21,441	30,539	91.8	86.6	5.3	6.8	2.6	5.9	7.9	12.7

of the largest suburban districts around Houston and Dallas. The striking increases in non-Anglo percentages in just seven years can hardly be ignored.

These figures become very important in the context of political socialization and mobilization. There is little doubt that the urban setting increases the potential for political organization and action. The isolation and poverty of rural East Texas and the ranches and farms of South Texas and the Rio Grande Valley are major obstacles to serious organizational efforts, contrasting sharply with the crowded residential ghettos and barrios of Houston, Dallas, San Antonio, and El Paso. Texas in the 1970s is characterized by significant and increasing concentration in urban areas of racial minorities with perceived serious grievances, These grievances, and even hostilities, are being and almost certainly

FIGURE 2–1
Non-Anglo population concentrations in Texas

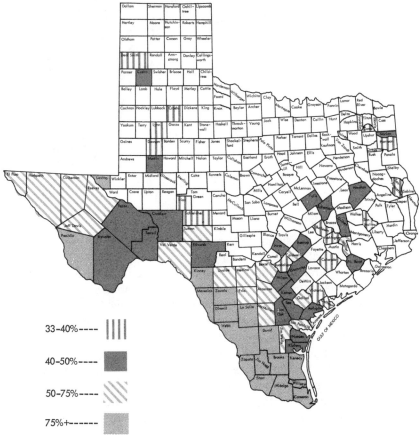

FIGURE 2–2

Mexican-American population concentrations in Texas

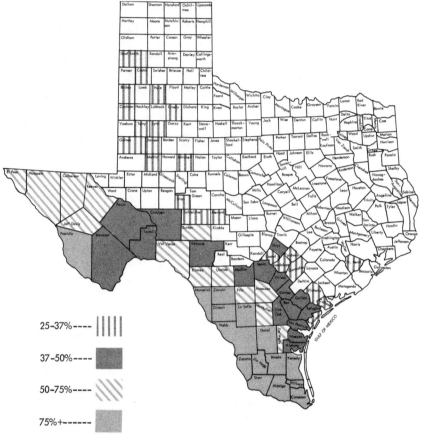

25–37% ---- |||||

37–50% ----

50–75% ----

75%+ ------

will increasingly be translated into demands on the system for ameliorative action.

Rural majorities This is not to suggest that all blacks and Mexican-Americans live in urban areas. The combined black-chicano population total is more than 50 percent in 33 of Texas' 254 counties. Only six of the 33—Bexar, Cameron, El Paso, Hidalgo, San Patricio, and Webb—can be described as essentially urban.

Figures 2–1, 2–2, and 2–3 illustrate the regional distribution of population, showing those counties and areas of the state having heavy concentrations of non-Anglo population. Perhaps the most striking point illustrated by the maps is the lack of overlap of Mexican-American and black populations. The overwhelming majority of the black people of

FIGURE 2–3
Black population concentrations in Texas

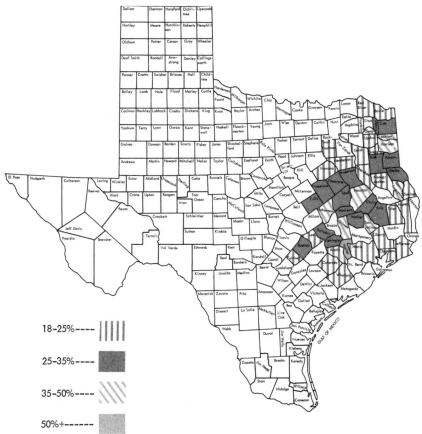

18–25% ---- |||||

25–35% ---- ▓

35–50% ---- ▨

50%+ ------ ░

Texas is found in East and Central Texas. In that general area, however, there has been a considerable dispersion of blacks into the large urban areas, to the point that currently in only one county (Waller) is there a black majority.

The concentration of Mexican-Americans is even more striking, although in a different part of the state. The area south of a line drawn roughly from El Paso through southwest Texas to Brownwood, back to Austin, and southeastward to Victoria contains a majority Mexican-American population. While much of that area is sparsely populated, rural, and poor, it includes more than a third of the state's area and population. Only in rural Caldwell and Gonzales counties is there over-representation of both blacks and chicanos.

SOCIAL CONDITIONS

Low income

By virtually any standard the bulk of the population of Texas is relatively poor, economically. In 1970, 22 percent of the population lived in families with incomes below the so-called poverty line, compared to a national average of 13 percent. An Office of Economic Opportunity study in 1970[4] reported that 26 percent of the population (in 850,000 families) had annual family incomes of less than $3,000. Forty percent of the households in Texas had cash incomes under $5,000; 77 percent had cash incomes under $10,000.

But blacks and Mexican-Americans are vastly poorer than the rest of the population. In 1973 nearly 40 percent of all non-Anglos in Texas had incomes below the poverty line, compared to 10 percent for Anglos. While less than 30 percent of the Anglo families made under $4,000, nearly 40 percent of Mexican-Americans and over half of the black families of the state fell under this total. Well over half (56 percent) of all chicanos and two thirds of all black families made less than $6,000 in 1970. The census of that year shows the following income breakdowns:

TABLE 2–3
Ethnic proportions of the population; by income levels

Income	Total population	Anglo	Black	Mexican-American
$1,000	8.5%	7.5%	14.7%	9.7%
$1,000–2,999	16.5	14.7	25.7	18.0
$3,000–3,999	6.9	5.9	10.0	10.4
$4,000–5,999	12.8	11.5	16.8	18.2
$6,000–9,999	23.9	24.5	21.3	25.3
$10,000–14,999	18.6	21.6	8.8	12.5
$15,000 and over	12.9	16.1	2.8	5.5

Source: U.S. Department of Commerce, *1970 Census of the Population, General Social and Economic Characteristics: Texas* (Washington, D.C.: U.S. Government Printing Office, 1972).

Other data show the same great disparities. Median family income for all families in 1970 was $8,500. Median income figures for blacks were $5,300 and for Mexican-Americans, $5,900. The figures for the Anglo population showed a per capita income more than double that of Mexican-Americans and 80 percent more than that of blacks. As detailed in Chapter 8[5] a close association exists between the economically deprived areas of the state and areas with high non-Anglo populations. This is true even though higher percentages of non-Anglo males and much higher percentages of non-Anglo females and youth are in the labor force, compared to the Anglo population.

Low status and low paying occupations

The obvious relationship between income and employment patterns is revealed in census and survey data. While unemployment in Texas has generally been lower than for the nation in recent years, as in national figures the rates for nonwhites in Texas remain about double that of Anglos. More important is the percentage of *working poor;* the Office of Economic Opportunity in the Texas Department of Community Affairs released figures of 1973 which showed that nearly one half of all poor adult males in Texas are employed but do not make enough money to rise above the poverty level. In 1970 HEW identified Texas as being the nation's leader—the state with the largest number of people in families headed by a person with a full-time job but still with income below the poverty line.[6]

The 1970 census shows the following occupational breakdown:

TABLE 2–4
Occupational breakdown of ethnic minorities

Occupations	Total	Black	Spanish-American
Professional, technical	13.9%	6.8%	7.2%
Managers, administrators	8.6	6.8	4.8
Clerical, sales	24.4	10.2	18.3
Craftspeople, foremen	13.8	8.3	14.3
Semiskilled	32.2	64.8	44.2
Farm workers	3.8	2.5	6.3

Source: U.S. Department of Commerce, *1970 Census of the Population, General Social and Economic Characteristics: Texas* (Washington, D.C.: U.S. Government Printing Office, 1972).

Blacks and chicanos are tremendously overrepresented in the low-paying, semiskilled occupations but vastly underrepresented in professional, technical, managerial, administrative, and even clerical and sales jobs. Blacks are even underrepresented in the craftspeople and foremen category.

Education

Another related area is education. Less than one quarter of the Anglo population has not completed nine years of school; 62 percent of Mexican-Americans and 43.5 percent of blacks never reach the same level.

Nearly 30 percent of Anglos have completed high school, compared to 15 percent of chicanos and 19.5 percent of blacks. At the college level the difference is staggering. Over 13 percent of Anglos have four or more years of college; less than 5 percent of blacks and chicanos in Texas have that much formal education.

Current data, for higher education especially, confirm the continuation of these patterns. In 1970, almost 16 percent of all undergraduates were non-Anglos; by 1976, this figure was still less than 19 percent. Given the very substantial increases in the non-Anglo populations of the state and the relative youth of those populations, this means that these groups continue to be underrepresented in the state colleges and universities by about 50 percent. Even these figures are deceptive when one considers that almost half the black undergraduates attend Texas Southern University and Prairie View, the stepchildren of the Texas university system, historically under-funded, understaffed, and generally offering a lower quality of education compared to even other Texas institutions. At the master's degree level the percentage attending these two schools is even higher. Similarly, almost 40 percent of Mexican-American students attend two schools, Pan American University and the University of Texas at El Paso.

The percentages and numbers drop even more sharply at the postgraduate levels. About eight percent of the Ph.D. students are non-Anglos. See Table 2–5. About 15 percent of all professional school students are non-Anglos, which is about the same as a decade ago. In 1970 there were 10 blacks and 40 chicanos among 1,500 medical students in the state. There are virtually no non-Anglos (or women) in veterinary medicine training. Less than 10 percent of the state's prospective at-

TABLE 2–5
College and university enrollments, by ethnic group, Fall 1976*

Level	Blacks	Mexican-Americans
Freshman	12%	10%
Sophomore	10	10
Junior	8	10
Senior	7	10
Totals	9.5	10
Postgrad and Masters	7.5	7.7
Ph.D.	4.1	4.1
Professional Schools	8.1	7.6

* These data overestimate the black and Mexican-American percentages since the data exclude students not classified as either Anglo, black, or Mexican-American.

Source: Reports of the Coordinating Board, Texas College and University System, 1976.

torneys are non-Anglos.[7] These data are particularly revealing in the contemporary setting after a decade or more of supposedly active recruitment of minorities through affirmative action programs at virtually every educational level.

Similar data are available for virtually every area of social or economic activity. Excepting a thin strata at the top, Mexican-Americans and blacks in Texas have not "made it" and are showing only slight improvements in an era with economic conditions and a national political climate more favorable to their progress than ever before.

SOCIAL STATUS AND RACE RELATIONS

The bottom of the ladder

This brief description of the social and economic conditions of the racial minorities in Texas makes painfully clear the relative and absolute deprivation of blacks and chicanos. However, the discussion may not suggest strongly enough the extent to which the non-Anglos have been relegated to the bottom of the status ladder.

While some black Texans became property owners (mainly small farmers in east and central Texas) during Reconstruction, these gains were wiped out during the post-Reconstruction era; and blacks in Texas have been subjected to intense discrimination until the mid-twentieth century. White Texans also easily forget that Mexican nationals once owned virtually all of the privately held land in what is now South Texas and were the legitimate political authorities in the region. Some Mexicans retreated back across the Nueces and finally the Rio Grande with the continuous incursions of whites into Mexican territory and the military defeats inflicted upon the Mexican forces. Also largely forgotten is the major role played by the Spanish-surnamed in the Texas independence movement, including martyrs of the Alamo, Goliad, and other battles of that era. Most Mexicans in Texas apparently stayed, and the Treaty of Guadalupe Hidalgo ending the Mexican-United States conflict of 1848 explicitly provided for the recognition of the property holdings of the Mexicans in the conquered and ceded territories.

The quick loss of properties held by both groups, after Reconstruction for blacks and after 1850 for Mexican-Americans, is symbolic of the continued treatment accorded both groups by white Texans.[8] Social and economic discrimination has been pervasive across the spectrum of activities, including major areas such as education (not surprisingly the U.S. Supreme Court case[9] challenging as unequal the method Texas uses to finance public schools came from an overwhelmingly chicano district in west San Antonio), jobs, housing, and credit. The combination of overt and subtle discrimination, lack of access to property and capital, and, finally, the inability to enter the political arena has kept the racial minorities in a highly subordinated status at the very bottom of the status ladder.

Responses of the dominant community

Two general responses are made to these observations. First, it is clear that some non-Anglos are moving up within the prevailing social and political structure. Therefore, many Anglo Texans argue that the reasons for the current low status of blacks and chicanos are not inherent in the kind of institutions and patterns of action, including political action, that prevail in Texas. In fact, it is argued that the low status may be attributable to some social and personal characteristics of the minorities themselves. However, even the briefest survey of the current conditions of the minorities in Texas reveals that the minority citizens that experience social mobility are exceptional cases and the mobility achieved is often relative to their own minority group, rather than vis-a-vis Anglos. The greatest recent improvements have been increases in income; yet, as late as 1970 less than 3 percent of Texas blacks and 5.5 percent of Texas Mexican-American families had incomes greater than $15,000, compared to a figure of more than 17 percent for Anglos. In terms of occupational status, educational opportunities, housing conditions, community leadership, and so on, chicanos and blacks are even now making few forward strides. The only highly visible indicator moving rapidly upward for these groups is the crime rate, as they move to urban areas with attendant family breakdown, stress increases, and greater opportunities for extralegal activity.

Another response of Anglos is that times are changing. Even if current data do not reflect these subtle changes, attitudes and behavior are undergoing a subtle transformation. While not denying this argument completely, especially as applied to young people in the state, it can be easily exaggerated. For example, a survey conducted in Houston in 1969–70[10] found continued strong evidences of Anglo hostility toward chicanos and especially blacks, even in an urban setting with a generally more hospitable climate toward racial interaction. When asked if they would be willing to admit a (not a sizable number, but a single person) black or chicano to their street, 14 percent of the Anglo respondents answered negatively toward chicanos and 44 percent would deny admission to a black. Fifteen percent of the Anglos would not want a chicano job supervisor, and 30 percent objected to a black in that position. Close kinship by marriage to chicanos was rejected by 50 percent of the Anglos and to blacks by an overwhelming 90 percent. When asked if minorities should be given special advantages for a limited time, 86 percent of Anglos disagreed. Only 5 percent of Anglos thought that the national government was pushing integration too slowly (compared to 22 percent for Mexican-Americans and 68 percent for blacks). Only 2 percent of the Anglos saw the need for more civil rights demonstrations (compared to 61 percent for blacks and 24 percent for chicanos). These findings are largely substantiated by earlier surveys in other Texas and southwestern cities.[11]

A 1972 survey[12] of Anglo attitudes toward Mexican-Americans in Lubbock, a city of 150,000 with about 17 percent Mexican-American population and a vastly different economic and social life from Houston, reveals quite similar findings in most respects. Over half (53 percent) of the Anglos thought Anglo-Mexican-American relations to be only average; an additional 17 percent thought relations to be "poor." Interestingly, and probably very accurately, the Anglos in Lubbock saw economic and social affairs as the areas of greatest disharmony. Rather small percentages (just over 10 percent) saw any serious chances for improvement in economic and social relationships. In this same vein, large majorities of the Anglos sampled favored bilingual education programs as electives, not requirements; only 12 percent approved of required courses in Mexican-American culture.

As in Houston, most Anglos in Lubbock are willing to work and associate with Mexican-Americans as long as the situation is controlled, but strong opposition is expressed on the issues of children playing together (33 percent "favored" but even more "opposed" or would only "tolerate" such action) and dating and intermarriage (about 15 percent favored, with nearly half opposed and an additional 15 percent "tolerating" this exceedingly sensitive issue area).

The Lubbock study does note significant areas of optimism, particularly in regard to the strong inclination among Anglos to regard Mexican-Americans as individuals rather than in group terms. Anglos did not think other Anglos to be prejudiced against Mexican-Americans and most thought legal equality, at least, to exist. An overwhelming majority thought there ought to be equal treatment among the different ethnic groups. However, over half of the Anglo respondents saw Mexican-Americans as less ambitious (60 percent), less law abiding (51 percent), and less dependable (50.5 percent) than Anglos. It should be remembered that Mexican-Americans are so few in number and so low on the status ladder in Lubbock that their "threat" to Anglos is still viewed as minimal, and tolerance involves little social and/or economic risk. Furthermore, the Lubbock data include no reference to blacks, a group usually regarded more negatively by Anglos in most of the state.

In more directly political matters the Lubbock Anglo respondents reflect a set of views that are undoubtedly widely shared within the Anglo community. While they thought about one quarter of the Anglo community had little if any interest in politics, they thought 60 percent of the Mexican-American community was similarly disinterested. Also, the Anglos had very low opinions of the potential effectiveness of Mexican-American political leaders. Forty-three percent ranked Mexican-American leaders as "poor" or "very poor," compared to 13 percent for Anglo leaders. Given a long list of local, state, and national offices, Anglos seemed somewhat favorable to Mexican-Americans only for local offices, especially the local school board. Even for the school board, only 25 percent of the Anglos were "favorable" toward a Mexican-American holding the job, while 27 percent would "tolerate" such a situation. Nearly 40 percent opposed a Mexican-American as governor and 44 percent disfavored a Mexican-American as president.

Anglo Texans seem to vote their opinions on these issues. A referendum in 1957 on integration of public schools (after national court action[13] declaring officially sanctioned segregation in violation of the Constitution) was turned down by a greater than three-to-one margin. A second referendum on that same ballot called for specific legislation perfecting state laws against mixed marriages and was passed even more overwhelmingly. In Austin, one of the more moderate Anglo-dominated areas of the state, an open housing referendum in 1966 was turned down decisively, even after national legislative and federal court action knocking down racial restrictions in the area of housing.

Interestingly, the Houston study found little difference in attitudes among different age groups, with the exception that young Anglos were a bit more favorable toward interracial marriage. Thus, while the times may be changing, they seem to be changing rather slowly. Obviously, these data reflect somewhat greater tolerance than was present a few generations ago, but equally obvious are the strong elements of hostility or at least grave suspicion.

A PATTERN OF POLITICAL INACTION

Structured apathy

One of the numerous ways in which the Texas political system exhibits characteristics of the systems in underdeveloped countries is in the pattern of participation. As noted elsewhere political participation in Texas is largely restricted to the more affluent, especially at the really meaningful levels of party activism, campaign financing, and Texas consistently ranks among the bottom five among the states in percentage of potential voters actually voting.

The patterns of domination by the few in Texas are only partially the product of low education levels, low incomes, and general conditions of relative deprivation. There is overwhelming evidence that the low participation rates in Texas, especially for the poor and the racial minorities, are products at least in part of calculated efforts by the political leadership of the state to maintain limited access to the political arena. A number of both formal and informal devices have been used to deny or restrain those whose entrance into the system might alter the prevailing patterns of rewards and punishments and threaten the system's stability.

For the lower social sectors in all systems the existence of artificial obstacles to their participation has a profound impact. The poor are burdened by physically and mentally deadening jobs, low income, and lack of sociopolitical awareness, the latter largely a product of low educational levels, consequent lack of understanding of often complex political activities, and lack of leisure time for the observation of and paricipation in politics. The imposition of further restraints has a striking negative impact on participation. Especially important are restraints on voting. While obviously a rarely decisive or even important means of exercising influence, voting is about the only ready means of influence for the vast bulk of the population, especially the less affluent, with their lack of access to other political resources.

The franchise denied

Historically, political elites in Texas have used a combination of constitutional and statutory provisions together with the actions of political parties and private citizens to effectively deny the ballot to large segments of the Texas population, especially the poor and particularly Mexican-Americans and blacks. The use of the "white primary," the poll tax, residency requirements, registration restrictions, the gerrymander, and other formal and informal restraints have kept the system free of potentially change-oriented influences.

The white primary   After Reconstruction the only viable statewide political organization was the Democratic party. By excluding blacks from the Democratic party (and its primary elections) Anglos denied blacks any effective political role in even local politics in Texas. Although challenged repeatedly in state and national courts, not until 1944 did the U.S. Supreme Court outlaw the white primary per se. As late as 1953, the federal courts had to deal with efforts by Texas political leaders to exclude non-Anglos from participating in Democratic primary elections.[14] Not until the 1960s did blacks in Texas vote in any substantial numbers.

Machine politics   Mexican-Americans were not given the blanket "get out and stay out" treatment blacks received during this period, but they were barred from participation in many local areas across the state. Where heavy concentrations of chicanos were found, a common strategy of Anglo leaders was the formation and use of the classic political machine, found in South Texas since before the turn of the century. A "carrot-stick" strategy served to institutionalize Anglo domination in even the overwhelmingly Mexican-American areas, and politically ignorant masses of Mexican-Americans in these areas often welcomed the activities of a patron or jefe to provide small favors and mediate between them and the political authorities. Combined with loss of jobs, physical threats, and other informal inducements that could be offered the chicano, the patron's favors usually proved sufficiently attractive to perpetuate the machine. Consequently, as late as the end of World War II, the overwhelming majority of potential black and chicano voters in Texas were either legally or informally barred from even voting or had their vote tied to the apron strings of one or another "boss" in a political "machine" arrangement.

Poll tax   Another major example of the restrictions placed on participation by lower social status groups is the poll tax, with an even later demise than the white primary. Initiated in 1902, the poll tax was a fee of $1.50 or $1.75, depending on the county, the payment of which registered the prospective voter. Its proponents argued the familiar "voting is not a right but a privilege" theme and cited the tax as a negligible burden serving only to keep the uninformed and casual observers off the rolls. The poll tax was outlawed in elections for federal offices by the 24th Amendment (1964). A federal court decision in 1966[15] outlawed the tax for all elections.

Voting data strongly suggest that people were kept off the rolls, to be sure, but those kept off were overwhelmingly the poor, including the nonwhite poor. Tables 2–6 and 2–7 illustrate the apparent effects of the poll tax on registration, both for the state in selected recent years and for counties with large non-Anglo population components. (More recent years are selected both because of our greater interest in the current scene and to avoid overlapping the effect of the white primary.)

The first nonpoll tax year is 1968 for the statewide figures and 1970 for the county level data in Tables 2–6 and 2–7. There is clearly a sharp break in the percentage of population registered and the percentage voting statewide between the years 1964 and 1968, even though in 1964 there was a native Texan heading the ballot at the presidential level, which probably increased registration and voting for that year. Perhaps a better contrast is that of 1962 and 1970, both nonpresidential years. In 1962 the governor's race drew 1.57 million voters, or 16.4 percent of the total population. Less than a decade later 2.3 million voted in the same race, 20.6 percent of the population. After removal of the tax there has been an average annual increase of nearly 3.5 percent in the numbers registered (not including the 18, 19, and 20 year olds in 1972).[16] (The 1974 decline appears to have been an aberration due to peculiar circumstances of that election.)

TABLE 2–6
Texas voter registration and election data, 1960–1976

Year	Voting age population registered	Voting age population voting presidential elections
1960	50%	41%
1964	51	44
1968	64	49
1972	69	45
1976	74	48
		Gubernatorial elections
1962	43	27%
1966	48	24
1970	63	35
1974	61	20

Registration data through 1966 are estimates based on the number of poll tax receipts, poll tax exemptions, and estimates of number of voters not required to hold exemptions.

Population data are from the 1960 and 1970 census reports and census bureau estimates.

Other registration and all voting data are from the Office of the Secretary of State, Austin, Texas.

Registration restraints The poll tax was tied to a set of registration procedures as important as the tax itself, maybe even more so, in inhibiting registration and voting. Until 1971 prospective voters still had to register annually, before January 31, and appear personally before the appropriate county official at the courthouse. Deputy registrars could not mail or bring in more than a single ballot at a time, effectively circumscribing any impact they might have in registering voters. The consensus of observers is that the Texas system until 1971 was the most restrictive in the entire nation. It has been estimated that annual registration accounted for 25 percent of the difference in registration and voting among the states.[17] An examination of the 1960 and 1968 elections revealed a strong association between annual registration, early registration cutoff, and low levels of voting in both years. Even more relevant to our interests here, the same study found that the impact of annual registration and early cutoffs was even greater for Mexican-Americans and blacks than for the total population.[18]

National court challenges, and legislative reactions to the challenges, in 1971 brought changes in voter registration procedures that may bring Texas into the 20th century, politically. The new registration system has already put hundreds of thousands of new voters on the rolls, on a near permanent basis. Most of these voters are of the less privileged social sectors, with vital, even if still unarticulated, stakes in changing the present patterns of distributing the state's resources. These increases

TABLE 2-7
Registration and turnout, selected counties, 1960–1974

County	1970 population Total	Percent non-Anglo M-A	Percent non-Anglo Negro	Percent non-Anglo Total	Percent of population registered° 1960†	1962†‡§	1970§	1972‡	1974‡§	Percent of population voting° 1960	1962‡§	1970§	1972‡	1974‡§
				COUNTIES WITH 45 PERCENT OR MORE NON-ANGLO POPULATION										
Starr	17,707	97.9	...	97.9	30.8	35.3	46.7	53.7	56.2	25.4	32.5	31.0	31.1	21.1
Jim Hogg	4,654	91.9	1.0	92.9	35.6	38.9	52.4	62.0	70.3	30.6	31.8	30.4	35.1	41.7
Zapata	4,352	91.5	...	91.5	33.5	38.2	52.5	64.5	66.8	21.9	30.7	26.1	31.0	28.3
Maverick	18,093	90.3	...	90.3	16.9	17.8	27.2	32.5	38.9	15.4	13.0	10.0	17.2	8.1
Webb	72,869	85.6	1.7	87.3	20.1	17.6	29.4	35.6	36.4	38.9	11.9	12.7	16.6	9.5
Duval	11,722	84.5	...	84.5	38.1	35.0	49.2	54.3	42.7	36.0	30.2	31.6	37.4	27.9
Dimmit	9,039	81.7	1.0	82.7	18.7	22.8	37.5	49.4	53.6	16.8	12.6	18.5	26.3	29.7
Zavala	9,275	81.6	...	81.6	14.7	15.6	35.1	47.2	57.4	12.5	10.9	14.0	42.0	40.8
Brooks	8,005	79.9	1.3	81.2	37.0	31.4	57.7	58.3	59.9	32.5	19.1	30.8	33.5	26.3
Hidalgo	181,535	79.1	0.8	79.9	18.7	16.8	34.3	49.4	46.0	37.3	13.3	16.2	22.4	9.7
Kenedy	678	78.5	...	78.5	20.4	19.0	40.9	45.3	46.0	16.9	13.8	23.0	30.2	22.6
La Salle	5,014	78.4	...	78.4	19.0	16.8	46.3	60.3	63.0	18.8	10.0	23.1	40.3	43.5
Kinney	2,006	72.2	6.0	78.2	27.4	23.2	49.1	53.9	70.5	27.4	17.3	29.9	...	27.2
Loving	164	77.5	...	77.5	42.5	45.1	56.7	53.0	49.4	39.4	31.9	40.2	53.0	27.4
Cameron	140,368	76.2	1.0	77.2	16.6	13.8	34.2	41.2	45.3	15.9	12.0	15.7	23.3	11.9
Willacy	15,570	76.8	...	76.8	21.7	19.3	37.8	45.9	42.7	18.8	11.3	18.9	23.3	11.3
Presidio	4,842	75.3	...	75.3	26.5	26.7	41.8	48.6	...	25.7	17.5	29.9	30.0	13.2
Frio	11,159	69.1	1.0	70.1	20.4	23.4	37.4	49.7	59.2	18.1	17.2	14.9	30.7	28.8
McMullen	1,095	67.9	...	67.9	42.7	40.3	53.2	58.3	56.4	34.8	28.7	33.0	36.2	23.7
Jim Wells	33,032	64.0	1.2	65.2	25.3	27.1	44.5	47.6	47.1	23.4	17.1	20.5	27.6	14.8
Jeff Davis	1,527	61.6	1.3	62.9	25.0	27.2	45.7	54.6	50.6	27.3	25.2	25.0	35.8	23.7
Hudspeth	2,392	60.4	1.0	61.4	25.7	25.1	37.6	45.4	61.0	22.6	12.8	24.8	26.5	36.3
El Paso	359,291	56.9	3.1	60.0	14.6	12.5	26.5	36.4	29.8	14.5	10.5	13.5	22.3	12.4
Val Verde	27,471	56.6	2.8	59.4	15.7	14.6	30.1	38.4	33.4	15.4	10.9	14.9	21.7	12.8
Reeves	16,526	53.3	3.2	56.5	21.7	21.5	29.9	41.8	37.5	21.0	14.0	14.7	23.0	8.3
Waller	14,285	3.5	52.6	56.1	24.3	22.1	33.7	47.8	37.3	18.7	16.2	16.7	25.6	11.5
Sutton	3,175	55.0	1.0	56.0	28.8	33.4	39.0	45.3	52.1	25.5	17.9	18.7	30.1	18.2
Caldwell	21,178	32.4	21.7	54.1	20.9	20.0	33.2	38.1	42.5	25.0	15.7	16.4	29.3	12.9
Uvalde	17,348	50.7	1.7	52.4	21.0	20.3	37.7	51.7	55.4	22.6	15.9	19.4	31.3	22.4
Atascosa	18,696	51.4	0.9	52.3	26.0	24.0	42.3	48.5	47.6	21.4	14.6	18.6	27.4	13.8
Bexar	830,460	45.3	6.8	52.1	18.2	17.7	31.3	40.2	38.6	20.2	14.9	15.8	26.9	14.2

County	Base													
San Patricio	47,288	49.1	2.4	51.5	21.1	18.6	39.8	45.4	42.7	20.1	11.6	16.9	26.2	10.0
Medina	20,249	48.5	1.9	50.4	22.5	21.5	35.7	45.1	50.4	21.4	18.6	17.7	28.2	17.0
Culberson	3,429	50.1	...	50.1	28.4	27.9	35.2	40.0	39.3	25.2	15.1	19.6	20.4	16.0
Goliad	4,869	37.6	12.0	49.6	26.1	24.5	50.3	52.2	56.6	29.6	18.5	24.9	29.5	15.0
Brewster	7,780	47.8	0.5	48.3	22.8	22.7	37.0	42.4	48.4	24.5	19.6	22.5	31.9	13.2
Kleberg	33,166	43.9	4.4	48.3	19.4	16.0	30.5	44.3	41.8	20.2	11.8	17.3	29.2	14.4
Nueces	237,544	43.6	4.7	47.3	21.3	18.5	38.3	46.3	40.7	28.4	14.2	17.1	31.5	15.3
Refugio	9,494	38.0	9.2	47.2	28.0	26.3	45.2	52.5	46.0	23.6	17.1	22.0	30.7	13.3
Gonzales	16,375	30.2	15.4	45.6	20.3	18.4	40.2	41.5	50.9	21.7	15.1	18.6	23.3	12.6
Totals	2,241,430													

COUNTIES WITH 35 PERCENT OR MORE BLACK POPULATION

County	Base													
Waller	14,285	3.5	52.6	56.1	24.3	22.1	33.7	42.8	37.3	18.7	16.2	16.7	25.6	11.5
Marion	8,517	...	44.7	44.7	22.3	19.6	45.4	54.9	60.3	21.7	13.2	20.8	30.1	16.8
San Jacinto	6,702	1.8	41.9	43.7	25.7	25.5	52.6	65.1	80.4	22.2	16.2	20.9	33.8	14.8
Houston	17,855	3.2	40.7	43.9	21.0	19.7	47.4	51.1	54.2	22.8	14.2	24.5	28.0	12.1
Harrison	44,841	...	36.8	36.8	21.0	18.6	43.1	49.6	46.3	19.6	16.8	22.5	28.7	13.2
San Augustine	7,858	...	35.6	35.6	29.7	25.1	46.1	55.0	53.2	24.7	15.0	18.0	28.6	11.3
Robertson	14,389	8.6	35.4	44.0	21.2	18.7	48.3	55.3	49.1	23.3	13.8	23.9	26.8	15.2
Grimes	11,855	9.5	35.2	44.7	19.6	20.9	40.7	46.5	50.4	22.2	13.9	21.2	27.8	13.5
Camp	8,005	...	35.0	35.0	28.6	27.1	50.8	61.0	59.0	31.3	16.2	25.2	32.5	15.0
Totals	134,307													

URBAN COUNTIES WITH LARGE NON-ANGLO POPULATIONS

County	Base													
Bexar	830,460	45.3	6.8	52.1	18.2	17.7	31.3	40.2	38.6	20.2	14.9	15.8	26.9	14.2
El Paso	359,291	56.8	3.1	60.0	14.6	12.5	26.5	36.4	29.8	14.5	10.5	13.9	23.3	12.4
Nueces	237,544	43.6	4.7	48.3	21.8	18.5	38.3	46.3	40.7	20.2	14.2	17.1	31.5	15.3
Hidalgo	181,535	79.1	0.8	79.9	18.7	16.7	34.3	49.4	46.0	17.3	13.3	16.2	22.3	9.7
Cameron	140,368	76.2	1.0	77.2	16.6	13.8	37.8	41.2	45.3	15.9	12.0	15.7	23.3	11.9
Webb	72,869	85.6	1.7	86.3	20.1	17.6	29.4	35.6	36.4	18.9	11.9	12.7	16.6	9.5
Totals	1,822,067													
State	11,196,730	18.4	12.5	30.9	23.4	21.0	37.1	46.6	44.3	23.4	16.4	20.6	30.7	14.8

* The voting base for all years is the total vote in the gubernatorial general election contest, which involves a larger total vote than any of the primaries, with the governor's race usually drawing more total votes than other statewide contests.

† The 1960 and 1962 figures are based on poll tax receipts and estimations of the population over 60 years of age. (Persons over age 60 did not have to pay the tax and did not have to file for exemptions in cities of less than 10,000. A standard formula is the addition of 25 percent of poll tax payers to the total, based on the ratio of those over 60 to the rest of the population.)

‡ The 1962, 1972, and 1974 percentages are calculated on the basis of 1960 (for 1962) and 1970 (for 1972 and 1974) population totals. In some counties, especially the growing urban counties, this procedure will slightly overstate the percentage registered and percentage voting. Most of the counties on this table, excepting the urban counties in the last section, have had relatively stable population totals for the past two decades.

§ The years 1962, 1970, and 1974 are nonpresidential election years. In Texas as elsewhere the percentage registered and especially the percentage voting declines sharply in non-presidential election years. The election of 1970 is remarkable in that the percentages are much higher than would be expected, based on past patterns. Most observers explain this sharp increase in terms of the removal of the poll tax and annual registration requirements.

in voter registration and turnout in Texas have occurred even though there has been a general national decline in popular participation, the addition of the 18-to-20 age group with their abysmal participation rates to the voting age population, and a dearth of candidates appealing to working and lower-class voters. Furthermore, much of the increase in the voting age population has occurred among lower-status groups, especially minorities, including a large and increasing legal and illegal alien population, which can be expected to have much lower participation rates than higher-status, better educated populations.

Other restraints on minority mobilization

The exercise of political influence and especially the development of independent political organization by the racial minorities has been inhibited by a number of factors beyond the general restrictions mentioned earlier.

Electoral majorities and apportionment   Probably the major inhibiting factor has been and remains the lack of popular majorities in but few electoral units. Blacks are an absolute majority in only one county in the state and constitute more than 40 percent in only three others. Mexican-Americans are a majority in 29 of the 254 counties and are 40 percent or more in 10 others. Thus, even in county-level elections (county judges, clerks, sheriffs, and so on) only in a few largely rural counties can chicanos or blacks control local politics, even with the most striking examples of bloc voting.

Apportionment of voting districts as a weapon to restrict the political impact of minorities has been very effectively used by Texas political elites. In fact, black and chicano voters living in metropolitan areas have been subjected to double discrimination as state and local political leaders have fought to maintain rural dominance at the expense of the cities. The entire decade of the 1960s was devoted to a "holding action" by state leaders as they fought the national courts over whether district lines (from county commissioners' courts to the state senate) could be drawn to underrepresent blacks, chicanos, and urban areas. By the end of the decade, after dozens of unsuccessful efforts to maintain the old system, it was relatively clear that the overt discrimination of past decades could not be employed. Less overt methods, such as gerrymandering and use of multimember districts, are still important, however.

The gerrymander can be used in one of two basic ways. First, if the minority is so large that it must be accorded some representation, then one district can be set aside for that group, enclosing as much of the minority as possible in that district. A good example is the congressional district in central Houston. This insures that the large minority population of the Houston area elects only one of five area representatives.

Where possible, a more common alternative has been to cut the minority community into pieces, attaching different parts to districts with Anglo majorities and completely eliminating minority voices. This has been the pattern followed in the Dallas-Fort Worth region, for example.

The multimember district is used for virtually all the state's municipal governments and school boards. This device enables a majority in an area to control a large number of seats on a city council or school board rather than dividing those seats according to population. Commonly, the majority will set aside one or two places for a token black or Mexican-American of acceptably "moderate" political views. Under national court pressure, the legislature has terminated the multimember state legislative districts, but multimember districts continue to be the rule for local governmental units. Lest one forget the intransigence of Texas elites on this subject it might be noted that in March, 1978, the U.S. Supreme Court overturned the state legislative district lines in Tarrant County (Fort Worth) on the basis that the districting there discriminated on the basis of ethnic identification.

The decades of discrimination against blacks and Mexican-Americans regarding the exercise of the franchise have created patterns of inaction that will not be broken overnight. The apathy and alienation among blacks and Mexican-Americans in Texas has become deeply rooted over several generations. The leadership of neither major party is seriously interested in mobilizing minority voters. The subcultures of both blacks and chicanos deemphasize conventional political action. Patterns of attitudes and action that have developed over several generations will be broken only very slowly.

Attitudes, alienation, and inaction

Probably the most extensive statewide survey of racially based differences in participation, party identification, and commitment to the system yet available was undertaken in late 1969.[19] Although the data refer only to the actual and not the potential electorate, the findings are very interesting. As the findings summarized in Table 2–8 illustrate, Anglos indicated greater political activism according to virtually every standard. Especially noteworthy are the figures for the categories "Worked for candidates" and "How often do you talk politics with your friends?"

The survey results confirm the generally assumed attachments of non-Anglo voters to the Democratic party. Over 40 percent of the surveyed Mexican-Americans think of themselves as strong Democrats and nearly nine of ten identify with that party. The appeals of Johnson, Truman, and Roosevelt to lower status groups, nonwhites, and Catholics only reinforced a pattern begun decades earlier in South Texas. This striking attachment is overshadowed, however, by the data for blacks. Almost

TABLE 2–8

Racial differences in political participation in Texas

	Anglo	Black	Mexican-American
Given money to campaigns	24%	16%	11%
Attended political rallies	32	18	22
Worked for candidates	24	21	13
How often do you talk politics with your friends?			
Frequently	27	23	14
Never	9	16	22

Source: Clifton McCleskey and Bruce Merrill, "Mexican-American Political Behavior in Texas," *Social Science Quarterly* 53, no. 4 (March 1973): 787.

two of three black voters in the survey identified as strong Democrats and nine of ten were either strong or weak identifiers. Only one in two Anglos identify with the Democratic party.

The voting habits revealed in the survey data largely conform to these party identifications, although Mexican-Americans seem to engage in more ticket-splitting and support for selected Republicans. Republican strength in general remains negligible, however.

Finally, the voters were asked about their perceived feelings of efficacy and alienation. While one in four Anglos surveyed perceived themselves as very capable of having a political impact, only one in ten blacks and Mexican-Americans felt similarly. At the other end of the scale, while one fourth of the Anglos indicated low degrees of perceived efficacy, nearly one in two blacks and chicanos were in this category. Concerning alienation, only one fourth of the Anglos had high degrees of alienation, compared to over half the black sample and more than one third of the chicanos. The intermediate (although usually much closer to the blacks) position of Mexican-Americans in this alienation pattern appears in most of the survey data gathered by Merrill, a point to which we return at the end of this chapter.

TABLE 2–9

Political efficacy and alienation among Texas voters

	Anglos (N 797)	Blacks (N 419)	Mexican-Americans (N 375)
Degree of efficacy			
High	24%	8%	10%
Medium	49	46	46
Low	27	46	44
Degree of alienation			
Low	45%	14%	26%
Medium	30	34	38
High	25	52	36

Source: Clifton McCleskey and Bruce Merrill, "Mexican-American Political Behavior in Texas," *Social Science Quarterly*, 53, no. 4 (March 1973): 795–96.

The political import of alienation and apathy

If close to 25 percent of the voters (and over 30 percent of the potential voters) in the state are non-Anglos, if those voters are largely found in particular regions of the state, and if the masses of those voters share not only general feelings of alienation and deprivation but also a generally "liberal" perspective on contemporary policy issues, one might imagine that the voice of the black and chicano citizens of Texas would be strongly felt in state politics. Instead, as two long-time observers have said, "so far as state government is concerned, the prevailing attitude is one of neglect and indifference." While that comment had special reference to Mexican-Americans, there is little doubt that the conclusion is at least as relevant for blacks.

There is almost literally no significant, serious legislation on the books in Texas designed to meet the specific needs of blacks and/or chicanos. For example, bilingual education has been for decades at the top of the list of desired state actions for chicanos, who watch their children consistently fail in the English-speaking (and thinking) school systems. Yet, the only bilingual programs in Texas before 1972 were nationally funded efforts. The state's political leadership has appeared unconcerned that Mexican-Americans in Texas have an average educational level of six to seven years.

Equally visible is the lack of black and chicano officeholders in the state. Table 2–10 illustrates the situation. In 1978, minorities hold three of 26 U.S. House and Senate seats, three of 31 state Senate seats, and 30 of 150 state Representative positions. The Democratic party, with its virtual monopoly on public offices, has *never* nominated a black or chicano for statewide office.

At the state government level, the proportion of non-Anglo representation is higher than ever before among elected officeholders but is still less than half the proportionate share in terms of population totals. At the appointive level, on the critically important state boards and commissions there is a near total absence of black representation and the Spanish-surnamed hold less than four percent of these positions, and even these are largely positions on the less important boards. In addition,

TABLE 2–10

Black and Mexican-American national and state officeholders

	Mexican-Americans						Blacks					
Office	1961	1965	1971	1973	1975	1977	1961	1965	1971	1973	1975	1977
U.S. Congressmen (26) ...	0	1	2	2	2	2	0	0	0	1	1	1
State Senators (31)	2	1	1	1	2	3	0	0	1	0	0	0
State Representatives (150)	5	8	9	9	13	17	0	0	2	8	9	13

excepting the five Mexican-Americans on the board of Pan American University, there is a near total absence of non-Anglos on the governing boards of the state's colleges and universities.

Some evidence indicates that the near total absence of minority representation is changing, at least slightly. In 1978, there were about 850 Mexican-American public officeholders in Texas (most of them either school board members or city government officers in small South Texas towns and counties). This is a substantially larger number than the figure for just a decade earlier. The number of black officeholders remains negligible, however. Furthermore, county-level data indicate that since the early 1960s there has been a marked increase in both registration and voting in almost all the counties with large minority populations.

Before becoming too excited over the impending black and brown takeover of Texas politics, the observer must note that in 1978 there were only nine Spanish-surnamed county judges among Texas' 254 counties and that the election of Texas' only black county judge in 1974 (the first since Reconstruction) was viewed as so peculiar that it made statewide headlines and drew national attention. Less than eight percent of the state's county commissioners are Mexican-American and black commissioners are virtually nonexistent, in a state where one in three citizens is either black or Mexican-American.

Much of the change noted above has been produced by *national* legislative, executive, and especially judicial actions. Court decisions requiring single member districting on the basis of population has sharply increased non-Anglo representation at the local government as well as state and national levels. Enforcement of the Voting Rights Act has undoubtedly increased black and Mexican-American participation, as has elimination of the poll tax, annual registration, and other registration restraints.

DIFFICULT CHOICES: NEW STRATEGIES

Alternatives for black Texans

The lack of response of the state Democratic party to the demands of the minorities, even though blacks and chicanos have overwhelmingly supported the party at both state and national levels, has brought increased agitation for different strategies. Leaders among Texas blacks have called for increased local organization of blacks independent of the Democratic party. However, given its responsiveness to blacks at the national level and the virtual impossibility of going their own way with their relatively small population base in the state, black leaders in Texas have continued to urge working within the framework of the Democratic party at the state and national levels.

The dilemma of blacks in most of the state is stark. On the one hand they can continue to vote a straight Democratic ticket and probably reap some rewards by helping to maintain Democratic party dominance in the national legislature and especially swinging the state for Democratic presidential nominees (as in 1960, 1968, and 1976), in which the vote of both minorities is crucial. At the same time straight ticket voting insures the continued domination of the conservative leadership of the state party and election of conservative Democrats to state and local offices, leaders whose responsiveness to the minorities in Texas has ranged from indifference to hostility.

Yet, like most voters, especially those of lower status background, black voters generally lack the organization, awareness, and sophistication to make the sometimes complex distinctions necessary to intelligently split tickets, discriminating among friendly and not-so-friendly candidates of the same party. This is well illustrated by the common occurrence of mostly black precincts voting for local conservative incumbents in Democratic primaries.

Furthermore, black voters have nowhere to go in terms of alternative parties or movements. The Republican party in Texas has distinguished itself largely by exhibiting even less interest than the Democrats in the economic and social issues that concern blacks. Also, blacks lack the population concentrations that would encourage anything other than local independent organization, which state laws discourage.

Consider Dallas county, for example, in which about 15 percent (over 250,000) of the state's black population lives. Until 1972, Dallas never had a black representative in Washington, never had a black representative in Austin, and never had a black city council member. Gerrymandering of districts, use of multimember districts (for state legislature, school board, and city council), the ingrained patterns of nonparticipation resutling from the white primary-poll tax days, and a variety of other techniques have had the effect of keeping black representation at a minimum. In fact, Dallas has rarely had representatives at any level who have paid much attention to the black community, given the strongly conservative orientation and the racial indifference and often hostility of the white majority in the area. Thus, at every November general election the voters of East Dallas and Oak Cliff get a choice between a middle class Anglo conservative Democrat and a middle class Anglo conservative Republican in virtually every contest on the ticket.

It is in the Democratic party primaries that blacks have their greatest opportunity to seriously affect the system and ultimately receive favorable state government policy outputs. In some few electoral units blacks can "go-it-alone" and nominate and elect black candidates. In most electoral units, however, black voting strength is insufficient to pursue this strategy and a coalition strategy is necessary. Unfortunately for the aspirations of black Texans, racial distrust and disharmony is sufficient to negate this option in most instances. Even if blacks have sufficient strength to win the Democratic nomination, Anglos, both Democrat and Republican, often unite in the general election to deny the victory. Thus far at least, the only black candidates to win the electoral districts not overwhelmingly black in composition have been those willing to largely ignore the black community's interests.

Since 1970, the utilization of federal court-imposed single-member districts in the larger cities of the state has made possible the election of several black legislators from Dallas, Houston, and San Antonio. One result has been the formation of the Black Caucus in the state House of Representatives. To the surprise of many observers, this often tenuous coalition has been able to extract from the overwhelmingly Anglo and conservative House some important rewards for blacks. Sometimes working with the Mexican-American representatives but more often pursuing a rather lonely road, this group has publicized the appalling administrative and academic conditions at predominantly black Prairie View A&M.[20] Even in the face of major opposition from supporters of Texas A&M, Prairie View's parent institution, the caucus was able to shame the House into formally investigating conditions of the school. The caucus has also secured substantially increased levels of funding for black colleges, such as Prairie View and Texas Southern, schools that have traditionally been ignored by the state's budget-makers. The establishment of a prison reform study committee and the creation of single-member districts for the Dallas school board are other examples of situations where the caucus has successfully organized enough support to achieve results with direct actual and potential benefit for blacks in both their own constituencies and beyond. The eight caucus members voted unanimously against the proposed new constitution in 1974, when only three more affirmative votes were needed for its passage. One of the caucus members argued that "racism lurked in every article except maybe the preamble and bill of rights."

The caucus and its individual members have become sufficiently well known that they receive communications and entreaties from blacks from across the state. In fact, perhaps their greatest contribution to this point has been their very presence as highly vocal and visible spokespersons for black interests.[21]

To "go-it-alone": The chicano option

The situation of Mexican-Americans in Texas is only slightly different from that of blacks. While they are more numerous than blacks, the strength of numbers is reduced by their greater integration into the Anglo population and the often lower degree of perceived discrimination and alienation.

Probably the greatest difference in the situation of blacks and chicanos politically is the concentration of chicanos large enough to form majorities and near majorities in most of South and Southwest Texas. This concentration presents at least the possibility of local chicano control over a wide region and provides the backbone for an independent political movement, La Raza Unida party (LRUP), with its first statewide efforts in 1972.

If double the LRUP gubernatorial percent of 6.3 percent in 1972 and 5.6 percent in 1974 is considered a significant vote for the third party, then about 30 counties demonstrated significant levels of support in those elections. (See Table 2–11.) Of the counties with Mexican-American majorities only the Parr Machine of Duval county and the virtually uninhabited areas of far West Texas failed to give significant support to the LRUP. It should be noted that the Democratic party nominee in both years, Dolph Briscoe, is a South Texas native, probably drawing greater support in the area than would ordinarily be the case.

As this country's history clearly shows, the organization of viable third party movements is extremely difficult in the single-member, winner-take-all electoral context, particularly when identifications with existing parties remain fairly strong. LRUP faces additional obstacles as well. It lacks money in a state with a well deserved reputation for having the most expensive public offices in the country. It has few well-known personalities to present as candidates. It lacks a strong widespread organization. It is perceived as a chicano movement and, as such, picks up support in the nonchicano electorate only from strongly liberal Anglos and then only when the Democratic party is offering no liberal-moderate alternative. LRUP must also contend with deeply ingrained Democratic party identification among Mexican-Americans. Furthermore, there has developed in several parts of the state, including urban regions of South Texas, pockets of liberal Democratic strength. Thus, LRUP often must field candidates against Democrats with at least similar perspectives and with Spanish surnames as well. Even Mexican-Americans sympathetic to LRUP are not inclined to give electoral or other support for fear of wasting their vote and/or effort.

In addition, two major recent blows have hurt the party badly. During his tenure as governor, Dolph Briscoe pursued what can be called something close to a vendetta against LRUP and especially its Zavala county leader and party founder, José Angel Gutiérrez. Briscoe, a very wealthy South Texas rancher from a predominantly Mexican-American area, wasted no opportunity during his term of office to punish what he has called a "communist" movement. The governor's attacks, verbal and actual denials of material governmental assistance, have undoubtedly damaged the party. The most devastating blow, though, was the arrest and conviction in 1976 of the two-time LRUP gubernatorial candidate, Ramsey Muñiz, on a charge of conspiracy to distribute marijuana. Just

TABLE 2–11

Areas of La Raza Unida strength (counties with 10 percent or more support for LRUP gubernatorial candidate)

	1972	1974
Zavala	52.2	53.8
Brooks	51.1	36.9
Jim Hogg	46.2	22.7
Maverick	37.2	24.9
LaSalle	36.5	39.0
Frio	33.4	24.2
Webb	31.8	32.1
Dimmit	30.7	26.9
Hidalgo	28.1	22.3
Kleberg	28.3	24.1
Brewster	28.1	12.8
Willacy	28.1	19.6
Jim Wells	27.8	21.2
Hays	26.7	10.8
Zapata	25.3	23.7
Val Verde	24.5	11.3
Bee	22.9	13.3
Jeff Davis	19.4	8.6
Nueces	18.5	20.2
Presidio	18.3	19.6
Starr	18.0	11.5
Travis	17.8	15.2
Crockett	17.8	14.5
Kenedy	16.1	3.3
El Paso	16.0	11.2
Reeves	15.9	4.7
Cameron	14.6	14.5
Bexar	14.4	11.3
Caldwell	14.3	7.2
Uvalde	13.6	10.5
Medina	12.0	4.4
Sutton	12.0	5.5
Crosby	11.7	5.1
Goliad	11.3	7.1
San Patricio	11.2	11.1
Calhoun	10.4	5.8
Wilson	10.1	4.8
Atascosa	10.2	3.6

Source: Compiled from official election returns, Office of the Secretary of State of Texas.

when it appeared that the party had attained a measure of legitimacy, recognition, and a solid 20 to 40 percent level of support in much of South Texas, this incident was critically damaging.

It appears that at least for the near future LRUP will be limited to maintaining its base in a few very poor, overwhelmingly Mexican-American counties of South Texas. There seems little chance of expanding the movement's base to even the more populous South Texas areas, and its role as a "spoiler" in statewide contests currently seems very limited.

Furthermore, LRUP's efforts to broaden its appeal to include non-chicano lower and working class voters, and especially the black voters of Texas, can be termed nothing less than a wholesale failure. None of the counties with large black populations has shown more than a token LRUP vote, and spot checks of largely black precincts in Austin and San Antonio reveal very low levels of support for Muñiz and other LRUP candidates.

Like almost all social groups, even ethnic groups, Mexican-Americans are not of one political mind, even though they share a wide range of fundamental views. One illustration, with political overtones, is the difference in opinions concerning identification. Many Spanish-surnamed individuals prefer the designation Mexicano, others Spanish-American, others Mexican-American, others chicano. Many, in fact, refuse the designation chicano, given its original reference (with derogatory implications), to lower class Mexican immigrants. Middle class Mexican-Americans with aspirations of becoming integrated into Anglo society are especially uncomfortable with the chicano movement. LRUP is perceived by many as being too "radical," separatist, nationalist, and obtrusive. Just as the Black Panthers or the NAACP do not appeal to all blacks alike, LRUP does not bridge the gaps among all Mexican-Americans.

Some evidence of recent years strongly suggests that Mexican-Americans may be considerably more conservative in their political views than previously believed, and especially as perceived by Anglos. A combination of religious, cultural, and political influences have produced a perspective that allows for considerable toleration, if not support of, conservative political perspectives. Authoritarian family structures, church officers with moderate to conservative social and economic views, and strong political machines that have at least provided a few elementary services—these are the kinds of influences that continue to inhibit independent action by Mexican-Americans and especially inhibit the support of an organization as strongly change-oriented as La Raza.

On the other hand, LRUP activities and chicano mobilization more generally have forced the two major parties to pay at least minimal attention to Mexican-American demands. For the Democratic Party, especially, it is no longer possible to either completely ignore chicanos or manipulate their support as in the past. While the Mexican-American community remains splintered and relatively apathetic, the rising numbers of Spanish-surnamed elected and appointed officials suggests changes in the patterns. And the dramatic increases in population, both natural and from legal and illegal immigration, in the overwhelmingly Mexican-American South and Southwest Texas area will ulimately change the character of the political order in that region and probably the state as a whole.

CONCLUSIONS

Texas has a very large minority group population. Blacks, Mexican-Americans, and other minorities make up about a third of the total population of the state. In this chapter we have analyzed the political role which ethnic minorities play in Texas politics, and we can now draw the following conclusions:

1. Although blacks and Mexican-Americans constitute a large percentage of the Texas population and have a large stake in changing the prevailing patterns of governmental and political rewards or penalties, ethnic minorities do not yet provide a serious political force in Texas. Voting turnout is low among blacks and chicanos, and their involvement in the crucial political activities beyond merely voting is minimal. Virtually no blacks and few chicanos serve in elected or appointive public office, and Anglo officeholders rarely have to provide more than symbolic rewards to their non-Anglo constituents. The Democratic Party, the traditional home of Texas' ethnic minorities, continues to be led by the conservative faction which has little interest in mobilizing working class people in general and racial minorities in particular. The propertied interests of the Texas establishment resist the mobilization of minorities because of their heavy economic stake in maintaining a large, unorganized, and politically docile labor force.

2. Texas' ethnic minorities share common problems, but geographical separation and intergroup competition for scarce resources (such as for jobs and housing) have meant that ethnic minorities are in conflict as often as they cooperate in the political arena. Cooperation among minority groups does exist in large urban areas, but the cooptation of Mexican-Americans in these areas by the Anglo political leadership has presented an obstacle (along with others) to lasting, institutionalized cooperation between blacks and chicanos.

3. There has been increasing political activity in Texas among blacks and chicanos, especially since the mid-1960s. A growing political organization of these groups has been made possible by federal court decisions forcing legislative reapportionment, federal government efforts to insure the political rights of minorities, the general success of the civil rights movement, the continued urbanization of blacks and chicanos with little relative improvement in their social and economic condition, and moderation of Anglo Texans' attitudes toward minorities.

4. One effect of the increased mobilization of ethnic minorities in Texas has been an increase in the representation of liberals in state politics. While recent court decisions threaten the democratization of the

system that has been largely responsible for the liberal gains, the heightened and better organized political activity of minorities should at least hold the ground gained in the past decade. Nevertheless, it is not possible at this point to determine whether liberal gains will be converted into the policy changes which are necessary to seriously and consistently aid the minorities.

5.   A less tangible impact of the increasing political mobilization of minorities has been to encourage a reorientation of Texas politics. The conservative leadership of the Democratic party has been required to make some difficult choices. If a female, Catholic, two-term state representative from Corpus Christi can, as in 1972, seriously challenge the choices of the leadership of the conservative faction, its domination of state politics may be cracking. Because blacks and chicanos are making their political demands more effectively, some traditional Democratic leaders (such as Lloyd Bentson, the Democratic senator from Texas) are seeking accommodation. Of course, the enhanced role of minorities in the Texas Democratic party has accelerated the movement of conservative Anglos into the Republican party—the so-called Connally alternative. If the heightened organization and mobilization of minorities causes Anglos to join the Republican party as an alternative to remaining in a Democratic party strongly influenced by minorities, this will be a godsend for Texas Republicans.

6.   Much of the political strength of the minority electorate in Texas is potential, not actual. The liberal Anglo-minority group coalition is only now capable of competing in statewide races. The prospects for this coalition are better in local contests, where political victories are attainable. Local political successes for ethnic minorities could be a starting point for making the serious policy changes which could alter the prevailing pattern of rewards and deprivations in the Texas political system.

The political mobilization of Texas' ethnic minorities will tend to destabilize a system that has been remarkably successful in avoiding political change. While changes may not be commensurate with those in other under-developed areas, common processes of political change are in motion in Texas. Having been passive subjects in a system that usually ignored them (and when it did not, they often wished it had), ethnic minorities currently are on center stage. Their political mobilization is crucial both to reshaping the general political process and altering the pattern of political outputs to fit the needs of all Texans in the last quarter of the 20th century.

CHAPTER THREE

Parties, elections, and interest groups

Th' dimmycratic party ain't on speaking terms
with itsilf.*

Within both the national and state political systems, the functions of
political parties include the nomination of candidates seeking public
office, the mobilization of popular support for candidates in competitive
elections, and, ultimately, the contribution of viable inputs into the policymaking process.[1] Traditionally, at least for the past century, the political
system of Texas has been characterized by one-party dominance. Until
1978, the highly factionalized Democratic party had, nevertheless, been
able to dominate electoral contests for virtually every office listed on
the ballot. Were it not for the election of U.S. Senator John Tower in 1961
(as well as his subsequent reelections in 1966 and 1972), several congressmen, a handful of state legislators, and some recent relatively close
gubernatorial contests, the Republican party in Texas would have been,
for all practical purposes, nonexistent. However, the election of Republican Bill Clements to the governor's office, the equally close reelection
of John Tower to the U.S. Senate, and a pick-up of two Congressional
seats to bring the total to four Representatives has breathed new life into
the state's Grand Old Party. Even so, the Republicans must build their
base at grass roots level if Texas is to have a viable two-party system
in the future. In addition, there are a number of other political, cultural,
and socio-economic factors which make politics in Texas unique.

The late V. O. Key, Jr., once observed that Texas is the only state of
the original Confederacy in which blacks are *not* the prime issue in political campaigns. Rather, he continued, the main concern of Texans
is "money and how to make it."[2] Oil, natural gas, sulfur, insurance, cattle,
and agribusiness are the significant commodities. It is in relation to the

---

* Mr. Dooley discusses party politics.

control of these economic resources that minorities, of which blacks are only a portion, may be viewed as a potential threat to white domination. Accordingly, on those occasions when the state government has attempted to limit suffrage it was done with the unexpressed intention to minimize the political *and* economic strength of chicanos, poor whites, labor, and blacks. As we shall see, the poll tax, the "white primary," and annual registration requirements have served well in these attempts to maintain the power of the white Democratic elite.

Today, however, the political system is undergoing a substantial change as clearly reflected by the results of the 1978 election. Primarily through inputs from the national level, including constitutional amendments, congressional legislation, and several important decisions of the Supreme Court of the United States, the franchise in Texas and elsewhere has been significantly broadened; so much so, in fact, that with few exceptions all citizens have the opportunity to actively participate. Accordingly, the system is becoming increasingly responsive to a heterogeneous electorate and thus is becoming more liberalized and unpredictable.

INTEREST GROUPS: PRESSURE AND LOBBYING ACTIVITIES

Americans are great joiners and organizers. When an organization forms for some recognized goal or special purpose, it may be termed a *special interest group,* particularly as it begins to promote that interest publicly. Unlike political parties, interest groups do not seek to capture office and operate the government but rather to influence government policy. Some writers term these groups *pressure groups* when they use publicity and propaganda, attempting to rally public support and acceptance of their common interest. This process has something of a "shotgun" effect. When an interest group aims directly at influencing state officials, particularly legislators, it uses the "rifle-shot" technique of hiring *lobbyists.* The term lobbying comes, of course, from the practice of interest group representatives positioning themselves in the lobbies of legislative and executive chambers.

The typical lobbyist is a former member of the legislature he is lobbying—or often a former executive aide.[3] This position gives him the contacts so important to his success, plus an intimate knowledge of the rules which govern the creation of a bill and its passage into law. Some lobbyists represent a half dozen interest groups or more. The most successful ones, however, represent one major interest group and they are highly effective and well-paid specialists. Lobbyists claim, and most legislators agree, that they perform a vital role in the complex life of the modern legislative process—they provide accurate and detailed information at a moment's notice on any aspect of a bill of importance to their interest group. Some of the less acceptable aspects of the job include the practice of providing meals and entertainment to public officials, and far more important, although a less known practice, of providing campaign contributions to favored public officials.

Appropriate to its freewheeling political milieu, the Lone Star State has far and away the largest number of registered lobbyists of any of the 50 states—a startling total of over 3,000![4] Well known are industry, professional, and labor group lobbyists, but there are also lobbyists for regional, ethnic, and consumer interest groups—or for practically any special interest conceivable. State lobbyists' most valuable contacts are governors and the presiding officers of the legislative chambers, in Texas the lieutenant governor and House Speaker. And, while lobbyists cultivate the entire legislative garden—no vote is unimportant—as professionals, they know that relatively few bills see the light of day after being assigned to a committee, and that those bills which are reported out of committee are often amended to the point of being unrecognizable. In appreciation of such realities, they concentrate on members of whatever committee is typically assigned bills affecting their interest group. Most particularly, however, they cultivate that committee's chairman and subcommittee chairmen.[5]

Veteran lobbyists do not wait for the start of the legislative session to begin work; they are active long before that. As Jim Wright, executive director and lobbyist for the Texas Association of College Teachers (TACT) puts it, "You've got to get your program before the committee members and the Legislative Budget Board months before the session begins. Good lobbying is practically a fulltime operation. By the time the session begins, it's often too late to get a reasonable bill organized."[6]

By early March of the regular legislative session in Texas, one can observe the interest groups, especially the new ones and the ad hoc, or current, single-issue interest groups, organizing in the capitol rotunda. They discuss the newspaper accounts of the previous day and await their legislative assignments from their respective lobby leaders. They may be Texas Baptists opposed to pari-mutuel horse racing or booze. They may be from such ethnic groups as the NAACP or LULAC. They could be Fundamentalists or Catholics opposed to abortion; women for (or against) ERA.; farmers or migrant workers; hairdressers or small oil operatives; saints and sinners in all colors, sizes, sexes, they represent a kaleidoscope of a state rich in cultures and natural resources. Commercial fishermen are pitted against sport fishermen over the limits on the catch of redfish (March 1977), or "Citizens to Protect the Constitution" (opposing a new constitution) facing "Citizens for the Texas Constitution" (who were opposed to the existing Texas Constitution) as in September 1975.

Which are the most important lobbies in Texas? It's somewhat of a moot point, since experts disagree. Some rate effectiveness on the amount of dollars a lobby gets out of the legislature, such as the half billion the highway lobby got in 1977. Others note that the Texas State Medical Association and the Texas Trial Lawyers Association (most legislators are lawyers themselves) are consistently most successful in blocking bills detrimental to their financial interests. Several labor groups stand out—the Texas AFL/CIO and the Truckers. Some place the Texas State Teachers Association (with over 140,000 members) at the top of the list. Here are some of the most significant ones, with their leading lobbyists:[7]

Texas State Teachers Association (Callie Smith)

Texas Trial Lawyers Association (Phil Gauss)

Texas AFL/CIO (Harry Hubbard)

Texas Real Estate Association (Gerhardt Schulle)

Texas Good Roads Public Transportation Association (Eugene Robbins)

Texas Railroad Association (Walter Caven)

Texas Motor Transportation Association (Terry Townsend)

Texas Automobile Dealers Association (Gene Fondren)

Texas Chemical Council (Harry Whitworth)

Texas Mid-Continent Oil & Gas Association (Bill Abington)

Of course, there are many others. Both the University of Texas and Texas A & M maintain a never-ending vigil to block attempts to give part of the state Permanent University Fund (PUF) to the many other public state universities. Since the leading legislators are apt to be graduates of one of these two schools, the legislature has been impervious to change. The strength of the University of Texas in the legislature is attested to by the fact that Big Jim Ferguson, the one governor ever impeached and convicted in Texas, came a cropper over differences with the University.

In 1978, there were 1,378 Political Action Committees (PACs) registered with the Secretary of State's office.[8] Texas even exceeds the rapidly rising national PAC registration for federal election activities. A good number of the big lobbies have PACs which dole out campaign largesse to favored officials. In 1975–76, special interest PACs gave at least half a billion dollars to candidates.[9] Top giver was the Texas Trial Lawyers' PAC called LIFT (Lawyers Involved For Texas) which received its money in small monthly donations from hundreds of Texas trial lawyers. They have a beautiful building just east of the capitol. LIFT spread some $86,000 among dozens of Texas officials. Close behind was TEXPAC, the

Medical Association's PAC. Number one on the receiving end was reported to be "That Maverick" state Senator Babe Schwartz of Galveston, whose $40,000 included $8,000 from the lawyers and $7,000 from the doctors.

Some of the active PACs include BALLOT (Bankers Legislative League of Texas), SALPAC (Savings and Loans), Morti-PAC (morticians), PAL (Pharmacists), HELP (hospital owners), LUPAC (Life insurance underwriters), AUTOPAC (auto dealers), CATPAC (contractors), TRANSPAC (truckers), and finally PAC-PAC (plumbers and air conditioners).

When you talk of Texas, you talk of oil. Whether it's off the coast, in the East Texas fields, or west in the Permian basin, you find people drilling, piping, hauling, refining, shipping, or looking for it. Texas alone produces one third of the energy used in the United States, making it literally the source of America's industrial lifeblood. Pipelines carrying Texas oil and gas stretch for thousands of miles across the country. The energy industry is the major source of capital and employment for congressional and state legislative districts from all over the state. As a consequence, Texans from the governor down to the man in the street generally identify with the industry. It's something of a psychological reflex —"What's good for the oil industry is good for Texas." The Texas Railroad Commission, which regulates intrastate oil and gas, is virtually a captive of the industry, even though its three members are popularly elected. Both U.S. senators and 23 of the state's 24 U.S. representatives openly support deregulation of oil and gas prices (although that would obviously be to the advantage of the industry at the expense of the consumer).[10] Even the majors and independents' lobbies are more of one mind these days, though the Texas Independent Producers Royalty Owners Association sometimes clashes with the oil majors' No. 1 lobbyist, the great Bill Abington (Texas Mid-Continent Oil and Gas Association). The independents favor increased domestic production and seek special tax breaks. In the 1973 legislative session, Abington nursed through the House a compulsory oil and gas unitization bill, but in the Senate he ran up against double-barreled opposition in the person of Peyton McKnight, who is not only an independent oil man but a state senator from Tyler. By a combination of common sense, uncanny timing, and by leading the bill into a labyrinth of procedural blind ends, McKnight beat the majors at their own game in a showdown final vote.

When a political candidate finds himself opposed by an interest group, he can often find another interest group to provide him with a political antidote. Thus when Governor Briscoe announced he was supported by two black ministers' groups in Houston, John Hill got the powerful Harris County Council of Organizations (black) to come out for him. But there are some big lobbies which are difficult to counteract. When Dolph Briscoe alienated the teachers by pouring millions into a highway bill (and then introducing the bill as "emergency legislation"), Hill scored a major political triumph—he got the first endorsement of any gubernatorial candidate in the 98-year history of the Teachers Lobby (TSTA) by pledging a $1.3 billion education and teachers' benefit package if elected. It paid off handsomely at least until his defeat by Clements in the November election!

Some of the most volatile reactions in this fiercely independent state result from efforts by organized labor—particularly in the person of the AFL/CIO's Harry Hubbard—to permit public employees the right to strike. The spectre of police and firemen on strike is just too much for the average Texas legislator. And the words "union shop" raise another red flag: even the AFL/CIO-endorsed Democratic candidate for the U.S. Senate Joe Christie openly disavowed the union shop in his 1978 campaign—all to no avail. About the only thing worse than supporting organized labor in most Texas political circles is to support a "gay rights" interest group. No Texas legislator has yet had the temerity to pick up *that* political hot potato.

With very weak lobbying restraints and a rich and complex cultural melange, Texas is by all odds the leading state in the number and scope of its lobbies. It almost seems that nothing else would be appropriate.

RULES OF THE POLITICAL GAME

Given the fact that there are few institutional barriers remaining between the citizen and the ballot box, the single most important question to be resolved by the individual is whether to vote or not. If the response is positive, the following items are significant considerations.

Qualifications

In the last 100 years, the national government has taken affirmative action in attempting to increase the power and size of the American electorate. Of the total of 12 amendments that have been ratified since 1870, 6 are devoted exclusively to that purpose: the extension of the right to vote to blacks (XV), women (XIX), and to citizens 18 years of age or older (XXVI); the expansion of the suffrage to include the election of U.S. Senators (XVII) and presidential elections in the District of Columbia (XXIII); and, finally, the elimination of the poll tax in primaries and general elections for federal office (XXIV). In addition, Congress has enacted national legislation which prohibits the use of literacy tests in federal and state elections and which eliminates durational residence requirements for presidential elections.[11] Under the terms of the law, the states must guarantee absentee voting. Finally, the Supreme Court held that durational residence laws as a means of assurance of minimal knowledge of the issues on the part of the voters are discriminatory. The Court suggested that 30 days might be an adequate residential period for the state to complete election administrative tasks, particularly those necessary to prevent fraud.[12]

The obvious effect of these federal requirements has been to reduce the discretionary power of the states over primaries and general elections. In the case of Texas, the few remaining restrictions on the franchise are of dubious constitutionality. For example, paupers supported by the county, "idiots and lunatics," and felons with such exceptions as the legislature chooses to make (such as, those whose rights have been restored by a full pardon), are prohibited from voting by the state constitution. Moreover, as a prerequisite to vote on local bond issues and public expenditures, the constitution determines eligibility on the basis of ownership or rendition of property. Similar restrictions and prohibitions in other states have been struck down by the federal courts.

For all practical purposes, any citizen 18 years of age or older who can show proof of residence in the state and county is qualified to participate in elections in Texas.

Registration

For 64 years, a 1902 amendment to the state constitution required all residents of Texas between the ages of 21 and 60 to pay a poll tax as a prerequisite to vote. Governmental authorities rationalized that payment of such a tax would serve as an efficient system of registration. More importantly, the tax originally served as a reaction to the Populist movement, a progressive coalition which threatened the solid Democratic South and which at the turn of the century had made significant inroads into votes of poor white farmers, blacks, and Mexican-Americans. With the disappearance of the Populists, the tax served as a constraining mechanism which conveniently discouraged the aforementioned groups from participation in the political process. However, by 1966 the last vestige of the tax was invalidated by a decision of the U.S. Supreme Court.[13] For a while, little else changed. Each voter will still be required to register each year between October 1 and January 31. Only during this four-month period was registration possible. In 1971, however, the legislature revised the law to create a new and, as it turned out, one of the most progressive registration systems in the country. Under this provision, individuals were required to register only once at any time during the year but at least 30 days prior to the election. Unless voters moved to another county, they were permanently registered so long as they voted at least once during a three-year period.

In 1975, the 64th Legislature enacted legislation which created a computerized voter registration system under which Texans were required to register between October 1, 1975 and January 31, 1976. They receive new registration certificates every two years, or register in person at the courthouse with the voter registrar, the county tax assessor-collector. Mailed in nonforwardable envelopes, this procedure makes it easier to eliminate from the rolls the nearly 30 percent of names presently listed which are believed to be improper.

Finally, in anticipation of federal action to extend the Voting Rights Act of 1965, the legislature provided that, in those counties with a Spanish-speaking population of five percent or more, all voter registration materials, as well as ballots, are to be printed in both English and Spanish. After Congress extended the Voting Rights Act to include Texas, all changes in state and local law affecting voting rights and procedures since 1972, including annexations and other electoral district adjustments, must be examined by the U.S. attorney general.

After a two-year battle in the federal courts, the Supreme Court of the United States turned down the state's attempt to avoid coverage of the act in *Briscoe* v. *Bell,* 432, U.S. 404 (1977).

The Texas election code

Despite the notable advance in the registration process, the bulk of Texas election laws as embodied in the Code remain outmoded and contradictory. Recent studies have demonstrated that the Code is a legislative patchwork containing inconsistencies and anomalies which hinder rather than facilitate the election process.[14] One author noted:

> If one wished to design an election system which was inefficient and guaranteed to produce errors, he would not need to exercise his imagination. He could simply copy the Texas election system.[15]

Obviously, the new system helps alleviate an almost endless list of problems: multiple voter registrations were commonplace; accurate totals of qualified voters were often unavailable in many counties; too little effort had been made to purge registration lists of the deceased or the relocated; improperly reported returns had often been recorded; arithmetic errors in tabulation of votes had been prevalent. Another related problem for Texas legislators had been that of the financing of political campaigns and the legal limits that should curb excesses. In 1971, the McKool-Stroud Primary Financing Law was passed as a first step. The 64th "reform-minded" Legislature attempted to create a permanent apparatus (a State Elections Commission) but failed at the end of the session. The more conservative Legislature of 1975 weakened the campaign finance law by exempting unopposed candidates, adding a clause requiring statewide candidates charged with violations to be tried in their home counties, changing the language of the law which had required contributions in excess of $100 to be made by check and raising the minimum figure over which reports must be filed from $10 to $50.

Finally, in 1977 the legislature repealed its two-year old limitation on statewide candidates of spending only ten cents for each Texan of voting age in first primaries and the general election. *Result:* Bill Clements spent nearly *eighty-two-cents* per eligible voter in his successful race for governor a year later.

THE ELECTION PROCESS

Primaries: The selection of elites

The sole function of the party primary is to select candidates for public office. While each party conducts its own primary including separate election officials and polling places, the bill is paid by the state. Texas has had mandatory primaries since 1903, and until 1973 any political party whose gubernatorial candidates garnered 200,000 or more votes in the last general election was required to conduct primaries for offices at the precinct, county, district, and state levels. Presently, only those parties receiving at least 20 percent of the vote are required to do so. The lesser parties must hold conventions.

With relatively few exceptions, the Democratic primary in this traditionally one-party state is *the* center of action. In the past, the selection of a candidate in the Democratic primary was considered tantamount to victory in the general election and, to a great extent, this remains an accurate axiom. Accordingly, in order to win nomination a candidate, under state law, must be selected by a majority not a plurality of voters. A second runoff primary would be required splitting the two top vote getters if no one receives a majority in the first contest. As in other one-party southern states, candidates must file with the party.

Rise of Republican primaries Only since 1962 in Texas has the Republican party regularly conducted party primaries. Before 1962, the party had been required to hold primary elections only in five election years, 1926, 1930, 1934, 1954, and 1958. Because of the lack of candidates, resources, and support, these primaries were not conducted statewide but only in selected counties, mainly in Republican "growth areas" (metropolitan and urban counties) and traditional Republican areas in the Panhandle and German counties of South Central Texas.[16] For example, the *Texas Observer* reported that Republican primaries were conducted in 1958 in only 61 counties. In 1962, in sharp contrast, Republican primary elections were held in all or in parts of a total of 215 of the 254 Texas counties.[17]

Clearly, the rather sharp increase in Republican activities in 1962 coincided with the return to power in Washington in 1961 of a moderate

Democratic administration under President John F. Kennedy. Conservative support for Republican statewide candidacies in the general elections increased immediately and dramatically, and in 1961 John Tower was elected in a special election contest to fill the Senate seat vacated by Vice President Lyndon B. Johnson. Despite the great upset election of 1978, the upsurge of votes for Republican candidates in Texas general

FIGURE 3–1

Votes cast for Democratic and Republican candidates in gubernatorial primaries and elections, 1958–1978

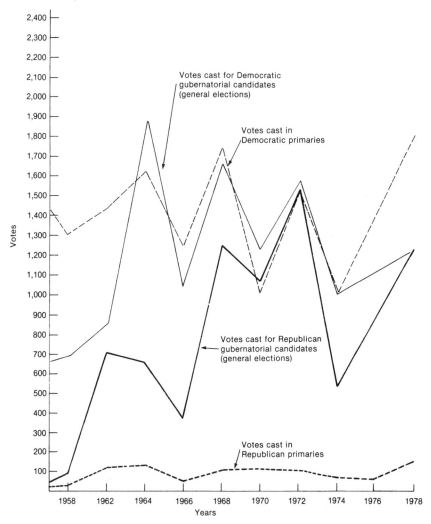

Source: Prepared by the authors from election data in *The Texas Almanac and State Industrial Guide* (Dallas: A. H. Belo Corp., biennial editions) and from various other sources.

elections for statewide office has not been matched, however, either by a large influx of new Republican state legislators or by significantly increased competition and activity in Republican primaries. On the contrary, most of the relatively small number of Texans who bother to vote in primaries still participate in the Democratic contests (see Figure 3–1). Indeed, the ballots cast in the Republican primaries average only 4.5 percent of the votes cast in the Democratic primaries in the same years (see Table 3–1). Using another measure, the statewide Republican primary vote has been only 11.7 percent on the average of the ballots regularly cast for Republican gubernatorial and senatorial candidates in the general elections.

No doubt the dominant political and cultural values, developed historically, underlie the habitual choice of most Texans to cast their ballots in Democratic primaries. Most of those voting Republican during the past three decades have called themselves "conservatives" rather than Republicans. The liberal-conservative struggles in the Democratic primary runoff elections seem to have held a fatal attraction for them, since the Democratic nomination contests have provided repeated opportunities for the minority-party adherents to provide the winning margin for conservative Democrats. To become a genuine aspirant to majority party status in the Texas legislature, the Republican party must be able to

TABLE 3–1

Participation and vote cast by members of parties and factions in Texas primaries, and general and presidential elections, 1964–1978

Type	Primary Dem.	Rep.	Other	General Elections Dem.	Rep.	Other	Presidential Dem.	Rep.	Other
Machine Democrat	X			X*				X	
Regular Democrat	X			X			X		
Liberal Democrat	X				X†		X		
Republican	X‡				X			X	
La Raza Unida			X			X	X		
Wallacite	X			X					X§
Other			X			X			X
	92%	2%	6%	53%	41%	6%	25%	45%	3%

* Machine (conservative establishment) Democrats will support the machine candidate in the primary even though other lesser known candidates may be more politically conservative. However, the regular Democrats, who are also politically conservative, generally maintain their ties with and vote for the party's candidate at the local, state, and national levels.

† In the general election, many liberal Democrats support the Republican rather than the machine conservative. If a conservative must be elected, they feel, let him be a Republican. If a La Raza candidate is running, a sizable number of liberals will support him.

‡ Only a relatively few Republican loyalists vote in the Republican primary. The vast majority vote "where the action is" in the Democratic primary.

§ The Wallacites are difficult to profile. They include a rather large number of erstwhile "populists" particularly in East Texas. Generally they will support the Democrat if an American Independent is not involved in the contest.

recruit more legislative candidates, attract abiding interest in Republican primary races, and contest the Democrats in the general election.

The presidential primary

In 1975, the legislature passed a law creating a presidential primary for election year 1976. Ignoring the charges of opponents who claimed that the political allies of Senator Lloyd Bentsen, Jr., pushed the measure through, the legislators provided that 75 percent of the state's delegation to the national conventions were to be chosen by the voters in each of either the senatorial or congressional districts, as determined by party leaders. The remaining 25 percent of the delegation were to be selected at the state conventions on the basis of the total vote received by each candidate in the primary. Critics, mostly liberal Democrats, insisted that this mechanism would enhance the presidential aspirations of Senator Bentsen because of the winner-take-all provisions in the district contests. As it turned out, such fears were groundless; a full three months before the primary, Bentsen, whose campaign had not really caught on, withdrew to avoid the onslaught of the Jimmy Carter "juggernaut"—in the primary and later in the general election in Texas. The law expired in 1977, so future legislation will have to be enacted if the primary is to continue. In 1978, Texas Republicans—who "stampeded" to support former Governor Ronald Reagan (R-Cal.) and had swamped President Ford in Texas' first presidential primary two years earlier—announced their support of Democratic backers for such a preference primary in 1980. *Reason:* their hero, Mr. Reagan, is expected to make another try for the top spot. In any event, if the presidential primary is renewed for 1980, the Democrats will have to contend with new rules enunciated by the Democratic National Committee two years earlier. These regulations make it much more difficult for an upstart challenge—California's Governor Jerry Brown, say—to defeat an incumbent: before, a candidate receiving *less* than 15 percent of the vote was not entitled to delegates from that state to the national convention; from now on, depending on the decision of the state's legislature, a candidate must receive *at least* 15 to 25 percent.

Elections: Mobilization of popular support

General elections Having selected their respective candidates for public office, the parties must engage in competitive elections. Since 1974, Texas has removed the election of its highest state officials from the presidential election calendar in compliance with an earlier constitutional amendment which changed the terms of the governor and related offices from two to four years. Such elections have since been held in the off years. Moreover in 1975 the legislature enacted legislation establishing four standard election days each year for most state and local elections. All such contests—excluding party primaries and wet/dry liquor elections—must be scheduled for either the first Tuesday after the first Monday in November, the third Saturday in January, the first Saturday in April, or the second Saturday in August.

The state is responsible for the funding and administration of elections with the secretary of state designated as chief election officer. Nevertheless, most of the actual election functions are performed by officials at the county level. While certain administrative tasks are performed by the county commissioners court, the county judge and the county election board (the clerk, sheriff, judge of the county and the chairpersons of the major parties' county executive committees), are the real work-

FIGURE 3–2
Administration of elections

Governor

Signs and transmits
certifications of election
to elected state and
district officials.

Secretary of State

Highest election officer:
Certifies state and district
candidates; issues directives;
lends assistance; maintains
records; canvasses votes in
special cases; and has
enforcement powers.

County Commissioners Court	County Election Board	County Clerk	County Judge
Determines voting devices to be used; authorizes expenditures for running elections; selects election judges; and canvasses the vote.	Responsible for distribution of election supplies.	Most important county election officer: Certifies county and local candidates; handles absentee voting in general and special elections above municipal level; canvasses and transmits county returns for state and district offices and presidential elections to Secretary of State.	Issues certificates of election to the newly elected county and precinct officials.

County Tax
Assessor-Collector

Voter Registrar

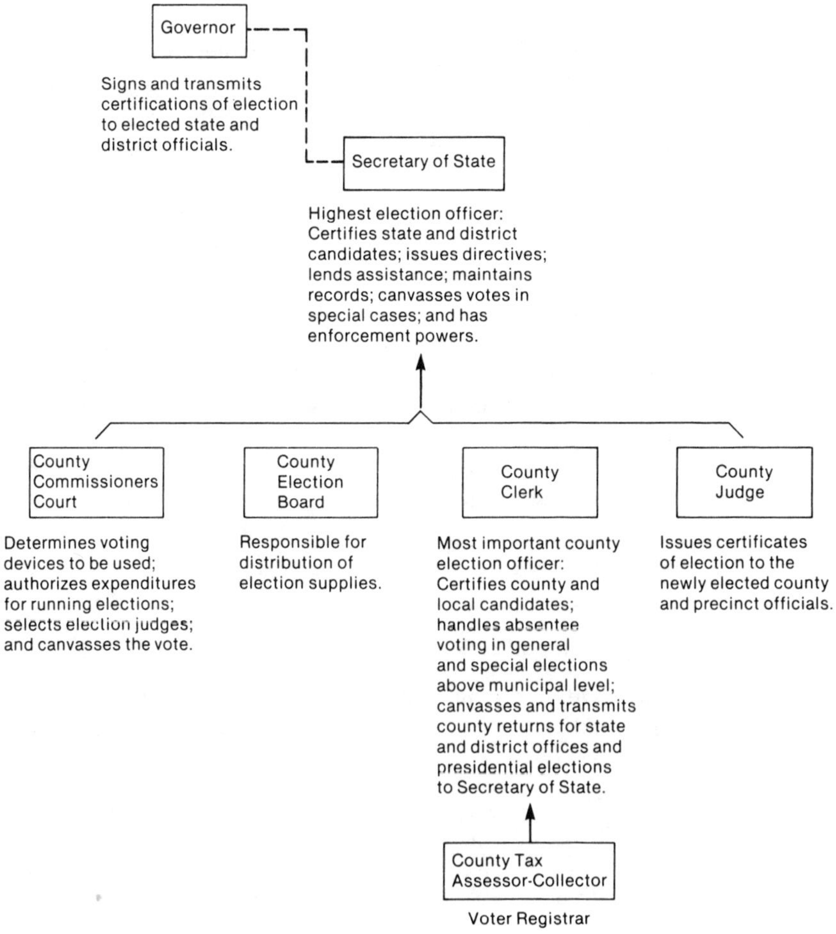

horses of the electoral process. The county judge certifies (in writing) the party nominees, whether by primary or convention, whose names will appear on the ballot in contention for county and local offices. The secretary of state certifies those running for state and district positions. Those candidates running as independents must present a petition signed by otherwise qualified voters who take part in no partisan primary or convention. The Election Code (Article 13.50) requires that the number of signatures on the petition must, at least, equal a specified percentage of the votes cast in the last gubernatorial election by the voters within the governmental unit sought: county or precinct office (5 percent); district office (3 percent); and statewide office (1 percent). In addition, the county clerk conducts absentee voting in all general and special elections except those at the municipal level. Finally, after the elections, the clerk canvasses and transmits the county returns for state and district affairs, as well as those for presidential elections, to the secretary of state.

The ballot used in general elections in Texas deserves some attention. Straight ticket voting is encouraged by the use of the party column ballot in which the names of the parties are listed at the top. In large metropolitan areas voting machines or computer ballots are used; while in less populated regions paper ballots are most commonly employed. Regardless of the type of voting mechanism, one may vote the straight party ticket by pulling the designated lever, punching the appropriate hole, or by placing an X in the box at the top of the column.[18] Many voters in Texas find the straight ticket designation the easy way out. The list of offices is often endless (the long ballot), but Democratic candidates are opposed in only about one third of the total number of contests. However, this trend may be changing somewhat.

The election of state legislators serves as a case in point. It is still true that for most Democratic candidates for the legislative nomination in the primary is equivalent to election save for the major metropolitan areas, where Republican legislative candidates have begun seriously to contest Democrats in general elections.

Yet, Republicans elsewhere are beginning to make impressive inroads into Southern state legislatures which were, until recently, almost totally Democratic in membership. By 1974, Republican state legislators controlled approximately one of four of the legislative seats in the six southern states on the periphery of the Deep South (Texas, Arkansas, Florida, North Carolina, Tennessee, and Virginia). In Texas, where the party's growth has not been as rapid as in the other states, 16 Republican representatives in 1975 were located in the following areas: Dallas (7), Houston (6), San Antonio (1), El Paso (1) and Midland (1). The three Republican Senators represented districts in Dallas, Harris and Tarrant counties. These numbers have remained essentially the same as of 1979.

Special elections These are issue-oriented nonpartisan elections held at the state and local levels which predictably arouse little voter interest. Also, special elections are held to fill vacancies (caused by death or resignation) in the offices of United States senator or representative or state legislator. More commonly such elections are conducted to test voter sentiment on those constitutional amendments not listed on the general election ballot. Here again, so many amendments have been submitted, particularly in recent years, that the typical voter could not realistically be expected to fully comprehend the nuances of each proposal.[19] Local options, depending upon provisions in the charter or laws, may include the filling of vacated posts and local propositions or referendums.

The degree of mobilization As in most one-party states, it is difficult for any party to mobilize support for its candidates. In Texas, voter participation is particularly low. Even in the more interesting presidential elections, rarely do more than 40 percent of the eligible voters in Texas actually participate. There are any number of possible reasons for this phenomenon but chief among them are the following: (a) approximately one third of the population in the state is composed of minority groups, primarily chicanos and blacks, who are less educated, have lower incomes, perceive that they have too little a stake in the action, and who, consequently, have no real incentive to vote; (b) traditionally Texas registration laws, even though recently reformed, have served to reinforce one-party domination and thus discourage voter interest; and (c) the predominantly conservative coloration of both major parties in the state leads the more liberal or progressive voters to the conclusion that even on those occasions where two-party competition exists, it makes little difference who wins.[20]

INTRAPARTY ORGANIZATION

Membership

The formalities The designation of party membership is a very loose procedure in Texas. Actually, there are no registered, card-carrying Democrats or Republicans since membership is determined depending on the primary or convention in which the voter participates. Under state law, once the voter has so acted he can participate only in that party's deliberations for the next voting year which concludes the following February, whether as a voter, party official, or party candidate. Accordingly, even though primaries are closed—that is, theoretically limited to members only—there is virtually no way to prevent opposition party members or independents from taking part on a year to year basis. This is particularly true of a great many Republicans who vote in important Democratic primaries, usually for the most conservative Democrat seeking nomination, only to return "home" by the time of the general election. This, of course, serves to maintain the control of the conservative Democratic machine at the expense of the liberal minority. It is for this reason that most liberal Democrats advocate changing to a system of party registration, some form of which is used in those states with strong two-party systems. Adoption of this approach would require the voter to declare partisan selection at the time of registration and then the voter would be eligible to vote only in that party's primaries. Supposedly, the voter would be required to officially declare in order to change party registration. Self-proclaimed independents would be registered as such and thus would be barred from participation in partisan deliberations. Such a measure providing for "party purity" was killed in conference committee during the last days of the 64th Legislature in 1975.

Permanent structure

The committees   In 1971, the legislature amended the Texas Election Code to require all political parties to file a detailed and specific set of party rules with the secretary of state.[21] The rules of both major parties are not dissimilar with respect to their permanent structures or committees, although, given the fact of one-party dominance, the Democratic party's remain the more important.[22]

Working from bottom to top, the *precinct chairperson,* elected by majority vote of the party primary for a two-year term, serves as the chief party administrator at the lowest structural level. Traditionally, he or she is appointed precinct election judge for all elections and is, *de facto,* a member of the county executive committee. Unlike the more powerful precinct leaders in politically competitive states, the precinct chairman has few formal powers. In Texas, the political strength of the precinct— fund raising, party loyalty, and voter turnout—depends solely upon the chairman's personality and determination.

The *county executive committee* is composed of the precinct chairmen of the county and a county chairman elected by a majority vote in the party primary for a two-year term. The committee and its chairman are extremely important in that they have the responsibility for administering the primary election and for coordinating the general election campaigns of the Democratic nominees within the county. Although the position of county chairman is not as powerful as it once was, the success or failure of the county organization will depend on his or her effectiveness, capabilities, and personality. The committee is authorized by state law to receive and file applications for a place on the primary ballot; to collect filing fees; to assess and collect election expenses; to appoint poll watchers; to determine the order of names on the ballot; to canvass primaries and certify the returns; and to set and publicize the times and places for precinct and county conventions. During the general election campaigns, the committee has the partisan responsibility to raise funds for local campaigns, as well as to support the slate of state-wide candidates; to produce election materials and coordinate services for local candidates; and, to establish committees to carry out other nonstatutory activities.

The composition of the *senatorial district executive committee* will depend on the size and makeup of the district. In those districts containing less than one county, the precinct chairmen constitute the committee, selecting one of their own as district chairperson. In those districts composed entirely of one county, the county executive committee serves as the district committee. However, if the district is made up of more than one county or parts of more than one county, then the district committee is composed of the county chairman of the district and one district committeeman elected by each group of precinct chairmen within that part of a county contained in the senatorial district. Thereafter the members elect their own chairman. The district committee is of little importance. Its main function is to fill vacancies in party nominations for district offices.

The top spot of the permanent structure is reserved for the *state executive committee* (SEC). The state convention meeting in September of each even numbered year elects a state chairman, a vice chairman, and a secretary. Usually, the party's gubernatorial nominee has a strong input into the selection of these officials. The state committee membership consists of 62 persons, one man and one woman from each senatorial district, elected by district caucus at the state convention. All members serve for two years until the next convention. The committee is legally authorized to receive and file applications for a place on the ballot in statewide primaries; to certify the names of all candidates for nomination to state offices; and to canvass the returns in primaries and runoffs for state and district offices. Perhaps, more importantly, the state executive committee controls certain aspects of the *temporary* organization of the party. It selects the location for the next state convention and has the authority to compile the temporary roll. After holding hearings, the committee may decide which of the contested delegations, if any, will be temporarily seated at the convention until such time that the final decision is made on the convention floor. Finally, the governor or the gubernatorial candidate of the party usually selects a full-time executive director who is paid to do most of the real work of the committee with respect to coordination of activities, fund raising, and public relations.

Temporary organization

The conventions If the permanent structure, or the committees, are viewed as the party elite, the relatively few who are chosen to engage in policy-making on a daily basis, then the temporary organization consisting of ad hoc conventions must be seen as the occasional pluralist input into the party apparatus. The conventions and primaries give the rank and file members the opportunity to select their leaders and to effectuate party policy. Except for the minor parties, the only nominations decided by political conventions in Texas are the candidates for presidential and vice presidential electors.

The *precinct convention* is held on the day of the primary election at 7:15 p.m. in most cases or between 2:00 and 9:00 p.m. in rural counties. The county chairman is responsible for deciding the polling place or location of the convention and for publicizing this information ten days in advance. All qualified voters who participated in the primary and who reside in the precinct are eligible to participate. The most important business before the precinct convention is the election of permanent officers, including the chairman and the election of delegates and alternates to the county or senatorial district convention. The apportionment of delegates is based on the number of votes cast in the precinct for the party's candidate in the last gubernatorial election.

The Democrats, for example, elect one delegate and one alternate for each 25 votes ("or major fraction thereof") cast. Regardless of the size of the vote, each precinct is entitled to at least one delegate and alternate. The delegate selection process is of particular interest in presidential years. Democratic party rules require proportional representation of the delegation on the basis of both presidential preference and of the diversity in population within the precinct—blacks, chicanos, women, and various age groups. As the qualified participants enter their names on the temporary roll, they indicate their presidential preference or opt for uncommitted status. On this basis, the convention subdivides into preferential caucuses provided that at least 20 percent of the total number of participants favor a particular candidate or are uncommitted. Those whose preference has less than 15 percent support are directed to the caucus of their second choice. Delegates and alternates are then selected by the respective caucuses by majority vote. The unit rule, under which the delegation as a unit reflected the choice of the majority to the exclusion of the minority, has been abandoned by the Democrats.[23] However, the convention may act as a whole in electing all delegates "at large" by a majority vote if a motion to that effect is supported by at least 70 percent of those on the roll. The delegation then chooses one of its number as delegation chairman.

The *county convention* is held in each county wholly contained within one senatorial district on the first Saturday following the primary. In those cases in which parts of the county are divided among different senatorial districts—Harris, Dallas, and Bexar at present—senatorial district conventions are held instead. The county chairman delivers the lists of all delegates and alternates elected by the precincts within the county, which constitutes the temporary roll. Thereafter the convention selects its permanent chairman and other officers, and selects its delegates and alternates to the state convention. The Democrats have established that the apportionment of the delegation should be one delegate and one alternate per every 300 votes cast in the county for their candidate for governor in the last general election. Again, the election of delegates is by caucus of precincts within the county or district.

The "regular" or September *state convention* is held on the third Tuesday of September and, of course, is composed of the delegates elected by the county or district conventions. The functions of the state convention include the election of permanent officers, the election of the members of the state committee, the adoption of a platform on significant issues for the November general election, the canvassing of the primary vote for statewide offices, and the certification of the party's nominees. In presidential years, a second conclave is held in addition to the one in September. The "presidential" state convention is held on the third Saturday in June following the runoff primary election and it is politically significant. The purposes of the convention are to select delegates to the party's national convention, to elect the national committee members, and to choose the official slate of presidential electors. The Democrats have a more complicated system for such tasks because of the procedures required by the national convention. To a greater or lesser extent, both national parties apportion the total allotment of delegates from each state to the national convention based on two considerations: (1) the total population of the state and (2) the percentage of the vote cast in the state or its congressional districts for the party's nominee in the last presidential election.[24] In 1976, the Republicans allowed voters in the party's presidential preference primary to elect the delegates to the national convention from the state's 24 congressional districts, rather than from the 31 state senatorial districts, as was customary. The voters chose four national convention delegates in each congressional district; thus the state convention was left to choose only four delegates and a slate of alternates. The Democrats at the state convention select 75 percent of their allotted number of delegates by senatorial district caucuses and 25 percent are elected by the convention at large. The convention is required to make "every feasible effort" to choose a delegation of minorities, women, and young people in "reasonable relationship" to their proportions of the state's population.[25] The convention must also choose persons to serve on the national committee. As an affirmation of loyalty, the Democratic committee members must positively declare in favor of the presidential and vice presidential nominees within one month after the national convention. Representatives serve four-year terms, Finally, the convention is required to select its slate of presidential electors equal to the total number of United States senators and congressmen representing Texas (26). The senatorial district caucuses have the responsibility for nominating the electors; however, since there are more districts (31) than the apportioned number of electors, the determination is made by those which cast the highest vote for the party's nominee in the last presidential election. The official slate must be certified to the secretary of state by the state committee chairman at least 35 days before the election.

THE PARTY SYSTEM IN TEXAS

From a philosophical or ideological perspective, as opposed to a politically partisan one, it would not be incorrect to say that Texas is dominated by the *conservative* party with Democratic and Republican factions[26] (see Figure 3–3). The philosophical differences between Republican John Tower and his Democratic challenger Bob Krueger in the 1978 Senate race were virtually nonexistent. The political spectrum contains a number of diverse components but the success of the conservatives in manipulating Texas politics has been overwhelming.

The Texas political system currently consists of four major and three minor components: (1) *Machine Democrats.* One of the three divisions within the state party, this faction represents the conservative "establishment" which has controlled the party structure, with few exceptions, since FDR's third term announcement in 1940. As the ruling elite, they operate as a clique supporting only group leaders for nomination and election, even against more conservative candidates. Since Adlai Stevenson's nomination as the Democratic presidential nominee in 1952 (when Machine Democrats rushed to vote for and swing the state into Republican Dwight Eisenhower's column), it has been customary for most of them to support the Republican presidential nominee—the notable exception being the backing of LBJ in 1964, himself a Machine Democrat. Other Machine leaders include (or included at one time): Allan Shivers, Price Daniel, Sr., Will Wilson, John Connally, Preston Smith, and, until nearly a decade ago, John Hill; (2) *Liberal Democrats.* The Machine Democrats' relentless opposition on the "left." This faction, nearly equal in numbers but usually not in political clout, espouses its views favoring civil rights and liberties, the advancement of education, spending for social welfare—proposals which infuriate the Machine faction—and steadfast support of party presidential nominees. In electoral contests

FIGURE 3–3
The political spectrum in Texas

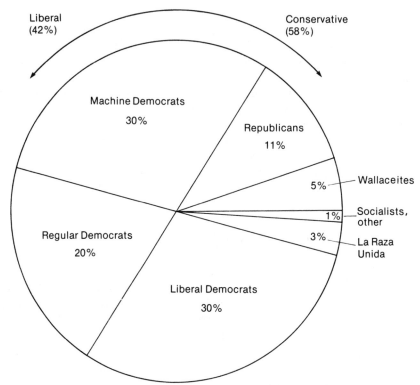

Source: Prepared by the author to reflect philosophical tendencies of the contending party and factional groupings in Texas.

between Machine or other conservative Democrats and Republicans (nearly always equally conservative) many Liberals support the opposition's candidate. It is hoped that by this process of elimination the control of the Democratic party will eventually shift to the Liberal faction. In fact, the election results of 1978 may serve to speed up this process considerably. The late James Allred and Maury Maverick, Ralph Yarborough, Bob Eckhardt, Don Yarborough (no relation to the former Senator), and Francis Farenthold are recognized as having been the most visible leaders of this faction; (3) *Regular Democrats*. While most are relatively conservative, the informal members of this group are traditional Democrats who, almost regardless of the nominee, support the party's candidate. To vote for a Republican, they believe, would be "treason" to their family, church, and home; (4) *Republicans*. Very few persons admit to being a member of this opposition minority party, but many Texans vote for its national candidates. As mentioned above, a number of registered Democrats are in reality "closet" Republicans. Despite disclaimers to the contrary, the leadership of the party has not attempted to expand for reasons of "dividing patronage among the fewest number." Party notables include John Tower, Bill Clements (an unknown Dallas oil millionaire until 1978), Hank Grover, Anne Armstrong, Ray Hutchinson, and relatively recent but not surprising converts, Will Wilson and John Connally (Weren't they once Machine *Democrats?*); the minor divisions include: (5) *Wallaceites*. Quasi-Populists located primarily in East Texas who, in the past, were attracted by the charismatic Governor Wallace (D-Alabama) and his antibigness in government, labor, and business views. With Wallace's political fortunes in decline since his defeat by Jimmy Carter in the 1976 presidential primaries, the importance of this faction (known as the American Independent Party) is also diminishing. Outside of motion picture actor the late Chill Wills (the voice of Francis the Talking Mule), there are no leaders who are well recognized; (6) *La Raza Unida*. An admittedly racially-biased party favoring "power to chicanos" which has also lost influence in recent years. Among other things the arrest and conviction of several of its leaders (primarily for possession and/or sale of illegal narcotics and dope) and their visiting Cuba's Fidel Castro and attempting to emulate his communist policies in small Texas communities, etc., have caused Anglo Liberal supporters to flee in droves. The future of this one-issue/one-race party is ironically like that of the Wallaceites without Wallace, fairly dismal. Party leaders have included Ramsey Muñiz, Jose Angel Gutierrez, Carlos Guerra, among others; and, (7) *Socialist Workers, etc.* This leftist faction and its splinter groups are composed primarily of disgruntled intellectuals, college students, and assorted dropouts. The effect of this faction on state politics has been, to paraphrase the words of a well-known politician, "that of a single snowflake on the Rio Grande River." Nonetheless, the cumulative effect of two or more of these splinter parties running candidates in tight state-wide races can have a decided impact. In 1978, the La Raza Unida and Socialist Workers Party candidates for governor drew 19,000 votes between them—the margin of difference between Clements and Hill. Over the years liberals and Republicans have been gaining strength and undoubtedly will continue doing so. Conservative Democrats have been losing ground and will lose still more, although they probably will remain the dominant faction in Texas for some years to come. The future prospects of the La Raza Unida party and the Wallaceites are not yet clear since they depend heavily on what path the national and state Democrats follow.

The Democratic party

From 1900–60, Texas was strictly a one-party state; Republicans never won elections and almost never tried to win.[27] Since 1960, Texas has been a "modified one-party state"; Republicans still seldom win elections, but they do usually wage energetic campaigns for at least one statewide office. As mentioned earlier, one of the reasons Republicans have made a better showing in the last decade and a half is that ideological divisions among Democrats since the 1940s gradually became too intense to be contained within the limits of the party primary, and they spilled over to the general election. Indeed, the Republicans would not have won the very close race for governor in 1978 had it not been for the support Clements received from the conservative followers of Dolph Briscoe. Typical of Texas politics, the former governor announced that he would vote the straight party ticket, while his wife and daughter actively supported Clements.

It was not always this way in Texas. The Democratic party which regained political control of the state from Republicans after Reconstruction was rather well united on principle. From the 1870s to the 1890s nearly all Democrats were white and conservative. They could easily agree on the necessity for purging the state of Republican officials by reducing the political participation of blacks, the mainstay of Republicanism. After some decades of trying various methods of persuasion and intimidation to break the blacks' will to vote, Texas Democrats finally resorted to legislation to eliminate virtually all black voters from the rolls. Poll taxes, literacy tests, and long residence requirements, all administered by antiblack Democratic officials, finished the job which violence and threats had begun in the 1870s.

At the same time that Democrats were wrestling with the problem of black voting and whittling the Republican party down to a nub, they found themselves under attack from the left. Economic hard times struck farmers a heavy blow, driving many off their own lands and into the status of mere tenants, and creating widespread political discontent in Texas and the nation. In the 1880s, this anger found an outlet in the Greenback party, which hoped to bring back prosperity by increasing the supply of paper money. Greenbackers organized throughout Texas and put up strong campaigns against the entrenched Democratic machine, polling over 40 percent of the vote for governor in 1882 and almost 30 percent two years later. Scarcely had this threat receded when there came an even stronger assault from the Populist party. Like the Greenbackers, the Populists represented the frustrations and fears of rural voters who felt squeezed economically by depressed prices and forgotten politically by a nation concerned with urbanization, immigration, and big business. On a platform of radical economic measures. Populist candidates came near to unseating the Democrats from the governorship of Texas, and they did take over control of several counties. In 1892, the Populist nominee for governor drew more than one fourth of the votes, rising to almost 40 percent in 1894 and 45 percent in 1896. Only sharp practices at the polling booths may have saved the Democrats from defeat.

However, Populist support dropped off sharply in 1898, and this was the last serious outside challenge to Texas Democrats until the present day. But in fending off the angry Greenbackers and Populists, the Democratic party itself became more liberal and produced within its own ranks candidates who began speaking and acting for the interests of the "common man." Governors Jim Hogg and Charles Culberson, holding office throughout the 1890s, were the first products of this liberal movement within the party. In fact, from then until the 1930s most Democratic governors were at least moderately liberal in their approach to economic questions, and there was not organized long-term conservative opposition to this. During these decades the opposing factions were not liberal versus conservative, but prohibitionist versus antiprohibitionist and Ku Klux Klan versus anti-Klan. Complicating the whole era was the man-and-wife political career of James A. and Miriam Ferguson. "Pa" Ferguson had been elected governor in 1914 but was impeached and removed from office in 1917 for various misdeeds. Barred from ever serving again, he simply had his wife run. "Ma" Ferguson was chosen governor twice (with "Pa" really running the state) and was defeated three times, so there was scarcely an election between 1914 and 1940 in which one of the Fergusons was not running.

"Fergusonism" thus became in itself a controversial political issue, cutting across all other alignments. Voters who agreed on the liquor question or the Klan issue might be on opposite sides of the Ferguson issue. Throughout the controversy and confusion, though, most of the successful Democratic candidates occupied the middle ground economically, proposing mild reforms but no major social or economic changes. This moderation enabled Democrats to have their disputes in the primary elections and to stick together in November against the almost invisible Republican threat. The only two major breaks in Democratic unity from the beginning of the century to the 1940s occurred over "Fergusonism" rather than economic policy. In both years when "Ma" Ferguson won the Democratic nomination for governor, her opponents were so disgusted at her victory that they gave strong support to her GOP challengers, enabling the Republican candidates to poll 41 percent of the votes in 1924 and 38 percent in 1932. Except for these outbursts, Democratic ranks remained unbroken until the Great Depression finally put an end to party unity. The divisions which grew out of the depression years still split Democrats into two warring factions.

Conservative Democrats: Presidential rebels In 1932 Texas Democrats gave Franklin D. Roosevelt an overwhelming ten-to-one mandate to bring the nation out of the deepening depression. But Roosevelt's programs of vast federal spending, increased governmental power, and stronger labor unions soon caused a growing number of conservatives to protest the speed with which the national Democratic party was moving leftward. By 1938 most of Texas' congressmen had deserted Roosevelt and joined the conservative coalition of Republicans and other southern Democrats in fighting most New Deal measures. By 1944 the conservatives actually gained control of the state Democratic convention. Calling themselves the "Texas Regulars," they put a slate of anti-Roosevelt electors on the presidential ballot and attracted 12 percent of the statewide vote, almost as much as the Republicans got. Harry Truman proved even less satisfactory; his close identification with the interests of labor unions and blacks enraged many old-line Texas conservatives. Some supported Republican Thomas E. Dewey in 1948, while others backed the splinter states' rights Democratic ticket, or "Dixiecrats." Truman still won a comfortable victory, but he lost more than one third of the vote to the combined opposition.

These defections of the 1940s were but the prelude to the massive conservative revolt of 1952 against Adlai Stevenson, the liberal Democratic nominee for president. So intense was the anti-Stevenson feeling that the Democratic Governor (Allan Shivers), the candidate for U.S. Senator (Price Daniel), and even the party's state convention itself actually endorsed and worked for Republican Dwight Eisenhower. Not surprisingly, Eisenhower won the state, with the great majority of his votes being supplied by rebellious conservative Democrats. This election began the modern era of presidential politics in Texas, and saw the emergence of a permanent block of "presidential Republicans"—conservative Machine Democrats who refuse to support their own party's candidates for president. Richard Nixon, hardly a popular candidate personally, was almost as successful as the war hero Eisenhower in winning these conservative votes. He missed carrying Texas by only 46,000 ballots against Kennedy in 1960 (although Kennedy's Catholicism was certainly a factor) and by only 39,000 against Humphrey in 1968, and swept the state by a landslide margin of more than 1 million votes over McGovern in 1972. Only when Lyndon Johnson himself ran for reelection in 1964 could the Democrats safely count on Texas' electoral votes for president. In the future the obvious willingness of hundreds of thousands of conservatives to reject a too-liberal Democratic nominee will make Texas a toss-up state in nearly every national election year.

The state machine While they are perennial rebels nationally against the national liberal wing of the Democratic party, the Machine Democrats are firmly in control of Texas itself. They have concentrated their efforts on holding the governorship because, although the office itself has little power, a liberal governor could use the prestige and moral leadership of his or her position to forward policies which might be damaging to conservative interests. Since the first eruption of ideological primary contests in the 1940s, Machine Democrats have never lost an election for governor, and only occasionally have they ever been closely pressed. From Beauford Jester's two-to-one landslide defeat of a liberal

University of Texas expresident in 1946 until the mid-1950s, there was no serious challenge to conservative leadership. Then, in a backlash against Governor Allan Shivers' support of Eisenhower for president, liberals mounted a determined effort to seize control of the party. Ralph Yarborough, who had lost heavily for governor in 1952, reduced Shivers' margin to only 53 percent in 1954 and only just missed defeating Shivers' conservative successor, Price Daniel, in 1956. Daniel won the Democratic nomination by only 3,000 votes out of nearly 1.4 million. Perhaps sobered by this near disaster, Daniel became noticeably less conservative in office. He won renomination against both a weak liberal and an untra-conservative, and by 1960 had become so moderate that he was able to gain liberal support to defeat a much more conservative challenger.

Growing conservative dissatisfaction with Daniel's record was largely responsible for his dismal showing in 1962, when he got one sixth of the votes in attempting to win a record-breaking fourth term. Daniel's defeat almost cost the conservatives dearly, however, because Navy Secretary John Connally (a then moderate Democrat not wholly acceptable to conservatives) just barely turned back the aggressive liberal campaign of Don Yarborough[28] by a 51–49 margin. This proved to be the last close call for conservatives, though, because Connally's bullet wound while riding with President Kennedy in Dallas gave him an unbeatable "martyr image," and he easily won two more terms. He was followed by Preston Smith, much more of a true conservative, who had little difficulty defeating Don Yarborough in 1968 and was unopposed in 1970. Like Daniel, ten years earlier, Smith suffered a humiliating defeat running for reelection in 1972, but conservatives lost nothing by this. Divided in the first primary, they found Dolph Briscoe quite acceptable in the runoff election and helped give him a healthy victory against Frances Farenthold, a hard-line liberal state representative. Having offended very few people in his first term, Briscoe easily swamped Farenthold by two to one in 1974 to serve the first four-year gubernatorial term since Reconstruction.

Secure until 1978, conservatives could look back on nearly three decades of factional strife with understandable satisfaction. Briscoe's 1974 margin almost exactly equaled Jester's in 1946. In the 15 elections between those two years, only three times had conservatives received less than 55 percent of the vote, and on five occasions there was no real liberal challenge at all. However, in the gubernatorial primary of 1978, Attorney General John Hill—once a Machine politician, himself—upset the attempt of the conservative Governor Briscoe to be the first to serve 10 years in the office. Hill, by receiving over 51 percent of the Democratic votes, mustered more than opponents Briscoe and former governor Preston Smith, thus avoiding a runoff. While no liberal, the former attorney general was certainly considered more consumer-minded, aggressive, and moderate than the incumbent. By showing his outward concern for the economic plight of the state's teachers and farmers, he managed to carry the typical liberal areas of Texas and a number of the conservative counties in the Panhandle (see Figure 3–4).

The conservative vote Examining the returns of the most recent hotly contested primary elections, one may readily see which counties consistently vote most heavily for conservative candidates. Fifty-five counties ranked in the top one third in conservative support in at least three of these four elections: 1968 governor (Preston Smith), 1970 senator (Lloyd Bentsen), 1972 governor (Dolph Briscoe), 1972 senator (Barefoot Sanders) and 1978 senator (Bob Krueger). The accompanying map reveals that almost every one of these counties is west of a line drawn

FIGURE 3–4
Philosophical breakdown of counties in Texas*

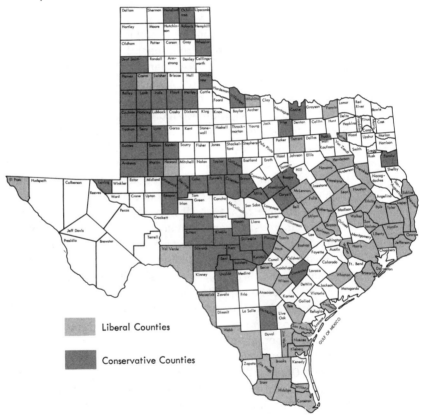

* Counties appearing in the most liberal or most conservative one third of all counties in at least three or four recent elections and never appearing in the bottom one third.

Source: Prepared by the authors from official election data in the Office of the Secretary of State.

from Fort Worth through Austin to Laredo. One group clusters in the Edwards Plateau north and west of San Antonio; another occupies a narrow swath running west from Waco to Big Spring and Midland; and the third large grouping is in the high plains area between Amarillo and Odessa. Ranking counties in this fashion has one major fallacy, however. Since so many small rural counties return very high conservative percentage margins, they crowd the larger counties out of the top one third in each election, and so the substantial conservative vote in urban areas is overlooked. These 55 counties are, however, a good indication of where rural and small town conservative strength lies. It is instructive to compare the people and the economics of these counties to the state as a whole. Clements carried most of these counties in his victorious campaign.

These conservative counties are smaller and less urbanized than the state as a whole. They have, on the average, only two thirds as many people as the typical Texas county, and over 60 percent of the residents are rural. Most of the heavily conservative areas are far more agricultural than the state is, and have comparatively little manufacturing. Finally, they contain almost no blacks (only 3 percent on the average), but quite a few Mexican-Americans (18 percent, just about the state average). Perhaps surprisingly, there is little difference between conservative and liberal counties in education, income, or percentage of people born out of state. There are slightly fewer poor families and uneducated people in the conservative counties, but the variation is not very significant.

What emerges as the picture of a typical conservative area is a small rural county, its people concentrating on farming, ranching, and trade. The area is stagnant or even declining economically, and has lost population steadily since before 1960. Its handful of blacks exert no influence to speak of, and its Mexican-American voters, while numerous, are not nearly so well organized and so independent politically as in the cities. Many probably vote as their Anglo employers or their conservative Mexican-American leaders dictate. Here, obviously, are people who are traditional in their ways, fairly homogeneous ethnically, and often suspicious of change. The state's headlong rush toward urbanization and industrialization has passed them by. They naturally feel a bit alienated from this brash newfangled Texas, and react with hostility to the demands of liberal candidates that the state's economic, social, and political structure be changed still further. They are individualists, unwilling to accept the idea that government should intervene in the workings of the economy or take money from one group of people in order to give benefits to another group. Organized labor, organized minorities, intellectuals, and others who demand that government take such forbidden actions are dangerous to the conservative tradition and naturally produce great opposition at the polls from these rural conservative voters.

Although the large counties in Texas are more liberal in their voting than the state as a whole, this does not mean that conservatives are necessarily weak in the cities. As a matter of fact, the mobilization of conservatives in the large metropolitan areas by Republicans contributed greatly to the "upset" of the century in 1978. It merely indicates that because so many small rural counties go conservative by enormous majorities of three and four to one, the conservative urban areas do not show up in the list of the state's 50 most conservative counties. Yet, among these large counties are Gregg (averaging almost 75 percent in its voting), Ector and Midland (almost 70 percent conservative), and many others which consistently reject liberal candidates. In fact, conservatives carried 15 of the 30 most populous counties in all four recent "bench-mark" primary elections (for governor in 1968 and 1972; for senator in 1970 and 1972). Liberal candidates were able to carry only 5 of the 30 counties every time.

What sort of urban county is most likely to vote for the conservative faction's statewide candidates? In some ways, conservative and liberal big cities are quite a bit alike, at least on the surface. One usually thinks, for instance, of poor people voting liberal and better-off people voting conservative. Yet the ten most conservative and ten most liberal urban counties have almost exactly the same per capita income, the same average house value, and almost the same percentage of both poor and upper-income families. Educationally, also, there is practically no difference between these two groups of counties. These figures should serve as a warning to use statistical averages very cautiously, because they do mask what is in fact a very sharp difference in the voting patterns of urban dwellers. Anyone who looks at the precinct-by-precinct election returns within the large counties will quickly see that the conservative precincts are in the upper-income, better-educated areas of each city, with the usual exception of university communities. Conservatives are weak in the faculty-dominated precincts around universities (which do have relatively high incomes) and in the lower-income working-class areas, and are weakest of all in the minority-group precincts, which normally have the lowest incomes and poorest educations.

Aside from income and education, the conservative large counties do have some things in common which they do not share with the big liberal counties. For one thing, they are generally smaller in population (Dallas is the only one of the conservative "top ten" counties having over 200,000 people and it was not surprising that the first Republican governor in over 100 years was a resident of this solid base), and are growing more slowly than the average for all major cities. The median age in the conservative counties is a full two years older than in liberal counties, which is in line with the general principle that older persons tend to be conservative. These counties also have fewer blacks and Mexican-

Americans than the average. Even the type of economic activity they engage in marks the conservative counties out as distinctive. They deal
much more in wholesale and retail trade, personal services, and agriculture, than in manufacturing or mineral production. The most conservative
urban counties have almost double the volume of wholesale trade and
sell almost three times the value of agricultural products per capita as
the typical liberal county. On the other hand, conservative areas manu-
facture less than half the per capita value of finished products and have
one third less mineral production than the liberal areas.

From these facts, it is apparent that urban conservatives, while in
many ways resembling rural conservatives, are basically different in
their economic orientation. Most small-county voters who consistently
vote conservative are associated in some way with agriculture and its
related activities. Obviously, few urban conservatives are engaged in
agriculture. Rather, they are likely to be professional, managerial, or
other white-collar workers, living in a "good" section of town. While they
share the rural conservative's dislike for an active and expensive government and may have little patience with the demands of blacks, Mexican-Americans, women, and others, many of them may respond favorably
to a candidate who speaks for urban versus rural interests and who
champions consumers against the "faceless" big corporations. It was
just such people who gave liberal Frances Farenthold a remarkably
strong vote in the well-to-do, well-educated conservative suburban areas
around Dallas and Houston in her 1972 primary race against rural-
oriented Dolph Briscoe, and John Hill against the same opponent in
1978. Here are potential defectors from the conservative ranks if liberals
are willing to woo them.

Liberal Democrats: The party loyalists   As conservative discontent
with the trend of the national Democratic party grew into open rebellion
after World War II, a large number of Texans still remained committed to
the liberal ideas of the New Deal period. Well satisfied that Democratic
presidential candidates after Roosevelt were carrying on and even expanding the social and economic programs of FDR, liberals became increasingly furious at those conservatives in Texas who claimed to be
Democrats for purposes of controlling state politics, but who turned their
backs on Truman, Stevenson, and later presidential nominees. Regarding national politics, liberals have always had two major goals: first, to
choose delegates of their persuasion to the Democratic national conventions, and second, to control the state party organization to insure that it
gives loyal and energetic support to the presidential ticket in November.

To obtain the first goal, it is of course necessary to control the election of delegates throughout the ascending process of precinct, county,
and state conventions. Anyone voting in the Democratic primary is entitled to attend the precinct convention held after the polls close, and

whichever side can "pack" the meeting with the most supporters is able to dictate the selection of delegates from the precinct to the county convention. The dominant faction in the county convention likewise sends its slate of like-minded delegates to the state convention. Finally, the state gathering selects the people who represent Texas at the presidential nominating convention.

Every four years therefore saw a fierce battle between factions for control of the various layers of conventions. Handicapped by the fact that their black, Mexican-American, and working-class voters often lacked motivation to attend precinct conventions, liberals usually lost these fights even in most urban counties. Although a strong liberal minority might sometimes emerge from the local conventions, it had to sit helplessly by and see the conservative majority in the state convention pick a nearly unanimous slate of conservative national convention delegates. In the 1948 convention, for instance, all of Texas' 50 votes were cast for Senator Russell of Georgia, opposing the renomination of President Truman and the inclusion of a civil-rights plank in the Democratic platform. In 1952, Texas again voted unanimously for Russell and in 1956 and 1960 for favorite-son Senator Lyndon Johnson. In each case these were the most conservative candidates available.

After the mid-1960s the situation began to improve slightly for the liberal minority. There was no effective opposition within Texas to the renomination of President Johnson in 1964, even though he had taken some remarkably liberal stands on social and economic problems. And in 1968 there was no conservative alternative again. The "establishment" leaders in Texas swung behind Vice President Hubert Humphrey in order to head off Eugene McCarthy, and while many liberals worked for McCarthy's losing campaign in Texas, there was perceived to be really little difference between the two candidates except on the Vietnam War. Humphrey was a confirmed liberal of long standing in domestic policy, and it could hardly have made Texas conservative delegates very happy to have to support him for president to avoid an even more obnoxious choice.

Beginning in 1972, the entire process of delegate selection was altered to conform to national party "reform" rules, greatly increasing the chances for substantial liberal representation at the national convention. Under the new rules, every sizeable minority (20 percent or more in that particular year) is guaranteed its proportional share of delegates to the next higher convention. Thus, if 30 percent, say, of those attending a precinct convention prefer a liberal presidential candidate, that candidate is entitled to 30 percent of the precinct's county convention delegates. Likewise, at the final level of the state convention a conservative majority can no longer deny a liberal minority its share of representation at the national convention. Because of much hard organizing work at the local level by both McGovern and Wallace supporters, those two candidates won the majority of Texas' 1972 Democratic presidential delegates. The "establishment" conservatives, who preferred Jackson or Humphrey, had to be satisfied with less than half the state's delegate votes. In 1976, the Democratic National Committee abandoned this rigid quota system of representation, much to the delight of moderate and conservative forces within the party. Employing the use of the presidential primary in the same year, Texas Democrats overwhelmingly gave their support to the moderate Jimmy Carter.

In state elections liberals have had a mixed record since the war. They have had some success in U.S. Senate contests, first with Lyndon Johnson and then with Ralph Yarborough both winning three times. But they have never yet been able to wrest the governorship from conservative or moderate "machine" candidates, and until recently seldom held any other state office. In the entire postwar era there actually have been only three strong liberal candidates for governor, contesting eight elections between them. Ralph Yarborough fought Allan Shivers twice and Price Daniel once from 1952 to 1956, increasing his vote each time until he very nearly slipped by Daniel in the 1956 runoff primary. His appeal was basically to urban workers, blacks, and Mexican-Americans, but also to farmers in anti-big business feeling.

When Yarborough went to the Senate, a young Houston lawyer named Don Yarborough then carried the liberal banner in 1962, 1964, and 1968. He ran remarkably well against John Connally in his first race, losing by less than 30,000 votes, and advance indications were that Yarborough might unseat Governor Connally in 1964 with the help of a hard fought Republican primary to drain off several hundred thousand conservative votes. Early editions of the Houston *Chronicle* on November 22, 1963, carried reports of an in-depth statewide survey indicating that Yarborough might have an even chance of victory the next summer. But that afternoon Connally rode in President Kennedy's car through downtown Dallas and was wounded in the assassination. Thereafter, he was of course impervious to challenge, and Yarborough, who stubbornly ran in 1964 anyway, lost badly in the primary. With Connally's retirement in 1968, Yarborough again emerged as the liberal challenger facing conservative Preston Smith in the runoff election. Smith picked up votes from most of the defeated first-primary candidates and won comfortably by 55 to 45 percent.

Smith in turn was defeated trying for a third term in 1972, when another energetic liberal entered the lists. Frances Farenthold had built a record as a hard-driving reformer in the Texas legislature, and although she had little campaign money she very surprisingly swept into a runoff with Dolph Briscoe. Hardly a firm conservative himself, Briscoe was still much preferable to Ms. Farenthold in the minds of conservative voters, and he won with no particular trouble. However, Ms. Farenthold (who ran again but lost heavily in 1974) opened up possible new avenues for liberal candidates at the top of the ticket. In addition to the usual social and economic issues aimed at workers and minorities, she campaigned heavily on the newer issues of environmental and consumer protection, and structural reform of government. These questions, partially cutting across the old liberal-conservative lines, had considerable appeal among well-educated suburban middle-class professionals, who in the past had been reliably conservative. In the whole state Ms. Farenthold ran 3 percent behind Ralph Yarborough (who was trying again for the Senate), but she led him by 8 percent in Harris and Dallas counties, the state's largest and fastest growing urban areas. (This unusually effective appeal to the middle class may have been a fluke, but if it were to become a permanent part of future liberal campaigns it might cut heavily into conservative strength in metropolitan areas, which, after all, contain a majority of Texans.) In 1978, liberal Joe Christie, former chairman of the State Board of Insurance from El Paso, was swamped 60–40 by conservative U.S. Congressman Bob Krueger of New Braunfels in the Democratic primary for U.S. Senator, and later the more conservative Clements eked out a general election victory in the governor's race over Hill.

One hint that liberals may, in fact, do better in future gubernatorial races is their striking but little noticed success in gradually taking over the lesser state offices. For more than two decades the only state office-holder who could be called at all liberal was Agriculture Commissioner John White (named as U.S. Undersecretary of Agriculture in 1977 in great part because of his early support of President Carter when still an aspiring candidate), known chiefly for his firm loyalty to unpopular Democratic presidential nominees. Then in the 1970 primary, an attractive young legislator with a moderately liberal voting record, Bob Armstrong, unseated the veteran land commissioner. Two years later, moderate William P. Hobby, Jr., a Houston publisher, won the lieutenant-governorship with liberal and urban support over a conservative brother of John Connally. The same primary saw moderately liberal John Lee Hill, also of Houston, defeat the staunchly conservative incumbent attorney general. Finally, an unabashed liberal and former secretary of state, Bob Bullock, took over the state comptroller's office in 1974. Bullock, a maverick of unbelievable proportions, personally disliked his peer, John Hill, with such intensity that he campaigned for his archconservative opponent, Dolph Briscoe, in the 1978 Democratic primary for governor. After Hill's unexpected defeat, Bullock might well be in the "driver's seat" for the gubernatorial nomination in 1984. Liberals thus hold four of the six offices below governor, where before 1970 they had had but one. Not only are these positions important in themselves in formulating state policy on a broad range of issues, but they also give liberal incumbents the exposure so vital in running a winning statewide race. If the Democratic party's liberal wing is willing to settle for these rather moderate men as its standard bearers in future campaigns for governor or senator, then conservative dominance at the top of the ticket may soon be ended.

Who are the liberal voters? The procedure for identifying liberal counties is the same as that used for conservatives earlier. A total of 58 counties ranked in the top one third of all counties according to liberal strength in at least three of four recent statewide elections, and none was ever in the bottom one third. A look at the map (Figure 3–4, page 100) reveals an obvious geographical contrast with the conservative counties. Only 7 of the liberal 58 are west of a line drawn from Fort Worth through San Antonio to Laredo. One large group of counties dominates southeast Texas from Beaumont, Galveston, and Houston on the Gulf northwest to Waco. Another cluster runs down the lower Gulf Coast from Corpus Christi to the Rio Grande Valley, while another third is centered on Austin and San Antonio. As expected, Hill carried these counties in his losing effort.

As this geographical pattern suggests, liberal candidates are heavily dependent upon the votes of minority groups. Nine of the top-ranked liberal counties are more than 75 percent Mexican-American; none of the top conservative counties are. Furthermore, the average liberal county has four times as many blacks as the average conservative county. Within counties, the same pattern appears almost every time; black and Mexican-American precincts, particularly in cities, often cast 80 percent, 90 percent, or even more, of their votes for liberals. Indeed, it would be amazing if this were not so since liberal Democrats have been in the forefront of those demanding better conditions for the ethnic minorities of Texas. A number of liberal leaders present and past are themselves Mexican-American or black, most notably U.S. Representatives Henry B. Gonzalez and Barbara Jordan, who announced her decision not to run for almost certain reelection in 1978.

Liberal counties tend to be larger in population and more urbanized than the average, and they are also growing faster than most counties. In a state where for so long rural areas had a far greater share of political power than their population warranted, people living in large, fast growing urban counties quite naturally felt aggrieved. The existing distribution of political power in Texas shortchanged these counties. With all their population, they were unable to control the legislature or elect an urban-oriented governor, and cities often received less than their due in the distribution of state money. Like the ethnic minorities, urban dwellers felt discriminated against. This feeling inclined them to vote for liberal candidates who seemed likely to correct the imbalance in the political system by giving more attention, more representation, and more money to urban areas and their problems. While liberals do not often carry large counties, they do run much better here than in the country-side. Of the state's 16 counties having over 100,000 population, 14 show up on the list of the 58 most liberal counties in Texas, and none makes the conservative top list.

As noted earlier, there is little difference, on the average, between liberal and conservative counties in the way of income or education, but this obscures the very real difference which does exist at the precinct level. Whatever a county's average level of income or education, within the county the poorer and less-educated areas will almost always be found giving heavy support to liberals, while the wealthier and better-educated precincts vote conservative. Finally, there is the matter of occupation and political affiliation. Liberal counties have about twice the number of factory employees and many fewer independent farmers than in the conservative counties. Since labor unions are one of the largest components of liberal politics in Texas, this statistic is not unexpected. If it were not for union money and organizing ability, liberal statewide candidates would run very poorly indeed. One of the prime reasons for Frances Farenthold's dismal showing in the 1974 gubernatorial primary was that the unions, which had given her considerable help two years earlier, were willing to accept Governor Briscoe for another four years in office. Even in 1978, with few exceptions, the unions refused to endorse the relatively more liberal John Hill over Briscoe in the gubernatorial primary, nor were they very active in the general election. This tendency of labor leaders to work with moderately conservative politicians has long been one of the chief complaints of liberal intellectuals, blacks, and Mexican-Americans.

As previously noted, large counties tend to be substantially more liberal than smaller ones. Even so, liberals have quite a varying degree of support in the state's 30 most populous counties, from a low of less than 33 percent of the vote in Gregg, Midland, and Ector, to a high of over 57 percent in Galveston, El Paso, and Nueces. Within counties, there is an even wider variation. Some minority precincts regularly vote liberal by upwards of 90 percent, while in wealthy Anglo precincts a liberal does well to reach 20 percent.

To avoid needless repetition of statistics, one may begin with the obvious inference that urban liberals have almost exactly the opposite characteristics of urban conservatives, who were discussed earlier at length. It is most important to realize that the almost identical average income, wealth, and education of liberal and conservative counties are quite misleading. Seldom will there be an exception to the finding that the poor and ill-educated make up the core of liberal strength in a large county. To this may be added such higher-income and better-educated groups as Jews, university professors, and an increasing number of liberal professional people. All these groups, either from a pressing personal economic need or from a more "idealistic" outlook, want changes in the state's political, economic, and social system. They want more influence for cities and minorities in the legislature and in other parts of the political structure; they want the state Democratic party to give full and loyal support to the national Democratic ticket, however liberal it may be.

The Republican party

From the 1880s through the 1950s, there was no effective Republican party in Texas. Ruled by a succession of petty "bosses," the party existed in name, but it was a mere shell, a means of distributing federal patronage whenever a Republican president happened to sit in Washington. In a space of more than two generations there were only three serious Republican campaigns for statewide office: the anti-"Ma" Ferguson outbursts of 1924 and 1932, and the anti-Johnson senatorial campaign in 1948. In each case, as in Herbert Hoover's presidential victory in 1928, it was disgusted Democrats and not the Republican party which gave body to these campaigns. Even when Texans deserted the Democratic national ticket regularly after 1948, there was no noticeable increase in Republican voting at the state level.

This situation could not last forever. Texas was changing too rapidly in its economic, social, and residential patterns to be long immune from the forces which produced two-party competition from one-party factionalism. The first signs of Republican life began to appear in the mid-1950s: a Republican congressman elected in Dallas in 1954 and reelected for a decade against both liberal and conservative challengers; a few Republican county officials elected in 1958; a strong third-place showing in the 1957 special Senate election against both conservative and liberal Democrats. The first real evidence of Republican strength occurred in 1960. Lyndon Johnson had accepted the Democratic vice presidential nomination on John Kennedy's ticket, enraging many conservatives. Some liberals, too, were angry at Johnson for his devious path in state politics previously. As insurance in case the national race failed, Johnson had pushed through the legislature a bill allowing him to run both for vice president and for reelection to the Senate. The situation seemed ready-made for a vigorous Republican opponent, and one came forward in the person of John Tower, a young political science teacher at Midwestern University in Wichita Falls. With a modest budget, Tower scoured the state for votes, using the slogan "Double Your Pleasure, Double Your Fun—Vote Against Johnson Two Times, Not One." He polled the amazing total of 42 percent against Johnson's 58 percent, while the Republican candidate for governor was drawing only 27 percent (a high vote in itself).

When Johnson resigned his Senate seat to serve as vice president, it was natural that Tower should be the Republican candidate for the vacancy. Since there are no party labels or primaries in special elections, and the filing fee is low, a record 71 people ran for the Senate. Having just finished a strong statewide campaign, Tower had a name as well known as any of the major Democrats. He easily led the first election with 31 percent of the vote, and edged past conservative Bill Blakley by 51–49 in the runoff. Many conservatives preferred Tower to Blakley, who had supported Kennedy for president in 1960, while many liberals felt both candidates were worthless and refused to vote. Tower's election proved that a Republican could win statewide and touched off a flurry of unfounded GOP hopes for a sweeping victory in 1962.

A record number of Republicans ran for office at all levels that year. Two were elected to Congress, the party's legislative ticket swept Dallas County, and almost two dozen county officials were elected. But of major victories there was none. A hard-hitting candidate for governor, Jack Cox, lost to Democrat John Connally by 54–46, and other statewide nominees ran further behind. The Republican organization was preparing another strong effort for 1964, hoping for some liberal victories in the Democratic primary, but Kennedy's assassination brought Lyndon Johnson to the presidency and unified the Texas Democrats. Many conservatives were still willing to support Republican George Bush against Senator Yarborough in 1964, but Bush did not manage to equal Cox's percentage for governor in the previous year. In 1966, Tower won reelection to the Senate (largely with liberal votes, against a conservative Democrat), but the GOP made little effort in other races.

Finally, in 1968 Republicans were ready to try again to break the Democratic hold on state offices. Johnson was leaving the presidency, George Wallace was splitting the Democratic party, John Connally was retiring as governor. But again there was disappointment; Paul Eggers ran a strong race for governor but garnered only 43 percent of the vote. In a return fight two years later he moved up to 46 percent, but neither he nor George Bush, who got about the same percentage running for the Senate, could overcome the handicap of the Republican party label. Henry Grover did no better in 1972 but nearly was elected governor anyway as the Democratic vote dropped to 48 percent because many Mexican-Americans voted for Ramsey Muñiz on the La Raza Unida ticket. This close contest gave Republicans high hopes for 1974 until Watergate, inflation, and recession buried the GOP under a two-to-one Democratic landslide. In the 1978 Republican gubernatorial primary an extremely conservative Dallas businessman (and former deputy secretary of defense under Presidents Nixon and Ford), Clements, easily upset former State Party Chairman Ray Hutchinson. Later, because of his successful effort to paint Hill as a "liberal" which attracted the support of many already alienated Briscoe supporters in West and Central Texas, the number of over-confident Democrats who stayed home in South Texas, the Panhandle (Hill lost 34 counties there that he carried in the primary), and Bexar and Travis counties, Clements astoundingly defeated Hill. Ultraconservative Deep South States such as Virginia, South Carolina, and Mississippi are increasingly showing a Republican take-over of state offices; viable two-party competition may not be far behind for the Lone Star State.

Who are the Republican voters? There are 48 counties which ranked in the top one third (according to Republican percentage of the vote) in all four recent closely contested elections: for governor in 1968, 1970, and 1972, and for senator in 1970. Another 44 counties were in the bottom one third in each of the four elections. As the map shows, there is no geographical pattern to Republican strength and weakness, unlike the sharp east-west division between liberal and conservative Democratic factions. One may find no less than six isolated areas where Republican candidates run well: in the Houston and the Dallas-Fort Worth metropolitan areas, in the deep East Texas and far West Texas oil centers around Tyler-Longview and Midland-Odessa, in the traditionally Republican "German" counties northwest of San Antonio, and in the Panhandle. No one characteristic ties these scattered centers together; some are heavily urban, others rural; some are oil-rich, others are agricultural or manufacturing centers.

In comparison with the 44 most Democratic counties, however, some points do stand out. The Republican counties tend to be densely populated; they average 50 percent more people than a typical Texas county, and 100 percent more than the Democratic counties. Furthermore, the GOP strongholds are more urbanized, faster growing, and contain more non-Texans. While the least Republican areas were losing one eighth of their population in the 1960s, the 48 banner counties gained 1,225,000 people, nearly 75 percent of the state's total population increase during the decade. A great deal of this gain came from outside the state, for the Republican counties average nearly one fourth of their people non-Texans, compared to barely one twelfth in the Democratic counties. Proof of these statistics is apparent in almost every one of the state's individual counties. Election after election, the Anglo-dominated urban precincts (even if only in a small town) will normally be more Republican than the Anglo rural precincts. Rural people are more tradition-minded than town dwellers in nearly every human society, and in Texas certainly a straight-ticket Democratic vote is among the oldest of traditions. Moving to a town or city helps loosen the hold of every sort of traditional behavior. One now sees more different opinions, observes that Republicans

FIGURE 3–5
Partisan breakdown of counties in Texas*

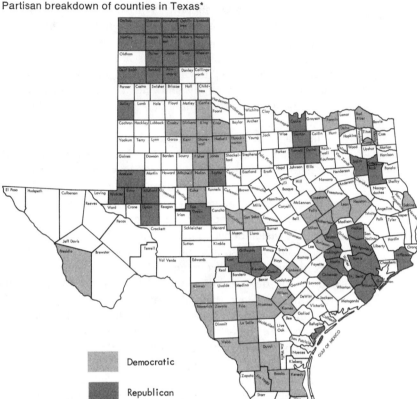

Democratic

Republican

* Counties appearing in the most Democratic or most Republican one third of all counties in at least three of four recent elections and never appearing in the bottom one third.

Source: Prepared by the authors from official returns in the Office of the Secretary of State.

do exist and are not all ogres, and feels the influence of out-of-state immigrants who are accustomed to two-party politics as a matter of course. Hence, a gradual willingness to vote Republican may appear.

The other major division between Republicans and Democrats is in income and education. On almost every measure, the 48 top GOP counties are superior to the bottom 44 counties. If one considers family income, the typical Republican county has 92 families living in poverty for every 100 families with over $15,000 income. In a typical Democratic county there are 380 poor families for every 100 which earn over $15,000. In education, people in the Republican areas have two full years more schooling than people in the least Republican counties. Looking at the extremes of education, the average Republican county has 60 percent more college graduates, and only half as many people with less than five years education, as the average Democratic county. What these figures say, of course, is simply that the higher a person's income and status in life, the more likely he is to vote Republican. This does not mean, however, that Republicans are more intelligent or better informed than Democrats, merely that they are better educated. Since income and education are rather closely connected, this is usually just another way of saying that Republicans tend to be richer.

Finally, the typical Republican county has more young people and fewer old folks than the Democratic counties. There is a difference of seven years in the median age of Republican and Democratic strongholds (28.2 years versus 35.3 years), and the Democratic counties have nearly twice as many people over age 65 as Republican ones. Again, one may say generally that older people are more fixed in traditional patterns than their children are, and therefore that Republicans have a much better chance of convincing voters under 30 to split their tickets than they do of persuading older voters.

While drawing profiles of "typical" voters is a hazardous business, it does appear that Republicans in Texas are likely to be young, well-educated Anglos earning an above-average income in an urban county, and living in the city or its suburbs. Many are newcomers to Texas, while others have recently moved from small towns or farms into the rapidly growing cities. In either case they have escaped the traditional straight-ticket Democratic voting habit of many older Texans. There is no doubt that they will some day constitute a major political force in the state, though they now have a long uphill fight to reach that goal.

The 30 largest counties, in which over 70 percent of Texans live, are considerably more Republican than the state as a whole. Fifteen of them are among the 50 most Republican counties in Texas, and only one is among the 50 most Democratic counties. However, there is great variation in party strength within these 30 large counties. Randall and Midland, the banner Republican counties, averaged more than 60 percent for GOP candidates in four recent statewide races, while Webb, the worst performer, averaged only 21 percent and Bell and Bowie were next with 35 percent each. Within this group of urban counties there is no particular association of size with Republicanism. The two most populous counties, Harris and Dallas, are also among the most Republican, but on the other hand Randall and Midland each has less than 70,000 people.

What is the typical urban Republican county like? By comparing the ten most Republican of these counties with the ten most Democratic, one may isolate the influences which seem to create Republican voters in the major cities of Texas. As was previously noticed in the state as a whole, the rate of population growth and the percentage of out-of-state immigrants both differ greatly according to the party affiliation of the area. The typical Republican urban county is growing at almost twice the rate of the typical Democratic county, and had almost 50 percent more non-Texans in its population. The Republican counties are also more highly urbanized; of the eight large counties over 95 percent urban, four are in the Republican "top ten" and only one is heavily Democratic. On the average, the ten large Democratic counties had almost twice as many rural residents as the ten large Republican counties.

As one might expect, the Republican urban areas have few Mexican-Americans—only about one fifth as many as the typical Democratic urban county. There is a higher proportion of blacks in the Republican counties, but this statistic is misleading and one should not conclude that urban blacks tend to vote Republican. An analysis of voting patterns within large counties confirms that both black and Mexican-American precincts are very heavily Democratic, usually by upwards of ten to one. The only exception to this in recent years was the 1970 election, when there was a heavy black and Mexican-American vote for the Republican candidates for governor and senator, Paul Eggers and George Bush. Since both candidates were perceived as moderately liberal, unusual for Texas Republicans, they ran far ahead of the normal party percentage in urban minority-group precincts, sometimes even polling a majority.

Economic status is very strongly associated with urban Republicanism, partly because the Democratic counties do contain so many low-income members of minority groups. The ten most Republican counties have many more families earning over $15,000 yearly, and many fewer living in poverty, than do the ten most Democratic counties. In fact, the typical urban Republican county has twice as many wealthy families as poor ones, while the typical Democratic county has half again as many poor families as rich ones. Along with income goes education. In the Republican counties people have about a half year more schooling than in the Democratic areas, but this seemingly small difference masks a greater gap. In the Democratic "top ten" more people had never reached the fifth grade than had graduated from college, where the Republican "top ten" counties had almost three times as many college graduates as people with a fourth-grade education.

Finally, the type of economic activity in which these counties concentrate has an impact on their party affiliation. Urban Republican counties are usually centers of manufacturing, mineral production, wholesale trade, or personal services. The ten large Republican counties, for instance, had almost twice the percentage of manufacturing employment, three times the per capita value of manufactured goods, twice the per capita value of mineral production, and wholesale trade, and almost twice the per capita value of personal service performed. Of course it is not the production of these goods and services, but the type of people who produce them that leads to Republican voting. Manufacturing establishments do have many blue-collar assembly-line workers who are likely to be Democratic, but they also employ great numbers of managerial and professional people, often born or educated outside Texas in two-party states. The same is true of mineral production (chiefly oil and gas). As for wholesale trade and services (such as tourism, recreation, and so on), these types of businesses employ mostly white-collar workers whose education and economic status are likely to make them more conservative (and therefore Republican) than the general population.

The Wallace voters

The lasting appeal of George Wallace to many Texas voters was one of the most noticeable phenomena of recent political history. From his emergence as a national candidate in the 1964 Democratic primaries, through his third-party presidential race in 1968, to his strong primary showing in 1972, Wallace had been able to count on a small core of fervent supporters and, occasionally, on a much larger number of more-or-less loyal voters. For a time during and just after the 1968 race it seemed that the Wallaceites might indeed form a permanent new party in the state. In that election Wallace polled more votes (19 percent) than any third-party presidential candidate in Texas history since the Populists in 1892. He carried a number of counties and gathered at least 30 percent of the vote in 43.

The distribution of the Wallace vote made fairly clear his long-term base of support. From Oklahoma to the Gulf he ran well in a solid band of East Texas counties, extending from the Louisiana border west to Paris, Palestine, and Huntsville. Here, blacks are a sizeable part of the population, and the race issue has never been far below the surface of politics. This area of Texas closely resembles the Deep South states where Wallace is seen as the defender of states' rights and a white-dominated society against an overbearing federal government. These same counties produced the bulk of Strom Thurmond's votes in 1948 when he ran for president on an openly anticivil rights Dixiecrat platform. In fact, out of the 19 counties which gave Thurmond at least 20 percent of their votes in 1948, 15 voted at least 30 percent for Wallace in 1968, and the remaining four did not fall much below that figure.

The most interesting aspect of these Wallace counties, however, is that many of them are also consistently liberal in Democratic state politics. Only one of Wallace's East Texas strongholds shows up in the list of top conservative counties, while 13 are among the most liberal counties. Does this mean that liberals who supported Ralph Yarborough, Don Yarborough, and Frances Farenthold are "secret Wallaceites"? Are they perhaps working-class Anglos from the oil fields, lumber mills, and factories of East Texas who are economic liberals but civil-rights conservatives? This is certainly a possibility since racial tolerance is often related to education, income, and occupation, with those lowest in these attributes being most hostile to economic and social advances by blacks. On the other hand, the seeming correlation may be misleading. These East Texas counties contain many blacks and industrial-oil-lumber workers who cast liberal ballots in state elections. The same counties also have many conservative Anglos who are most afraid of black progress (because they are closest to it and most affected by it). There might be little overlap between the two types of voters, even though both occupy the same counties. This problem will require detailed investigation of the precinct-by-precinct returns for the 1968 election.

About the other group of Wallace counties, there is little mystery. These are clustered in far West Texas Permian Basin oil and cattle country around Midland and Odessa. Few blacks live here and, although Mexican-Americans are present in some numbers, the dominant tone of politics is not ethnic tension but pure and simple economic conservatism. Four of the eight western Wallace counties are on the heavily conservative list, while none shows up on the liberal roll. This part of the state is so conservative that in 1960 it found even the Republican party too liberal and voted heavily for a candidate of the far-right Constitution party who wanted to abolish the federal income tax (among other things). Whoever seems most against federal power and federal spending will get the backing of these people, and in 1968 Wallace seemed to fit that description. There are, of course, also many such voters in the large urban areas; they do not show up on maps because their numbers are lost in the heavy liberal and Republican turnout in most cities. But if one looks at precinct figures for 1968, the urban Wallaceites become visible. Many precincts, particularly in Houston and Dallas, were more friendly to Wallace than the East Texas counties were. The same thing occurred in 1972 when Wallace's supporters made a massive effort to win delegates to the Democratic national convention. They actually wound up controlling several big-city senatorial districts as well as the rural and small-city East Texas area, and gave Wallace an impressive share of the state's delegates.

What is the future for these people, who make up perhaps one fifth of all Texas voters and who dominate several congressional districts? A really energetic local organizing campaign after 1968, with the creation of a party structure at the county level and the running of scores of local candidates in 1970, might have turned the Wallace movement into a permanent force in state politics. However, by deciding to work within the Democratic nominating system for 1972 after nearly being killed by an assassin's bullet during the Maryland primary and after losing to fellow Deep Southerner Jimmy Carter in the Florida and Texas primaries of

FIGURE 3–6

The counties in Texas showing a preference for George Wallace or La Raza Unida

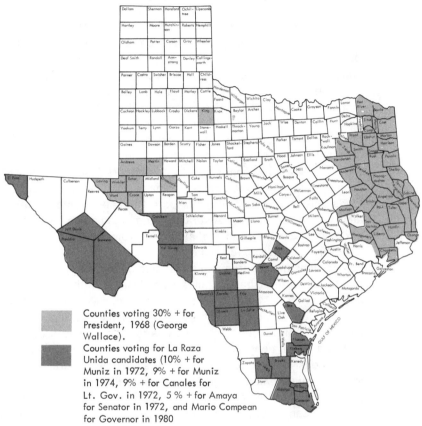

Counties voting 30% + for President, 1968 (George Wallace).

Counties voting for La Raza Unida candidates (10% + for Muniz in 1972, 9% + for Muniz in 1974, 9% + for Canales for Lt. Gov. in 1972, 5 % + for Amaya for Senator in 1972, and Mario Compean for Governor in 1980

Source: Prepared by the authors from official returns in the Office of the Secretary of State.

1976, Wallace eliminated any real chance of such a party. Moreover, by 1978 the once spunky Governor suddenly announced his withdrawal from a sure-bet race to fill a vacated U.S. Senate seat in Alabama and, apparently, his retirement from politics. The American Independent Party without Wallace will have little influence with Texas voters. Instead, most of his supporters continue to be Democrats, at least to the extent of voting in Democratic primaries and (usually) for local Democrats in November. They are quite willing, though, as they showed in 1972, to reject a Democratic candidate whom they regard as too liberal. They will continue to represent an opinion that statewide Democrats would be foolish to ignore, but if reasonable attention is paid to their views they will probably remain Democrats for some years to come.

La Raza Unida

During the same years that the Wallace voters failed to evolve into a separate political party, a group of "militant" Mexican-Americans did produce Texas' first long-term third party organization in this century. Dissatisfied with decades of neglect and discrimination by state Democrats, and not attracted to the even more conservative Republican party, a number of Mexican-American leaders decided that there was real potential for a new party oriented toward the needs and desires of their particular ethnic group. Along with like-minded organizers in several other southwestern states, they began building the structure of a predominantly Mexican-American political institution, the La Raza Unida (or United People's) party. While the leaders insist that they welcome support from blacks, students, women, and liberals generally, the attitude and very name of the new party indicate an interest in appealing almost solely to Mexican-Americans, and doing so on the basis of ethnic pride and a common sense of alienation from the old political system. In 1972, the La Raza Unida gubernatorial candidate, Ramsey Muñiz, was able to draw heavily from students in some university communities, and among some few liberal Anglos who disliked both major party candidates. But by 1974 and certainly by 1978, most of this outside support disappeared, as non Mexican-Americans came to perceive La Raza as overly militant, indeed, almost hostile to other ethnic groups.

The areas of consistent La Raza voting support in both 1972 and 1974 are obviously limited to counties where Mexican-Americans are present in substantial numbers. Even in this area, the new party has not overpowered the opposition. In the 15 counties which are more than 75 percent Mexican-American, Muñiz could average only one third of the vote in 1972. Outside these ethnic core counties and university centers he did very poorly indeed. In 1976, the LRUP ran only one half of the total number of candidates in local elections that it had slated two years earlier. In explaining the low vote percentages, it should be remembered that many Mexican-American voters are not yet able to cast independent ballots; they are swayed by local bosses in such counties as Duval (85 percent Mexican-American, 7 percent for Muñiz). Many others are simply traditional Democrats; they feel their people have a better chance of making political, social, and economic progress by helping liberals take over the dominant Democratic party. Voting for La Raza, they think, merely divides the ethnic bloc and weakens its political effectiveness. Finally, for reasons stated earlier in this chapter, any statewide influence that LRUP might have had, e.g., in 1972 when its "spoiler" role almost cost the Democrats the governor's office, has nearly disappeared. Its only remaining clout is restricted to several local communities such as Zavala County in South Texas. *Only* if the Democratic party reverses its tendency of recent years and deliberately turns its back upon Mexican-Americans and their needs is it likely to be able to hold the loyalty of this group even against an ethnic-oriented party like La Raza. In fact, both Tower and Clements increased the amount of chicano support for Republicans over that experienced before 1978.

The future of Texas politics

By 1979, the long-term future for moderate and liberal Democrats looked as dim as was the outlook bright for Republicans. It will surely be some years before any group completely succeeds in ousting the conservative Democratic "machine" from control of state politics. Two developments will help both groups of challengers: the extension of the "one man-one vote" rule in legislative and county redistricting, and the growth of metropolitan areas. In recent years Harris, Dallas, and Bexar counties changed to single-member legislative districts, and because of recent litigation in the courts negating multimember schemes the other large counties have had to follow. When all the members from Harris County, for instance, were elected at large, it took a great deal of money to wage an effective countywide campaign. Machine Democrats naturally had easiest access to the type of financing required, and both liberals and Republicans were hard put to raise funds on this large a scale. In addition, a countywide election enabled conservatives to play off the other two groups against each other. In the Democratic primary, most Republicans would show up to help conservatives defeat their liberal challengers. In the general election, enough liberals would obligingly vote straight Democratic and help the conservatives (who had beaten them in May) to turn back any Republican challenge.

Single-member districts deprive conservatives of both these advantages. While a 75,000-person district is not small, it can be covered reasonably well in door-to-door campaigning with minimal expense for major advertising. Thus, a large volunteer organization (which both liberals and Republicans are more likely to have) and a small budget becomes much more effective than a large budget and a poor organization. Furthermore, districts dominated by blacks, Mexican-Americans, or working-class Anglos, where almost any Democrat can win in November, are not likely to nominate conservatives in the primary. The Republican districts will go ahead and nominate conservative Democrats in May, only to defeat them with conservative Republicans in November. Only those marginal districts with a mixture of populations will still provide the conditions which allow a conservative to win in May and a Democrat to win in November, and there are not likely to be many of these. The most extreme example of what single-member districts can do is shown in Harris County. In the era of countywide elections conservatives usually won most, and sometimes all, of the county's seats. After 1972, when single-member districts were first used, Harris County elected 14 liberal Democrats, 3 moderates, no hard-line conservative Democrats at all, and 7 Republicans (nearly all strict conservatives). Dallas County, which used to be almost unanimously conservative, is now about evenly divided between liberal Democrats, conservative Democrats, and conservative Republicans.

Population shifts within the state will also work to the advantage of the antiestablishment groups. The most striking things which liberal and Republican counties have in common are their above-average size, heavy urbanization, and rapid growth. Conservative Democrats tend to be rural or rural-oriented, and their influence cannot help but decline as rural counties continue to lose population. City growth produces both a larger number of working-class people (who vote liberal), and a larger group of professional and managerial people (who vote Republican). Also, the larger any urban area becomes, the more single-member districts it will contain and the more homogeneous each district will probably be. This process will gradually produce more and more heavily liberal and moderate districts, and fewer mixed districts where conservatives have the advantage. The "big four" metropolitan counties contained 62 of the 150 state House districts after the 1971 redistricting, and will unquestionably increase their share, perhaps to more than 70, after the 1980 census.

Liberals have potential sources of future growth. The two bedrock liberal voting blocs, blacks and Mexican-Americans, have been attempting to increase their political influence in several ways. First, their percentage of the state's population is gradually rising. This is only a long-term trend, but it should add something to liberal strength with each passing election. Second, a larger percentage of voting-age persons in these two groups is registering to vote. This has been especially noticeable since the state adopted a permanent registration law in 1972. Third, despite 1978, those blacks and Mexican-Americans who do vote have an increasing tendency to do so in an organized fashion for liberal candidates, rather than following the lead of some *patron* who swings the minority-group vote to a conservative candidate. Finally, the advent of single-member legislative districts; equal-population legislative, senatorial, and congressional districts; and redrawn county commissioners' and justice of the peace precincts—all should help to improve the chances of electing liberal black or Mexican-American candidates.[29] Of course, these projections must be evaluated by a jaundiced eye after the *close* reelection of Senator Tower and the election of Bill Clements as Governor. It will remain to be seen if the Republicans can now build a solid base for a two-party state, or if the Machine Democrats, now "stung," will reinforce their efforts in the future to regain absolute control of their party and thus to reinstate one-party dominance in Texas.

Another help, though an erratic one, for liberals has been the extension of the vote to young people between 18 and 21. College students, particularly, were active in the 1972 primary and general election campaigns, and student-dominated precincts usually produced large majorities for liberal candidates in the May primary. In some local races, the student vote made the decisive difference in allowing liberal victories. However, student enthusiasm quickly declined. In the 1974 and 1976 primaries the voter turnout in student precincts was lower than among any other group and seemed to hold true in 1978. This erratic pattern will no doubt persist in future years, but at least on occasion liberals can expect substantial help from student voters *if* the issues arouse their interest.

For now, the Machine still sits in the "driver's seat" in Texas politics, since both Regular Democrats—Briscoe and Hill—have vacated the scene. As always Machine Democrats dominate the state legislature, particularly the appropriations processes in both houses. On the other hand, the liberals controlled both state conventions in 1976—almost ousting Briscoe's handpicked chairman, Calvin Guest, except for the unprecedented intervention of Jimmy Carter who pleaded for party unity —and they also dominated the State Democratic Executive Committee (SDEC) by 1978.

Finally, the future of Texas politics may well depend upon the actions or inactions of the aggressive Bill Clements as the Governor. His political "ancestor" during the Reconstruction period was so unpopular he had to be removed at gun point. "The times—they are a changing!"

CONCLUSIONS

In this chapter we have been able to establish these general conclusions about political parties and interest group politics in Texas:

1. Texas politics is very much one of interest-group influence. Although there is disagreement about which are the most influential lobbies in Austin, major influence is exerted by business groups representing real estate interests, railroads, trucking companies, automobile dealers, the chemical industry, and oil and gas interests; labor groups such as the Texas AFL–CIO; professional groups representing such occupations as teachers and lawyers; and such major institutions as the University of Texas and Texas A & M. Oil is so important to the Texas economy that its interest constitutes the major "mobilization of bias" of the political system.

2. Party politics in Texas has been dominated by the Democratic party, although Republicans have made some inroads in recent years. Both Democratic and Republican parties are formally organized into precinct, county, district, and state chairmen, committees and conventions. But the key to Texas party politics is to be found in its domination by

an unofficial conservative party with Democratic and Republican factions. The Texas party system's main components are the Machine Democrats, the Liberal Democrats, the Regular Democrats, and the Republicans. The Machine Democrats make up the conservative establishment of the Democratic party, thus controlling the formal party organization.

3. The "main event" in Texas election politics is the Democratic party primary. The state's election laws are devised in such a way as to insulate state contests from national political trends—by electing state officials at times other than presidential election years. Because general election competition is minimal, voter turnout in elections is low. The well organized supporters of Bill Clements took advantage of this fact in the last gubernatorial election.

4. Despite the central control of Texas politics by the traditional establishment, winds of change are blowing. Changes in districting the Texas legislature will weaken the grip of conservatives on state politics, and shifts in the population to metropolitan areas will benefit anti-establishment groups, and provide new political opportunities for influence in Texas politics by blacks and Mexican-Americans. To top it off, it appears that the Republican "pack is back!"

CHAPTER FOUR

The legislature at work

One of the most significant actions that state
legislatures can take is simply to meet.[*]

Among accounts of memorable experiences of editor and author Willie
Morris is a lively and delightfully irreverent description of the Texas
legislature in the early 1960s.[1] Deals were cut in secret, lobbyists reigned
supreme, "good old boys" from the rural areas ran the show, all progressive legislation was suspect, and tired and cynical newsmen filed absurd,
routine, stereotyped reports with the establishment press. Working with
Morris at the time to cover the Texas legislature was Robert Sherrill,[2]
of whom Morris comments: "Sherrill came to scoff, but I think he remained as long as he did because there was so much to scoff at."[3]

Of his own preconceptions, Morris observed, "I was no novice. . . .
My tenure on *The Daily Texan* had given me some early taste of the
extravagant world of Southwest politics, though I think I still vaguely
suspected there might be some *science* lurking in it, even in a state
capitol."[4] After a time, Morris said, he began to understand and accept
such politics and politicians "quite simply, as a reflection of the broader
system. . . . This legislature was no worse than many, considerably more
entertaining than most."[5]

Things have changed some, but not much. Texans are more numerous, the space age has arrived, people are more sophisticated, and
issues arise more insistently. But power in the legislature is still centralized, groups still dominate, and the role of the legislature is still generally conservative, passive, and noninnovative.

In this chapter we look into the world of the Texas legislature, at the
structures and processes but most of all at the men and women who
run it and participate in it. For "the legislature is a human group, engaged in the process of making collective decisions face to face."[6]
Citizens need to know how the legislature works and for what ends.

---

[*] *Intergovernmental Perspective*, 4, no. 1 (Winter 1978): 17.

LEGISLATIVE ORGANIZATION

Bicameralism, representation, and legislative sessions

The Texas legislature is two separately elected and organized bodies, the House of Representatives with 150 members, and the Senate with 31 members. Senators have four-year terms, while representatives are elected for two years. Since representation in both houses must be based upon population—and population is not evenly distributed in Texas—each senator represents a larger slice of Texas than a representative. Differences in size of membership and terms—plus slightly different institutional values, norms of behavior, and rules of procedure— lend a distinctive flavor to the proceedings of each branch.

The legislature convenes in regular session the second Tuesday in January of odd-numbered years for a maximum of 140 days. Only Texas among the large industrialized states retains the biennial session of drastically limited duration. Special sessions, called by the governor (who also stipulates the legislative subjects to be considered), are constitutionally limited to 30 days each. Although back-to-back sessions may be called, governors fear that frequent use will bring popular reprisals at the polls. Between 1961 and 1979, chief executives called only a total of 13 special sessions, resulting in the addition to sessional time of only 27 days each biennium.

Presession, postsession, and interim activities

While no provisions exist for presession organizational time or for postsession meetings to consider overriding gubernatorial vetoes,[7] several arrangements exist to expand limited legislative time and to provide for its better utilization.

> *Orientation conferences:* Postgeneral election sessions sponsored by the Lyndon B. Johnson School of Public Affairs feature veteran legislators, presiding officers, legislative staff, seasoned administrators, and guest lecturers on legislative procedures, activities, and upcoming issues and problems.

> *Bill drafting:* While the attorney general and the Legislative Council are available for this purpose, in practice, lawyer members of the legislature and counsel for interest groups draft many bills—and many of these serve as substitutes for others' bills. Substitute bills are freely used, and many standing committees see their work frequently discarded when their bills reach the floor.

> *Prefiling bills:* About 30 days before a session, members may prefile their bills, and nothing prevents appropriate standing committees from beginning work on these measures.

Interim committee work: Most standing committees operate for significant amounts of time during the interim between legislative sessions. Standing committees are staffed for research, study, and reports. Members receive travel and enlarged expense accounts for conducting hearings and for other expenses.

Organizing a new legislature

Every two years, in the first several days of each regular session, the Texas legislature must perform tasks of reorganization and renewal. The House of Representatives is simply 150 members-elect. Members must be sworn, the speaker selected, rules adopted, and committees and their chairpersons appointed. And in the Senate also, although that body does have a presiding officer and one half of its membership, no rules, committees, or staffs exist until a new legislature is organized. The two-year period of time between the beginning of regular legislative sessions is called a legislature and is given a number. For example, the Legislature of 1979–1981 is the 66th Texas Legislature.

In addition to organizational activities, the beginning of a regular legislative session is marked also by several ritualistic functions, including receptions, swearing-in ceremonies, a state of the state address, and, at intervals, inauguration of a new governor and lieutenant governor. These preliminary activities may be quite extended, impinging seriously upon the already brief sessional time. No regularized, efficient, impersonal institutions, such as party caucuses and party committees, exist in the Texas legislature to settle many of the issues of organization before the opening day of the legislative session. If selection of the speaker does take several ballots, naming standing committees, committee chairpersons, and housekeeping staff personnel may involve bargaining for a week or more after the speaker's election. Further, a new governor is inaugurated a week after the convening of the legislature, and members are prone to wait for direction in policymaking. Finally, if a new lieutenant governor has been elected, the Senate will wait until he or she is installed (a week after the legislature convenes) before adopting permanent rules and organization, operating in the meantime under temporary rules and arrangements, except for installation of basic staff officers.

Legislative staffs and services

Four different types of staffs are found in each house to aid in the work of the legislature.[8]

Housekeeping staffs: A set of "officers and employees" serve the needs of the legislative houses as a whole. Responsible for clerical and administrative tasks are the Chief Clerk and several other titled clerks. Sergeants at arms, doorkeepers, parliamentarians, and chaplains maintain order and decorum, limit access to the floor during sessions, assist in rules interpretation, and open the daily sessions with prayer. Housekeeping staff perform duties under direction of presiding officers and Administration Committees. Personnel in the House are selected by the speaker. In the Senate, members caucus on opening day of the session to nominate housekeeping and other staff personnel, as well as to adopt the Senate budget, formulate the staff personnel classification and pay schedules, and nominate the president pro tempore. Senate employment tends to be more stable and less tightly controlled than in the House of Representatives.

Leadership staffs: Staffs of the speaker and the lieutenant governor vary from 16 to 20 employees, including executive assistants, press secretary, speech writer, secretaries, receptionists, and clerks. Presiding officers are also assigned Capitol apartments and personnel to care for these spaces.

Committee staffs: Staffing of standing committees became extensive and less haphazard in the 1970s. Best staffed of all are the House Appropriations and Senate Finance Committees, which are served by the increasingly numerous and highly professional staff of the Legislative Budget Board, discussed below.

Members' staffs: Texas pioneered staff for individual members of the legislature. Each legislator receives, besides per diem pay, several thousand dollars, both in session and during the interim, for an administrative assistant, an administrative secretary, and other full-time and part-time employees. Texas legislators, unlike members in about one half of the states, receive specially assigned and plentiful office space in the Capitol.

In addition to staff services, members enjoy computerized operations (see below), a joint media office for public relations and reelection services, and a variety of services provided by four permanent legislative agencies.

The legislative agencies

Joint legislative committees, composed of the presiding officers and other members appointed by the speaker and lieutenant governor, oversee the work of the legislative agencies.[9]

Legislative Reference Library: A specialized staff of 11 librarians and clerical employees serves the reference needs of legislators, answers inquiries from the public, and serves as a point of contact with other state legislatures and research organizations on legislative matters. The Library is the official depository of state documents.

Legislative Council: An expert staff of 95 persons provides bill-drafting services, conducts authorized research, performs special projects (such as codification of Texas statutes), and operates the computerized Legislative Information System of Texas (LIST). LIST combines bill and journal preparation and printing operations and prepares and prints the various House calendars. At the end of a day, complete and corrected texts of all bills, schedules, and journals are available to all legislators. Other components of LIST include (1) a bill status and history system, (2) a statutory research and retrieval system, and (3) a system which integrates bill-drafting and search and retrieval to facilitate better bill-drafting services.[10]

Legislative Budget Board: Charged with preparing the state's budget, drafting appropriations bills, making performance reports of state agencies, and projecting cost estimates of proposed new programs contained in bills before the legislature is a staff of 60 persons. Housed and staffed by the Performance and Evaluation Section of the Legislative Budget Board is the Sunset Advisory Commission, which reviews the operations and functions of each state agency every 12 years.[11]

Office of the Auditor: A specialized staff of 145 persons postaudits the financial transactions of state agencies, administers the state's job classification plan for state employees, and advises state agencies about their records management and accounting programs.[12]

Legislative employment and costs

The level of full-time legislative employment of housekeeping personnel and employees of the permanent legislative agencies has increased rapidly, from 276 persons in 1969 to 616 or more in 1979.[13] Part-time patronage positions may double the employment figures in some months.

The legislature is not a very expensive branch, however. In 1979, total costs of legislative operations, salaries, services, upkeep of spaces, staffing, facilities, and legislative agencies represented only about .35 percent of the total state government budget.

LEGISLATIVE LEADERSHIP

A "no party" legislature

Leadership selection, powers of presiding officers, place of the lieutenant governor in the political system, leadership styles, and major operations of the legislature all reflect a central fact, that the Texas legislature is truly a "no party" legislature. Only in four other American states is there a total absence of party caucuses, leadership posts, and committees.[14] Only party labels and some party sentiment exist.

Leaders are not nominated in party caucuses: The speaker does not represent a majority party caucus. The lieutenant governor is an "outsider," elected by popular vote. Candidates for speaker and lieutenant governor take their candidacies outside the legislature, where successful contenders endure long, expensive, lobby-dominated campaigns.

No majority or minority floor leaders exist: In the House, personal cohorts of the speaker stalk the floor on bills in which the speaker is interested. If other bills reach floor consideration, factional leaders work the floor for votes. In the Senate, a very small body of 31 members, controversial bills reach floor consideration only by a two-thirds vote. Leaders of a conservative "directorate" watch over floor action.

Legislative programs do not receive caucus discussion: The unifying influence of party is nonexistent, legislators scattering their influence to the four winds of a pervasive and unsettling factionalism based variously on cults of personality, transient issues, economic interests, ideology, urban and rural problems, or traditional geographic regionalism.

Party committees do not nominate standing committee membership: The speaker and lieutenant governor appoint all standing or legislative committees and all chairpersons, subject to no party caucuses. No general seniority system exists.

Centralized, personal leadership

What exists in the Texas legislature is a leadership structure which is highly centralized, personal, and often utilized in an arbitrary fashion. The absence of party structures and mechanisms leaves no alternative but to place unusually strong formal powers and authority in the hands of the speaker and lieutenant governor. Drawing upon the Constitution, tradition, statutes, and rules, which they write, legislative presiding officers feed upon an extremely impressive group of personal prerogatives and powers unequaled in most states and unmatched even in the United States Congress. See Table 4–1. These prerogatives affect every structural and procedural aspect of the Texas legislature and have a particular impact on public policy.

The "speaker's team"

The leadership structure, or inner circle, in the House is called aptly, the "speaker's team." A closely knit group of personal friends and fac-

TABLE 4-1

Formal powers of Texas legislative presiding officers

In the political leadership system:
1. Appointment of all chairmen and vice chairmen of standing committees.
2. Appointment of all chairmen and vice chairmen of standing subcommittees (Senate only).
3. Appointment of housekeeping or leadership committees.
4. Appointment of the speaker pro tempore (House only).

In the committee systems:
1. Appointment of all standing committees, subject to only a fragile and very limited seniority rule in the House.
2. Appointment of all subcommittees (Senate only).
3. Appointment of all select, conference, and interim study committees and their chairmen and vice chairmen.
4. Determination of the jurisdiction of committees, either ad hoc or through writing the rules.

In the staff system:
1. Appointment of all officers, employees, and personnel except members' staff assistants.
2. Appointment without respect to seniority of all members and chairmen and vice chairmen of the administration committees.
3. Direction and supervision of all officers, employees, and personnel of the housekeeping and other staffs through control of the administration committees.
4. Control over the physical areas of the Capitol which are designated for utilization of the two houses.
5. Service on and appointment of members of the legislative staff agencies.

In the system of rules and procedures:
1. Writing the rules.
2. Application, interpretation, and enforcement of the rules through direction of the staff and through control of the respective rules committee or subcommittee.
3. Referral of all bills to standing committees.
4. Presiding over the activities of the chambers, including recognition of members to speak.
5. Scheduling bills for floor debate (House) or recognizing members (Senate) to move that bills be taken up out of order for floor consideration.
6. Full participation in the Committee of the Whole.

tional associates of the speaker, the team includes the speaker pro tempore, heads of housekeeping, scheduling, and strategy committees (House Administration, Calendars, and Rules Committees), and other chairpersons and vice chairpersons of major standing committees. All of these positions are filled by appointment of the speaker. For the flavor of the House leadership and its operations through a view of the role of the head of the House Administration Committee, see Figure 4-1.

Race for the speakership

On the contest for the speakership hang the threads of selection of all other leaders of the House. The constitutional prescription for se-

FIGURE 4-1

MAILED FIST IN VELVET GLOVE

Pete Laney's a fine example of "the mailed fist in a velvet glove," a House member said of the man who controls many of the privileges state representatives enjoy.

Little things like parking places, office space, expense accounts, and choice seats on the floor mean a lot to politicians. Laney and his House Administration Committee say who gets what.

. . .

Like [Speaker] Clayton, he is a High Plains farmer. His home at Hale Center is only 35 miles from Clayton's in Springlake, and the two worked at Water, Inc., before Laney came to Austin.

Propping his cowboy-booted feet atop the coffee table in his fourth floor office, with its view down Congress Avenue, Laney said:

"I try to do what I think is right and the way I think the people of Texas would like us to run our business. If I do things that give me credit for being a hatchet man, I guess it comes with the job."

Among the things for which Laney and his committee take credit are consolidation of House printing and bill distribution with the Legislative Council at a saving of about $250,000 and reduction of between-sessions staff by nearly 50 percent.

Critics say Laney is arbitrary and uses his position to reward his (and Clayton's) friends and punish their political enemies.

. . .

[One] . . . member said requests for new seating assignments on the floor generally were ignored.

"But Laney and [Tom] Uher [another Clayton ally] were moved over near [speaker candidate] Buddy Temple so they could keep an eye on him," he said.

Clayton denied that was the reason for the shift.

"We just wanted people to get to know each other better. . . . We had Red Square [the liberals' corner] and Constitutional Avenue [the conservatives' corner—called "Red Neck Square" by some liberals]. Now we have a good scattering."

Source: *The Houston Post,* April 3, 1977, p. 24A. Reprinted by permission of Associated Press.

lection of the speaker is deceptively simple—election by the membership of the House from among the 150 representatives. Before this election, however, is a selection process quite unlike that in most legislatures, where party caucuses nominate candidates and the winner is selected from the majority party.

Two patterns of leadership selection and succession have emerged during the past three or four decades,

A traditional pattern of highly fractionalized processes of leadership selection, to 1961, used again in 1973 in the "reform election" of Price Daniel, Jr. and in 1975 in the election of Billy Clayton, and

An advance, multiyear pledge system of leadership selection, 1963–1971, based upon the appropriations process, restored in 1977 in the reelection of Speaker Billy Clayton.

In the old, outmoded traditional pattern, a dozen members of the House initially announced their candidacies for the speakership. The race featured a frenetic pace of bargaining for support of legislators by would-be speakers and their lieutenants, with deals secured by pledge cards signed by each member. The object, of course, was to secure at least 76 first-choice pledges in order to be elected speaker. The tendency was to get a first-ballot winner because only two candidates, a liberal and a conservative, tended to come down to the wire.

One tactic of a front-runner candidate was the "weekend blitz" involving

Simultaneous telephone appeals to "soft" holdouts to get on the bandwagon before it is too late,

Media attention to exaggerated pledge claims, and

Increased inducements to legislators to switch.

Under superbly timed, coordinated martial tactics in a highly fragmented and individualized legislative system, most legislators found that they would rather switch than fight.

In the meantime, candidates took their races outside the legislature, usually before small, select groups, such as Rotary Clubs, prayer breakfasts, local Chambers of Commerce, and cadres of local followers and opportunists. Commonly, only lobbyists and opinion leaders were aware of the intensity, scope, stakes, and costs of lengthy successful campaigns.

Most candidates could not stand the tempo and expense for long, and they dropped out. By the time the regular legislative session convened, the field usually had been reduced to the two ideological candidates mentioned above.

However, from 1963 through 1971, an informal line of succession was established through an advance multiyear pledge system, which made the long, expensive speakership campaign unnecessary. Members were asked early in the regular legislation session of 1963 to pledge to the speaker and to someone else for several succeeding speaker elections. Involved was the appropriations process.[15] Kingpin of the system was the chairperson of the House Appropriations Committee. The head of this powerful, strategic committee selectively lent aid to pet local projects of members and lobbyists, built financial support from lobbyists and others for the speaker's contest, produced support or opposition to members' ambitions, utilized a network of local supporters in the legislative districts, and generated substantial statewide contacts and political clout to line up, years in advance, pledges for members in the line of succession—Byron Tunnell, Ben Barnes, and G. F. "Gus" Mutscher.[16]

In 1973, in the wake of the Sharpstown Bank scandals, the multiple pledge succession cycle was broken. A wide-open race in the old tradition occurred in 1973 and again in 1975. Price Daniel, Jr., was installed speaker in 1973 with the backing of the reform elements. Another race in the old tradition took place again in 1975 after a promise by Daniel of a one-term speakership for himself.

Although reform legislation sponsored by Daniel produced a system less corrupt and less authoritarian than in the heyday of Gus Mutscher, the reformers failed (as reformers are wont to do) to offer an alternative system of leadership selection and power. The multiple-pledge succession arrangement has now produced, for the first time in the history of the Texas House of Representatives, a third-term speakership. Further, insiders and members know, for they have advance-pledged, who most probably will be the next speaker, barring any factional or other upset. Because members must advance-pledge before they receive their committee assignments and other considerations, gone are the serious challenges of conservatives by liberal Democratic candidates. Thus, the legislative leadership is given even greater stability and predictability by the advance, multiyear pledge system and by low legislative turnover and the power of the lobby. But it is based on power outside the legislature in the hands of dominant economic elites.[17]

Speaker contest as basis of legislative cohesion

Working alliances with lobbyists are functional to the Texas electoral system, the House leadership system, and cohesion in producing public policy outputs. As stated by former Speaker and Lieutenant Governor Ben Barnes[18]

> A candidate for speaker must be acceptable to lobbying interests, especially those representing clients who are a prime source of political contributions. . . . Support from lobbyist groups assures contacts with individuals who are in a position to influence to some extent the votes of other legislators.

Ideological and policy dispositions of speakers are apparently carried over strongly in appointment of committee chairpersons, selection of members of more prestigious "little legislatures," appointment of speaker pro tempore, and selection of members of housekeeping, scheduling, and strategy committees. Further, legislators who do not pledge multiyear find themselves consigned to "Siberian committees" from which they are not heard again.

The "speaker's team" may be the major cohesive force in the House. But by and large, the House is cohesive only on certain bills in which the team is interested. (They could not care less on secondary matters.) "To get along, go along" is a dominant norm. But in the majority of bills, factionalism, personalism, individualism, localism, and weak institutional values prevail in the Texas House.

The Senate "directorate"

The leadership team in the Senate can be described rather accurately as a directorate of senior, dominantly conservative Democrats, plus the lieutenant governor.[19] As in the House, these influential members deal themselves the most important committee chairs.

Because of tradition, popular election of the lieutenant governor, and small size of the Senate (with its club-like atmosphere), the lieutenant governor is more dependent upon his branch's membership than is the speaker. Indeed, the Senate "directorate," in league with powerful forces outside the legislature, often is able to get one of their own elected lieutenant governor.[20] The race for the office still usually features a conservative and a liberal in the open Democratic runoff primary, but all modern Senate presiding officers have been conservatives. They do not run as part of a slate, either with the governor or with other elective officials on the long Texas ballot. Instead, among contestants for statewide office in the open primaries, the tradition is "Every person for himself, and the Devil take the hindmost!"

The lieutenant governor, unlike the speaker, is not formally a member of the legislature. But like the speaker, he or she is easily established as the major force in the legislative body.[21] While the trend among the 39 states with a lieutenant governor is to retain the office as an *executive* post, in Texas, the modern office—a creation of Allan Shivers, 1947–1949[22]—has developed into a very powerful *legislative* position in Texas state government and the most powerful lieutenant governorship in the nation. It is interesting to note that prerogatives of the Senate's presiding officer are not based in the Texas Constitution or statutes; *they are a gift of the conservative majority in the Senate.*[23]

LEGISLATIVE COMMITTEES

"Little legislatures"

Standing committees in U.S. legislatures process the thousands of bills and resolutions which are introduced regularly. Called "little legislatures" for their specialization and activities in considering bills, they ordinarily leave an indelible imprint on measures which survive for floor debate and ultimately reach the governor.

Texas' legislative committees, on the other hand, have been labeled "poorer performing" for their lack of responsibility for killing bills and for low autonomy in the legislative process. Committee work is not performed well and an unusually large number of bills is reported out of committees. Consequently, bills are disregarded on the floor.[24] On an index of formal authority of committees in state upper houses, Texas

Senate committees ranked 48th, with only the Florida and Hawaii Senates having lower scores. In the Texas House, on the other hand, standing committees have more autonomy, ranking 22d and at the mean of U.S. lower house committee autonomy scores.[25] Bills in Texas which survive the calendar system and reach floor debate often fall victim to numerous amendments and even to whole substitute bills, particularly in the Senate. One important bill received a total of 19 changes offered by senators who were not even members of the standing committee which considered the measure.[26]

Downgrading the committee process necessitates, of course, calendar manipulation and control of the floor, so that only the "important" bills of the thousands reported out of committees receive floor consideration. These procedures, in turn, facilitate the tradition of passage of hundreds of local bills without the slightest consideration by the entire legislature.[27] Low autonomy of standing committees is directly related to legislative goals of leadership teams in the legislature. Other factors which serve to downgrade committee importance in the Texas legislature include:

Brief sessional time,

Failure of members to build expertise because of relatively low rates of tenure and no seniority system, or limited seniority in the House,

Existence of a large number of "waste heap" committees to which no bills of consequence are referred by presiding officers, overworking a few committees,

Political referral of bills to committees which have no expertise in the subject, especially in the Senate,

Relatively poor and haphazard staffing of committees from staff pools, and,

Knowledge that bills on which much committee work is expended may be disregarded on the floor.

Committee appointments

Standing committees, as we have seen, are named at the organization of a new legislature every two years. In the Senate, all committees, including chairpersons and vice chairpersons of committees and subcommittees, are appointed by the lieutenant governor. In the House, the rule is the same except that subcommittees and subcommittee chairpersons may be appointed by the parent committee chairperson. Also in the House, a limited retention seniority rule exists by which the speaker must retain from the preceding legislature one half of each committee's membership, but only if members eligible so request. Normally, only about one fourth of committee members are appointed on the basis of retention seniority, and this retention rule does not hamper greatly the speaker's overall authority.

See Table 4–2 for the list of standing committees and subcommittees in the House and Senate during the 65th Texas Legislature. All of these committees are not equal in the lawmaking process. The little legislatures which deal with appropriations, taxation, oversight of state agencies, and, on occasion, apportionment are ordinarily much more powerful than the others. Appointment to the housekeeping committees, unlike in most legislatures, is very important to members because they place legislators in the leadership group. Their duties are not strictly clerical and administrative but are related to strategy and legislative goals of the leadership teams in the legislature.

Legislators naturally compete for the choicest committee assignments. As we have seen, in the House the most coveted posts are rewarded to members of the personalistic and ideological coalition which serves the interests of the speaker's team. In the Senate, two conditions seem to be of top importance in determining choice committee assignments: (1) ideological affinity with the conservative "directorate" and (2) willingness to follow established procedural traditions and norms, especially having to do with placing leadership authority in the lieutenant governor, handling executive and judicial nominations, and retaining mechanisms for policy control by the "directorate." Aid during members' reelection campaigns and lieutenant governorship contests, along with past friendships, count as additional considerations in committee appointments, but these factors interweave, in any case, with the former standards.

Special committees

Besides the standing committees, the Texas legislature uses select or special committees composed of members of one or both houses for ad hoc and limited purposes. A particular kind of joint select committee is a conference committee, composed of members of both houses to compromise differences between House and Senate versions of the same bill. All special committees, like all standing committees, are named by the legislature's presiding officers.

LEGISLATIVE PROCESSES

The orderly conduct of legislative activities is provided by both informal and formal mechanisms or processes. Heaviest reliance is upon informal and external management techniques and practices, such as:

Strong, centralized authority in presiding officers and other leadership,
Dependence upon the lobby for information and services,

TABLE 4-2

Standing committees and subcommittees in the 65th Legislature

House of Representatives 28 committees, 23 subcommittees	Senate 9 committees, 10 subcommittees
"Big three" committees	"Big three" committees
Appropriations	Finance
Ways and means	State affairs
State affairs	Elections
Executive departments	Nominations
State institutions	Jurisprudence
General matters	Civil matters
Housekeeping committees	Criminal matters
House administration	Housekeeping committee
Calendars	Administration
Local and consent calendars	Rules
Rules	Other committees
Other committees	Economic development
Agriculture and livestock	Intergovernmental relations
Business and industry	Education
Industrial development	Human resources
Consumer protection	Consumer affairs
Constitutional amendments	Public health
Criminal jurisprudence	Natural resources
Energy resources	Agriculture
Higher education	Energy
Senior institutions	Water
Junior institutions	
Public education	
Elections	
Environmental affairs	
Pollution control	
State parks	
Wildlife preservation	
Financial institutions	
Health and welfare	
Public welfare	
Health	
Mental health and mental retardation	
Aging	
Insurance	
Intergovernmental affairs	
Urban affairs	
Local government	
Judiciary	
Workmen's compensation	
Judicial affairs	
Judicial districts	
Labor	
Liquor regulation	
Natural resources	
Regions, compacts, and districts	
Social services	
Correctional institutions	
Rehabilitation	
Transportation	
Rail transportation	
Motor transportation	
Air and water transportation	

Source: Texas Legislature, *House Journal*, 65th Leg., Reg. Sess. (January 12, 1977), pp. 48–58 and *Senate Journal* (January 12, 1977), pp. 72–73.

Endowment of conference committees with broad prerogatives,

Reliance upon general and item vetoes of the governor, and

Dependence upon in-session and postsession advice and opinions of the attorney general to give meaning and application to statutory enactments.

These informal, customary requisites interact with and modify the sets of formal rules and regulations.

Rules of procedure

Legislative rules of more than 70 pages are rewritten every two years in both houses,[28] but basic practices remain very much the same. Besides reflecting traditional legislative practices, each set of rules reveals something also of the personality, leadership style, habits, and values of each speaker and lieutenant governor. For example, House rules of 1973 and 1975 reflect the different perceptions of Speakers Price Daniel, Jr. and Billy Clayton of the events which occurred under Speaker G. F. "Gus" Mutscher, 1969–1973, and of the public's reactions to the Sharpstown scandals.

Although legislative rules outline the duties of presiding officers and staff, provide committee and subcommittee selection, enumerate minimal standards of decorum and conduct, and perform other functions, setting the formal stages in the passage of bills is their most prominent and helpful characteristic. Both houses and the governor are involved in the steps in the passage of legislation.

Steps in the passage of a bill

Given below, in summary, are the legislative procedures (required alike in both houses) for bill passage and possible actions of the governor. All legislative bodies use essentially similar legal processes. In the 65th Texas Legislature, 2,267 bills were introduced in the House and another 1,336 in the Senate, of which 439 House bills and 458 Senate bills were finally enacted.[29] To understand how this winnowing of bills takes place, one must know much, besides these formal steps, of the informal requisites of the legislative system, particularly practices involving floor action. This is true because, as we have seen, committee work is stifled and frequently disregarded.

1. *Introduction.* In either body, or both houses simultaneously, sponsors file bills with Clerk (House) or Secretary (Senate), who gives them numbers, e.g., House Bill 1 or Senate Bill 10.

2. *First reading.* Referral of bills to standing committees by presiding officers constitutes first reading. A bill received from the other

branch (after passage there) may be referred to a committee. A committee may refer a bill to a subcommittee.

3. *Committee hearing.* A public hearing, with testimony from interested individuals and groups, may be held. If a committee or subcommittee makes no decision for public hearings, the measure dies.

4. *Committee report.* All manner of changes in a bill may be made in committee. An executive (closed) session of the committee is held to decide whether to report the bill and whether to recommend passage. Minority reports may also be filed. No report means that the bill dies.

5. *Placement on calendar.* Reported from committee, a bill is placed on a calendar (schedule) of bills. Bills may be taken up for floor debate out of order. This is commonly done in the Senate. In the House, which adheres more closely to its (eight) calendars, rules designate certain days for working each schedule.

6. *Second reading.* Taking the bill up for floor debate constitutes second reading. A bill may be debated in full and amended, or a substitute accepted.

7. *Third reading and passage.* After elapse of a legislative day, a motion is in order to take up a bill for final passage. No amendments may be added except by two-thirds votes. Rules may be suspended to allow second and third readings on the same day.

8. *Conference committee action.* If the bill is not identical with the bill passed by the other house, presiding officers appoint, upon request of the bill's sponsors, member conferees to compromise differences. A report of all issues resolved in conference is made to both houses. If conferees cannot agree, the bill dies.

9. *Acceptance of conference committee report.* Motions to accept the report, without amendments, are in order. If either house rejects the report, the bill dies. Members may agree to send the bill back to conference for further efforts at compromise.

10. *Signatures.* Presiding officers sign the bill, enter the fact in the House and Senate *Journals,* and send the measure to the governor.

11. *Action by the governor.* The governor may take one of several actions, as follows:

    a. *Sign the bill.* A bill becomes statute law when signed if it is an emergency bill passed by four-fifths majorities in both branches; otherwise, the bill becomes law 90 days from the end of the session.

    b. *Withhold signature.* Bills, if not vetoed, can become law without the governor's signature. During the session, if a bill remains unsigned for 10 days, it becomes law (subject to time limitations stated above). After legislative adjournment, if a bill remains unsigned for 20 days, it becomes law (subject to time limitations stated above).

c. *Veto the bill.* The governor may return a bill with his objections (in a veto message) to the legislature, which, if it is still in session, may vote to override. Governors may veto separate items in appropriations measures.

d. *Ask for recall of the bill.* Threatening to veto, the governor may ask the legislature to recall a bill to make changes to meet the governor's objections. Recall requires a two-thirds vote in both houses. The bill must then be debated and passed again in each house.

Suspension of the regular order of business in the Senate

While the House has a system of eight calendars of bills which are subject to floor action, the Senate has only one general calendar. The House order of business is almost always followed, but in the Senate the calendar is almost always suspended. The practice of bypassing the calendar is a device by which the lieutenant governor and 11 senators (one third of the membership, plus one) effectively control the flow of bills for floor action.

The system works as follows. Many spurious bills are prefiled or filed early in the session, get immediate committee reports, and are placed high on the general calendar. Logjams are produced all along the schedule of bills when senators decline to take up their own bills for floor debate. "Because a few controversial ones, with authors who want no action, get to the top of the calendar and stay there all session, the calendar system is meaningless. . . ."[30]

To get a bill taken up for floor debate for second reading, a sponsor then faces three immediate obstacles.

The sponsor must get floor recognition from the lieutenant governor, who may withhold it.

The sponsor must obtain a two-thirds vote to suspend the rules to take up the bill out of order.

The sponsor must be willing to trade votes or bargain for votes to obtain recognition and the two-thirds vote for suspension of the rules.

A rigidly controlled vote of 11 senators can defeat any precocious attempt to suspend the rules to allow just any measure to advance to floor debate.

An alternative to suspension of the rules is to take up a measure by unanimous consent. To guard against being caught by surprise, as he was in the 63rd Legislature, Lieutenant Governor William P. Hobby instituted a practice (later placed in the rules) designed to further strengthen the Senate "directorate" in policy matters. A so-called Intent Calendar was established by which senators day-to-day must give the lieutenant governor 24 hours notice, in writing, of their intention to ask unanimous consent or to move to suspend the regular order of business. The secretary of the senate is charged with preparing the list of bills, incorporating them in the daily schedule, printing the schedule in the *Journal,* and distributing a copy to each senator. Except by unanimous consent, no member who has failed to give notice will be recognized by the lieutenant governor. The effect of the Intent Calendar is softened by the practice of senators who want a chance for their bills to be taken up to give notice every day of their intention to ask unanimous consent or to move to suspend the regular order of business.

The suspension device for determining legislative outputs is really a "double obstacle" system. In practice, a bill's sponsor must obtain recognition and a two-thirds majority twice—once to take up the bill on second reading and again to take up the measure immediately for third reading and passage. Otherwise, the bill must lie over to another legislative day. Another legislative day may never occur, by the tactic of simply recessing the Senate daily. Once a bill clears these hurdles, only a simple majority is then necessary for final passage. Struggles in the Senate may be all for naught if the bill is held hostage somewhere in the House.

The functional consequences of Senate floor practices are, of course, conservative and undemocratic impacts on public policy. Procedures can be used to prevent a positive legislative program or a program countenanced by a majority of that body. So far, in the hands of conservative Democrats, these mechanisms have been used to destroy liberal Democratic legislative goals. In the hands of liberals or Republicans, they could sweep in other directions.

Fear of changed control of the Senate poses a study in the dangers of personalism and factionalism in the legislative process. It also raises the stakes outside the legislature in the open primaries, in both legislative and executive contests for public office. For only by renomination and election of incumbents—or their designated ideological and factional heirs—can there be assurance that the legislative system will continue to serve traditional personal and policy ends. With the exception of traditional restraints on voting and other deficiencies of the input structure, legislative practices probably serve, more than other conditions, to establish the characteristics of the electoral process in Texas, including

Modes of campaign contributions,

Levels of campaign spending, and

Patterns of recruitment of candidates for legislative, executive, and judicial offices.

Abuse of local and consent calendars in the House

Calendars facilitate legislative effort by establishing schedules of floor action on bills. The House rules provide for periodically working each of eight separate calendars. See Table 4–3.

These House calendars establish different classes of bills by

Level of priority,

Subject matter,

General or local effect, and

Contestability.

As examples, the Major State Calendar lists all measures deemed by the speaker and members of Calendars and Local and Consent Calendars Committees to be of prime importance and general effect; the Local Calendar contains bills of interest to local interests on which no opposition is expected (or wished); the Consent Calendar is a schedule of uncontested bills of general or statewide applicability.

For quick floor action, if not to hide the real nature of measures, the calendars committees may permit placement on the Consent or Local Calendar bills which are distinctly far-reaching and controversial, or which, when passed, violate a clear constitutional proscription against

TABLE 4–3
House calendars

Emergency calendar	Lists all revenue and appropriations bills and matters demanding immediate attention or which are designated by the governor as emergency measures.
Major State calendar	Lists all measures of prime importance and general effect.
General State calendar	Lists all bills and resolutions which are deemed of secondary importance.
Consent calendar	Lists all uncontested bills of general or statewide applicability.
Local calendar	Lists bills confined to subjects of interest to specific localities or on which little or no floor opposition is expected or desired.
Constitutional amendments calendar	Lists all joint resolutions which propose Texas amendments or call for ratification of federal amendments.
Resolutions calendar	Lists nonemergency and nonprivileged simple and concurrent resolutions.*
Motions calendar	Lists all memorial, congratulatory, and mascot motions.

Simple and *concurrent* resolutions deal commonly with internal matters and expressions of opinion, but the former are passed only by one house and are not sent to the governor. Actions of both houses which do not go to the governor are designated as *joint resolutions,* such as resolutions which propose constitutional amendments.

local and special legislation. Pressures are particularly strong in the waning days and hours of a session to bypass the Major State and General State calendars. Rules have been tightened to allow members to "tag" bills on Local and Consent calendars, that is, to simply challenge bills and call for general floor debate, forcing them to be removed and rescheduled on the Major State or General State Calendar. Rescheduling during final days of a session usually has the effect, of course, of killing the measures.

The spirit of localism in the House, strengthened by traditional norms and sanctions, discourages the practice of tagging, so that scores of general interest and proscribed bills find their way each session to the Consent and Local calendars. The abuse is so widespread that in matters affecting local governments, a hodgepodge of numerous statutes exists, so that it is difficult in many subject areas to know what the law is.[31] Further, the practice violates rights to discuss controversial public issues and the ideal of "local self-government."

The "free" conference committee

The two houses separately adopt a set of joint rules which govern ceremonial and bill-making activities which are common to both houses, including

Communications between the two branches,

Joint sessions (as when the governor addresses the legislature),

Appointment of joint ceremonial and study committees,

Enrolling and signing bills (after their passage) by presiding officers,

Times and conditions of adjournments, and

Appointment of conference committees to adjust differences between House and Senate bills.

Appropriations measures, apportionment plans, tax bills, and other major pieces of proposed legislation nearly always differ in House and Senate versions and have to be compromised by conferees appointed by the presiding officers, usually in the waning days of the session.

Normally, compromises are produced in conference committees from alternatives fully discussed on the floor. But in appropriations measures, "free" conference committees commonly go beyond items and money figures in House and Senate bills, adding new spending purposes and raising or lowering spending figures well beyond amounts considered on the floor of either house.[32] Rejection of the blatant excesses of the free conference committee means an unwanted special session, and presiding officers and conferees can assume the attitude "take it or leave it." No bills carry over to another session.[33]

Although the "free" conference committee is prohibited by the joint rules, traditional practices (in the context of the crush of time created by limited sessional length) tend to hold sway against legal regulations. Even if the joint rules are not suspended, as they were in 1975,[34] the conference committee of five representatives and five senators is the scene of some of the wildest horse-trading in Texas. In the 65th Legislature in 1977, bargaining sessions took two weeks, even after negotiations over increased state aid to public education were separated from the main attraction.

THE TEXAS LEGISLATOR

In the remainder of this chapter, we focus on the Texas legislator and his perceptions of other actors in the legislative process. Except for legal qualifications, terms, compensation, and selection, the Texas Constitution and statutes tell us little. What type of person offers himself or herself for legislative service? What factors induce individuals to become candidates? How do legislators perceive their roles and duties, and how do they relate to other participants in the legislative process?

Legal qualifications, terms, compensation

Common to all the states are certain legal qualifications to be a legislator

Minimum age—21 for representatives in Texas, 26 for senators

United States citizenship

Minimum residence—in the district one year for members of both Texas houses, plus two years in the state for representatives, five years for senators

Qualified voter

House and Senate members have two-year and four-year terms, respectively. Senators' terms are staggered, so that approximately one half of the terms expire every two years. Thus, we have state legislative, congressional, and judicial elections every two years, while our executives are elected every four years, in nonpresidential years.

Although Texas legislators have been paid annual salaries since 1961, their remuneration ($600 per month, set in the Constitution in 1975)[35] is low compared with legislative salaries in other populous, urbanized, industrialized states. These funds are supplemented by an expense allowance of $30 per day in session, a travel allowance of 16 cents per mile, and very liberal year-round staff and contingency allowances. But Texas ranks 26th among the American states in legislators' total compensation. Legislative pay contrasts sharply with the 1979 annual salaries of $51,900 for highest appellate judges and $71,400 paid to the governor.

Personal, political, socioeconomic backgrounds

While many Americans are geographically mobile, the persons they elect as their legislators are tied to their states and localities. Most Texas legislators were born in Texas, and many of them were born in the districts which they represent.[36] Members of the Texas legislature reflect quite strongly the dominant social values and political culture of Texas.

Although legislators are not geographically mobile, they are extremely mobile professionally. Most legislators' fathers were farmers, craftsmen, foremen, managers, and proprietors. By and large, voters select legislators from gregarious, socially ambitious, educated, fairly young, politically sophisticated, male persons.

A look at social attributes confirms the high social status of House and Senate members. Predominantly white, Anglo-Saxon, Protestant, professionally trained persons (mainly lawyers) comprise about 90 percent of the group. Only nine women, 12 blacks, and 15 Hispanics served during the 65th Legislature, 1977–1979.

House members, at least, do not perceive themselves as career politicians. Although many have held party posts prior to election to the House, for most, legislative service is their first governmental position. Most refuse to identify themselves as politicians, reflecting the political culture and the average tenure level of only about four years. Among members of the Texas Senate, on the other hand, average tenure runs about 11 years. Almost 20 years average tenure was accrued by the 13 senators in the 65th Legislature with the longest service, with low retention related only to certain districts. Very few Texas Senate and U.S. Representative positions regularly come open for most Texas legislators.[37] If service in the Texas House is a dead end for most House members, they are satisfied with a respectably brief apprenticeship in the legislative marketplace to consolidate friendships and connections for success in law, banking, timber, insurance, agribusiness, and finance.

Selection

Selection of public elective officials consists of three different stages or processes: recruitment, nomination, and election. An additional process, called apportionment, establishes the geographic limits of the legislator's district and sets the number and characteristics of constituents. While constitutions and legal codes formally prescribe something of the manner, conditions, and rules for three of these processes, recruitment patterns are informal and subject largely to unwritten standards. In all four processes, too little is known about such matters as agents of recruitment, inducements to candidacy, influence of groups, sources and classes of campaign supports, campaign structures, and political factionalism.

Recruitment Filling public offices is not automatic. Many tasks and activities must be performed. For one thing, the pool of interested, qualified citizens is low. Persons somehow must be induced to offer themselves for legislative and other offices. Inducements may take several forms—promises of investment of money, time, and personal influence and other resources, such as group and newspaper endorsements. Or candidacy may derive from personal ambition, drive, or socialization. Spinoff benefits, such as media coverage and word-of-mouth publicity during campaigns, may be expected by all would-be candidates, but these resources may not materialize, particularly for legislative candidates.

In some states, party organizations and leaders may figure prominently as the major agents of legislative recruitment. In other states, parties must compete with organized interest groups, ad hoc organizations, friends, family, and influences which induce self-recruitment. In Texas, a one-party state in legislative elections, one recruitment pattern is found for the Democratic party and another for the barely visible (in state, district, and local elections) Republican party.

The Democratic party, because of factionalism and other factors, employs little legislative recruitment activity, the officialdom acting principally as a "holding company" for the conduct of primary elections and for other official functions.[38] In the Republican party, on the other hand, intensive recruiting activities have emerged in the major cities, but they are not very successful outside the safe Republican districts which were produced by the single-member district system. Many of the problems of Republicans stem from the party's strident, if not extreme, conservatism and exclusiveness, resulting in failure to broaden the party's base to build local organizational strength. Too, many conservative voters are apparently satisfied with Democratic legislators. Would-be Republican candidates often cannot be persuaded that they can be elected when the Democratic label in Texas implies conservatism on legislative issues.

By default, self-recruitment is the most common form of candidate inducement in Texas. Although a variety of people and organizations may be consulted by would-be legislative candidates, most legislators are self-starters who, for a variety of personal reasons, jump at the opportunity to run for the legislature when vacancies occur.[39]

In Texas politics, then, personal and family political backgrounds, self-interest, a sense of obligation to social and governmental systems, a personal interest in politics, and an opportunity to serve are factors in the pattern of self-recruitment. The reason for an increased number of legislative candidates in recent Democratic primaries seems to be related largely to greater issue orientation among the young and perhaps to a decreasing rate of turnover of legislators, not to additional recruiting agents.

Nomination   Nomination of legislators in Texas since 1906 has been by direct primary election. Although since 1962 the Republican Party has regularly conducted primaries, Republicans had difficulty until the 1970s launching primary elections outside Republican "growth" areas in the cities. In 1978, Republican party primaries still were not held in all of Texas' 254 counties. Further, most of the relatively small number of Texans who bother to vote in primaries (about 20 to 25 percent of the possible qualified electorate) still participate in Democratic primaries.[40] Liberal-conservative battles in many of the contests in the open Democratic primary seem to hold an habitual fatal attraction for the small group who label themselves Republican and the much larger group of self-styled "independents." Examples exist of Republican candidates attempting to vote in the Democratic primary!

Election   For most legislative positions, then, nomination as a Democrat is still tantamount to election, as it has been for a century. Although Republicans constitute nearly one fourth of state legislators in five states on the periphery of the Deep South, the least success (12 percent) is experienced in Texas. In 1977–1979, only 18 of 150 representatives wore Republican labels. These legislators represented districts in Dallas (7), Houston (6), San Antonio (1), Fort Worth (1), Lubbock (1), Midland (1), and Dalhart in the Texas Panhandle (1). The three Republican senators (of 31 members) came from districts in Harris, Dallas, and Tarrant counties. Except for one representative from a traditionally Republican rural area, Republican legislators were elected from urban areas where a majority of Texans reside. By all indicators, Republican chances are much better than their current showing in the legislature. As we saw in Chapter 3, it is in the state's metropolitan areas where

Substantial out-of-state immigrants greatly augment Republican strength,

Huge population, combined with small, single-member districts, enhance opportunities for Republican success,

Socioeconomic indicators (high educational levels, affluency, and managerial and professional status) duplicate those found important outside Texas in Republican voting, and

Majorities are often found for Republican presidential candidates.

Apportionment   One of the constitutional duties of legislators every ten years after each national census is apportionment of the Texas House and Senate and for Texas' delegation to the national House of Representatives. Should the legislature fail to apportion state legislative seats, both House and Senate, in the first legislative session following the decennial census, the duty falls to the Legislative Redistricting Board, an ex officio body composed of the lieutenant governor, speaker, attorney general, comptroller of public accounts, and commissioner of the

General Land Office. No alternate state constitutional remedy exists for failure to attend to congressional reapportionment.

Apportionment refers to the twin processes of

Allocation of legislative seats or places among the geographic areas or political subdivisions in Texas and

Districting, that is, drawing boundaries of the represented geographic areas.

For example, from 1970 census figures, it was determined, on a proportionate population basis,[41] that Dallas county was due an allocation of 18 Texas representatives. The legislature had also to decide where to draw boundaries of 18 single-member districts. The federal judicial requirement of single-member districts means that in metropolitan areas (where segregated and socially stratified neighborhoods exist) legislative representation tends to tap socioeconomic, racial, ethnic, and political groupings. When single-member districts were instituted in Dallas county by federal court order in 1972, representation there changed from white, Anglo-Saxon, conservative Democrats to a mixture of Republicans, liberal Democrats, conservative Democrats, blacks, and Hispanics.[42]

Legislative roles and norms

Roles are derived from expectations of legislators themselves and of other individuals (particularly of persons in groups and institutions with which legislators interact) about legitimate behavior or conduct in their positions of authority. In this brief treatment of legislative roles, we examine the perceptions of legislators in three dimensions.[43]

Areal focus—representing districts Texas legislators tend to adopt a district focus rather than (1) to assume a state or regional orientation or (2) to attempt to compromise district and state interests and responsibilities. A district orientation is strongest among legislators who encounter opposition at election time and whose districts contain governmental institutions dependent upon state moneys.

District orientation is congruent with the disintegrated political institutions and bases of authority and with Texas political culture, especially with the value of "local autonomy." Justified as an extension of the principle of local control is the long-standing tradition of members to defer to the wishes of a single senator or representative on bills which "affect district interests." Known historically as the "local bill racket,"[44] the practice is frequently a ploy to avoid scrutiny by local majorities or by the whole legislature. Not only local interests but a set of state and national interest groups apparently wish to perpetuate the myth of "local control." By supporting a rash of "local bills," the legislator may bask in the sunshine of the speaker's approbation, reap a reputation of "effectiveness," and secure future campaign support.

Another price is paid by the legislator for his or her support of the local bill racket. The legislative leadership has the ability to manipulate local interests, either directly or by raising their anxieties about ample funding of local governmental institutions. Local interests can be counted on to pressure their legislators to swing into line on bills of general and fundamental importance to the "leadership team" at the state capital. Professors Donald S. Lutz and Richard W. Murray, in finding lopsided majorities on most of 12,215 legislative roll call votes (1961–1969), speculate that a potent *leadership-lobby combination* overrode individual legislators' preferences and constituency interests on most major policy issues. Very low salience of the Texas legislature with the majority of people in the districts seems to contribute to this state of affairs. Specifically, legislators had little to fear from local elites as long as leadership and lobby were not offended enough to *intervene* in the legislative districts. Interestingly, only *social issues* were of high enough salience to Texas constituents to produce close roll call votes in the Texas legislature—such issues as liquor by the drink, Sunday closing laws for businesses, parimutuel betting, prostitution, and welfare "fraud."[45] What is termed a "religion-morality" domain of highly volatile issues has been discovered in other state legislatures as well.[46]

Style—trustee of constituents' welfare   Because Texas lawmakers are decidedly the products of the cultural values of their districts, many members are unlikely to perceive any great difference between representing their districts and following their own best judgments. Few modern Texas legislators seem to face the classic dilemma of Edmund Burke—whether to follow "the mandate of the citizens of Bristol" or to answer the dictates of conscience tied to a wider horizon than constituency preferences. Texas legislators, in common with other state lawmakers, most often adopt the role of *trustee*. In this role, they emphasize their own judgments, convictions, and outlooks as reponses to legislative decision-making—a Burkean outlook widely divergent from the rather commonly held folk wisdom that legislators should and must follow the will of the majority of their district constituents. The obvious explanation is that people are unable, and often do not wish, to articulate and communicate their sentiments on complex issues. Further, as we have seen, organizational linkages (input structures) which could transmit messages either do not exist or do not function well.[47]

Decision-making—mastering legislative routines and procedures
Most state legislators perceive their task as ritualistic, that is, of mastering rules and routines, rather than approaching their function as "inventors" in a creative manner to leave an indelible imprint on public policy. The role of *ritualist* is apparently dominant in all state legislatures.

A budget, for example, is seen principally as following rules and negotiating bargains, not as a task of putting together a policy document to best allocate scarce societal resources. A drive for expertise in the rules and routines, as well as a secondary orientation of a need to discover and articulate public opinion (the role of *tribune*), derive from concern of Texas legislators for best representing the interests of their districts.

Relatively few Texas legislators view their role as *broker* or referee of conflicting group or individual demands. In the system of powerful interest groups around Texas state government, a brokering of not very intense interest conflict is apparently done principally at the top by the "leadership team." A former member of the House remarked, "A critical juncture in the education of a House member may come when he . . . faces the increasing visibility of a power system within the House allied with a power system outside the House, all under the Speaker's aegis."[48]

Brokering by the leadership involves the following elements:

Establishing formal and informal "rules of the game" for political activity, including policymaking,

Setting legislative and electoral agendas,

Defining or redefining issues which come up for discussion and action, and

Limiting the scope of conflict over political issues.

In any social system, elites work to define and propagate dominant social and political values, myths, rituals, and institutions.[49] The system of distribution of power and the prevailing belief system "predispose the decision-maker to view the claims of certain groups as 'reasonable' or 'essential' and the claims of other groups as 'questionable' or 'outrageous'."[50] The status quo seems "reasonable" and "essential," under most circumstances, at least. This is one of the reasons why state legislators do no approach their statute-making function in innovative ways.

Legislative norms

In addition to the standards of decorum and conduct contained in the formal rules of each house of the legislature, legislators find they must abide by numerous *unwritten* standards of interpersonal conduct. Texas House members in 1971 expressed 31 different customary norms, mores, folkways, or conventions. Two types of legislative norms are prevalent in Texas.

Highly personal norms common to most state legislatures These norms facilitate performance of duties in a nonacrimonious atmosphere, involving admonitions to assume a "responsible, modest, impersonal, conciliatory" manner with due regard for other members' rights and feelings. Concerned more with "appearances" than substance, these norms fail to come to grips with finer moral distinctions having to do with exercise of power, responses to group tactics, and concentration of formal authorty in top leadership.

Norms fixed by characteristics of the Texas political system   Going along with the "team" was the second most frequently mentioned norm in the Texas House in the 62nd Legislature. Typically stated: "One rule is to pledge to the Speaker for a term. You support the Speaker as the House leader. If you are on the Speaker's team, you must go along."[51] That the leadership is the most visible and powerful element affecting the status and ambitions of legislators[52] is to be expected when we review the major features of the legislative system

Lack of party structure.
Uncertain gubernatorial leadership.
External influence in leadership selection.
Powerful interest groups.
A spirit of localism and individualism.
Open Democratic primaries.
Tradition of limited access to voting.
Great formal powers in the leadership.
Limited, biennial sessions.

Sanctions   Norms are enforceable through sanctions, a system of rewards for acceptable behavior and deprivations for poor observance of peer and leadership standards. Only a few legislators fail to perceive a system of sanctions. Heading the list of potent punishments designed to encourage adherence to the norms is obstruction of members' pet bills—a denial of "effectiveness" and standing which could prove fatal to career plans. Other, secondary sanctions include "the silent treat-ment," exclusion from social groups, and denial of common legislative privileges.

LEGISLATORS' INTERACTIONS AND PERCEPTIONS

By now we realize that legislators do not act alone to make policy. Other actors, inside and outside the government, with whom legislators interact, such as lobbyists, are called "role reciprocals" because of their mutual interdependence with legislators in the legislative system. Pat-terns of legislative behavior are developed around others. Perceptions of legislators of these other legislative actors determine and reinforce these patterns and tell us much about how policy is made.

Party actors

Only party labels and low levels of sentiment prevent a party void in the Texas legislature, at least among the dominant Democrats. Party labels are dimly perceived as having some kind of importance, at least at election time, and party sentiment is more widespread and deep-seated than one might expect. However, for the foreseeable future, party is not expected to be a focal point for organization, leadership, and voting in the Texas legislature. Party caucuses, committees, leadership posts, cohesion, and competition have never been tried. Only a small portion of members (about 12 percent) is regularly elected as Republicans, and persons in that faction apparently consider themselves conservatives first, Republicans second. As Republican Representative Chase Untermeyer of Houston complained in the 65th Legislature, "Under Speaker Bill Clayton . . . Republicans are major players on the Speaker's 'team.' . . . By failing even to . . . caucus and coalesce around a spokesman we have missed countless opportunities."[53]

Republicans working with conservative Democrats is more than a product of common ideology. It is also an accommodation to power and political culture. No doubt partisanship and party organization would violate important norms and activate serious sanctions. In the 62nd Legislature, hostility to the short-lived (one session) Republican caucus and floor leadership was widespread, most (Democratic) members judging the Republican faction as "ineffective," composed of "publicity seekers," and guilty of "opposition for the sake of opposition."

Lobbyists

If party is practically nonexistent, organized interest groups are quite visible and their activities manifest in the Texas legislature.[54] Lobbyists and lobbying are considered by nearly all legislators as proper and legitimate, and they are viewed as potent forces. Further, bases of group powers are perceived and articulated, and members are willing to rank groups in terms of their imagined strength in both legislative and electoral arenas.

Information, persuasion, influence Legislators regard *reliable information* as the strongest basis of group influence, while lobbyists see their own basic function as *persuasion*.[55] Legislators, then, are far more likely to view lobbyists as service agents than opinion manipulators, grossly underestimating the persuasiveness of skilled lobbyists and overestimating their own ability to judge the quality of information transmitted by groups.

Lobbyists are valued also as sources of influence with other political actors, being commonly asked to test and build public opinion and help to plan legislative strategy around specific proposals. Thus, lobbyists have learned to function in subtler ways than in crude activities which are attributed to them in the folklore of lobbying.

Influence in legislative districts Interest group reputation for strength in the legislature rests less on success in direct contacts with legislators than it does on reputed influence of interest-group money and membership in legislators' districts, particularly in campaigns. Election of "friendly" and "right-thinking"[56] members, solons point out, makes lobbying unnecessary. Hence, legislators are wary of all broad-based groups (bankers, teachers, unions, retail merchants, chambers of commerce, and the like) which have, or are reputed to have, large potent memberships and networks of relationships with other powerful organizations.

But reluctance of legislators to discuss constituency power structures hampers efforts to cross-check data on groups.[57] Further, rankings by legislators of group strength differ from session to session.[58] Notably, only a few members openly claim that lobbyists exercise dominant influence in important legislation.[59] Lobbyists may, on occasion, cancel out influence. But it may mean that lobbyists are subtle and skilled. Lobbyists probably deal, in the main, with presiding officers and others in the leadership teams. To get definitive answers, political scientists need to select key decisions and study the structure of actors and decisions around each. A major problem, of course, is that it is very difficult to obtain access to private organizations and to public and private discussions of policy.

Registration and disclosure   Adequate disclosure and reporting legislation of 1973 provides names and organizations of lobbyists and details monetary resources. But such information only hints at the extent of lobbying, gives information about only one resource (money) in elections, and allows us to see something of legislators' financial holdings, if we can process and analyze it. A registration and disclosure act correctly identifies persuasion as the function of lobbyists and recognizes that lobbyists also lobby executives. Disclosure of names, addresses, employers, specific bills in which interested, membership totals, expenditures by spending categories, and lobbying methods is required. A campaign reporting and disclosure measure requires disclosure and reporting of all campaign contributions and expenditures. Finally, an ethics statute requires reports of financial holdings of legislators, constitutional executives, and appellate judges.[60]

The governor

As we shall see in Chapters 5 and 6, the governor's leadership in the legislative process derives mainly from the authority and prestige of the office. The chief executive, of course, commands no cohesive legislative majority and may remain "neutral" in leadership selection. Although the meagre formal legislative authority—which includes calling special sessions, sending messages to the legislature, designating emergency measures, and exercising general and item vetoes—serves to thrust the governor into the policymaking process, it is through informal leadership tools and authority in administration that the chief executive leaves a positive imprint upon public policy.[61]

Perceptions held by legislators focus nevertheless on the governor's small arsenal of constitutional powers. Further, the minority who attribute influence to informal leadership tools tend to emphasize simply the governor's personality and popularity with specific interest groups.

Legislators' responses understate the proven legislative influence of the chief executives who cultivate strong informal bases of authority. A recent national survey found that on key issues, legislators look inward to their own information sources, and governors are seen as reacting to only a few current issues of greatest concern to their respective states. Governors are not perceived as setting legislative agenda or engaging regularly in legislative decision-making processes.[62]

Heads of administration

Because of both legislative and administrative disintegration, various uncoordinated relationships exist between legislators and the administrative system. Not much is known beyond the more formalized and structured interactions of legislators and administrators. And not much is known of legislators' perceptions of administrators in the legislative process. Agency representatives come to the legislature for appropriations and, perchance, additional authority. Undoubtedly, many bills are administration measures, and agency heads appear regularly and often before legislative committees. But legislative sessions are short and infrequent, and agency heads are pleased to rely upon their own devices and upon particularly intimate relations with their clientele groups. Legislative oversight is sporadic and defective because of the unstable committee system and other political conditions, even though many of the traditional management tools are held by officers legally responsible to the legislature (see Chapter 6).

Attorney General

Of particular importance in legislative-administrative relations is the office of the Attorney General. Besides drafting bills, the attorney general acts as the official adviser of the legislature on the constitutionality of bills. Further, administrators' questions about implementation of public policy provisions, including the legal effect of statutory enactments and the intent of the legislature, are also referred to the state's chief legal officer. In the absence of court decisions and clarifying statutes, which often reflect the attorney general's views, the advisory opinions of the attorney general stand as policy directives. The opinions, regarded usually as authoritative by other political actors, give the attorney general a key policymaking role in Texas.[63]

Capitol correspondents

Even when the legislature is not in session, 40 or more Capitol correspondents regularly report on state government matters, and the number swells to nearly 100 reporters during regular sessions.[64] Physically close to legislators in adjacent offices and press rooms and at press tables on the floor of the House, these newspersons are an educated, attentive, skilled, sometimes cynical elite who represent a very important channel between legislators and attentive publics.[65]

Tension normally marks the interaction between legislators and news media representatives. Legislators entertain mixed feelings of respect and suspicion of correspondents' potential political influence, and they tend, alternately, to shower media representatives with fawning attention and to threaten their floor privileges. Legislators naturally want legislative issues handled in what they consider to be a "fair, responsible, and objective" fashion, and they want their roles in the legislature presented in a sympathetic, if not favorable, manner. Reporters, for their part, often fuel their stories with "unfavorable and sensational" observations, and the reporting of scandal always produces strain, with demands for "reform" often following. By focusing upon some issues to the exclusion of others, the media can become, in effect, agenda-setting, somewhat undermining prerogatives of legislative leadership to set the program and priorities of the session.

Dominance of the Texas establishment press has been offset since the late 1960s by enlargement of the Capitol media representation and an influx of younger, energetic, more critical newspersons. Viewing their prime role as one of public advocacy, they are more interested in investigative reporting, with the result that the public is receiving more meaningful reportage of Texas legislative affairs.

CONCLUSIONS

A state legislature is a relatively large and complex human group representing the diverse interests, concerns, and attitudes of the state's citizens. It is also a political institution, both wielding the legal powers of statute lawmaking and subject to organized political influences and leadership. The Texas legislature at work is a fascinating object of political inquiry, and our analysis of its performance yields the following conclusions:

1. Although the Texas legislature has achieved a high level of professionalization and "procedural efficiency" in legislative operations, it operates under two severe limitations: lack of time and lack of effective party organization.

2. The Texas Senate is given very strong leadership by the lieutenant governor. Although listed in the executive article of the Constitution, and

"only a heartbeat away from being governor," the lieutenant governor receives a legislative salary and in practice is one of the strongest of the nation's lieutenant governors. Although chosen from outside the Senate (no legal provision prevents the Senate from choosing its own political leadership), the lieutenant governor is given great power in the Senate by that body itself. The Speaker of the House of Representatives is formally elected by House members, but in reality the election of Speaker is grounded in the exercise of power by the dominant economic elites outside the House.

3. It is possible to produce a cohesive legislative majority only on policy matters which have high priority for the leadership teams, or on such moral issues as liquor by the drink. When it comes to ordinary policy issues, the legislature's performance is characterized by low cohesiveness, factionalism, localism, individualism, and weak institutional values.

4. The major function of the legislature is statute lawmaking, where the focus of activity is on both committee work and floor action on bills. Committees in the Texas legislature have had little autonomy, and their work is often neglected. In consequence, floor action on bills is of paramount importance, and floor procedures are enhanced in significance. The rules of procedure have served the legislative leadership well, permitting manipulation of calendars, barriers to consideration of all but high priority bills, and the practice of rigging the results of conference committee activities. The rules of the legislative game are never neutral, and Texas legislative leaders are specialists in using the rules of procedure to secure legislative actions which they favor.

5. Texas legislators are, for the most part, "home grown." They are closely tied to their districts, and tend to conceive of their role as legislators in terms of speaking for the voters in their own constituencies. They also tend to perceive their essential task as mastering the rules and routines of the legislative process, leaving to the leadership teams the function of brokerage among the demands of the huge, powerful array of interest groups.

6. When legislators make public policy by enacting legislation they act together with other political actors, official and unofficial, inside and outside the governmental structure. The most significant of these other actors is that of lobbyists, who offer valuable services to legislators and are skilled in information and persuasion. The governor is the next most influential political actor in making public policy, but his impact is greater at the stage of implementing policy rather than at the stage of its initiation.

CHAPTER FIVE

The governor

A leader is best when people barely know
that he exists. . . .

WITTER BYNNER

With the constitutional separation of the governor and the legislature,
the fragmented political system, and the long ballot, few formal ties exist
between the chief executive and the legislative bodies in Texas. The
governor is not a member of the House or Senate. He has no command
over a majority of legislators, and he exercises little control over selection of legislative leadership. Even in such executive functions as budgeting and management of administration, the governor of Texas is a *weak*
executive; his formal administrative powers lend little support to the direction of state policy matters.

Nevertheless, the governor can use effectively the authority and prestige of his office and many advantages of his position, along with meagre
constitutional and statutory duties, to build influence with the legislature.
Clearly, a distinction exists between the authority and powers of office
and the skills which may be used to exploit and enhance prestige and
prerogatives of office. The expertise employed may be largely a function
of the governor's personality in dealing with the duties of the governorship.

The governor is a single individual, and many people find it easier,
especially in times of emergencies, to fix their attention upon the governor rather than focus upon 181 separate legislators situated in two
separate bodies. And studies demonstrate that the governor is deemed
responsible for the general well-being of the state, including policymaking and policy implementation. Being the ceremonial head of the community, the governor, if he can identify closely with the public, may become chief spokesman of the people.

The governor and the legislature work together more often than not,
for the formal constitutional duties, if they do not give the chief executive

the upper hand, thrust the governor into the policy-making process in Texas. The legislature needs to have the policy preferences of the governor and to know which bills carry the sponsorship and backing of the executive if for no other reasons than to help set legislative priorities for the short biennial sessions, to understand what the governor is likely to veto, and, more than that, to provide constructive and efficient utilization of legislative time by shaping measures which will avert a gubernatorial veto produced by passage of bills which public opinion counts as not important.

HISTORICAL SETTING OF THE GOVERNOR'S OFFICE

Background

Texas is one of the most interesting and singular of states. Wrested from Mexico, it became an independent republic, then a slave state of the Old South,[1] with its population concentrated in East Texas. Expanding west, it became celebrated as a frontier state with such stories as those of Judge Roy Bean, "The law west of the Pecos," becoming legendary. After a prolonged and bitter Reconstruction period, great livestock empires, such as the celebrated King Ranch, were carved out. Then as barbed wire and railroads eclipsed the long drive, the rail and livestock industries came to the forefront of Texas politics, with a now fading counterpart of small farmer populism. With the turn of the century, Spindletop signaled the birth of an entirely new basic industry in the state, creating the proverbial Texas oil barons, the gigantic petrochemical complexes of the Gulf Coast's Golden Triangle, and an important source of state income.[2] Today, Texas is the greatest producer of livestock and petroleum in the country.

Despite sectional feelings which were once intense enough to have brought sporadic threats of secession from West Texans and the fact that the state has a 13 percent black population concentrated in the east[3] and an 18 percent Mexican-American population concentrated in the south,[4] there is no pernicious division to the population as a whole— such as the piedmont-mountaineer cleavages of the Appalachian states, or mountaineer versus delta planter division of Tennessee. Sectional differences have not predominated in Texas gubernatorial campaigns.

Not surprisingly for a state with interestingly diverse geographical and ethnic components, it has produced some unique governors, albeit universally white, Anglo-Saxon, and Protestant. The incomparable Sam Houston, who schemed with his friend Andrew Jackson to gain Texas for the Union, served as U.S. senator from the Lone Star State for over 13 years. Despite his increasingly unpopular pleas for maintaining the Union, he was elected governor in 1859, but following Lincoln's inauguration, when Texans voted to secede against Houston's wishes,[5] he retired, and died within several years. Houston was something of a tragic hero, and his name was given to what has become the largest city in the state, and the fifth largest urban complex in America. Appropriately, Houston is also near the site of the battle of San Jacinto, where Texas independence was finally won.

In the explosive atmosphere of 1873's electioneering, the Democrats' Coke defeated the Republicans' Davis two-to-one in a contested election fraught with illegalities from double voting to false countings. The reaction to the radical Republicans' Reconstruction period was extreme, and the 1876 constitution was a child of this period.

A great Texas governor of the post-Reconstruction era, indeed of the past century, was big Jim Hogg,[6] a New South progressive Democrat who had opposed the unhealthy monopoly influences of the burgeoning railroad combines as attorney general, and who was elected governor in 1890 on the promise that he would curb their abuses. As chief executive, he created the famous Texas Railroad Commission, regulating freight and passenger rates. In the next century the Texas Railroad Commission became the most famous regulatory commission in the United States next to the federal government's Interstate Commerce Commission as a consequence of having been given control of oil and gas production in Texas.[7] Hogg's impact extended for several decades. His trustbusting reformist policies expanded under Governor Thomas M. Campbell, whom Hogg endorsed in 1906.[8]

But the growth years which culminated in the dizzy boom of the 1920s changed Texas' gubernatorial campaigns from a choice of populist versus conservative to issues of personalities and generalities. The period was dominated by the incredible Texas political phenomenon of "Ma" and "Pa" Ferguson, a couple who held the governor's chair in 1915–17, 1925–27, and 1933–35. A rural stump-speaking demagogue, James E. Ferguson is best known as the only Texas governor ever impeached and convicted (1917).[9] He attempted to avoid impeachment by resigning the day before the judgment. In 1925, he got the legislature to grant him amnesty on impeachment, but this was ruled unconstitutional by the attorney general, and the 1927 legislature repealed it. He ran for president on the American party ticket in 1920. Finally, advertising "two governors for the price of one," he got his wife, Miriam A., "Ma," Ferguson, elected to the state's highest office. Thus, "Big Jim" or "Farmer Jim" served vicariously as the state's chief executive, ensconcing himself in an office next to hers. Ferguson was not all sham, however. He did much for rural education, was sympathetic to the plight of poor farmers, avoided the race issue, and, in fact, took a courageous and notable stand against the Ku Klux Klan.

Taking a leaf from Ferguson's book was an individual of perhaps lesser ability, another zany Texas political figure, W. Lee O'Daniel, governor in 1939 and later U.S. senator. He made extensive use of the radio; first to sell flour, and later to sell himself to the people of the state, explaining the ten commandments, promising pensions, and writing folksy songs for his hillbilly band, the Light Crust Dough Boys. After gaining special backing from rural sectors, farmers, the poor, and the elderly, he consistently acted against their interests, meanwhile accepting extensive support from conservative millionaires. "Pass the biscuits, O'Daniel" was not the brightest star among Texas governors.

Perhaps the truest liberal-activist governor in history was James V. Allred, a man whose policies were in response to the Great Depression and whose programs paralleled the New Deal of Franklin D. Roosevelt.

Since that time, the governors of Texas have been more typically of the conservative wing of the Democratic party. In the 1950s, Allan Shivers twice promoted the presidency of the Republican Dwight D. Eisenhower. John Connally, the governor in the 1960s, became a Republican in 1973. Governors Preston Smith, Dolph Briscoe and Republican Bill Clements were millionaires,[10] conservatives, and rather bland in comparison with the flamboyant Ferguson-O'Daniel governorships of earlier days.[11] The 1972 Briscoe campaign featured short television spots urging Texans to "pull together." He based his 1974 platform on the promise to hold the line on taxes, a pledge which he honored with relish.

Attorney General John Hill's narrow victory over Governor Briscoe in the May, 1978 Democratic primary came as a surprise. Briscoe took the traditionally conservative counties, whereas Hill won in the traditionally liberal counties. One telling exception, however, was the panhandle where the third candidate, Lubbock's Preston Smith, drew enough conservative votes away from Briscoe to give an edge to Hill.

In the November general election, there was a veritable bombshell—the election of the first *Republican* governor in the state in 106 years in the person of the irrepressible Dallas oilman Bill Clements. It was perhaps the biggest upset in the history of Texas state politics, although the narrow victories of Smith over Paul Eggers and Briscoe over Henry Grover had indicated that the Republicans were gaining strength since the 1960s. Every major poll had predicted an easy democratic win. Shocked pundits searched for an explanation. Some said Blacks and chicanos had not turned out in sufficient numbers. A few noted that the miniscule Raza Unida vote for Mario Compean might have drawn more than enough votes from Hill to make up Clements' 18,437 vote margin. Some blamed the failure of Governor Briscoe to campaign for Hill (wife Janie made open statements in support of the Republican Clements). The principal reasons for the dramatic Clements victory however, were that

Hill's supporters were lulled into a sense of complacency coupled with the aggressive, well-organized, high-roller campaigning of Clements (who had buried the highly respected Ray Hutchinson in the Republican primary).

As surprising as Clements' election was, it continued a Texas political tradition—that of electing conservatives to the highest state office.

Qualifications, salary, term of office, and succession

The governor of Texas must be a citizen of the United States who has been a resident of the state for at least five years preceding his election. He must also be at least 30 years old and while in office may not "practice any profession and receive compensation, reward, fee, or the promise thereof . . . from any person or corporation."

The governor's salary is set by the legislature, and at $66,800 in 1977 he was the second-highest paid chief executive among the 50 states.[12] In addition, the governor is allowed the use of the executive mansion in Austin, including the cost of maintenance, and in appreciation of the state's geographic expanse, the governor enjoys the optional use of an aircraft in the performance of his duties.

By a constitutional amendment passed in 1972, the governor's term of office was increased from two to four years, effective starting in 1975.[13] While Texas does not permit the popular recall of its governor,[14] the constitution does provide for impeachment, the aforementioned conviction of Governor James Ferguson being the only case of a major state official so removed. Unlike many other governors, the chief executive of Texas may hold successive terms and is not limited as to the number of terms served. In Alabama, however, the governor cannot serve successive terms. Governor Wallace got around this limitation by having his wife, Lurleen, elected to the office while he governed vicariously through her, much in the manner of Texas' team of Ma and Pa Ferguson. By virtue of his election to the first four-year term in Texas history in 1974, Governor Dolph Briscoe served six years, but he could not eclipse the record-setting seven and a half years of Allan Shivers. The proposed constitution of 1976, which was defeated three-to-one at the polls, would have limited the governor to two four-year terms much in the spirit of the U.S. Constitution's 22d Amendment.[15]

If the governor should die, resign, become incapacitated, or be removed from office (impeachment and conviction being the only way), or if he or she[16] should leave the state for any reason,[17] the lieutenant governor assumes the executive powers, and in line of succession thereafter come the Senate's president pro tempore, the speaker of the house, the attorney general, and the chief justices of the several courts of civil appeals (in their districts' numerical order).

In the event the governor-elect should die before taking office, for example between the election in November and the first Tuesday after the new legislature organizes itself in January, the lieutenant governor-elect "shall act as governor until the next general election." If both the governor-elect and lieutenant governor-elect die or are disabled, the senate's president pro tempore and the speaker of the house must call a joint session of the legislature to elect replacements for both offices.

GOVERNOR'S ROLE AS POLICYMAKER

Legislative responsibilities

Twentieth century America has seen a vast increase in the powers of government and a particular increase in the power of the executive, although the powers of state executives have only more recently been recognized as requisite to meeting the problems of the Industrial Revolution with its societal readjustments in an increasingly complex and urbanized setting. The bureaucratic complexities of American government have really burgeoned especially since the days of Franklin Roosevelt's New Deal, which has been a prototype for bureaucracies at all levels of American government since. Modern executive staffing and statewide perspectives give many governors a superior concept of approaches to problem-solving than prevails in their respective legislatures.

The veto

Perhaps the governor's most important legislative function is the seemingly negative exercise of the executive veto, a power which is traceable back through five state constitutions without a break since statehood in 1845. While we have noted that the president's powers are far wider than those of state governors', the veto is an exception. About half of the states, including Texas, provide some form of item veto which permits the governors to negate any single item in a bill passed by the legislature without having to reject the rest of the bill with it. This greatly reduces the legislature's potential for logrolling extraneous and sometimes costly items into law by forcing the executive to accept unwanted items in order to get the major elements of a desirable bill. While the Texas Constitution limits the item veto to appropriations measures, these bills are so important that the net result is a significant enhancement of the executive power in the passage of legislation. Typically, the legislature takes many weeks to get organized and for the new members to become familiar with the legislative regimen. Important appropriations bills, on which the entire budget hinges, are characteristically passed in the closing days of the session. Once the legislature has adjourned, the governor's item veto on appropriations bills becomes all-powerful.[18] The governor then has 20 days to kill any item, filing a message with the secretary of state to make the action official. The majority of ordinary bills are presented to the governor while the legislature is still in session, which leaves the governor only 10 days, not counting Sundays, in which to send a message containing his objections to the house where the measure originated. As with the national Congress, the executive veto can then be overridden by a two-thirds vote in both houses. Unlike the president, however, the governor does not have the option of a "pocket veto." Any bill not vetoed becomes law with the passage of 10 days during the normal session, or 20 days after adjournment, as applicable, unless the governor expressly exercises the veto.

Recommending legislation

Thus, while the Texas governor lacks the political convenience of the pocket veto, he has the far more formidable item veto over appropriations bills. And the veto power is much more than a last-ditch negative factor: the implied threat of its use can and does have significant influence on the structuring of legislation, particularly of appropriations bills. Vetoes are seldom overridden due to the two-thirds requirement in both houses, and item vetoes more often than not come after adjournment and hence cannot be overridden.[19]

Despite the American tradition of exercise of power through separation of powers, governors as well as presidents are expected to set the policy direction of each new administration by addressing each regular legislature as it opens its sessions. The governor's state of the state address parallels the president's state of the union speech. He is particularly enjoined to assess estimated tax revenues. Borrowing from the precedent of Washington's farewell address, the governor is also expected to assess the condition of the state at the close of his term.

> The Governor shall, at the commencement of each session of the Legislature, and at the close of his term of office give the Legislature information, by message, of the condition of state, and he shall recommend . . . measures . . . he shall present estimates of the amount of money to be raised by taxation . . .[20]

After presenting his policy message with appropriate media coverage and fanfare, the governor subsequently needs to draft legislation on virtually every significant subject of legislative concern, the proposals being prepared by the governor's office. A governor with a popular mandate can put heavy pressure on the legislature to enact his proposals by categorizing them as emergency measures. This overcomes the strictures barring action on ordinary legislation in the opening 60 days of regular sessions when legislators are getting organized and preparing bills in committee. It also permits the governor to introduce bills in the final 60 days when new bills are customarily barred to diminish the customary pileup of last-minute bills which would prevent adequate deliberation. Thus the governor can use the emergency category to gain consideration in 120 of the normal 140 day limit to regular sessions, making the governor's potential for leadership in formulating legislation quite formidable.

CALLING SPECIAL SESSIONS

The trend in twentieth century state government in the United States is a switch from biennial to annual regular sessions. This is due to increasing demands by citizens in the areas of welfare, education, criminal law and juvenile problems, and more recently in transportation. Scarcely a year passes without someone proposing an amendment creating annual sessions for the Texas legislature. Virtually all proposed new constitutions require annual sessions for state governments. Even though Texas has resisted the change into the 1970s, the demands of modern state government have often required a special session in the even-numbered years[21] in addition to the regular sessions of the Texas legislature which are held in the odd-numbered years. Normally, the governor exercises constitutional power to call special legislative sessions for budgetary purposes (when state expenses are overrunning revenues), or to adjust Texas laws to federal grant-in-aid programs where state inaction might cause a loss of federal assistance. Since it is a considerable inconvenience for many legislators to meet in the unscheduled special sessions, the governor does not call them on whimsy.[22] The lawmakers can adjourn the special sessions at their own initiative, but the nationwide trends is for state legislatures to meet in regular sessions annually to meet the constantly increasing demands being placed on state governments.[23]

Setting legislative priorities

Delivering his speech in person in the first of his annual state of the state messages to the legislature, the governor outlines legislative priorities. Newly elected Governor Dolph Briscoe in 1973, after stating a desire for cooperation to provide unity, alluding to the greatness of republican government and America's status as a melting pot of different races and nationalities, and paying obeisance to the free enterprise economic system as fostering "the greatest material and spiritual prosperity ever achieved by mankind,"[24] set the parameters of his legislative program in 14 policy areas: government ethics, lobby control, constitutional revision, law enforcement, penal code revision, drug traffic and abuse, vocational education, economy in government, executive budgetary management, pollution abatement, conservation of natural resources, crisis in energy, welfare, and consumer protection.

Rich in platitudes and references to the dominant political and social values, a new governor's initial message to the legislature reveals perhaps for the first time his positions on a variety of issues and usually reflects, in large measure, a studied concern for the maintenance of the status quo. In modern times, any chief executive's attitudes have great significance for future state policy, for in cataloging the major concerns of the leadership structure and indicating the parameters of public "solutions," public problems are defined and the range of acceptable solutions are outlined, setting for some period of time the scope and calibre of the activities of state government.[25]

As an example, the initial Briscoe message in 1973 was prominent for its "no new taxes" pledge. Accordingly, all legislative action during the 63d legislature, regular session, was dominated by the governor's dogged determination, apparently popular, to keep government spending "within the state's means." The governor was able to prevail, although strong pressures existed for additional funding in many policy areas, particularly the avowed need to equalize educational opportunities between impoverished and wealthy school districts. In 1979, Governor Clements promised even greater devotion to cost-cutting and fiscal discipline. His message reflected a businessman's dedication to planning and balanced budgeting, with implications that the Texas bureaucracy might be trimmed. He wanted to protect the state's oil resources from further federal controls. Educational considerations were classroom discipline and periodic recertification of teachers with the overall objective being an improvement in quality.

Beyond the constitutional and traditional message activities of the governor and the content of the messages themselves, we know little of certainty in Texas of the web of processes, priorities, and personalities involved in the development of the legislative program of the state. Further, we know little of the resources upon which the content of the messages draw—whether from inputs from campaign promises, the party platform, the personal predilections of the governor, close advisers, lobbyists, or the public. Of necessity, much of which we know is simply descriptive of piecemeal activities, impressionistic, and speculative.

THE GOVERNOR'S EXECUTIVE POWERS

The political and legislative powers of the governor have already been described in large measure in connection with the legislative responsibilities. Later, we will see his role as party leader. First, he has a variety of executive powers.

Appointive powers

The governor appoints a temporary replacement to fill any vacancy in the office of a U.S. senator from Texas. The appointee holds office until an election is organized. However, the governor cannot appoint replacements for Texas representatives to the Congress since the U.S. Constitution requires all members of the House to be popularly elected. The governor does fill many state and district office vacancies (the major exception being seats in the state legislature), but appointments to vacancies in elective posts terminate with the following general election. Governor Briscoe was extremely circumspect in making appointments in his first term, and was criticized for leaving some posts vacant too long. Partly this seems to have stemmed from his desire to select persons who were well known to him, and partly from a desire to find and appoint a number of qualified minority group members. Many appointments require persons with extensive professional or technical qualifications, and for a number of appointments the governor is restricted to selecting candidates from a list drawn up by state or private agencies.

While appointment is potentially an enormous power for administrative control, the Texas governor's appointive powers are heavily restricted. Because of the long ballot election of multiple state executives, only four officials with state administrative capacities are appointed by the Texas governor: the secretary of state, the commissioner of labor statistics, the director of the Department of Community Affairs, and the adjutant general. None is a top decision-maker. Still, the governor does appoint about 700 people, and this sometimes might lead one to conclude that he can eventually attain overall control of the executive branch of government, especially in the course of a four-year term. But the fact is that the cumulative effect of these many gubernatorial appointments is severely blunted by a practice known as "senatorial courtesy" under which a governor's nominee must be approved by the state senator from his home district. The forces behind this practice are the senate rule that confirmation hearings must transpire in executive sessions (which are closed to the public and the press) and the constitutional stricture that such nominees receive a two-thirds vote of approval in the senate (whereas the president needs only a simple majority approval in the U.S. Senate for the bulk of his appointments— even for ambassadors and supreme court justices). Thus, the Texas senate has close controls over the governor's appointive powers. Any real change here would require modification of these legislative restrictions,[26] but this became most un-likely after Dolph Briscoe nominated his barber to the Coordinating Board of State Colleges and Universities and followed that up with per-haps the ultimate in appointive fiascos—the nomination to a state agency of a man who had *died* some months previously.

Removal powers

As for the removal power of a state official by executive authority, it is virtually nonexistent, except for the governor's own staff.[27] Removal is in the hands of the legislature through a cumbersome impeachment process closely akin to that of the federal Constitution, by legislative address (a step just short of impeachment which is effected by a two-thirds vote of both houses), or by the heads of various boards and agencies through powers conferred in a variety of ways by the legis-lature. Interestingly, the legislature could just as readily confer such removal powers on the governor by providing that the agency positions were to be held at the pleasure of the governor. While this has never been done, it was significant that the 1974 legislature sitting as a con-stitutional convention, recommended that the governor be given removal powers for cause, subject only to approval by a majority of the senate.

Law enforcement

While the constitution directs the governor to "cause the laws to be faithfully executed," it simply does not give him the powers nec-essary to do so. The governor does have control over the small force of Texas Rangers (less than a hundred officers) and during times of emergencies and special situations he has some powers through the Department of Public Safety. As with militia powers, the governor's authority in law enforcement is basically restricted to emergency and highly specialized situations. A more significant figure in law enforce-ment is the attorney general, the highest legal officer in the state, and a person who is elected altogether independently of the governor. Further-more, much of the day-to-day power is exercised by local officials, thus further diffusing enforcement authority.

The state constitution declares that the governor is:

> . . . Commander-in-Chief of the military forces of the State, except when they are called into actual service of the United States. He shall have the power to call forth the militia to exercise the laws of the State, to suppress insurrections, repel invasions, and protect the frontier from hostile incur-sions by Indians . . . . (Article 4, Section 7)

The governor appoints an adjutant general to administer the Texas forces for him. In emergencies such as the disorderly days of the Texas oil rush, or during natural disasters or riots, the governor can declare martial law and send the National Guard to affected areas, but the Guard cannot be used to impede federal laws or constitutional rights. The president can nationalize the Guard at any time.

In addition to this force, there is a Texas State Guard, dating from World War II, which serves as a military police and internal security support system for the National Guard, but it is not subject to federal mobilization. The highlight of its activities is its annual paid drill. Otherwise it remains unpaid and immobilized and awaits the rarity of a gubernatorial call for assistance.

Interstate rendition and clemency

Article 4, Section 2 of the U.S. Constitution requires that felons who flee from one state to another must be returned (interstate rendition is the correct form; the popular term used is "extradition," but technically this is a proper description only for such agreements between countries). Since each state is sovereign and independent relative to its neighbor, governors have from time to time refused to return out-of-state felons to their home state for prosecution. Even the Supreme Court of the United States had ruled that interstate rendition was "mandatory but unenforceable."[28] The Fugitive Felon Act of 1934, however, made it a federal crime to flee from one state to another to avoid prosecution. Consequently, today it is rare to find problems emanating from requests for rendition.

The governor appoints one of the three members of the board of pardons and paroles, and with the approval of at least two of the members, he can grant reprieves (temporary suspensions), commutations (reduction of punishment), pardons (full commutations) and remit fines and forfeitures.

By his own authority, the governor can revoke a parole or any conditional pardon and grant one 30-day stay of execution of the death sentence (a reprieve) in any capital case.

Budgeting

Given the lack of control over budgeting and fiscal management and the disintegrated administrative system, it is probably not realistic to expect a carefully considered, comprehensive legislative program to emanate from the governor's office in Texas. As a result of the independence of bureaucratic chieftains, the governor's staff probably cannot look to the agency heads as a major source of programmatic ideas. Further, Texas has two budgets, and no agency has budgetary execution powers. In practice the Texas legislature largely disregards the governor's budget for that of their own Legislative Budget Board (LBB). Nor does Texas grant the governor authority to oversee the execution of the budget.

Thus the budget is of limited value in Texas as a tool of gubernatorial policy influence, including building power with the legislature.[29] The governor retains only an initiative for focusing public and legislative attention on the policy issues related in a broad way to program priorities and taxing and spending, a function quite different from the role of the U.S. president. The latter uses budget-making and budget-execution powers for such purposes as soliciting suggestions for the administration's program, communicating to agency heads and party leadership, White House spending and policy expectations, seeking opinions from congressional leadership about administration goals, writing the budgetary and other messages for communication with Congress and the public, drafting administration bills for new programs and modification of old policies, negotiating through White House office legislative liaison personnel with individual congressmen for support of administration bills, and managing and executing the budgetary spending figures on specific programs to ensure the carrying out of the policies in which the president is interested.

Federal grants-in-aid

Although the governor's budgeting powers are highly circumscribed, there has been a growing trend in the 1970s for the federal government to send monies to the states or communities within the states for projects which it wishes to stimulate. What this adds up to in Texas is that some of these federal grants-in-aid go directly to the governor's office and he controls them. Some projects, however, go directly to lower levels of government such as regional councils or cities.

A struggle for money and the patronage and power associated with it has developed between governors and state councils of government (groups of approximately ten counties united for a special purpose, such as flood or crime control). Recently, the governors, by virtue of their greater political clout in Washington, have been gaining control of the lion's share of federal grants-in-aid. In controlling these millions of dollars flooding into his state, a governor can avoid having to use state money for a number of state programs and can claim that he "held the line on taxes" or allowed "no new taxes," when in fact government spending programs may have increased significantly.[30]

We have noted that the governor has a virtual veto of funding in many federal grants.[31] This is increasingly the case since the issuance of the Office of Management and Budget's (OMB's) Circular A95, commonly referred to as A95 Review, which requires federal allocations to go to a central clearing house and the governor's Office of Budget and Planning. Thus, while the governor might not have direct power over the funds, he is made the final review officer, or chief planning officer, and under one such hat he can in fact exercise a veto.

Since federal grants-in-aid now involve many millions of dollars in Texas, this phenomenon has significantly increased the governor's power base, and it is one which is not yet understood by most Texans.

THE GOVERNOR AS PARTY LEADER

Despite severe constitutional restraints, the governor of the state of Texas is ex officio his party's titular head, and in presidential election years he heads the Texas delegation to his party's national convention. As chief executive, he holds the top political office in state politics, and has customarily been of the conservative wing of the Democratic party.[32,33] While U.S. representatives from the Lone Star State may call on the loyalties of personal followings and important factions within the state party, the major positions of party power in the state are those of governor, lieutenant governor, speaker of the house, attorney general, and a coterie of little known lobbyists. However, it is rarely the case that the influence or prestige of an incumbent Democratic governor or the Democratic party's gubernatorial nominee is eclipsed.

Until Clements took office in 1979, Republican candidates were not similarly blessed. Since they had not been successful in a century, they had never received the exposure and publicity of their opposites, and, of course, had never had the chance to dispense patronage as governors. Thus, although the 1972 Republican candidate gained in party status by virtue of the fact that he lost the general election to Dolph Briscoe by only 1 percent of the popular vote,[34,35] Henry Grover was something of a maverick and far less influential than Senator Tower among state party councils.[36] Before Clements the chairman of the Republican state executive committee and the national committeemen were the perennial party leaders, with greater power than their Democratic counterparts since they were not overshadowed by a governor of the same party.

In the case of the Democrats, despite virtually continuous struggles to control the state Democratic party leadership, the Democratic state executive committee customarily closes ranks to operate in concert with its party's gubernatorial nominee and his associates. For political expediency, the governor may sometimes attack a faction of the party, but a more typical role is increasingly that of peacemaker, mollifying dissidents, working for overall harmony and party unity, and raising party funds.[37]

On January 19, 1974, when the perennial dispute in the state Democratic party erupted over precinct conventions selecting delegates to the national Democratic convention, the majority conservatives proposed a winner-take-all solution, while the minority liberals sought proportional representation. Governor Briscoe brought about a truce and compromise insuring proportional representation of minorities without changing party rules. This was a significant improvement over his performance at the 1972 Democratic party's national convention in which, as governor and head of the Texas party's delegation, he vacillated between Wallace and McGovern, shifting uncertainly after repeated deferments to the latter to the bitter dismay of the Wallaceites.

The governor's power was temporarily reduced in 1976 when the state legislature ordered Texas' first presidential primary be held to aid favorite-son candidate Lloyd Bentson (see Chapter 3). As to who would control the state Democratic party in the wake of its first loss of the governorship since Reconstruction, there were plenty of candidates. Hill said he would be willing to assume leadership—after all, he had defeated Briscoe in the party primary. Briscoe all but said he would run again, suggesting that he considered himself still the party chief. Houston's Billy Goldberg, as state party chairman, certainly had a strong claim. And in theory, incumbent Senator Lloyd Bentsen could marshal some support. As the highest Democratic officeholder in state politics, however, Lieutenant Governor Bill Hobby was *finally* recognized as party boss. Clearly, the Democratic state party organization was in some disarray in the wake of Clements' completely unexpected takeover of the governorship, but it seemed certain, after reorganizing, to continue its domination of Texas state politics.

MODERNIZATION AND REFORM

From time to time it has been apparent in Texas that the governor and the state's foremost executive officers have been rivals, sometimes of the keenest sort. The result inevitably reflects itself in the performance of the executive branch of government. On some occasions, the lieutenant governor (Ben Barnes), or the attorney general (John Hill), has eventually run for the top office against the governor he was supposedly supporting. On the national level presidential candidates select their running mates at their respective parties' national conventions, thereby ensuring that every potential vice president is the personal choice of the presidential candidate. Thus, from the start, they are personally and ideologically compatible, and are considered by the voting public to be a political "package."[38]

The power of the lieutenant governor of Texas on the state level is far greater than is the power of the vice president on the national scene. Both are presiding officers of the upper house of the legislatures at their respective levels, but the vice president's powers in the U.S. Senate are largely ceremonial—so much so that he more often than not leaves the work to the president pro tempore, and he in turn often defers to the dean of the senate, who may even leave it to a junior senator. The real power in the U.S. Senate is vested in the majority leader. By contrast, visitors to the Texas Senate will be impressed by the fact that the lieutenant governor is virtually always present and personally in control of all proceedings in the chamber. In fact, the lieutenant governor is powerful enough to truly damage the governor's programs and policies right there in the Senate where he is dealing with an organization in which he appoints every committee chairman, assigns all bills to whatever committee he sees fit,[39] and appoints the majority of the members of every committee.[40] Furthermore, the lieutenant governor can use his scheduling powers to severely limit debate. Finally, he may cast what the state constitution describes as the "casting" vote to break a tie, since a bill which ends in a tie is defeated. The Vice President of the U.S. has the same limited voting power.[41]

But the lieutenant governor is by no means the only member of the executive branch with an independent power base.[42] In the nineteenth century Texas established a multiple elected executive, so that with the exception of the secretary of state, whom the governor appoints, other major offices in the executive branch are independently elective. They need no approval from the governor, and many typically hold office for many years. In some respects, the governor might be regarded as simply *primus inter pares*. The Constitution of Texas provides:

> The executive department of the state shall consist of a Governor, who shall be the chief executive officer of the State; a Lieutenant Governor, Secretary of State, Comptroller of Public Accounts, Treasurer, Commissioner of the General Land Office, and Attorney General.[43]

If one wanted to increase significantly the power of the governor and improve the cohesiveness of the executive department at a stroke, perhaps the most productive step would be to give the governor appointive power not only for the office of lieutenant governor, but also for all the other officers of the executive department as well excepting only the attorney general, whose operating independence is essential. The comptroller would continue to be checked by the state auditor so that fiscal integrity would not be threatened.

Dozens of agencies have been created by statutory legislation and a few boards and commissions have been established by constitutional amendment, yet all but a dozen or so of the state's 130–40 operating agencies (there are over 230 state agencies altogether) are headed by boards or commissions, or in other words, by multiple executives.[44] These boards and commissions, in turn, commonly hire an executive director, much like a school board hires a superintendent of schools.

The executive director is responsible to the multiple executives of the board—and not to the governor, who has virtually no administrative control over him.

Since the Texas governor now enjoys a four-year term, his appointive powers will become more telling, for, with the multiple executives of the state's various boards serving staggered terms, it takes about four to six years for the governor's appointments to constitute a majority. One way to speed this process up and to eliminate duplication and rivalry is to consolidate and significantly reduce the number of boards and agencies and to make the heads of the new agencies single executives who are nominated and dismissed by the governor. In addition, the reduction of the constitutional requirement for two-thirds senate approval of gubernatorial nominees to a simple majority approval would loosen the throttlehold the Senate now exercises over the governor's appointive powers.

No academic investigation of governmental administration seems to end without a plea for the extension of the merit system of requiring scholastic accreditation and/or competitive exams in a greater number of job areas. More professional and technically competent administrative personnel are seemingly more necessary every year as administration becomes more complex.

Last, but not least, integrating the innumerable agencies into a score of departments under the control of the governor would place the executive department in a position to formulate a comprehensive and meaningful budget, which then might well eclipse the Legislative Budget Board's budgeting capabilities. At present there is no single head to budgeting efforts for the state.

In general, reform of the Texas executive department would be based on greater centralization and coordination of executive effort. It is not likely that Texans are ready for this yet. It is definitely not going to come through any constitutional change if the state legislature is to be the agent of reform.[45]

After the 37-man Texas Constitutional Revision Commission submitted its proposals for a new state constitution in 1973, the state legislature used the commission's proposals as a takeoff point for drafting a new constitution in 1974 when it convened as a constitutional convention. Entitled *Constitutional Convention Progress to Date and Highlights of Major Proposals,* the draft was distributed to the convention for guidance in constitutional revision and in the case of the executive article was close to proposals of the final draft. Since the entire work of the convention was defeated by three votes in the fall of 1974, nothing came of it; then in 1975 it surprisingly passed the legislature late in the regular session and was thereafter defeated by the voters that November.

Basically, the legislature, like the commission, sought to retain the weak, multiple, independently elected executive and envisioned meaningful reforms mostly in administrative areas—such as in permitting governors to designate the chairmen of state boards and commissions, in most instances, every two years and allowing them to appoint one third of all the members of such organizations within four months of their own inauguration, and in permitting them to remove appointive (but not the elected) officers of state for cause, subject to senate approval. The legislature would have limited most government agencies to a ten-year span, requiring legislative review before statutory renewal for an ensuing decade. In total, these reforms would have been an important step in the direction of developing "administrative efficiency," but there was no move to consolidate the overlapping multiplicity of agencies and commissions, except under the aegis of the legislature itself. This would have given the legislature, not the executive, more control.

Most political scientists hold that the governor should enjoy increased power in the budgetary process and in the appointment, direction, and removal of lesser officials in the executive branch.

CONCLUSIONS

Texas governors have sometimes seemed to be larger than life, or smaller; few have been uninteresting politicians. In this chapter we have sketched the history of the Texas governorship and investigated the contemporary political role of the governor. Our inquiry leads us to draw the following conclusions about the Texas governorship:

1.   While the governor is constitutionally weak, his four-year term and his control of increasingly large federal grants make him a formidable political leader if he is an active politician and maintains his popularity.

2.   The governor's influence upon the policymaking process depends upon the visibility of the office, the need for giving priorities to policy proposals because of the brevity of legislative sessions, the extent of support from strong economic interests, a large staff, and the ideological and policy affinities which the governor has with the leaderships of other segments of state and local governments. These considerations may lead to strong gubernatorial influence despite the governor's weak formal powers, the disintegrated political and administrative systems, and the existence of few formal ties to the legislature.

3.   The executive powers of the Texas governor are very limited. He has limited control over the administrative apparatus, his appointive power is constrained by the powerful intervention of the state Senate, and his powers in the state budgeting process are greatly circumscribed.

4.   The Texas governor has an important role as a party leader, but

other offices, such as that of lieutenant governor, provide important bases of political power as well, and provide competition for the governor in performing party leadership roles.

5. The governor is a key political figure in Texas; potentially he is the focal point of political activity in the state. The governor is also a key legislator—his item veto on appropriations bills and his postadjournment veto power make him indeed a formidable opponent of legislation inimicable to his taste.

In his function as chief executive officer, the governor continues to labor under severe disadvantages, notably the independently elected plural executive, which places potential rivals high in the executive branch, and the continued limitations to his control over a still fragmented bureaucracy—one which could use major consolidation, coordination, and the heavy application of a merit system in hiring.

Overall, the defeated revised constitution of 1975 attempted to move in the direction of modernizing the executive department and contained the seeds requisite for significant enhancement of gubernatorial control and direction of the state administration, especially for governors who win consecutive four-year terms. Real executive direction depends heavily on the governor's own capabilities. With a popular mandate, leadership capacity and the support of the chief legislative officers, future governors of the Lone Star State have the potential for significant executive control of state affairs—even if they happen to be Republicans!

CHAPTER SIX

State administration

The largely unpublicized decisions ... in administrative organizations determine who gets what, but the news focuses on elections and on the pronouncements and decisions of executives, legislators, and high courts.

MURRAY EDELMAN*

Most employees of state government work in state administration in the executive agencies which deliver public services and regulate the activities of individuals and groups. State bureaucrats, as these public employees are called, have achieved much notoriety in recent years for their increased numbers, amounts of money consumed, and in the volume, diversity, and visibility of their activities.

While their activities are performed pursuant to broad legislative authorization, bureaucrats have great discretion in terms of when and how to carry out or implement government policies. And they are delegated limited policy-initiation authority by the Texas legislature because of the complexity of modern problems and inability to foresee contingencies. As a result, bureaucrats produce a large body of rules, regulations, decisions, and actions which touch our daily lives at many points. Oddly, "the news focuses on elections and on the pronouncements and decisions of executives, legislators, and high courts,"[1] rather than on the work of administrators. The *Texas Register,* issued weekly by the Office of the Secretary of State, contains administrative rules, regulations, and proclamations, and it gives us an opportunity to gauge the amount of these rulings and their impact.

In policy-initiation activities of administrators, we observe operations which we saw as common in the legislative process in Chapter 4, such as hearings, investigations, studies, consultations, consideration of petitions for proposed services, deliberations, and building of relationships with other governmental branches and with interest groups. Acting

---

* *Political Language: Words That Succeed and Policies That Fail* (New York: Academic Press, 1977), p. 77.

in the interests of agency clienteles or of the bureaucracy as a whole, bureaucrats often also behave like lobbyists, drafting and proposing legislation, testifying at hearings, rallying support, mobilizing opposition to threatening measures, assigning staff as "legislative liaison officers," and entering into alliances with other agencies and groups.

Besides implementing and initiating policy, bureaucrats also commonly engage in judicial-like procedures, in which they hear appeals from their own actions, rulings, and decisions. Many complaints are handled simply and informally to explain, modify, or uphold policy. Other complaints result in more formal, extensive, and complicated judicial proceedings, which may be appealed to the judicial branch, where bureaucrats may be asked to argue their cases and defend their actions and decisions. Thus, we see bureaucrats engaging in *implementation* of policies, limited policy-*initiation,* and limited adjudication of policies.

In this chapter, Texas administrative structures and characteristics, the role and influence of the governor in state administration, and the public personnel system are viewed. Little is known about the 93,000 state bureaucrats beyond aggregate features, such as the number of them covered by the merit system and the ethnic, sex, and salary and occupational features of state employment. A recent sample and study of 13,000 upper-level state administrative officials found a high degree of professionalization of the public service, as measured by educational attainment, professional certification, membership in professional societies, and attitudes. Many state agencies apparently are managed by administrative and professional elites, but their public service roles seem tempered by a sense of public responsibility.[2]

FORMAL ADMINISTRATIVE STRUCTURES

Citizen boards and commissions

Many of the top executive officials of Texas travel to Austin only occasionally and receive only daily pay and expenses for their work. This is so because the typical Texas administrative unit is the multimember board or commission, and statutes provide that these board members be only part-time officers. Altogether, some 400 to 500 intelligent, enthusiastic, enterprising, mostly middle-management business types dominate the Austin bureaucratic scene. Representing a variety of geographic and corporate interests of Texas, these "amateur bureaucrats" ride herd over a wide variety of government programs. About 60 of these "citizen boards and commissions" exist of the type which preside over separate agencies in Texas state administration. Figure 6–1, which shows the Texas Water Development Board arrangement for the Texas Department of Water Resources, is a typical example of the part-time citizen board

180

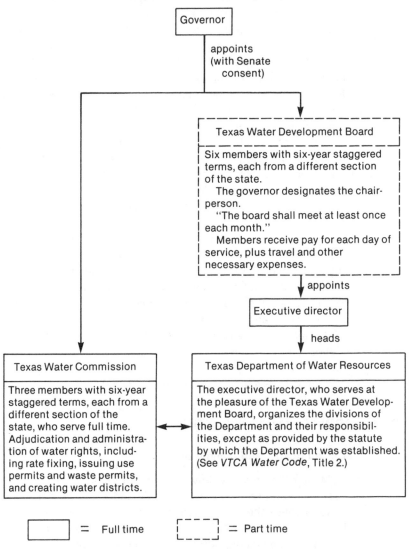

FIGURE 6–1
Typical board or commission arrangement in Texas administration

Governor

appoints
(with Senate
consent)

Texas Water Development Board

Six members with six-year staggered
terms, each from a different section
of the state.
　　The governor designates the chairperson.
　　"The board shall meet at least once
each month."
　　Members receive pay for each day of
service, plus travel and other
necessary expenses.

appoints

Executive director

heads

Texas Water Commission

Three members with six-year
staggered terms, each from a
different section of the
state, who serve full time.
Adjudication and administration of water rights, including rate fixing, issuing use
permits and waste permits,
and creating water districts.

Texas Department of Water Resources

The executive director, who serves at
the pleasure of the Texas Water Development Board, organizes the divisions of
the Department and their responsibilities, except as provided by the statute
by which the Department was established.
(See VTCA Water Code, Title 2.)

☐ = Full time　　☐ = Part time

structure.[3] (For contrast with a single-headed department, see Figure
8–6 in Chapter 8.)

　　Citizen boards such as the Texas Water Development Board establish most of the state's programs, appoint full-time executive directors
of their agencies, approve agency personnel and budgets, and establish
policy guidelines and rules of administrative procedure. Some 30 other
citizen boards and commissions operate with very small staff or with

personnel supplied by other agencies, or they meet infrequently, if at all. In addition to the citizen boards are seven full-time regulatory and claims boards and a large number of professional and vocational licensing and examining boards. See Table 6–1 for the classes of Texas boards and commissions, with examples.

Agencies with single heads

While the boards and commissions of all types are heavily dominant among the units of the Texas bureaucracy, there are ten departments and agencies which have single administrative heads. These units are

TABLE 6–1
Classes of Texas boards and commissions

I. Citizen boards
Important examples of these boards, which number almost 100, are the following:
State Board of Education (21) (elective)
State Board of Public Welfare (3)
State Highway and Public Transportation Commission (3)
Texas Board of Health (18)
Texas Board of Corrections (9)
Public Safety Commission (3)
Texas Water Development Board (6)
Coordinating Board, Texas College and University System (18)
Texas Air Control Board (9)
Parks and Wildlife Commission (6)
Texas Alcoholic Beverage Commission (3)
State Securities Board (3)

II. Full-time regulatory and claims boards
Railroad Commission of Texas (3) (elective)
State Board of Insurance (3)
Public Utilities Commission (3)
Texas Water Commission (3)
Board of Pardons and Paroles (3)
Industrial Accident Board (3)
Texas Employment Commission(3)

III. Professional licensing and examining boards
Thirty-three professional groups have secured governmental endorsement of vocational and professional qualifications and standards. Ten other agencies license such professions as teachers, commercial driving instructors, and insurance agents. Examples include:
State Board of Barber Examiners (3)
State Board of Medical Examiners (9)
State Board of Morticians (6)
Texas Board of Plumbing Examiners (6)

IV. Ex officio boards
Some part-time boards are comprised in whole or in part by officials who are given statutory duties on boards *in addition to* their regular and primary responsibilities. A good example is membership of the treasurer and banking commissioner, along with a citizen member, on the State Banking Board.

TABLE 6–2
Agencies with single heads

Elective heads	*Appointive heads*
Office of the Attorney General	Office of the Secretary of State
Office of the Comptroller of Public Accounts	Adjutant General's Department
	Department of Community Affairs
Office of the State Treasurer	Teaxs Department of Labor and Standards
General Land Office	
Texas Department of Agriculture	Office of State-Federal Relations

listed in Table 6–2. Note that only five of these department heads are appointed by the governor. The other heads are elected. As a result, Texas has the long ballot, by which in addition to the governor and lieutenant governor, a total of eight executive officers (including the three members of the Railroad Commission of Texas) and numerous appellate judges are elected on a statewide ballot.

Fragmentation of services and regulatory authority

The Legislative Budget Board, which is responsible for studying state agency performance, divides state programs and services into six broad functional categories (exclusive of professional and vocational licensing and certification services), as follows:

General government services (executive staff, financial services, central management operations, and intergovernmental units)

Health and welfare programs

Economic development programs

Natural and recreational resources programs

Public safety programs

Programs in education

The Board found numerous agencies operating in each program area. See Table 6–3. Many state agencies have programs in more than one of the six basic functional categories. A major functional consequence of so many offices, agencies, departments, boards, and commissions is fragmentation of services and regulatory authority.

In some areas, such as in regulation of financial institutions, the legislature has authorized "umbrella" boards to oversee several administrative agencies. For example, the Finance Commission, a nine-member board, provides overall policy and supervisory control of three agencies: Banking Department, Savings and Loan Department, and Office of the Consumer Credit Commissioner. Typically, however, this integrative arrangement is partially vitiated by the existence of additional financial

TABLE 6–3
Number of state agencies operating in six basic policy areas

Functional category	Number of agencies with programs
General government	17
Health and welfare	19
Economic development	13
Natural and recreational resources	20
Public safety	42
Education (exclusive of universities)..........	3
Total	114

Source: Legislative Budget Board, *Performance Report to the Sixty-fourth Legislature* (Austin: Legislative Budget Board, 1975).

regulatory boards: Banking Board, State Securities Board, and Credit Union Commission. Further, the concept of public regulation is weakened by provisions for "self regulation" in the requirements that (1) costs of regulation be borne by fees charged the regulated corporations and (2) the public boards be comprised of active members of the regulated enterprises. In this pattern of economic self regulation, statutes require that four members of the Finance Commission be active bankers with no fewer than five years executive experience each and that two commissioners be building and loan executives with like experience.

In a variation of the umbrella organization, which leads to disintegration rather than integration, single-headed departments serve as umbrellas for additional boards and commissions. Some 43 Texas agencies, commonly boards and commissions, receive their appropriations through some other administrative unit. For example, the Department of Agriculture handles funding of the Pink Boll Worm Commission, Poultry Improvement Board, and Dairy Advisory Committee.

Auxiliary or housekeeping services

In another facet of administrative disintegration, the governor has little control and direction over most of the traditional auxiliary services.[4] These aids, many of which are financial,[5] are services which are supplied in common to all or most of the state agencies. Thus, they are often called housekeeping services. They include central purchasing and procurement, building and property services, central accounting, tax administration and collection, custody of funds, performance auditing, records management, data processing services, and budgeting. As seen in Table 6–4, these housekeeping operations are *diffused* in several state agencies, several of which are under the direct control of the *legislative*

TABLE 6–4
Central management operations, performance by

Management operations	Legislative agencies	Elective officer	Appointive board	Office of the Governor
Budgeting	X[a]			
Personnel classification	X[b]			
Personnel merit system	X[c]			
Performance auditing	X[a]			
Post auditing	X[b]			
Appropriations accounting		X[d]		
Tax administration		X[d]		
Custody of state funds		X[e]		
Legal services		X[f]		
Central purchasing			X[g]	
Property services			X[g]	
Records management			X[h]	
Comprehensive planning				X[i,j]
Planning coordination				X[i,j]
Research and program development				X[i,j]
Federal programs coordination				X[i]
Information and computer services				X[i]

Key: [a] Legislative Budget Board
[b] Legislative Audit Committee
[c] Merit System Council
[d] Comptroller of Public Accounts
[e] State Treasurer
[f] Attorney General
[g] Board of Control
[h] Library and Historical Commission
[i] Budget and Planning Office
[j] Interagency planning councils

branch. On the other hand, note the existence of *newer* operations of policy leadership and management in the Office of the Governor, including comprehensive planning, coordination of planning activities, research, program development, and federal programs coordination.[6]

By taking a brief look at the agencies which perform auxiliary services, we see what is meant by housekeeping services, with relevant examples. In addition, we view some of our major executive and legislative officials.

Comptroller of Public Accounts   The comptroller is central accounting officer and principal tax administrator and collector. A close relationship with the taxation and appropriations committees of the legislature is assured by the "pay-as-you-go" provision of the Constitution, which requires that the comptroller submit in advance of each legislative session a statement of the financial condition of the state, together with estimates of anticipated revenues. Unless an appropriations measure can receive a four-fifths majority vote of the total membership in each legislative branch, all appropriations bills—unless accompanied by revenue bills—must propose expenditures not in excess of the comptroller's estimates.[7]

In connection with his duties as central accounting officer, the comptroller preaudits expenditures, authorizes spending, and issues warrants on the state treasury. Questions about legislative purposes, legislative intent, prior statutory approval of programs, and constitutional spending limitations are referred to the attorney general, who ordinarily issues written opinions concerning these matters.

Attorney General   By the Texas Constitution, the attorney general is the state's lawyer, representing the state in all suits and pleas to which the State is a party and furnishing legal advice to the governor and other state officials and agency heads. Through advisory opinions, the attorney general shapes administrative processes, content of agency rules and regulations, and interpretation and implementation of statutory enactments.[8]

State Treasurer   Actual custody of state funds is in the state treasurer who, like the comptroller and attorney general, is a separately elected executive official.

State Board of Control   With more than 700 employees, the gubernatorially appointed three-member Board of Control provides central purchasing and other central services, including business machines repair, mail and messenger service, stationery supply, automated services, property accounting, and telecommunications services. In addition, the agency is charged with modernization and remodeling of government buildings, acquisition and coordination of building sites, and planning, design, and construction of new state structures.

Texas State Library   Responsible for retrieving, indexing, and storing semi-active files of Texas state agencies is the records management division of the Texas State Library. An ex officio Records Preservation Advisory Committee, composed of the state librarian and six other state officers, aids in identification and protection of essential records for preservation by the state.

Legislative Budget Board   Comprised of legislative presiding officers, heads of fiscal committees, and other legislators, this board is responsible for preparation of Texas' biennial budgets. After formal preparation of the budget for the legislature, the staff of the Board serves as staff also to the appropriations committees. In this way, the Board maintains control of the budget through the legislative appropriations process.

As an adjunct to its duties of preparing budgets, drafting appropriations bills, and staffing appropriations committees, the staff of the Board compiles performance audits of the state agencies and institutions by conducting a continuous performance review of programs against statutory duties, of unit cost management tools, of workload efficiency data, and of program output standards adopted by the Board. As an aid to zero-base budgeting, the Board compiles and makes a performance report to the legislature every two years.[9]

Legislative Audit Committee   Postauditing the financial records of the more than 200 state departments, agencies, boards, commissions, and educational institutions is the work of the state auditor, who is hired by the Legislative Audit Committee. The auditor is also the state's efficiency expert charged with suggestions for economy, accounting systems improvements, increasing performance capabilities, and assistance in records management and data retrieval systems for all state agencies. An additional duty of the staff of the Legislative Audit Committee is to administer the state's job classification plan for state employees. As we shall see in the last major section of this chapter, Texas has no central personnel office.

Sunset or sunrise?

Focusing public and legislative attention on overlapping and duplicating responsibilities of numerous state agencies was one concern of those who urged passage in 1977 of the Texas Sunset Act. Another matter was whether the existence of some agencies could be justified in terms of performance or public need. Starting in 1977, the Sunset Advisory Commission, a joint committee of the legislature, reviews the operations and functions of each state agency every 12 years. Unless the legislature acts to continue existence of an agency, it is automatically abolished.

Staff and housing of the Sunset Advisory Commission is provided by the Legislative Budget Board, Performance and Evaluation Section. In its first two-year cycle, 1977–1979, the Commission reviewed operations of 26 agencies, most of them the licensing boards for architects, automobile dealers, barbers, certified public accountants, cosmetologists, lawyers, morticians, nursing home administrators, pest control businesses, private employment agencies, real estate brokers, and surveyors. Others reviewed were commemorative commissions, such as the Battleship

Texas Commission. Exceptions to these two classes were the Texas Turnpike Authority and Board of County and District Road Indebtedness.[10]

The sunset process begins with agency self-evaluation, moves through public hearings, and ends with findings and recommendations to the legislature. The major problem, of course, is to develop evaluation criteria, including measures of efficiency, impact, and performance, which is complicated by need for data. What may appear as relatively simple turns out to be infinitely complex technically and fraught with political considerations, including determining legislative intent and articulating programmatic goals.

Probably the most salutary effect of the sunset process is to focus some public attention on state agency activities. No doubt licensing boards have received little public and legislative scrutiny, being made up of members of the regulated profession or vocation, preparing their own budgets free from the appropriations process (by funding their activities from their own collected fees), and paying scant attention to consumer complaints. A report by the staff of the Sunset Advisory Commission on the Texas Private Employment Agency Regulatory Board "showed that 46 percent of all complaints referred to the department . . . [in 1977] were dismissed, another 41 percent found invalid, and the disposition of 13 percent was not indicated."[11] Likewise, the Commission reported that the State Board of Morticians had taken no action on most of its consumer complaints— those dealing with price and quality of service—on the grounds that "these types of problems do not lie within its jurisdiction."[12] The Board of Morticians later changed its policy, the members reporting that the sunset process had been most "educational" for them.[13]

How important are formal structures?

No doubt, Texas with its 177 boards and commissions of all classes bears little resemblance to the state government reform model of a few single-headed departments under the control and supervision of a strong governor with powers of appointment and removal, budgeting, administrative reorganization, and the like.[14] Formally, Texas bureaucracy is certainly characterized by (1) a fragmented administrative structure of autonomous administrative units under numerous boards and commissions and elective heads of administration; and (2) a chief executive who lacks some important formal powers, as in budgeting and removal of executive heads.

Assessments of state administration have been too heavily influenced by a large body of reform literature to present a balanced picture. Most textbooks on the Texas governor and state administration carry several pages of scoldings about weaknesses of the governor and the existence of "an administrative jungle." These strictures are followed by a standard, prescribed list of reforms which Texas *ought* to adopt.

This reform approach is limited and unrealistic. It centers its attention on *formal organization and powers,* and it probably overestimates what can be accomplished by legal and structural change. It overlooks *patterns of informal authority* and practice which grow up in a political system through the continual impact and interaction of specific environmental forces with the political system. These patterns, of course, *become traditional and legitimate* for the major political actors, and they often prove much more important than formal organization in establishing characteristics of administration and of administrative performance.

As we shall see in the remainder of this chapter, reformers who limit their attention to formal structures and powers overlook the cumulative impact of several energizing elements in Texas, including:

> Broad economic and social change, the mass media, and high visibility circumstances and issues which everywhere heighten public expectations about gubernatorial influence and give executives extra opportunities for policy initiatives
>
> Effects of new legal positions of the governor as "chief planning officer," "federal systems officer," and coordinator of state-local programs, together with the rise of large programmatic staffs in the Office of the Governor
>
> A large network of political relationships (based on a gubernatorial patronage system), which serve to tie administrative units to other parts of the political system and to give the governor and other political actors sufficient support to preserve the political regime and their political goals.

We turn now to a consideration of the more informal and extralegal aspects of administration in Texas.

THE GOVERNOR IN STATE ADMINISTRATION

The plural executive system

Executive leadership in Texas, at least formally, is clearly plural, fragmented, and centered in autonomous boards and agencies. As we have seen, most agency heads are named and supervised by multimembered, mainly part-time boards and commissions. Although the governor appoints these board members, they serve commonly for six-year, staggered terms, so that only one third of board membership is appointed every two years. As we saw in Table 6–2, of the full-time, single heads of administration, the governor appoints only five.

A chief functional consequence of the plural executive and of other structural arrangements in state administration is to deprive the governor of some important *formal* tools of policy direction and supervision. Besides the lack of appointment and direction of executive directors of most executive agencies, the governor's formal removal power is practically nonexistent.

Nevertheless, recent governors have worked out a circuitous "one-shot removal power,"[15] which has been bolstered by tradition and numerous advisory opinions of the attorney general. Upon expiration of a board member's term, the governor may let the incumbent holdover continue to occupy his or her position, subject to the governor's removal at any time (by the act of sending the name of a successor to the Senate). Allowing board members to serve at the governor's pleasure gives the governor more effective policy direction of the member. Besides, an interim appointment can be made at any time the Senate is not in session, which does not subject the nominee immediately to the scrutiny of Senate confirmation proceedings. If the holdover arrangement proves unfruitful for the governor, the chief executive may terminate the agreement, thereby regaining the patronage plum.

The number of holdovers in state administration is sizable. The Committee on the Executive of the Constitutional Convention of 1974 showed that at points in time in 1968, 1970, and 1974, retainees numbering 196, 176, and 300 were serving past the end of their appointive terms.[16] The governor loses neither political, policy, nor ideological power bases by holdovers, because all Texas governors for 40 years have been conservatives with similar policy concerns and outlook.[17] As a result, remarkable stability and tenure patterns are found in the topmost echelons of Texas state administration.[18]

Another informal arrangement, common in Texas as elsewhere, serves to give the governor a form of removal and policy direction. This is an understanding with the appointee, as a condition to nomination and appointment, that he or she will vacate the post upon request. The countervailing tradition, however, of "a long term of service as compensation for willingness to undertake government tasks without emolument" is very strong in Texas.

Patterns of formal and informal authority

Besides formal restraints in appointments and removals, additional limitations hamper the governor's policy directive capacity. As we have seen, legislative agencies exercise budget authority and many traditional housekeeping functions. On the other hand, the governor has the item veto, a four-year term with legally unlimited tenure, a formidable set of modern administrative management tools, and a bountiful patronage base derived from appointments to the numerous multimember boards and commissions.[19] Table 6–5 attempts to summarize the governor's formal and informal administrative authority. As we shall see in a later section of this chapter, gubernatorial authority in administration

Tends to be highly dependent upon particular circumstances or situations,

Rests upon a large reservoir of modern management tools and resources, and

Is augmented by the governor's other roles in state government.

The patronage system: Patterns of cooption

Keystone of the governor's informal authority in state administration is the patronage system. To the critics of Texas state administration who characterize the governor as a "weak" executive and the system as "an administrative nightmare," it can be pointed out that on this base the chief executive builds a formidable system of supports for gubernatorial authority and influence which reach into every part of the Texas political system. Board members are active and influential citizens in every region of Texas, and in recent years all governors have had the tenure to appoint a majority or more to every board and commission.[20]

A complete and balanced account of the governor's scope of authority in appointments must consider traditional patterns of *cooption,*[21] which enlarge the governor's patronage system to include judicial positions and elective posts in the executive branch. Mention has already been made of the extensive holdovers on the citizen boards, which is a form of cooption of board members from previous administrations.

In the formally elective judiciary and in the parts of the executive branch which are elective, it is traditional practice for judges and administrators to submit retirement and other resignations not at the end of elective terms but after their own reelection, so that governors may name replacements until the next general election. Appointees to these low visibility elective positions have the advantage running as incumbents in the next election. This system aptly has been called an *appointive-elective* process.[22] On the Railroad Commission of Texas, for example, which was established in 1891, most of the 28 members (to 1979) have had initial appointment by governors. More than ten years average service points again to the long tenure characteristic of state administrative officialdom.

In the same manner, an appointive-elective process is fixed in the Texas judiciary. Most judges first reach the bench through gubernatorial

TABLE 6–5
Patterns of formal and informal bases of gubernatorial authority in state administration

	Formal authority	*Informal authority patterns*
Appointments	No appointment of heads of most state agencies; appointment of numerous boards. Board members have staggered, six-year terms, require Senate confirmation.	Powerful base of political, policy, ideological support derived from appointment of citizen boards. Traditional pattern of cooption enlarges patronage base to include judicial and elective positions. Appointment of all board members by lengthy tenure enhanced by four-year term (no legal limitation). Holdovers require no Senate confirmation. Interim appointments are made. Governor retains initiative, although must consult, as courtesy, with nominee's senator.
Removals	Almost nonexistent authority to remove department heads.	"One-shot removal authority" and other informal practices and understandings.
Budgeting	Governor is termed "chief budget officer," but authority is in Legislative Budget Board.	Programmatic planning, coordination of programs, and setting of spending limits through use of staff and item veto.
Vetoes	Item and general vetoes furnish a strong negative in policy.	Threats of vetoes, with reliance on his or her publicity organs and the mass media, generate policy support.
Management	No traditional housekeeping tools in budget execution, personnel, and performance auditing.	Use of newer policy leadership and management tools of comprehensive planning, coordination of state-local programs, control of federal programs, data information systems, and research and policy analysis.
Staff	Huge staff; authority to assign duties.	Use of staff offices in crucial situations to enhance authority, such as building power bases through appointments of influential citizens and authorization of local programs.
Elites	Major political figure, titled as chief executive, chief planning officer, chief budget officer.	Attention to popular expectations and symbols of office. Entree to economic elites. Direct, intimate relations with powerful interests, enhanced by little citizen participation, noncompetitive elections, other conditions.

appointment. This selection process "cuts out not only the electorate but also party leaders not in the governor's personal circle."[23] Enlarging the number of positions, the legislature during the recent Briscoe administration created scores of new district-level courts, all of which were subject to first-time appointments. Often, in practice, judicial and administrative appointments cut across one another. Further, promotions to higher positions in either branch set off a long string of vacancies and nominations.

Close political friends of the governor in both legislative bodies may be in a strong position to influence, but not dominate, gubernatorial patronage. Patronage matters, including recruitment, nomination, and appointment, are handled by a top assistant in the Office of the Governor. Nominations must be submitted, of course, as a formal requirement to the Texas Senate for confirmation, which takes a two-thirds vote of members present. Although the senator in whose district the nominee resides is consulted beforehand as a matter of courtesy, the governor retains the initiative in patronage. Senatorial courtesy is seldom invoked, and ordinarily only in administrative nominations. On occasion, the governor withdraws a name from Senate consideration when he receives word of some unanticipated objection to a nominee. But most of the hundreds of biennial nominations are duly, if not hastily, confirmed. In a period of 15 legislative days in the regular session of the Sixty-fifth Legislature, the Senate consented to a total of 622 executive nominations affecting 209 boards, advisory councils, and university regents. In addition, 35 judicial nominees and three district attorney nominees, affecting 37 different courts, were consented to.[24] Even at this pace the 140-day session ended with scores of nominations yet to be confirmed.

Thus, the patronage system, while undergirding the governor's influence and authority, also provides formal, legitimate, and direct points of *access* and communication between the dominant interests and the state capitol. No thorough empirical studies exist of the number and types of corporate and geographic interests which have built this system of *direct interest representation* in state government.[25] One judgment is that a loose alliance of affluent economic groups comprise the pressure system in Texas.[26] Tending to substantiate this conclusion is the report that in 1969 more than 100 members of the Texas Research League, generally acknowledged to constitute the business elite of the state, were serving as gubernatorial appointees on state boards and commissions.[27] There is no reason to believe that the relationship has changed.

The ideal of popular democratic control of government, particularly of bureaucratic structures and processes, is difficult to achieve in any environment. As in most state bureaucracies, each major agency tends to operate as a somewhat autonomous subgovernment supported by dedicated revenues, defended by influential legislators and powerful lobbyists, and closely associated with its functional counterpart in local and national governments. More study is needed of the Texas interest-group system, appointive processes, and backgrounds and values of nominees to know just how narrow a complex of interests exercises dominant influence in the policy process. We do know that the dominant values of the political culture in the larger political community come to be pervasive throughout the halls of government. And we have seen major deficiencies of the input structure, including limited political participation, low levels of voter turnout, disintegrated nomination processes, and noncompetitive elections. Direct interest representation in Texas state administration is so strongly entrenched—and the benefits apparently so great—that lengthy sessions of the legislature (until recently, an amateur body) have not been considered essential by many national and state interests.

THE CITIZEN GOVERNMENT MODEL

The term, *citizen government* model, is how we characterize an administrative system which features a network of direct interest representation and informal arrangements which tie the administrative branch to the other parts of the political system and which generates supports for the regime and its values. As we have seen, the model thrives on a patronage system of influence from gubernatorial appointments to administrative and judicial positions. The patronage system is supported by other, mainly informal practices, such as patterns of cooption, and by some salient features of the political institutional system, such as brief legislative sessions, a fragmented, open primary nomination system, and noncompetitive elections.

The notion of full-time, direct interest representation in the administrative and judicial branches is presented schematically in Figure 6–2. Note the linkages to (1) recruitment, nomination, and electoral activities (for legislators, governor, other elective executives, the lieutenant governor, and judges) and (2) the part-time legislature. Note also the role of legislative presiding officers (speaker and lieutenant governor) and the governor as brokers between dominant economic elites and state government. To keep the model simple to show the main lines of relationships, part-time relations between the governor and the legislative branch and its officers are not illustrated.

Officials on the dominant boards and commissions, elective executives, and judges are not ordinary citizens, either in their socioeconomic status or in their public service priorities. That is why the term, "citizen government," is in quotation marks. The "citizen government" model probably means elitist patterns of domination of policymaking, while giving the appearance of embracing (1) the notion of wide participation

194

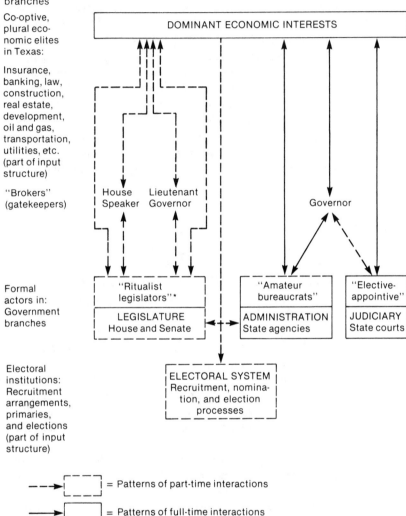

FIGURE 6–2

Direct, full-time interest representation in Texas administrative and judicial branches

Co-optive, plural economic elites in Texas:

Insurance, banking, law, construction, real estate, development, oil and gas, transportation, utilities, etc. (part of input structure)

"Brokers" (gatekeepers)

Formal actors in: Government branches

Electoral institutions: Recruitment arrangements, primaries, and elections (part of input structure)

DOMINANT ECONOMIC INTERESTS

House Speaker   Lieutenant Governor

Governor

"Ritualist legislators"*

LEGISLATURE
House and Senate

"Amateur bureaucrats"

ADMINISTRATION
State agencies

"Elective-appointive"

JUDICIARY
State courts

ELECTORAL SYSTEM
Recruitment, nomination, and election processes

- - - ▶ = Patterns of part-time interactions

⎯⎯▶ = Patterns of full-time interactions

* See *Legislative roles and norms*, Chapter 4.

in state government and (2) the pluralist idea of the existence of a large number of competitive and countervailing interest groups.[28]

"Citizen government" seems to be useful in several respects to undergird the bias of economic elites for small government and the penchant of the mass of people for democratic symbolism. It leaves the impression that

Government is simple enough to be run by any citizen,

The mass of people and their interests are well represented in government by a system of competitive and countervailing groups, and

Small, part-time, parsimonious government is all that is needed in Texas.

What are the political consequences? They are not entirely consistent with the populist idea of "every man a king," the pluralist ideal of competition among groups, or democratic ideals of popular representation. The system

Reinforces elitist decision-making structures by direct formal representation of dominant economic interests in administration;

Strengthens tendencies toward autonomous administrative units independent of gubernatorial and legislative direction, supervision, and oversight;

Enhances the importance of administration, in its priorities, spending levels, and day-to-day implementation of programs, while downgrading decision-making in the legislature (a part-time institution); and

Reinforces tendencies toward small government, the status quo, and noninnovative public programs in Texas.

If all this is so, the system can be faulted not so much on grounds that it is weak, disintegrated, or "an administrative jungle." More justifiable concerns probably lie in the following areas:

How strong is the dominant interest system as compared with other input arrangements?

How vital are input structures in transmitting others' demands and supports?

Do informal administrative processes operate in congruence with democratic theory?

What are the levels of public services, and are public needs being met by the policy system?

Are government processes understood by the average citizen?

THE OFFICE OF THE GOVERNOR

Staff organization

Major management resources of the governor lie in the organization, specialization, and use of modern staff. As the intimate "official family" of the governor, the staff can be organized in any manner and assigned duties at the discretion of the chief executive. Not needing confirmation by the Texas Senate and lacking ties to other institutions, staff personnel are ordinarily free of strong countervailing loyalties to interest groups, administrative agencies, and the legislature. They are placed beyond the realm of regular legislative oversight of administration, and most chief executives claim some degree of executive privilege in the confidentiality of their official duties.

Heading the Office of the Governor is the governor's executive assistant. For more than two decades, the staff has had two functionally separate, but interdependent, parts, a political section headed by several administrative assistants and a program development section headed by program directors.[29]

Political section Located in this section are approximately 50 persons who constitute the governor's top political advisors and their staffs. Administrative assistants handle the governor's routine political and administrative tasks in press and public relations, legal matters, legislative liaison, appointments, itinerary, clemency and parole matters, military affairs, and liaison with administrative officers, including relations with the Office of the Secretary of State on rendition of fugitives from justice. Included also are special assignments involving nonroutine matters. Much continuity of personnel exists in this section, unlike in many other states, because of the ideological and partisan affinity of the succession of conservatives who are elected governor in Texas.

Program development section In this section are approximately 400 persons who are employed not so much for their loyalty to the governor or for concern with efficient, courteous contacts with the public but on the basis of a large variety of professional and technical skills and qualifications. (Added to this group are approximately 250 employees in the Department of Community Affairs.)[30]

This section of the staff has become, since the administration of Governor Price Daniel, Sr., 1957–1963, rather highly institutionalized, with much continuity in personnel, programs, and activities. Although succeeding chief executives have tended to shape the section to their needs, the basic structure has remained the same. Component parts of the program development section are

Budget and Planning Office

Office of Criminal Justice Planning

Committee on Aging

Personnel and Employment Opportunity Office

Office of Migrant Affairs

Greater South Texas Cultural Basin Committee

Film Commission

Energy Office

Coordinating Office for the Visually Handicapped

Commission on Physical Fitness

Activities of the more important of these executive staff agencies are sketched in the next section.

Policy leadership and management

The governor is the state's chief planning officer empowered to provide policy leadership. The governor's Budget and Planning Office aids and coordinates planning activities of substate councils of governments (COGs),[31] acts as central clearing house for local government project requests in many federally aided programs, promulgates rules for federal-local cooperation, and creates a series of state interagency councils to facilitate planning, coordination, and supervision of state services.[32]

State-level interagency planning councils garner much of the information about the needs of Texas in specific program areas. Chaired by the governor, and most of them staffed by the Office of Budget and Planning, the interagency councils promote a degree of programmatic consolidation at both state and local levels in an otherwise highly disintegrated state administrative structure.

Research, statistical coordination, and policy analysis The Budget and Planning Office, along with the Department of Community Affairs, undertakes research and data collection projects, which provide to both state and local governments information on such subjects as manpower resources, health care, environmental problems, and criminal justice. The Department of Community Affairs collects, publishes, and disseminates data on more technical subjects, such as local finance, employment systems, housing conditions, poverty, demographic characteristics, and land-use patterns. Planning staff in the Committee on Aging, Criminal Justice Council, the Energy Office, and interagency councils plan, coordinate, and evaluate programs in particular target areas. Useful in planning and assessing the economic impacts of selected government economic transactions, public policies, and government programs is the model of the Texas economy which has been developed. The Budget and Planning Office prepares and assesses the data in terms of program costs and alternatives, for the purpose of programmatic recommendations to the governor and the political staff section.[33]

Control of federal programs The Office of the Governor has become the chief channel of federal funds for federal, state, and local programs. Planning programs, requesting funds, and coordinating federal projects, the governor's "federal systems officer role"[34] provides the governorship additional resources to meet constituency and consumer demands, some control over fragmented programs, and legitimacy to act in a larger policy capacity. Liaison with the national government is provided by the Texas Office of State-Federal Relations. Consisting of 17 employees, most of whom are located in Washington, D.C., this agency works for Texas interests in the capital, providing federal agencies and the Congress with information about programs, problems, preferences, and policies in Texas.

Politically, the governor's role as "federal systems officer" has meant jobs, services, and programs to key supporters, state and local interest groups, and units of local government. Administratively, contrary to the board and commission structural arrangement, the Department of Community Affairs facilitates delivery of services to constituents in such policy areas and programs as community development and planning, drug abuse, public employment, early childhood development, housing, antipoverty, and model cities. Thus, the governor, if he or she so desires, is assured of a positive, continuous involvement and influence in these programmatic areas. Annual reports of all federal funds received, with their intended usage, are made by the Budget and Planning Office to the legislature for review and use by the appropriations committees.

The governor's staff is seen as the really crucial element in developing the strength of the governor in state administration.[35]

Gubernatorial big government

The most obvious and startling changes in the Office of the Governor in the past ten years have been in the increase in personnel,[36] the amount of money budgeted for the Office, and the portion of federal financing. In the 1970s, total funds increased nearly fourfold, while the portion of federal moneys averaged about 85 percent annually. If the impact of the staff depends upon the governor's political leadership and effective utilization of personnel, the wherewithal comes from the national government! In addition to funding of the Office of the Governor, a large portion of federal grants to state agencies and local governments ($2.7 billions in 1979) are channeled through the Office.

In a situation filled with irony, a huge, oversized staff—a gubernatorial big government—exists in a regime which values small government. In addition to the impact of federal aid and national programmatic standards, several other interacting environmental, structural, political,[37] and personal factors have conspired to bring about this situation:[38]

> *Size of state.* Texas ranks third in population and second in geographic area.
>
> *Administrative disintegration.* Because executive agencies are not

organized around broad and coordinated functions, the governor needs interagency staff.

New functional categories. As new concerns arise or are forced by national initiatives, Texas agencies, traditionally organized, have newer programs tacked on. Planning and coordinating staffs are necessary for state and local governments to accept federal moneys. The complexity of government services increases technical staffing.

Protective reaction of state elites. Frightened by national initiatives in policymaking and by grants for social services to urban elements, the state's conservative leadership moved to enlarge and strengthen the *intermediary position* of the governor between national and local governments.[39] This movement, in large measure national in scope, also included shifts in programmatic emphases (through bloc grants, for example, in criminal justice) to other groups.

Rising public expectations. The increasing complexity of social problems and the high visibility achieved by the governor through the mass media make the chief executive more and more a focus of public expectations and demands. Responses included enlarged staffs, altered agendas, and extra opportunities for policy initiatives.

Governor's style and personal interests. A governor attuned to public relations will increase his or her political staff and delegate functions to programmatic aides. Current interests and projects of the governor, to the extent that they are not sidetracked by "crisis" situations,[40] will also shape staff organization and intervention of the governor in operations. In the Briscoe administration, adjustment of the state allocation of moneys to local school districts became a major concern, and the Governor's Office of Education Resources (GOER) was established to work, not too successfully, on a revised formula.

Broad social and economic change. Urbanization, industrialization, increase in exportable capital, population mobility, increase in service industries, and great technological growth mark broad economic and social change in the past four decades in Texas. In this environment, the most hardened advocates of laissez faire see advantages in the use and control of public power for the ends of economic development and prevention of regulation of private economic activity. The current Texas establishment "grew out of the New Deal, preserving the reliance of business upon government, but dispensing with the social concern that grew out of the Depression."[41] Viewing government as a positive tool for creating "a favorable climate for business," elites have moved a step away from a traditionalistic emphasis upon an extremely small role for government. The chief executive has benefited enormously from these changes.[42]

PERSONNEL ADMINISTRATION

Small government–public employment in Texas

Government employment at state and local levels is one of the fastest growing sectors of the labor market, having doubled in the past decade. Texas public employment, on the other hand, is relatively small (only 4.9 percent of the state's population, estimated at nearly 12.5 million persons). Further, it has experienced only one half the growth rate of all the states. Total U.S. state-local employment is about 13 percent of the national work force, while Texas state-local employees constitute about 11 percent of the Texas work force.

Another characteristic of public employment in Texas is the comparatively large number of employees of local governments. See Table 6–6. While Texas ranks 39th among the states in state personnel, it ranks 15th in local employees. Heavy employment in education exists at both local (school district) and state levels. Note that in state employment, total personnel, exclusive of college and university staffs and employees, is only 93,558, giving Texas a rank of 44th among the 50 states!

TABLE 6–6
Public employment in Texas

Level of government	Number of employees	Number/10,000 population	Texas rank among states*
Federal (civilians)	149,638	120	4
State	159,243	128	39
Education†	65,685		
General control‡	1,494		
All other areas	92,064	75	44
Local	446,456	358	15
School districts	266,882		
Municipalities	111,643		
Counties	52,697		
Special districts	15,234		

* Rank is in full-time equivalent employees, except federal, which is in total number of civilian employees.

† Includes higher educational instructional, 19,668; higher educational non-instructional, 43,353; state agency employees, 1,294; and other state educational personnel, 2,370.

‡ Class includes legislators, judges, and central staff agency employees of state government.

Source: U.S. Department of Commerce, Bureau of the Census, *Public Employment in 1976* (Washington, D.C.: U.S. Government Printing Office, 1977).

State employment figures spell "small and negative government" in Texas. In Chapter 10 we shall see the fiscal aspects of this phenomenon in the state's taxation and expenditure figures. We have suggested in preceding chapters that the state's relatively low per capita wealth (a ranking 33d among the states) does not fully explain the presence of extremely small government.[43]

Classes of state employees

Working at the state level are 1,294 nonteacher employees of the state agencies of education and 92,064 noneducation public personnel. These 93,358 state workers occupy two major employment and salary categories:[44]

Classified employees. A little more than 50 percent occupy the 1,300 positions listed in the current appropriations measure and are paid annual salaries which are provided in the accompanying salary schedule. See Table 6–7. These classified employees have two subclasses

TABLE 6–7
Classification salary schedule, fiscal 1979

Salary group	Salary steps							
	1	2	3	4	5	6	7	8
2	6624	6852	7080	7320	7560	7812	8076	8352
3	7080	7320	7560	7812	8076	8352	8628	8916
4	7560	7812	8076	8352	8628	8916	9216	9528
5	8076	8352	8628	8916	9216	9528	9840	10176
6	8628	8916	9216	9528	9840	10176	10512	10872
7	9216	9528	9840	10176	10512	10872	11232	11616
8	9840	10176	10512	10872	11232	11616	12000	12408
9	10512	10872	11232	11616	12000	12408	12816	13248
10	11232	11616	12000	12408	12816	13248	13692	14148
11	12000	12408	12816	13248	13692	14148	14628	15108
12	12816	13248	13692	14148	14628	15108	15624	16140
13	13692	14148	14628	15108	15624	16140	16692	17244
14	14628	15108	15624	16140	16692	17244	17832	18420
15	15624	16140	16692	17244	17832	18420	19044	19668
16	16692	17244	17832	18420	19044	19668	20340	21000
17	17832	18420	19044	19668	20340	21000	21720	22428
18	19668	20340	21000	21720	22428	23196	23952	24768
19	21000	21720	22428	23196	23952	24768	25608	26448
20	22428	23196	23952	24768	25608	26448	27348	28248
21	23952	24768	25608	26448	27348	28248	29208	30168

Source: Texas Legislature, *Supplement to House Journal,* Text of Conference Committee Report, H. B. 510, 65th Leg., Reg. Sess., May 24, 1977, V-22.

merit system employees and
spoils system employees (the larger group).

Exempted employees. Four subgroups of noneducation personnel are
exempted from the classified system. (These are listed from largest
to smallest group.)

Hourly wage earners. Most are maintenance personnel and technicians and full-time employees of the Texas Department of Highways and Public Transportation. Uniformity of wages is attempted
by having wages per year approximate annual salaries paid certain lower paid salary groups in the classified system.

Miscellaneous employees. These are personnel paid entirely from
federal moneys, employees of semiautonomous agencies,[45]
trainees, and part-time and temporary employees, including consultants paid by fees.

Top administrative and professional personnel. Officials appointed by the governor, directors of agencies, under boards and
commissions, and professional groups, such as medical doctors,
are prominent in this subclass. Salaries are much higher than the
top range of the classified system and are commonly set by the
legislature as line item positions in the appropriations bill. This
subcategory also includes positions excluded by executive order
of the governor.

General control personnel. This small subclass is comprised of
legislators, judges, central staff agency employees, and elective
executive officials.

Personnel classification structure

The state's classification structure imposes a degree of uniformity
among agencies in (1) the classification of positions and (2) the salaries
of personnel filling these classified positions. Before enactment of the
Position Classification Act in 1961, rates of pay and job classification
systems varied from agency to agency, even among merit system employees. The current appropriations measure contains the applicable
list of 1300 classified positions and an accompanying salary schedule.
See Table 6–7. The bill contains in addition much detail in such matters
as reclassification, political activity, holidays, vacations, hiring policies,
travel on official business, acceptance of gifts, use of alcoholic beverages on the job, authorization of pay telephones, and annual reporting.

Job titles (not shown in Table 6–7) are matched to the salary groups,
on a scale of 2 through 21. Within each of the 20 salary groups are eight
salary steps. For example, state employees whose job titles and descrip-
tions place them in Salary Group 2, Step 1 receive (fiscal year 1979) an

annual salary of $6,624, or $552 per month, the lowest salary in the classified system. Highest salaried personnel receive $2,514 per month. As we have seen, salaries of top administrative personnel and certain professional and technical personnel are paid at rates substantially higher than employees in the top classified positions. Agency heads in 1979, for example, were paid an average of about $40,000 annually, with constitutional department heads, such as the attorney general, receiving $45,200. Hourly wage personnel, while exempted from legislative classification schedule, are usually the subject of agency classification and pay schedules. Part-time and temporary workers may be paid at rates substantially below the beginning salaries in the classified system.

Personnel management structure

No central personnel agency The Texas personnel management system contains no central personnel agency. Like administrative practices in general, the system is decentralized and disintegrated. Further, public personnel management, like most other management operations, is controlled by legislative and other actors, the governor having authority only in marginal matters and in concert with other actors.

The following officials hold personnel management responsibilities:

Legislative Budget Board, chiefly responsible for the appropriations bill, which contains personnel classification, pay schedule, and other details about personnel matters.

Classification Officer, makes salary recommendations for the appropriations bill and gives agency personnel officers limited assistance and advice about personnel matters. (The Classification Officer is an official appointed by the state auditor with approval of the Legislative Audit Committee. *See below.*)

Attorney General, issues, upon request, advisory opinions on interpretation, application, and constitutionality of personnel policies.

Comptroller of Public Accounts, maintains payroll system, issues state warrants, and affects personnel policy by enforcing compliance of agencies with basic policies involving payment of salaries.

Legislative Audit Committee, has authority to reclassify personnel positions. Reclassifications can mean additional pay raises within an agency and closer adherence to the principle of "equal pay for equal work." (The Legislative Audit Committee is a joint legislative committee of the legislative presiding officers, chairpersons of revenue and appropriations committees, and other members.)

Governor, has authority to exempt positions, by executive order, from the classification schedule, thereby correcting errors in the appropriations bill, providing new positions, and complying with federal and state equal employment opportunity plans. In addition to monitoring agency affirmative action plans, the Governor's Personnel and Employment Opportunity Office provides technical assistance in personnel management practices.

Agency heads and personnel officers, design and administer personnel systems and affirmative action plans.

Personnel system variation among agencies State personnel policies are promulgated in several statutes and in each general appropriations bill. Oftentimes, statutory language is not consistent among legislative enactments. Agency heads and personnel officers treat the Classification Act of 1961 and statutory amplifications only as *guidelines,* with the result that wide variation exists among agency personnel practices and systems and no certainty even that general qualification requirements for personnel are followed. Legislative review of personnel practices is ordinarily only cursory, more often related to saving money and cutting back positions than with unified, sound personnel management practices.[46]

Agency centralization If state personnel standards, activities, and practices are scattered and not uniform among the agencies, personnel authority within each agency is highly centralized in the director of the agency. Recruitment, screening and testing, hiring, promotions, development and administration of training programs, grievances, counseling, dismissals, and personnel records and files are all centralized in the agency staff for personnel, if not in the executive director of the agency. Most agencies operate under the spoils system, and many of them have less than standardized recruiting and hiring practices, promotion policies, and tenure and retention standards.

The merit system

Texas' partial merit system Another structural characteristic is a partial merit system. About one third of the classified personnel are in the merit system, which was created in 1940 as a response to federal requirements. Not all federal grant programs are required to use merit personnel. In fact, only ten administrative units are under the merit system. See Table 6–8. While in some of these agencies all personnel must be covered, in others only a fraction of total employees are under the merit system. Further, all Texas agencies which receive and dispense federal funds are not required to participate. Altogether, the ten covered units employ 50,000 persons; approximately 17,000 are merit system employees.

Merit System Council The Texas merit system is administered by the Merit System Council, a three-person, gubernatorially appointed,

TABLE 6-8
Texas agencies with employees covered by the merit system

Texas Employment Commission
Department of Health
Department of Public Welfare
Department of Mental Health and Mental Retardation
Air Control Board
Surplus Property Agency
Texas Commission on Alcoholism
Governor's Committee on Aging
Drug Abuse Division of the Department of Community Affairs
Division of Disaster Emergency Services
    in the Department of Public Safety

Source: *Handbook of Governments in Texas.*

nonsalaried board, the members of which are recommended by the three members of the Texas Employment Commission. One shortcoming is that the council and the merit system are financed by merit system agencies, which naturally wish to keep costs as low as possible. Another drawback is operation of the system under a joint agreement of member agencies with scarcely any oversight to assure compliance with the terms of the agreement.

Shortcomings of merit system operation   In the ideal, important differences exist between merit system operations and a spoils system. In practice, recruiting is neglected, tests do not tap necessary qualifications, on-the-job requirements are relaxed, and high turnover levels result from failure to adhere to salary, promotion, and tenure policies. In salary administration, for example, the merit system works well only in the Texas Employment Commission, where personnel salaries are spread across the salary step structure.[47]

But the system is working better than in nonmerit employment, where employees cluster largely in salary Steps 1 and 2 of the various salary groups. The reason for this is frequent legislative pay raises, with failure of the legislature to authorize merit raises. The problem comes about in this manner. When a legislative pay raise is voted, a new salary schedule is constructed by dropping the first or second steps in all salary groups and adding one or two new columns (Steps 1 and 2) to the left. Refer to Table 6-7. Thus, all employees in Step 3 in one biennium find themselves in either steps 1 or 2 in the new schedule (depending upon the size of the pay raise). Granting authority for supplementary pay raises would allow personnel officers to move their employees across the steps. "Merit increases require authorization in appropriations bills, and the legislature has provided only sporadically for such increases."[48] In the absence of this authority, Texas nonmerit personnel become impacted in lower pay steps. As we shall see in the next section, other conditions contribute to this problem.

Personnel problems

Impaction of personnel in lower pay steps   As we have seen, no administrative mechanism provides progression of nonmerit employees along salary Steps 1 through 8, with the result that two thirds of classified personnel are set in the first two steps. Contributing to this condition are hiring only in Step 1, high turnover, and little utilization of longevity pay increases. Poor salary administration naturally produces great injustices, which may have a devastating effect on morale and retention rates.

Personnel turnover   Besides other adverse effects, turnover is very expensive. Replacements must be recruited and trained. Studies demonstrate a turnover of 25 percent annually, with a resulting tenure of less than five years among the bottom 50 percent of permanent employees.[49]

Salary levels have increased substantially in recent years, annual increases having been voted in every biennial legislative session since 1965. As a result, Texas ranks 27th among the states in the average earnings of full-time state employees.[50] Only one in five resignees in one recent year gave inadequate salary as the primary reason for leaving public service, pointing to the existence of other detrimental influences on retention.[51]

Employee-employer relations   While Texas public employees at all levels have the right to join unions or other organizations,[52] Texas has "the most inclusive and severe strike ban of any state."[53] And only a peculiar kind of collective bargaining *by employees* is permitted, for the law allows no organization or union to act as bargaining agent of employees. Any collective bargaining contracts are void.[54]

Yet, unionization and de facto bargaining are occurring in Texas' major cities. Unionization of municipal employees is extensive but not dominant. Organizational representation in grievance procedures are not prohibited, and some local governments use their own negotiating procedures by ordinance or by informal or ad hoc action. Results of these discussions and negotiations are stated in "municipal working conditions" papers, but not in signed contracts. When discussions break down between city officials and sanitation workers, transit employees, firemen, or policemen, strikes and sick-ins often occur. Some militant local employees have been able to force public referenda in municipalities to gain increased wages or reduced hours.[55]

In its *legal* posture, Texas moved in 1973 from "avoidance and silence" concerning methods of resolving worker-management disputes to special consideration for fire-fighters and police. The Fire and Police Employee Relations Act guarantees collective bargaining, arbitration procedures, and judicial remedies for these two classes of municipal employees, if approved in local option elections. But the local referendum, a feature in statutory law unique to Texas in labor relations, has been a costly bar. Bitterly fought, it has been overcome in only a few municipalities.[56] Meanwhile, unionization grows apace and ad hoc bargaining arrangements continue.

On the state level, public employees are far less militant, unionization has been largely unsuccessful, and the Texas Public Employees Association (TPEA) has been committed to narrow statutory goals through lobbying efforts with the legislature and administrative management. The TPEA, which has grown in recent years to 40,000 members, is being challenged by more militant employee organizations and by its more activist membership. In a recent firing of the TPEA executive director by the TPEA board, the deposed director of seven years attributed his dismissal to his pursuit of two legislative goals desired by TPEA membership: (1) a central personnel agency with authority to set uniform personnel policies and regulations and (2) special grievance procedures for complaints against supervisors, with TPEA assistance to an employee in such proceedings. It was reported that state agency heads saw the proposals as threats to their authority in personnel matters. "Part of the conflict," one source reported, "is that the [TPEA] board has always been dominated by agency upper echelon folks, while the membership is comprised of working stiffs."[57]

Equal employment opportunity   Texas legislation stating the principle of equal employment opportunity without regard to race, religion, color, or national origin dates from 1967, and it was amended in 1971 to include women. Not until 1973, however, was affirmative action required, and this under pressure from federal agencies and from urban minority legislators elected from Texas districts produced by federal judicial reapportionment decisions. After a false start,[58] affirmative action was placed in the Office of the Governor in the Personnel and Employment Opportunity Office, which is charged with reviewing, approving, monitoring, and evaluating the plans of all state agencies. Operations have been hampered by the absence of a central data and personnel information system. Manpower needs, turnover data, and the like were maintained, if at all, on the agency level, except for scattered information. As a consequence, the Personnel and Employment Opportunity Office has had to establish a central data system in order to compile recruiting information on minority and women and to coordinate aggregation of data for reporting to federal agencies.

Four major statistical reports of the Texas Legislative Council since 1969 tell us what we know about (1) employment by sex, ethnic origin, and race and (2) salary and occupational statification in the state bureaucracy.[59] Looking at total state employment, the surveys indicate a decided decrease in the proportion of males, from 60.7 percent to 51.8 percent. Among ethnic groups, black males are still the object of sexist bias, having declined from 43.4 percent in 1968 to 34.7 percent in 1976 of total black employment. See Table 6–9. Hispanic females, on the other hand, have made the greatest gains in female employment, moving from one third to one half of their ethnic group.

A bleaker picture for all Hispanic employees, male and female, is revealed in Table 6–10. Although substantial gains have been made, to 12.9 percent of state employment in 1976, Hispanics constitute about 19 percent of Texas' total population. Blacks, on the other hand, come close in state employment (11 percent in 1976) to approximating their proportion of the total population of Texas. But percentage figures obscure the fact that the net employment gain for blacks from 1968 to 1976 was only 6,584 persons (exclusive of employees in the state's colleges and universities), while that of Hispanics was only 6,611 additional employees.[60]

Perhaps a better estimate of whether affirmative action programs are working is seen in salary and occupational data. Since 1968, salary increases have gone disproportionately to white males so that median salaries of this group is from $2,233 to $4,739 higher than for any other group.[61] See Table 6–11. Acute wage differentials between male and female employees are revealed also in the number and percentage who receive $13,000 or more in annual salaries. Only 3.6 percent of black and Hispanic females draw the highest salaries. Among whites, more than three times as many male employees as white female employees are top-salaried.

TABLE 6–9
Proportion of males and females in ethnic groups in state employment

	1968		1972		1974		1976	
	M	F	M	F	M	F	M	F
Whites	62.1%	38.9%	61.4%	38.6%	59.4%	40.6%	54.5%	45.5%
Blacks	43.4	56.6	38.1	61.9	36.3	63.7	34.7	65.3
Hispanics	67.9	32.1	57.1	42.9	55.5	44.5	50.7	49.3
Other	50.4	49.6	64.6	35.4	47.5	52.5	50.9	49.1
All groups	60.7	39.3	58.7	41.3	56.8	43.2	51.8	48.2

Source: Texas Legislative Council, *Employment in State Government,* Staff Reports 60–4, 62–1, 63–1, and 64–1 (Austin: Texas Legislative Council, January 1969, 1973, 1975, and 1977).

TABLE 6–10
Ethnic groups as percent of state employment

	Years			
Groups	1968	1972	1974	1976
Whites	82.9%	79.9%	79.2%	75.6%
Blacks	9.2	10.1	8.8	11.0
Hispanics	7.8	9.0	11.6	12.9
Other	0.1	1.0	0.4	0.5

Source: Texas Legislative Council, *Employment in State Government,* Staff Reports 60–4, 62–1, 63–1, and 64–1 (Austin: Texas Legislative Council, January 1969, 1973, 1975, and 1977).

While the percentage of blacks and Hispanics receiving top salaries is low, significant gains have been made since 1968. In 1968, only 0.27 percent of blacks and 0.6 percent of Hispanics received more than $9,215 annually. In 1976, 4.9 percent of blacks and 9.4 percent of Hispanics made $13,000 or more annually. In contrast, however, 25.5 percent of white employees were paid top salaries.

Reflecting salary data, the modal occupational category of all males except blacks is professionals. Black males are still heavily impacted where they were in 1968, in service/maintenance jobs. All women, too, except black women, are heavily concentrated now as in 1968 in office and clerical jobs. Black women in 1968, heavily impacted in personal and domestic service work, have moved up in large numbers to paraprofessional positions, such as library assistants, police auxiliary personnel, research assistants, medical aides, home health aides, and child support workers.

Affirmative action programs are working very slowly. Further, results are very uneven across agencies because of the wide variety in quality of agency plans and difficulties of monitoring and enforcement in a highly fractionalized administrative structure. With imaginative and force-

TABLE 6–11

State employees by ethnic group and sex: Number with high salaries and median salary and modal occupational category

Ethnic groups	Number in group	Salaries of $13,000 plus		Median salary	Modal occupation*
		Number	Percent of total		
Whites					
Males	35,743	13,342	37.3	$11,699	2
Females	29,824	3,357	11.3	8,160	6
Blacks					
Males	3,289	247	7.5	7,646	8
Females	6,200	222	3.6	6,960	5
Hispanics					
Males	5,677	853	15.0	9,466	2
Females	5,519	196	3.6	7,333	6
Other					
Males	231	98	42.4	11,736	2
Females	223	33	14.8	7,644	2

* The mode is simply the category which contains the largest number of employees. The occupational categories are as follows:
1. Officials and administrators
2. Professionals
3. Technicians
4. Protective service (security) workers
5. Paraprofessionals
6. Office and clerical workers
7. Skilled craft workers
8. Service/maintenance employees

Source: Texas Legislative Council, *Employment in State Government,* Staff Report No. 64–1 (Austin: Texas Legislative Council, January 1977).

ful efforts in the Office of the Governor, equal employment practices should be realized in time.

CONCLUSIONS

Most of the daily work of state government is done by bureaucrats, usually dedicated public officials who carry out state programs and have regular contacts with the state's citizens. Our analysis of state administration in Texas indicates that:

1. Administrative officials are not mere ciphers, mechanically going through the motions of carrying out policies fully dictated elsewhere. While the central function of administrators is to implement government programs, bureaucrats engage continuously in a range of activities which are intended to influence policy, to initiate and change policy, and to adjudicate political differences.

2. Texas administration has as its main structural characteristic multi-member boards or commissions. There are few state agencies which do not have so-called independent boards superimposed over them. Members of these governing boards have long, staggered terms and are not formally removable by the governor; so the chief executive has scant ability to supervise the top officials of the state administration.

3. The regulatory authority of state administrative agencies is weak because of multiple agency responsibilities, overlapping authority, co-optation of board members by the regulated agencies, the fee system of agency funding, and the lack of oversight of agency operations by the legislature.

4. Although the formal control which can be exercised by the governor over the administration is limited, his political influence over the system is considerable. He can use his appointment power to influence the course of decision-making by governing boards. His patronage not only builds his own influence and authority but also permits a means of access to the administration by the dominant economic and social elites in the state, which strengthens decision-making by the few. The capacity of the governor to exert an influential presence in administration is also enhanced by the substantial staff of the Office of Governor, an important administrative unit in itself.

5. State administration in Texas is small in numbers of employees, heavily infected with political patronage, uncoordinated, and plagued by questionable employment conditions. Texas ranks 44th among the states in numbers in state employment (not counting university employees); a "spoils system" characterizes 80 percent of its state employees; there is no central personnel agency so that personnel practices vary widely among agencies; and there is high turnover among employees.

CHAPTER SEVEN

The courts, criminal justice, and civil liberties

The generality of men are naturally apt to be swayed
by fear rather than by reverence, and to refrain from evil
rather because of the punishment that it brings, than
because of its own foulness.

ARISTOTLE

THE TEXAS JUDICIARY

General Lawrence S. Ross, an Indian fighter who was later to become governor of Texas, was an important figure at the state's constitutional convention in 1875. Arguing a lost cause for a decent salary for state judges, Ross pointed out that "unjust and oppressive laws may be repealed, but unjust and oppressive judgments rendered in the laws, and affirmed in the higher courts are inrepealable and fixed and the luckless citizen is wronged without remedy and his wrongs do not even attract attention. . . ."[1] No doubt, Articles XV and I of the Texas Constitution, which established the state's court systems, have produced a long line of "wronged" citizens. Today, following the defeat of the revised constitution, there remains an antiquated, overloaded, and vastly inefficient judiciary.

Ideally, the functions of the courts should include the following: (1) the administration of criminal justice with full procedural safeguards resulting in a fair and speedy trial; (2) the impartial adjudication of civil controversies; (3) the efficient resolution of divergent legal claims of individuals and of government under law and equity by properly trained personnel; and (4) a minimum of overlapping jurisdiction and an equalization of court dockets, ensuring sufficient, not excessive, court financing. Even a cursory examination of the Judiciary Article shows that it falls *well* short of the ideal.

Structure of the courts

Under the Texas Constitution there are five levels of courts: (1) municipal courts and justice of the peace courts; (2) county courts; (3) district courts; (4) the courts of civil appeal; and (5) the supreme court and the courts of criminal appeals. Not surprisingly, the nature and judicial importance of each level can be evaluated in terms of the qualifications established for the judges:

Court	Methods of selection and qualifications
Municipal (two years)*	Elected or appointed either as required by the city charter (home-rule cities) or as determined by the governing body (general law cities).†
Justice of the Peace (four-year term)	Elected; qualified voter of the state.
County courts (four-year term)	Elected; be well informed in law of the state.
District courts (four-year term)	Elected; 25 years of age; citizen of the United States and the state; practicing lawyer or judge of a court, or both combined, for four years prior to election.
Courts of civil appeals (six-year term)	Elected; 35 years of age; citizen of the United States and the state; ten years service as practicing lawyer or judge of record or both.
Court of criminal appeals (six-year term)	Same as above.
Supreme Court of Texas (six-year term)	Same as above.

* Although the term of office was originally set at two years, a 1958 amendment permits any city or town to adopt four-year terms for all officers including judges. Moreover, in several home-rule cities, the term of office is unlimited depending on the designation of the governing body.

† In 1912, the Texas Constitution was amended to provide for home rule, stating that cities with populations over 5,000 might have their own charters; those under 5,000 are considered general law cities.

The inferior courts

Municipal courts Created by statute in 1899, these bodies were known as corporation courts until 1969. While there may be more than one court within the territorial limits of the city, only one judge serves on a given court and his or her qualifications are established by local law. The jurisdiction of municipal courts extends to criminal offenses in notation of local ordinances. These courts also have concurrent jurisdiction with the justice of the peace courts in those criminal cases—petty and misdemeanor—involving fines not in excess of $200.

Justice of the peace courts Article V, Section 18 of the Texas Constitution provides for the division of each county by the county commissioners court into no less than four or more than eight precincts. Such divisions must be made on the basis of population.[2] Within each precinct a justice of the peace is elected, except in those with a population of 8,000 or more, where two such justices are elected. Justice of the peace courts have both criminal and civil jurisdiction. The former extends to all criminal matters where the possible penalty or fine does not exceed $200. The latter includes all civil cases, not otherwise delegated to higher courts, where the amount in controversy is $200 or less. However, in 1978 the voters approved a constitutional amendment which authorizes the legislature to expand the jurisdiction of the courts in civil cases, concurrently with the county and district, where the amount in controversy exceeds $500 and does not exceed $1,000. Under Texas law, a person charged with a misdemeanor or involved in a civil case may request a jury trial in a justice of the peace court or any other trial court of the state. Such juries have only six members. Except as otherwise provided by law, civil cases can be appealed to the county court if the amount in controversy exceeds $20.

In recent years, the justice of the peace courts have been subjected to a great deal of criticism.[3] The primary thrust of such attacks has been aimed at the fact that the justices, who are not required to be lawyers, have relatively broad judicial discretion. They are recognized as magistrates and as such may conduct criminal investigations and hold preliminary hearings to determine whether the sufficiency of evidence warrants further criminal proceedings including indictment by a grand jury.[4] Moreover, except for the four most heavily populated counties (Harris, Dallas, Bexar, and Tarrant), the justice of the peace serves as coroner by holding inquests upon the occurrence of death in certain cases.[5] Finally, because of their civil authority, the justices of the peace serve as small claims judges, which is a very important function in urban areas. Indeed, when measured against the lack of established qualifications, the office of justice of the peace is quite powerful.

Partially in response to the criticisms leveled at the justice of the peace system, the legislature enacted laws requiring non-lawyer justices or those who had not served more than two terms to take 40 hours of legal training in a state-supported college or university within one year of assuming office, and thereafter 20 hours of such training annually.[6]

County courts Under the constitution and laws of the state, there are three general classifications of courts at the county level: (1) the regular county court; (2) specialized county courts; and (3) the county commissioners court. The county judge serves as the elected magistrate of the *regular county court.* In all but the largest counties, this court has a number of important functions. It has general probate jurisdiction over wills including the settlement, partition, and distribution of the estates of the deceased. The court can appoint guardians of, and transact all business for, minors, idiots, lunatics, and other persons who are legally incapable of managing their affairs, as well as for common drunkards.[7] In addition to the appeals reviewed from the justice of the peace courts, the regular county courts have *original* jurisdiction in all civil cases where the amount in controversy exceeds $200 but is not in excess of $500 and *concurrent* jurisdiction with the district court where the amount falls between $500 and $1,000 excluding suits for recovery of land. Moreover, the regular county courts have original criminal jurisdiction extending to misdemeanors when the fine imposed exceeds $200. These courts have the discretionary power to issue writs to enforce their jurisdiction.

In those counties with heavier populations concentrated in large urban areas, some of the functions of the county courts have been shifted to *specialized county courts* to assist in easing the heavy volume of litigation. Such courts include county courts at law, county criminal courts, and county probate courts.

Finally, the Constitution establishes administrative bodies with limited judicial powers, the *county commissioners court.* Known as county boards in other states, these courts have primarily quasi-legislative, quasi-administrative functions. The county commission is composed of a commissioner elected from each of four commission precincts within each county and the county judge.

District courts   Article V, Section 7 of the Texas Constitution designates that the district courts are the primary trial courts in the judicial system of the state. The legislature has the sole responsibility for the number of district courts and the geographic area over which they exert jurisdiction. At present there are 245 district courts, each serving at least one county, with one elected judge within the district. These courts have original civil jurisdiction of state suits attempting to recover penalties, forfeitures, and so on; divorce cases; slander and defamation suits for recovery of damages; controversies concerning property; contested elections; and "general control over executives, administrators, guardians, and minors as provided by law." The district courts also have appellate jurisdiction over those civil controversies appealed from the county courts, particularly in probate matters and supervisory control over the county commissioners court.

In addition to civil controversies, the district courts have original jurisdiction in cases of criminal felony and all misdemeanors involving official misconduct. They have the power to punish those guilty of contempt of court with a maximum fine of $100 and three days of imprisonment. In such cases, a jury of 12 members is provided; however, in civil litigation, the request for a jury must be made by the party to the suit who is willing to pay the jury fee. Texas employs the alternate juror system and in certain cases requires less than unanimous verdicts.

The district courts, as can be imagined, are terribly overworked. In the last ten years an additional 63 courts have been created and, while there has been some improvement in the total number of cases disposed of by the judges, the backlog of litigation has increased by 40 percent.[8] This increase has for the most part taken place in the 16 metropolitan counties where the population exceeds 100,000. By 1971, the average number of cases per judge in these counties had grown to 1,500 while the average annual load for judges in nonmetropolitan counties was only 765. Presently, 55 percent of the district courts are located in the urban counties but they dispose of approximately 70 percent of the cases filed. The situation is expected to become even more critical in the future, since some studies suggest that the yearly case load will increase by more than 50 percent by 1980.

The higher courts: A judicial Janus

Janus, to ancient Romans, was a two-faced god of gates and doors, who looked in different directions. This Roman god serves as an appropriate characterization of the higher courts of the state which consist of two divisions; one adjudicates solely civil cases, the other solely criminal. This system has proved to be so cumbersome, that virtually all of the various committees and groups having any input into the 64th Legislative Session advocated its abandonment in favor of a unified system. In fact, the proposed judiciary article was approved by the requisite two-thirds vote of the convention members, mandating this scheme for unification; however, such revision will obviously not take place in the near future.

Courts of civil appeals These are intermediate courts of appellate jurisdiction. The state is divided into 14 supreme judicial districts with a court in each. Presently the courts are located in Amarillo, Austin, Beaumont, Corpus Christi, Dallas, Eastland, El Paso, Fort Worth, Houston (2), San Antonio, Texarkana, Tyler, and Waco. A panel of three judges—a chief judge and two associate justices—serves on each court with six year overlapping terms, as elected by the voters of the district. The number of judges sitting on these collegial panels is now subject to change since the approval by the voters of a 1978 constitutional amendment which permits the legislature to increase the number, to permit a court of appeals to sit in sections, and to require a concurrence of a majority of justices to decide a case. As provided by the state Constitution (Article V, Section 6), the courts of civil appeal may review any civil case, except for probate matters, from the inferior courts where the amount in controversy exceeds $200. Moreover, they have jurisdiction over challenges to the validity of civil statutes including revenue laws. Finally, these courts are empowered to review all appeals involving cases of slander, divorce, contested elections and interlocutory orders as provided by law.

The Texas court of criminal appeals Given the Janus-like structure of the state courts, it could be said that this court serves as the supreme court for criminal appeals. Until 1977, the court was composed of five justices (with the assistance of two commissioners), elected statewide, with six-year overlapping terms. In that year, however, the voters approved a constitutional amendment which changed the court in the following ways: (1) it increased the number of justices from five to nine; (2) it allows the court to subdivide into three separate three-membered panels, each of which would hear and decide different cases; and, (3) the only time that the court would have to act as a single body of nine members—instead of three separate courts—would be to hear appeals involving capital punishment. As in the past, the court has appellate jurisdiction in all cases where the fine exceeds $100.

For years the Court of Criminal Appeals has been particularly overloaded with casework, primarily because of two factors. First, the lower intermediate appellate courts do not have criminal jurisdiction and therefore appeals are made directly from the district and county courts. Second, Article 44.24 of the Code of Criminal Procedure requires the court deliver a written opinion in every case that it adjudicates so that by 1971 each justice was writing an average of 212 opinions during the term.[9] Despite the fact that the court has had the assistance of two commissioners since 1971, which in fact made it a seven-member tribunal, the individual caseload remains much greater than that of the other appellate courts. It is hoped that the 1977 amendment will alleviate this critical situation.

The Supreme Court of Texas The court is the highest court for civil appeals in the state. The nine member tribunal has appellate jurisdiction in all civil controversies except those in which, by law, a determination by the lower appellate court is final: legal variances, substantive errors or disagreements over questions of law arising from the courts of civil appeal, controversies involving the construction or validity of statutes or revenue provisions of the state, and cases in which the Railroad Commission is a party. Moreover, the legislature has given the supreme court a certain amount of policy-making authority, primarily with respect to the operations of the state bar.

Other legal agencies Included in this category are those offices or groups invested with varying degrees of responsibility by either statutory or constitutional mandate.[10] The constitution created the positions *notary public* and the *State Judicial Qualifications Commission.* Notaries public are appointed by the secretary of state for a term of two years and have "the same authority to take acknowledgments of proofs of written instruments, protest instruments . . . administer oaths and take depositions, as is now . . . conferred by law upon county clerks."[11] The only established qualifications for the position of notary are that the person must be a citizen of the state, a business owner, employee, or resident of the county and at least 21 years of age. Created in 1965, the *State Commission on Judicial Conduct* (formerly, the State Judicial Qualifications Commission) was composed of nine members chosen by the supreme court

FIGURE 7–1

The judicial Janus

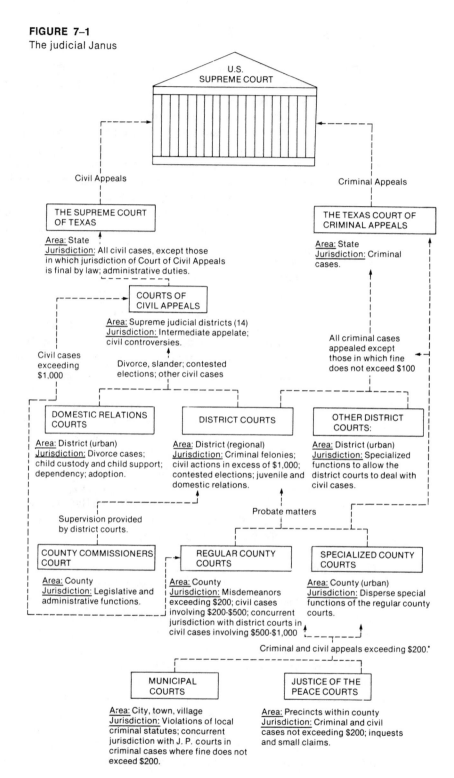

* Civil jurisdiction is subject to change by legislature after voter approval of a 1978 constitutional amendment.

and the governor for six-year overlapping terms. Its principal task is to investigate complaints or reports relating to the misconduct or disability of judges sitting on all but the municipal and justice of the peace courts.[12] However, in recent years (1975–1978), there were at least *ten* public officials—district judges, present and former representatives in the legislature or its offices, school board officials, and even a Texas Supreme Court Justice—indicted by grand juries, convicted, disbarred or all three for criminal offenses. Since a number of these were judges accused of official misconduct, the Commission was besieged by its critics with accusations of being extremely lax, if not a complete failure, in fulfilling its responsibilities. Moreover, since its creation the Commission has investigated complaints against 378 judges; of this total, formal charges have been brought against only 12; and, unbelievably, formal hearings were held in only *two* of these cases!

Defenders of the Commission argued that the prime cause of its supposed "inaction" was the lack of cooperation on the part of lawyers in bringing charges for fear of losing cases before the accused, but not removed, judges in the future. Nonetheless, in 1977, voters approved a constitutional amendment that: (1) changed the name to the State Commission on Judicial Conduct (SCJC); (2) expanded the membership from nine to *eleven;* and, (3) increased its investigative powers.

Those offices created by the legislature include the *state prosecuting attorney,* appointed for term of two years by the court of criminal appeals, who primarily represents the state in those criminal cases appealed to the U.S. Supreme Court; the *state bar,* which consists of all practitioners of law in Texas, has relatively little official authority but remains a vitally important pressure group in the machinery and procedures of government; the *Board of Law Examiners* consists of five members chosen by the supreme court for a two-year term makes the determination as to which candidates qualify to practice law in the state; the *commissioners of deeds* are those persons appointed by the governor for a two-year term—as required by federal law—who have basically the same authority as notaries public; and, finally, the *Texas Judicial Council* which is composed of 18 members, primarily state court judges, and which has the responsibility of continuously examining the structure and procedures of the state courts, both criminal and civil.

The movement for modernization

The final reading of the proposed judiciary article at the constitutional convention, issued July 7, 1974, and later reapproved by the 64th Legislature less than a year later, called for a unification of the criminal and civil courts.[13] However, Proposition 2 (Article V) suffered the same fate as the other portions of the proposed revision. It would have resulted in the following judicial structure.

FIGURE 7–2
The unified plan

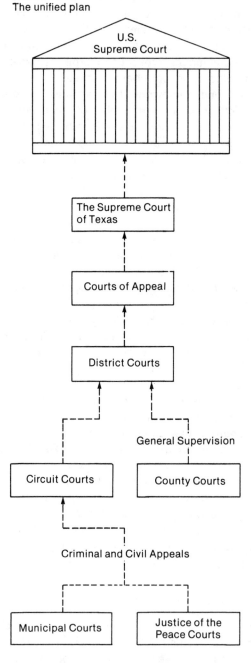

The judicial power of the state would have been vested in the *supreme court,* as court of last resort, and in the inferior state courts. The *civil courts of appeal* would have been transformed into intermediate appellate courts of criminal and civil jurisdiction. The *district courts* would have remained essentially the same; however, there would have been a revamping of the county courts below. The legislature would have been allowed to create new *circuit courts,* which would have essentially absorbed the functions of the county, and specialized county courts. Such courts would have served two or more counties, but no county would have had more than one court. On the other hand, the county commissioners court would have simply become the county commission. Despite sizable opposition on the convention floor, the proposed article would have preserved the justice of the peace courts, as well as the municipal courts as they exist at the present time. Finally, the article would have permitted the nine-membered supreme court to divide into sections of no less than five members and would have allowed a limited right of appeal on the part of the state in criminal cases. The qualifications for judges established by the article would have allowed only justices of the peace to escape the requirement to be a licensed lawyer practicing in the state. However, on November 4, 1975, the judiciary article went down to defeat with the rest of the proposed document, leaving Texas as the only state with a dual system of courts.

Aside from the structure of the judiciary, there remains a defect that would not have been rectified even if the proposed document had been given life—the partisan election of judges. In Texas, Jacksonian Democracy and the long ballot virtually run riot. We Texans elect practically *every* official—except for a penumbra of state boards—holding a municipal, county, or state position. Not uncommonly, voters know little of the real qualifications of candidates vying for public office but rather rely on preconceived notions of qualities that are consistent with our somewhat parochial environment. Voters are more inclined to elect Harry Hamburger to the position of judge because he has stated that he is a long-time resident of the community, a veteran, a member of the First Baptist Church, a civic leader, and a Rotarian, rather than to seriously question his legal background and experience. As folksy as this might seem, it is considered by some a *terrible* way to select public servants. If any such office should not be elective in nature, it should be that of judge, whether justice of the peace or supreme court justice. An alternative method of selection is the *American Bar Association* or *Missouri Plan,* by which the governor appoints judges from a list of qualified candidates submitted by the state bar. Periodically, the electorate would have the opportunity to vote whether to keep or remove them from office based on their judicial performance to date. If a majority of voters opposed their continuance, the original procedure would be repeated and the governor would appoint a new judge.

The thrust for reform was brutally brought home to the voters of Texas after first the Democratic nomination and then the election of Donald P. Yarbrough, whom many had confused with well-known liberal campaigner Don *Yarborough,* also from Houston, as a justice on the Texas Supreme Court. After his nomination in 1976, Yarbrough was found guilty of legal malpractice and fraud in a Houston civil lawsuit. After his election, criminal convictions and disbarment followed. Texans, it seemed, had elected an apparent criminal with knowledge aforethought. Thankfully, before his impeachment proceedings were concluded in the Texas legislature, Yarbrough resigned in July 1977. Undoubtedly, the shock of it all forced such establishment types as Texas Supreme Court Justice Charles Barrow and former Justice Tom Reavley to advocate elimination of the election of justices to the Supreme Court in favor of some sort of merit-selection process.

CIVIL LIBERTIES

This section describes the system of civil liberties and the criminal justice system as outputs of the political process to the extent that both are products of the legislature, the source of laws, and the judiciary, which interprets the laws. The process in which the legislature and judiciary produce these outputs, in essence, is a conversion process in which a variety of inputs—popular demands that racial minorities accept the existing social order of Anglo dominance, public disinterest in, if not hostility toward, such esoteric issues as civil rights and individual liberties, attitudinal residuals from the frontier era and agrarian society with respect to law and order, precipitant expectations stemming from a below-average level of educational attainment—are in turn produced as outputs.

Until very recently the Texas political elite has consisted almost entirely of representatives of the most socially and politically retarded regions of the state. Not surprisingly this elite, which is empowered to deal with issue areas on which the general citizenry has few strong feelings (for example, civil liberties and criminal justice), has had a fairly free hand—too often at the expense of constitutional guarantees. The following examples tend to support this contention:

Pointer and another man were arrested for armed robbery in violation of the Texas Penal Code.[14] During the preliminary hearing (the examining trial), neither of the men had counsel and counsel subsequently failed to cross-examine the victim whose testimony was later instrumental in obtaining convictions. Prior to the trial, the witness for the prosecution moved to California and the transcript of his examining testimony was admitted over the objection of defense counsel. The Texas Court of Criminal Appeals upheld the convictions and the case was then brought to the

U.S. Supreme Court. In a 9–0 decision, the Court reversed, holding that the Sixth Amendment's guarantee that the accused is "to be confronted with the witnesses against him" is fundamental to a fair trial.[15] Accordingly, the state had violated the due process clause of the Fourteenth Amendment by allowing the use of the transcript.

In the second case, Jackie Washington, an 18-year-old Dallas youth was convicted of murder with malice and was sentenced to 50 years in prison. The facts surrounding the case were somewhat hazy, but this much was clear: Washington, jealous over the fact that his former girl-friend was dating another boy, and several friends attempted a confrontation at the girl's house; one of the friends, Charles Fuller, had brought a shotgun; in the melee that followed shots were fired and the girl's boy-friend was killed. Washington and Fuller were charged separately as coparticipants in the murder. During his trial, Washington maintained—and it was later verified—that Fuller's testimony showed that he, not Washington, had actually fired the shots even though Washington had tried to dissuade him. The trial judge refused to allow Fuller to testify citing two Texas statutes which provided that persons charged or convicted as coparticipants in the same crime could not testify for one another although there was no bar to their testifying for the state.[16] On appeal, the Texas Court of Criminal Appeals held that Washington had not been denied a fair trial; however, the U.S. Supreme Court disagreed. In a unanimous decision the Court reversed the convictions on the grounds that the Sixth Amendment's guarantee of "the compulsory process for obtaining witnesses on behalf of the accused" is enforceable against the states by way of the Fourteenth Amendment.[17] As to the legality of the Texas statutes, Chief Justice Warren said in part:

> The rule disqualifying an alleged accomplice from testifying on behalf of the defendant cannot even be defended on the ground that it rationally sets apart a group of persons who are particularly likely to commit perjury. The absurdity of the rule is amply demonstrated by the exceptions that have been made to it. . . . To think that criminals will lie to save their fellows but not to obtain favors from the prosecution for themselves is indeed to clothe the criminal class with more nobility than one might expect to find in the public at large.[18]

The facts are *inescapable:* in each case, the trial court had denied a procedural right, personal and present, to the accused; in each case, the highest Texas court for criminal cases had held that the defendant had not been denied a fair trial; in each case, attorney general lawyers had argued the cause of the state before the Supreme Court, only to have the convictions reversed; *ironically, in each case, not only had Texas officials violated the Constitution of the United States but the state constitution as well.* Our highest ranking legal technicians had blinded themselves to the fact that the Texas Constitution in Article I, Section 10, provides that "in all criminal prosecutions the accused . . . shall be confronted by the witnesses against him and shall have compulsory process for obtaining witnesses in his favor."[19] If the purpose of the Texas "bill of rights" has been to make inviolate those rights listed from abridgement by the state government, its viability has been at best questionable, at worst it has been nonexistent.

National and state linkage

The basic function of civil liberties within the context of the Texas political system is to limit governmental power for the protection of individual rights and to safeguard these rights from potential abuses arising in the political arena. Traditionally, civil liberties encompass those fundamental rights which are guaranteed to all persons, citizen and noncitizen alike, under the United States Constitution.[20] They primarily take the form of restraints on governmental authority and are found, for the most part, in the First, Fourth, Fifth, Sixth, Eighth, and Ninth Amendments. The First Amendment freedoms of speech, press, assembly, religion, petition, association, privacy and academic freedom are *substantive* or tangible rights. The remaining guarantees are *procedural* in nature and are structured at the pretrial (Fourth, Fifth), trial (Sixth) and posttrial (Eighth) stages of criminal procedure. Those liberties not expressly written in the Constitution, but which may be implied, are protected by the Ninth Amendment which provides that the "enumeration . . . of certain rights, shall not be construed to deny or disparage others retained by the people." Until 1925, it was generally an accepted doctrine that these civil liberties restrained only the national government.[21] However, in *Gitlow* v. *New York* the U.S. Supreme Court rendered a landmark decision that would directly affect state and local government for years to come. It held that the Fourteenth Amendment which forbids a state from depriving a person of his "life, liberty or property without due process of law" could be used as a *modus operandi* to apply essential guarantees of the Bill of Rights to the states. Specifically, it incorporated the First Amendment's guarantee of freedom of speech and press into the term *liberty* so that henceforth state and local governments could no longer feel free in arbitrarily or unduly restricting speech without a controlling justification for doing so. This judicial doctrine of incorporation has progressed to such an extent that today nearly every one of the liberties listed in the Bill of Rights has been made enforceable against the states, with the notable exceptions of the Fifth Amendment's guarantee of indictment by a grand jury for serious crimes and the Eighth Amendment's ban on the imposition of excessive bails and fines.

In addition, every single one of the liberties contained in the First,

Fourth, Fifth, Sixth and Eighth Amendments is also guaranteed by the Texas Constitution of 1876. Functionally, the state bill of rights should make the state, not the federal courts, the guardian of our liberties, but as the *Pointer* and *Washington* decisions have demonstrated this has not been the case.[22] The future of the criminal justice system in Texas, including the rights of those accused thereunder, will depend upon: (1) the actions taken by the legislature in rewriting the Constitution; (2) the adherence to the resultant document by state officials; and (3) the future deliberations of a more "conservative" U.S. Supreme Court since 1969.

The Supreme Court in transition

During the 16 years in which Chief Justice Earl Warren presided over the Supreme Court (1953–69) critics charged that because of the judicial activism of the "liberal" majority the Court was exceeding its constitutional authority and usurping the powers of Congress and the states. This criticism was particularly acute with respect to decisions which further expanded the rights of the accused in state criminal proceedings. Of the total number of decisions which incorporated a procedural right of the Fourth, Fifth, Sixth, and Eighth Amendments, the Warren Court had handed down all but four. The performance of the Court became an issue in the presidential election of 1968. Opponents openly accused the Court of causing breakdown of law and order in the United States at the expense of the victims of crime and the police. In fact, prior to his election, Richard M. Nixon pledged that if elected he would appoint:

> . . . strict constructionists who saw their duty as interpreting law not making law. They would see themselves as caretakers of the Constitution and servants of the people, not superlegislators with a free hand to impose their social and political viewpoints upon the American people.[23]

During his tenure, former President Nixon had the opportunity to place four justices on the Court: Chief Justice Warren E. Burger (1969), Justices Harry M. Blackman (1970), Louis Powell, and William Rehnquist (both 1972). His successor, Gerald Ford, named John Paul Stevens in 1975. The net effect, as verified by a number of recent decisions, has been to tilt the philosophical balance to a more conservative position. At least a majority on the Court are less likely to further expand the rights of free speech and press, to require the strict adherence to the "one man-one vote" rule in the drawing of congressional and state legislative districts, and most certainly they appear to be willing to backtrack from further expansion of the rights of the accused.[24] Quite obviously, the nuances of criminal procedure in Texas and other states will be reflective of the future deliberations of the High Court.

THE CRIMINAL JUSTICE SYSTEM

The courts

The administration of justice in Texas is hampered by its antiquated court structure. Moreover recent studies have shown that this cumbersome system may be contributing to the rise of urban crime.[25] There are nine types of lower courts beneath the district court level: county courts, county courts at law, county civil courts at law, county courts for criminal cases, county criminal courts, county courts for criminal appeals, county probate courts, municipal courts, and justice of the peace courts. With such dispersion of adjudicative authority, little focus can be achieved in handling classes of civil and criminal cases. In addition, serious overcrowding of dockets is commonplace.

Since 1962, the rate of increase in cases filed in the district court has been appalling. By 1971, the number of civil cases had increased 50 percent; while the number of criminal cases filed had increased 150 percent. Despite the addition of 63 new district courts, the district judge in a metropolitan county today must handle an average of 1,500 cases per year.[26] Aside from awaiting initial disposition of cases, county court dockets have burgeoned because of the appellate system. Presently, individuals who are adversely affected by the decision in a justice of the peace or a municipal court has the right to a new trial (*de novo*) by appealing their case to the county court or county court at law. This time-consuming process benefits individuals who are charged with misdemeanors or who are involved in minor lawsuits, but it taxes the administration of justice to the utmost. Moreover, individuals involved in a serious criminal case or lawsuit have the right only to one trial. Most importantly, the *de novo* appeals system has led to, at least, nonenforcement of the law. Since some county judges refuse appeals in minor cases, many cases are merely dismissed without a trial.

This distressful situation is even more disturbing in that roughly nine out of ten Texans have their only judicial contact with the lower courts during their lifetime.[27] Through the process of political socialization the lower courts become, whether wrongly or rightly, the transmitters which shape public opinion of the entire judicial structure. The picture formed is too often a poor one; however, there at least exists the possibility of reform.

Recent improvement plans, including the Chief Justice's Task Force Proposed Judiciary Article, recommend that all lower court judges meet specific qualifications and that they be paid by the state. Since these courts would be courts of record and review, every judge would be part of unitary judicial system with centralized administration. The ultimate goal, of course, is to provide proper administration of justice, as well as the uniform application of the law. As the task force reviewed the problem:

> The organization of the Texas judiciary is presently not responsive to the needs of Texans, particularly in the criminal area. The end result of the war against crime is in the courtroom, where appropriate justice is meted out to convicted offenders. *The finest police forces and the most accomplished lawyers amount to nothing if the courts are not equal to the task.*[28]

It concluded:

> The deterrence of law breakers depends in large part less on the severity than the swiftness and certainty of punishment. If punishment is slow, uncertain, and not appropriate to the crime, then we might well ask who will be deterred. Certainly not the guilty, who prosper under the current system. And the innocent, who do not need deterrence, will only suffer as they do now.[29]

The Texas Penal Code

It is hardly a secret that the occurrence of crime is increasing nationally and in Texas. The estimated crime rate in the state for 1969 was 4,074 offenses per 100,000 persons, with crimes against property (burglary, theft, etc.) far out-pacing crimes against the individual (murder, rape, robbery and aggravated assault).[30] However, statistics also reveal that the rate of arrest or clearance rate for crimes against the individual (63 percent) far exceeded that for property-oriented crimes (24 percent). Space does not permit adequate discussion of the debate over the roots of crime itself, except to recognize there exists ample evidence to support the view that societal factors—mental illness, poverty, inadequate housing, improper environment during the developing stages of life—are nutrients for crime. Still others argue that persons who perform continual criminal acts simply *want* to be criminals. In any case, the occurrence of crime in society makes it necessary to enforce substantive laws dealing with offenders.

The antiquated Texas Penal Code was adopted in 1854. Although the code has been formally revised on numerous occasions, an earnest attempt to reform it completely has occurred only recently. For the past seven years a special state bar committee has worked to produce a new code in order to streamline criminal justice in Texas. This committee on revision made an effort to sound out the views of practicing prosecutors, defense attorneys, and judges, and presented the proposed Code to the 63d legislature in January 1973 for its consideration. After some modifications were adopted (for example, possession of marijuana under four ounces was set as a misdemeanor; reinstatement of the death penalty for certain crimes), the proposal was approved by the legislature in June 1973. The major objectives of the proposed penal code, as outlined by Chairman T. Gilbert Sharpe of Brownsville, include the following.[31]

1. Consolidate, simplify, and clarify the substantive law of crimes.
2. Modernize a Penal Code designed for the preindustrialized, rural, and underpopulated Texas society of a century ago.
3. Identify and prohibit, with as much precision as possible, all significantly harmful criminal conduct.
4. Rationally grade offenses, according to the harm they cause or threaten, and sensibly apportion the sentencing authority between the judiciary and the correctional system.
5. Codify the general principles of the penal law.
6. Collect in a single code all significant penal law, transferring to more appropriate locations in the statutes regulatory and similar laws that merely employ a penal sanction. (The present code devotes 60 articles to the subject of theft, 57 to official misconduct, 38 to malicious mischief, and 35 to bribery).

Perhaps the most important change in the revised code is a grading system by which all offenses fall into one of three categories of misdemeanor or one of four classifications of felonies instead of spelling out specific penalties for each offense. However, the existing practice of setting the punishment for offenses by either the jury or trial judge is retained.

During its operation, the revision committee was attuned to relevant decisions on criminal procedure announced by the U.S. Supreme Court. For example, the landmark decision striking down the death penalty left the question of capital offenses in serious doubt. Seven of the justices indicated that the death penalty was not conclusively rejected and suggested that a properly drawn and administered statute could survive a challenge in the Court.[32] Based on that dictum, the committee submitted Section 19.03 (the Capital Murder section) which assigns the death penalty "under certain aggravated and extreme conditions"—murder of a prison guard by an inmate, murder in connection with a robbery, forcible rape or sexual abuse, or kidnapping—"or where the murder is done with extreme atrocity or cruelty under circumstances which show exceptional depravity on the part of the actor." In June 1973, Governor Briscoe signed this statutory proposal into law. The governor and legislature were vindicated by the subsequent decision of the U.S. Supreme Court which upheld Section 19.03, in *Jurek* v. *Texas*, 428 U.S. 262 (1976). However, in an apparent move to avoid future challenges contending that capital punishment carried out by use of the electric chair constitutes a "cruel and unusual punishment," the legislature approved a 1977 proposal which calls for the carrying out of the death penalty by use of lethal injections—a supposedly more humane method of imposing the "Big Sleep."

The procedural rights

The investigatory process Although there are variations in procedures and institutions from state to state, the basic stages of criminal procedure are the same: (1) investigation, (2) accusation, (3) trial, and (4) custody and corrections. Despite the fact that a great number of crimes go unreported, the investigatory process begins only with reliable input—a report or "tip" that a crime has been or is being committed as conveyed to a law enforcement agency. Most commonly the agencies involved are the municipal police and county sheriffs, deputies and constables; however, depending on the nature of the crime and the jurisdiction, the investigation may be carried out by the Department of Public Safety. In any event, the investigation may lead to the issuance of a search warrant in order to ascertain evidence relating to the crime. The officer must swear or affirm "probable cause"[33] before a magistrate, usually a justice of the peace or a district judge. If the judge decides that sufficient probable cause exists, that is, that the person(s) named in the warrant may well be involved in the commission of an offense. The search warrant must "particularly describe" the persons to be searched and the things to be seized. Since *Mapp* v. *Ohio* (1961) state and local officers have become aware that the products or evidence resulting from an *unreasonable* search are inadmissible in court. *Reasonable* or permissible searches include those conducted with a proper search warrant. In addition, the following searches are generally permissible in the *absence* of a warrant: (1) those performed in connection with, or incident to, a valid arrest; (2) where the officer has probable cause yet lacks sufficient time to obtain a warrant, *e.g.,* in the case of a moving vehicle; and (3) if voluntary consent is given to be searched.

It may be assumed as a postulate of judicial reasoning that any evidence found during the course of a reasonable or proper search is admissible, even though not related to the crime under investigation.

The accusatory process After the investigation has been completed and sufficient evidence has been gathered, the accusatory process begins. The proper magistrate, upon a submission of the sworn statement of the officers, issues an arrest warrant to be presented to the accused. (Of course, if the officer is present during the commission of a crime a warrant is not necessary). At that point, the right of counsel begins.[34] In

Texas, for serious misdemeanors and felonies, the arresting officer must inform alleged offenders of the *Miranda* "litany," that they have the right to remain silent, that anything they say will be used against them in court, that they are entitled to the presence of an attorney and further that if they cannot afford counsel, one will be provided for them by the court *prior* to any questioning if they so desire. If the accused wishes to waive these rights and make a statement he is required to sign an affidavit to that effect. He is then confined—for a reasonable period—until he can be brought before a magistrate. At this time the magistrate presents the charges and again informs the accused of his constitutional and statutory rights. If the accused wishes to waive these rights, he again must sign a statement so stating. Hereafter, if at any time he wishes to claim his procedural rights, he may do so; any incriminating statements made prior to that claim cannot be used by the prosecution unless the accused perjures himself on the witness stand.[35] Depending on the seriousness of the offense and the evidence presented, the magistrate will either issue a warning or complaint, call for an examining trial if requested, and thereafter commit or release the individual. If the accused is subject to a grand jury trial for a felony, the judge has the discretion to set bail bond.

Defendants are then bound over for the grand jury although they may choose to waive this guaranty. Initially, grand jurors are selected by a grand jury commission from taxpayer rolls and eventually by drawing certain of these names at random from a jury drum. The purpose of the grand jury is to assure that no person shall be brought to trial on serious criminal charges unless this impartial group of citizens has good reason to believe that the accused may be guilty. If sufficient evidence establishing a causal relationship between the alleged offender and the crime is lacking, the grand jury will present a "no bill" or "pass." However, it is more likely that the grand jury will indict the individual if the performance of grand juries in recent years is a reliable indicator. The district clerk, upon receiving the indictment returned by the grand jury, issues the writ of attachment, or *capias*,[36] and sets a new bond. The case is then placed on the docket to await trial.

In recent years, however, not all state officials have been satisfied with decisions of local grand juries or of their operations. For example, in 1976–1977, there occurred a number of instances of police "lawlessness and brutality" in which persons—most notably minority group members—in the charge of local officers were killed. Of particular notoriety were the cases of Richard Morales, who was shot while in the custody of the Castroville police chief, and of an arrestee, Torres, who was (while handcuffed) thrown over a bridge by Houston police officers and was subsequently drowned. Grand and petit juries seemed reluctant to act, and when they did the sentences were minor. In response, then Attorney

FIGURE 7–3
The criminal process*

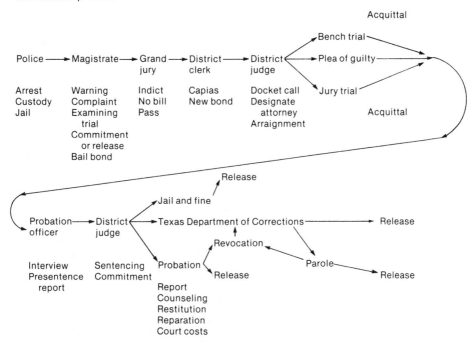

* An abbreviated diagram of the criminal process as it is generally practiced in the district courts of Texas. Some Texas courts are without probation officers and may omit this function in the process. Moreover, there may be steps in the process that are combined in a single hearing. (As conceived by District Judge Terry Jacks of the 22d District.)

General John Hill suggested that the following steps be taken: (1) the creation of statewide 12-membered grand juries in cases where local juries are hesitant in investigating police misconduct. Such a panel would be named by the governor and the chief justice of the state Supreme Court; (2) the enactment of a state civil rights law and a human rights commission to enforce its terms; and, (3) failing all else, to request the direct involvement of the U.S. Justice Department to prosecute federal civil rights violators. It remains to be seen whether Governor Clements will push for the passage of any of these proposals into law.

The trial process begins in court, when the district judge presents the defendant with several important questions: Does he or she desire counsel? Can he or she afford an attorney? Does he or she wish a jury or bench trial? If the accused is an indigent, the district judge will designate an attorney to plead the defense. After consulting with a lawyer, the defendant chooses which plea to enter. There is, of course, the option of plea bargaining through which the defendant agrees to plead guilty in exchange for a concession on the part of the prosecution, for example, a lesser charge preferred, recommendation of a lighter sentence or even probation. Because of the overcrowded dockets of district, as well as other, courts, the judge will regularly agree to such a bargain. Once the plea has been entered the actual trial begins. If the petit (trial) jury is to be used, the selection of veniremen (jury members) is one of the most important elements in the adversary system. The names of jurors are selected from voter registration rolls. Thereafter, experienced prosecution and defense lawyers—and unfortunately most working in the prosecutors' office are only recently out of law school—will carefully pick, choose, and eliminate veniremen because of prejudices which may adversely affect their cause—socioeconomic background, race or ethnic origin, political views, or any number of factors.

If the defendant is not acquitted and is found guilty, the next step provided at the district level is consultation with the probation officer. Based on an interview with the offender, the probation officer submits a presentence report to the judge; however some Texas courts are without probation officers and may omit this function in the process. In most cases, the district judge passes sentence; however, if a jury trial was used, the defendant may choose sentencing by the petit jury.

Post-trial procedure Commitment to a penal institution begins the third stage of criminal justice in Texas—*correction* and *rehabilitation.* Municipal and county jails are temporary custodial facilities for those taken into custody following arrest and those convicted of misdemeanors. Texas jails are substandard by virtually any criteria: they are operated without any state guidelines or control, they lack any professionally trained corrections personnel, they are run by municipal and county law enforcement officers, and in the main they are dirty honeycombs of confinement characterized by inadequate facilities, sexual assaults, poor food, official neglect, and public indifference.[37] The rate of recidivism among convicted persons having served their sentences in county and municipal jails is extremely high—about four times higher than those who have served sentences in the state prison system. The probation picture is somewhat brighter. Although most county probation departments are understaffed and underfunded, they have done amazingly well. Giles W. Garrison, Travis County chief probation officer, relates that 90 percent of all probation cases in the county run their course without revocation; in misdemeanor cases, the percentage is just short of 100.[38]

Convicted felons who are sentenced to confinement are sent to one of 14 Texas penitentiaries.[39] These prisons come under the jurisdiction of the Texas Department of Corrections. Its nine-membered Board of Corrections, headed by the director, is appointed by the governor with the concurrence of the Senate. The board has three primary functions: (1) to protect society from the criminal offender; (2) to provide a program of humane treatment; and (3) to develop a program of rehabilitation which will fit the offender for reentry to society.[40] In all, the board has had some measure of success in that not only are Texas prisons rated above average when compared to those of other states, but the rate of recidivism stands at only 20 percent. In 1977, the 65th Legislature increased funding to add 500 new guards to the penitentiary system and increased the budget by an additional $78 million for new construction, including the construction of a prison hospital in Galveston.[41] To a great extent the *treatment* program, which is devoted to the well-being, vocational training, health, and records of inmates, is responsible for the success of the state penal system. For example, the Pre-Release Center initiated at the Jester Unit in Richmond in 1963, helps ease the difficult transition from imprisonment to freedom and thus decreases the recidivism rate. The 61st Legislature, viewing the success of the program, authorized a work furlough plan for inmates at Jester. Aside from vocational training, educational advancement is also strongly encouraged. More than eight out of ten convicted felons in Texas are elementary and high school dropouts: half have less than a fifth grade education; approximately, one out of six are illiterate, and more than half are under 25 years of age. Efforts have been made to provide inmates with accredited courses ranging from the 1st to 12th grades within the prison system itself. In addition, programs are offered for qualified inmates, in cooperation with the penal institution, at a number of junior colleges and colleges in the state.[42]

In the past, a person convicted of a crime and sentenced to no more than 15 years was *entitled* to bail pending appeal of the conviction; however, the 65th Legislature put its foot down on this policy also. Since 1977, the judge has the authority, under law, to deny bail in such cases if he believes the defendant might commit another offense when released or might not return to court on the appointed date. Moreover, in the same year the voters approved a constitutional amendment which gives judges the authority to deny bail if the defendant had committed a felony while out on bail from an earlier felony charge or if the defendant had been convicted for a deadly-weapon-related felony.

Whatever the attributes of the Texas corrective and rehabilitation program, the recidivism rate—one out of five convicted offenders are returners—remains too high. Perhaps the optional plan would be to increase the number of offenders who are placed on probation or parole. This suggestion, however, is fraught with difficulties.

These changes were obviously recognized by what has become known as the "law and order" 65th Legislature which took a conservative, anticrime approach to policy-making in this area. In 1977, it enacted laws which: (1) took away from judges the power to grant probated sentences to persons convicted of violent crimes or who used a gun or deadly weapon during the commission of an illegal act. Only a jury can grant probation in such cases and, even then, only after the defendant has served a mandatory number of years (maximum of 20 years); (2) created a statewide adult probation system replacing the former county-administered system; (3) provided for the mandatory supervision by the state of all individuals released from prison early because of their good conduct as an inmate; (4) innovated a "shock probation" program under which judges can send first-time offenders to prison for a while *before* releasing them on probation; and, (5) for the first time permitted and encouraged parolees to make restitution to their victims through work furlough earnings or other court-supervised arrangements.

With respect to probation, the trial judge may probate the sentence of first offenders of less serious felonies. Like probation for misdemeanors, the offenders must walk the "tight rope" of revocation and confinement if while remaining in society they fail to meet the terms of their probation. The obvious advantage is that the convicted felons may live with their families and retain meaningful employment without the serious physical and psychological effects of imprisonment. However, the state probation program is totally inadequate because of too few trained probation officers and lack of adequate funding.

Those offenders who have demonstrated good behavior during the first one third of their sentence, or for 15 years, whichever has come first, are subject to possible parole. The ultimate decision to allow such inmates to rejoin society on a trial basis is made by the three-membered Board of Pardons and Paroles (BPP). Here again, staff and funding are insufficient to the task. Today there is only one trained parole officer for 100 parolees and, unfortunately, one third of those paroled find themselves recommitted to serve out their original sentences for failure to comply with established rules of conduct. Even if things are in the defendant's favor, it is extremely difficult to obtain a parole. In 1977, the BPP approved only 5,000 out of a total of 17,000 applications for parole. Former Governor Briscoe, a hard-liner on "law and order," approved only 3,800 of these. Complete pardons are even *harder* to come by: in the same period, the BPP approved only 1,500 of 4,200 and Briscoe approved only 368 of this inumber. If anything, Governor Clements may be expected to be even more stingy on granting paroles and pardons. One can only hope that more "Atticas"[43] will not result before much needed reform of the rehabilitation process, nationally and in Texas.

Juveniles The subject of juvenile offenders—those between the ages of 5 and 17—is somewhat an ambiguous one. Theoretically, juveniles do not commit crimes and they are therefore tried in civil proceedings. However, in the past decade, decisions by the U.S. Supreme Court have had the effect of casting doubt on this theory. Specifically, the Court has held that in juvenile court proceedings which determine delinquency and which may result in the child's commitment to an institution, the child and/or parents or guardian must be: (1) provided with sufficient notice to permit preparation of defense to charges, (2) informed of the juvenile's right to counsel including a court-appointed attorney if necessary, and (3) extended the privilege against compulsory self-incrimination and the guarantees of confrontation and cross-examination.[44] In addition, the Court has held that "proof beyond a reasonable doubt is among 'essentials of due process and fair treatment' required during the adjudicatory stage when a juvenile is charged with an act which would constitute a crime if committed by an adult."[45] Finally, the president's Commission on Law Enforcement and Administration of Justice reported that an astonishing number of juveniles were placed in correctional institutions for offenses that would not be considered crimes if committed by adults, for example, smoking, drinking, using vulgar language, violating curfew laws, patronizing bars.[46] Accordingly, the commission recommended the organization of local youth services bureaus to facilitate those youthful offenders who the juvenile courts felt could best be handled outside the juvenile justice system.

The juvenile judge has extensive powers in attempting to strike a balance between the general welfare of the youthful offenders and the interests of the state. Depending on the nature of the case, the judge may require closer supervision by the child's parents, require the child's participation in a local rehabilitation program if one is available, or, if necessary, place the child under the jurisdiction of the Texas Youth Council. The three-membered council has a staff of nearly 500 employees and is responsible for administering correctional facilities for delinquent children; for providing a program of care, treatment, education, and training aimed at rehabilitation and reestablishment in society of delinquents; and for providing for the supervision of paroled juveniles released from the state training schools.[47] Presently, the Gatesville State School for Boys and the Crockett State School for Girls care for an average of 2,400 juveniles ranging in age from 10 to 18. The council is also responsible for the maintenance of three state homes for dependent and neglected children located in Waco, Corsicana, and near Monahans. Despite these facilities, the same types of problems that plague corrective and rehabilitative programs for adults adversely affect the juvenile system of criminal justice.

Texas Youth Council statistics show that the delinquency rate in Texas has increased steadily, particularly in metropolitan areas, since 1952.[48] However, state juvenile facilities remain overcrowded and understaffed in the face of increased appropriations. More disturbing is the fact that the training schools too often turn out future adult criminals instead of rehabilitated children. The solution to this problem may well be found in local programs which divert young people from the juvenile or criminal justice systems.[49] A prime example is the Youth Services and Resource Bureau (YS & RB) in San Angelo.

The YS & RB, funded by matching grants from the Texas Criminal Justice Council and the federal government under the Omnibus Crime Control and Safe Streets Act of 1968, began its operations in January 1970. The main purpose of the program was to divert troubled and troublesome children from corrective institutions by coordinating community resources to deal with youths' problems before they reached serious proportions.[50] Young people are referred to the YS & RB by the schools, law enforcement agencies, parents, or by other young people. When the YS & RB receives a client, he or she is interviewed at length by a counselor who, through an analysis of this personal information, attempts to isolate the child's problem. The difficulty may have arisen from a variety of sources: drug abuse, learning disability in school, emotional strains in the home, sexual behavior, and so on. Once the client's problem has been identified, he or she is referred to the agency most qualified to provide appropriate professional aid. Although the child is not coerced to do so, an appointment is set up by the board and, with the child's and parents' permission, the file is turned over to the agency. The YS & RB follows up on each referral to determine the results of the appointment. If the referral source is in the process of effectively dealing with the child's problem, the file is closed; however, if the client is unresponsive or the agency is inadequately equipped to solve the problem, the YS & RB continues to counsel the youth or attempts to arrange an appointment with another agency.[51]

Although it is still too early to evaluate the overall effectiveness of the operation in San Angelo or to endorse its adoption in other communities in the state on the basis of its diversion rate, the Texas Research League advocates that its operation be continued. The cost-benefit ratio would seem to justify this conclusion. Within the last several years, the average cost of sending a boy to a state training school for an average of 9.8 months was $5,000; for a girl, the average cost of commitment for 11.5 months was more than $6,000; while during its first year of operation, the YS & RB served 125 young people at an average of just over $277 per client.[52] If the program had managed during that time to keep just 70 young people (or 69 percent of its clients) out of state training schools, it would have paid for itself.

Even so, some state authorities remained skeptical. In 1976, former Governor Briscoe refused to release one half of the $4 million that the legislature had appropriated for the community-based programs until he had seen the effectiveness of the first $2 million that had already been expended.

Prospects for change   There are too many political and social "ifs" involved to accurately predict the future of criminal justice in Texas; however, there exist several guideposts which might be used to appreciate new trends. First, despite the fact that the constitutional proposal suffered humiliating defeat at the polls, the need for change remains. Only with a revamping of court functions at the local level, can overly burdened court dockets be alleviated so as to facilitate the administration of justice. Second, the adoption of the revised Penal Code, as approved by the legislature, should have the effect of bringing our confused patchwork of criminal statutes into the 20th century and of providing more reasoned enforcement of laws covering victim-oriented crimes. Third, the growth of law enforcement degree programs in state colleges and universities can provide better trained and more respected personnel. Since 1970, state law has required that local peace officers receive at least 140 hours of training. This requirement includes not only local on-duty experience but also permits officers to enter college degree programs which give academic exposure to public administration, civil rights and civil liberties, minority group relations, business administration, and sociological and psychological approaches to law enforcement problems. Undergraduate and graduate courses are presently offered at Southwest Texas State University in San Marcos, Sam Houston State University at Huntsville, and Baylor University in Waco. Finally, public concern exists for effective law enforcement and for our judicial and corrective processes. More and better equipped personnel at all levels will not be made a reality by the use of car bumper stickers proclaiming "Support Your Local Police." Only when public interest focuses on the inadequate salaries paid to officers and the public accepts the real possibility of an increase in local taxes will the incentive for skilled manpower be likely. Only when public outrage centers on the indecent and inhumane treatment inflicted on many inmates by their keepers and their peers and awakens governmental interest will our corrective institutions begin the difficult, but not impossible, task of providing meaningful rehabilitation instead of serving as breeding grounds for more hardened criminals to be unleashed upon society.

CONCLUSIONS

We have seen that the judicial system in Texas falls well short of the ideal. In this chapter, we have analyzed the strengths and shortcomings of Texas courts, and can draw the following conclusions:

1. The court system, and especially the district courts, bear a burden of work *far* in excess of what they can do effectively. The two-pronged structure of the highest courts, with civil and criminal divisions, has not been very workable. The inadequacies in the structure of the judicial system in Texas call for the establishment of a unified court system.

2. The civil rights of Texans are not well protected by the judiciary even though the protections of the federal Bill of Rights are also guaranteed to Texans, to be enforced by state courts, in the Texas Constitution. The state courts should be the leading protectors of civil liberties in Texas, but the federal courts have been the chief guardians of these rights.

3. The antiquated state court system hampers the administration of criminal justice, and much improvement is needed in Texas' correction and rehabilitation processes.

CHAPTER EIGHT

Metropolitan and rural problems: The intergovernmental context

The confusion of jurisdictional authorities . . . is a
property of federalism, . . .

EUGENE LEWIS*

Probably the most meaningful regional distinctions in Texas today are those which separate and differentiate urban Texas and rural Texas. Such forces as high population mobility, in-state migration, emigration from outside the state, modern communications systems, technology, and increased educational attainment have submerged many of the older cross-state distinctions. As we saw in Chapter 1, four of five Texans live in metropolitan areas and other urban places. In the rural sector, however, dwell 2.4 million people. Politics, public problems, occupations, life-styles, social indicators, outlooks, and economic opportunities offer enough contrast in urban and rural areas of Texas to warrant separate and extensive treatment in a textbook about the Texas political system.

THE URBAN CONDITION TODAY

During the late 1960s and early 1970s, the central theme in the study of the problems which beset people in our highly urbanized areas was "the urban crisis." A rather shapeless symbol of what was wrong with urban life, the urban crisis denoted a large unconceptualized set of ills —racial conflict, physical decay, citizen alienation, unmet psychological and tangible needs, breakdown of community spirit, loss of leadership, and relatively impotent local governments dominated by special interests.

The problems which constitute the urban crisis were—and still are— very real, but the crisis conception of urban America is inappropriate in characterization and deficient in conceptualization for the 1980s.

---

* *American Politics in a Bureaucratic Age: Citizens, Constituents, Clients and Victims* (Cambridge, Mass.: Winthrop Pubs., Inc., 1977), p. 13.

Changes in urban America and in interdisciplinary studies of urban problems have produced newer outlooks and unifying themes for thinking and studying about urban problems today.[1]

Several broad, related substantive concerns permeate the scholarly literature. These themes, only loosely tied to transient issues, attempt to place urban America in an historical, developmental context, demonstrating the modern city's very deep roots in the past. Newer, unifying theoretical perspectives include:

Functional aspects of cities as governments, as service-delivery mechanisms and as instruments of social control and conflict resolution;

Problems of representation, responsiveness, and service-delivery inherent in bureaucratization of city services;

Difficulties in urban governance and management of the modern city in the context of present environments;

Problems of equitable distribution of essential municipal services;

The relationship of private and public institutions in the urban context;

The potential effects of scarcity on services and levels of political conflict;

Long-term outcomes (consequences) of locational decisions having to do with siting private and public institutions and services; and

Impact of forms of municipal government on politics and service patterns in urban areas.

These themes will be sketched briefly in a general way to demonstrate the complexity of urban environments and institutions (public and private), the links of urban America with the past, and the probable shape of urban America tomorrow. Probably too little attention is given here to suburbanization and to the potential of county government as an alternative and supplemental local service mechanism. At any rate, the student is urged to observe modern urban life and institutions all around him or her and to draw upon the select bibliography for a richer understanding of this dynamic, unfolding panorama.

Impact of municipal forms

A continuing interest is the study of the effects of the adoption years ago in most mid-sized American cities of the council-manager form of city government, with its professional manager, nonpartisan ballot, and at-large representation of city councilpersons.[2] A reaction to the bossism, ward politics, and political corruption around the turn of the century, the reform spirit of yesteryear affects in some degree most U.S. cities today.

The study of municipal reform structures offers an opportunity to note the impact of input structures and governmental forms on representation of interests, establishment of service priorities, distribution of private resources, and styles of governance.

A central conclusion is that "a middle-class efficiency ethos"[3] was imposed on city government with the adoption of the reform structures. These organizational arrangements poorly represent ethnic groups, depress overall spending, prefer certain types of public programs, enhance the power of business elites, and promote bureaucratic independence, efficiency norms, and rule-making.[4] Political scientists, professional administrators, legislators, and judges are now noting these effects and looking, when pressures arise, for more neutral forms. What this tells us, however, is that means and ends are connected—that the rules which are set and the structures which are used determine, in some measure, who is represented, the nature of political conflict, the types of issues which are raised, and the nature of programs adopted.

Government as instrument of social control

In a broader, historical, and social maintenance context, urban machines are now seen as a set of mechanisms to absorb discontent, institute arrangements for delivery of public services, and increase the power of dominant urban classes, whose interests the bosses and machines served. "The machines stressed ethnicity, not class; community, not work; concrete rewards, not ideology. . . . They facilitate the expression of potentially explosive redistributive issues in distributive terms; . . ."[5] In other words, the machines built political and economic power on communities of immigrants through the use of jobs and other patronage influence. The results were socialization of immigrants in U.S. values, development of their political skills, "shifts in the definition and expectations of public policy, and disaggregation of conflict."[6]

During the time of the urban machines, as now, someone has noted, U.S. society is more successful at defusing discontent than with solving problems. Insulation of wealth from political power, of bureaucracies from responsibility, and of city governments from demands of minority-group politics continue to be social control tactics today, it is charged. One group of observers sees U.S. municipal institutions, machines, or reform structures as reflections of capitalist values and modes of production—as setting class patterns and establishing coercive, symbolic, and institutional buffers between the wielders of power, private and public, and the people.

The rise of the "new urban machines"

The large, modern service bureaucracies in U.S. cities have been dubbed by Theodore J. Lowi as "the new urban machines."[7] It is contended that our municipal services—police protection, water supply, mass transit, solid waste disposal, health care, fire protection, and others—are delivered by "relatively irresponsible centers of power, insulated from the direct control of mayors and councils and the indirect power of citizens."[8] Scholars focus on the results for society of these insular municipal service organizations—citizen alienation, hostility, feelings of impotence, distrust, and denial of their legitimacy (right to exist). Discontent arises as much from unsatisfactory routine contacts with bureaucrats[9] as it does from obvious lack of links to public control and distribution of services according to their own internal rules (rather than under guidelines set by governing bodies). Society, some scholars think, will have to be concerned with establishing symbolic and participatory mechanisms to give popular majorities more control. What forms these will take is anyone's guess. In the meantime, questions of popular control of service bureaucracy may serve to distract people from questions of equitable service delivery.

Municipal bureaucracies as service-delivery mechanisms

Apart from questions of democratic control and their irresponsible and autonomous nature, bureaucracies are judged also in terms of equitable distribution of their services. Studies show biases more than extreme, conscious inequities. Allocation of services and regulations are determined by the bureaucracies' own "task performance rules."[10] "Organizational rules simplify decision-making and provide 'objective' solutions to distributional tasks, but they sometimes have distinct distributional outcomes."[11] They may also institutionalize bias in services, without realizing it, thereby projecting well into the future distributional inequities and building a backlog of antagonism for bureaucrats and their service bureaucracies.

Concerns over distributional inequalities tap older socioeconomic, racial, and institutional bases of city life. Distributional concerns magnify race because blacks are still the poorest and most deprived of urban populations. If city political structures, such as at-large representation of city councilpersons on city governing bodies, have the effect of excluding blacks or other groups from full representation, then distributional problems tap the question of changes in government structures. The issue of private power, an old concern, takes on a new dimension in the politics of service distributions if private power acts to insulate itself from questions of equity in "who gets what." City service institutions, highly bureaucratized and manipulated by economic elites, become unresponsive to questions of equitable distribution of city services.

Locational problems in equitable service distribution

Service distributional problems must be conceptualized as broader than simply, "Does every family receive individualized services, such as water supply or sewerage disposal?" Although that, of course, is very important, the total distributional pattern—of private facilities and services as well as public benefits—must be taken into account, including access to jobs, acceptable levels of income and buying power, and quality of life, as measured by such things as clean air, low levels of noise pollution, educational and recreational facilities, and adequate housing.

Such services as highways, water facilities, and communications and transportation networks are located, sited, or placed at different geographic points for the general population. The population, in turn, is stratified socially and by income and its parts confined within specific geographic subareas. These geographic, spatial, or siting aspects contribute to a distributional effect of uneven distribution of services and regulations, not to mention taxation, fees, and other costs.[12] Even in the siting of the most basic public and private services is found the establishment of patterns of differential net costs among consumers of these services, that is, the same basic service is relatively inexpensive for some persons and grossly expensive for other persons within the target group. Further, for poor people, "resource alternatives are minimal."[13] The affluent can buy better education or clean water, but the less affluent are saddled economically with existent public services.

In addition to quality of life consequences, the location of public and private facilities and services affects property values, the tax base, the accessibility and availability of jobs, and other valuable considerations. A strong relationship exists between the existence or nonexistence of a range of adequate public services and housing values, rents, and land values.[14] These consequences, in turn, affect family residential locational choices and the resultant pattern of residential locations, socioeconomic and racial stratification, and segregation.[15] Spatial outcomes of increased land values and the like may even have a redistributive effect on incomes, of making the poor, in the long run, relatively poorer than before.[16]

The point is that locational or siting decisions made by both private and public actors can have differential, even opposite, effects on different persons in a city or metropolitan area. An airport can be an essential public facility for some persons, a nuisance for others. Highways can be major arteries for commerce, instruments of pollution and congestion, and essential connecting links to jobs. These services, in addition, are apparently being manipulated everywhere by elites to reap direct and indirect unearned economic windfalls and political advantage. Policy scientists are trying to build theory for adequate study and assessment of consequences of locational decisions.

Distributional solutions to redistributive problems

Other concerns about equitable distribution of services arise from decreasing resources in a period of low economic growth. The major concerns are the levels and scope of political conflict which may be generated by "the politics of dividing up less."[17] Other unknowns are the shape of future urban political coalitions and problems of urban governance.

During periods of large annual economic growth rates, a larger and larger budget made possible a steady increase—or made credible *promises* of future increases, eventually—in the allocation of public benefits to additional recipients. This historic U.S. process forestalls concern with equity among recipients and of redistribution of wealth to the poor by holding out the promise that eventually most persons will come to participate in an ever expanding public and private economic windfall.[18] The utility of economic growth as a conservative force in society is well stated by Charles Maier, "Growth served as the great conservative idea for a generation [after World War II]: conservative in that it forstalled [sic] claims for redistribution on the left or authoritarian search for power on the part of the right."[19]

The condition of limited economic resources, scholars feel, may set off not only higher and wider levels of conflict but class conflict as well. Society will be harder pressed to defuse discontent by *payoffs*. More overt coercive controls may be proposed by some political leaders and private groups, which will convert considerations of equitable services to civil rights debates, or even class issues. Certainly, more conflict between "haves" (the more affluent) and "have-nots" (the poor) will result; for the issue of "who gets what" in a growing economy will have been changed to "who gets how much of limited services." The question of distribution of services will have been converted by economic forces to the question of *redistribution* of resources. If so, the nature of politics in urban areas will be qualitatively different from past patterns of distributive policies, in which most groups quietly built subgovernments in policy specific areas (such as education) to negotiate and logroll larger and larger programs and expanded benefits.[20]

Governing and managing modern cities

Are cities governable under the circumstances and the conditions discussed above? Can the urban bureaucracies be made responsive to citizens more than to their own working rules and biases? Will urban politics escalate to class struggles? If not, what forms will adversary coalitions take? "No doubt we will witness the formation of new alliances and coalitions across racial, ethnic, and class lines in an effort to influence the allocation of very scarce resources."[21]

Can any mayor, no matter what his or her style may be, build a stable supportive coalition on such a potentially conflictual and ideological base? So far, the federal government's infusion of money and policy guidelines tends to dampen both class politics and to equalize, at least on a minimal basis, resources between central cities and suburban areas within the same metropolitan region.

The study of recent mayoral leadership behavior can yield some answers. One such research effort found at least five approaches to the job.[22] But mayors were found to operate under such changeable circumstances that any one approach can lead to different results at different times. Whatever the style—as ceremonial head or noninnovative caretaker, on the one hand, or executive or program entrepreneur, on the other hand, the mayor had to perform three key daily processes:[23]

Agenda-setting (deciding what tasks to undertake),

Network building (establishing and maintaining a network of cooperative relationships), and

Task accomplishment (undertaking tasks).

Ignoring any one of these processes brings a multitude of annoyances, and the mayor is well advised to build a carefully selected, competent staff and use these persons to compensate for any weaknesses or needs in the processes. The mayor must figure out what the key elements or variables are in each of these three processes, with their interactions, in order to assure himself of significant impact on his city, whichever role he or she decides to assume.

A disturbing trend: All of the 20 mayors studied found, without exception, that their jobs were dead ends. Mayors' positions are unattractive and do not lead to higher political office.[24] Many of the mayors were short-tenured, and they left office without public confidence or approbation, a situation which embittered some of them. Apparently, urban political leadership is getting difficult to find, leadership skills harder to develop and use. Rewards for public service are apparently few or nonexistent, especially at the mayoral level of the U.S. political system.

Texas is still experiencing economic growth, and its cities are at an earlier stage of development than is found in most U.S. cities. Texans can learn from the problems experienced by older sections of the country. But it remains to be seen if Texas' institutions can build effective and far-sighted political leadership. Local and state governments, with adequate planning and programs, have time to avert some of the shoddier manifestations of the urban condition today.

URBAN SPRAWL

Urban sprawl is a manifestation of the flight of people to the suburbs. It is a condition in which large, low-density metropolitan population spreads out over larger and larger geographic areas, gobbling up land and other resources, requiring more complex and extensive freeways, making traditional urban services much more expensive and difficult to supply, and contributing to congestion and water and air pollution.

Texas pattern

In the rather typical demographic patterns in Texas are seen the process and characteristics of urban sprawl.

Intrastate migration During the past 15 years, the dominant migration streams have been *within* the state and have constituted a flow from rural areas and small towns and cities into the six largest metropolitan areas, plus a flood outward from the central cities to the suburbs. For example 45 suburban neighbor cities of Houston, Dallas, San Antonio, and Fort Worth experienced a growth rate during the 1960s of more than 100 percent. Some of these cities, such as Irving, now rank among the 30 most populous municipalities in Texas. While metropolitan area population was increasing by 1.5 million persons, 146 of the state's 254 counties experienced net population losses.

Physical growth of central cities Ambitious municipal annexation policies are chasing suburban populations. During the 1960s, the state's four largest cities annexed 230 square miles of development, a 25 percent increase in the total size of these areas.

Decreasing population density As a result of land acquisition and continued suburban movement, population densities in the major cities and their suburbs declined substantially to a level considerably lower than density in the nation at large. This occurred during a time when total population aggregations of the central metropolitan cities were growing wildly (see Table 8–1). In 1970, the population per square mile in Texas' largest cities was only 60 percent of the density in 1960!

TABLE 8–1
Area and population density of selected Texas cities

City	1950 Area	1950 Density	1960 Area	1960 Density	1970 Area	1970 Density
Houston	160.0	3714	328.1	2859	447.0	2757
Dallas	112.0	3704	279.9	2454	296.5	2848
San Antonio........	69.5	5641	160.5	3650	184.1	3553
Fort Worth	93.7	2757	140.5	2301	211.2	1863
El Paso	25.6	4499	114.6	2414	119.5	2697
Lubbock	17.0	4199	75.0	1716	75.7	1920
Amarillo	20.9	3535	54.8	2513	61.3	2072
Beaument	31.4	2994	70.8	1683	71.7	1617

Source: Texas Urban Development Commission, *Urban Texas: Policies for the Future* (Austin: Texas Urban Development Commission, 1971), p. 19.

Types of land development

The U.S. Advisory Commission on Intergovernmental Relations catalogs three basic types of land development which occur in the process of urban sprawl.[25]

Low density land usage Single family houses are built on large acreage lots, consuming large amounts of land and resources and promoting long-distance commuting, traffic congestion, pollution, inadequate services, and other inconveniences.

Strip development Narrow bands of more specialized and expensive projects consisting of motels, service stations, garages, automobile sales enterprises, specialty houses, restaurants, tourist attractions, and scattered residential construction are built along interstate highways.

Leapfrog development Residential and other developments leapfrog farther and farther away from the central city in search of cheaper land or vacation sites, leaving in their wake large patches of undeveloped land areas. In Texas, pressures which produce this type of resource development include few controls on speculation in lands and developments, conditions which generate a spirit of "flight to suburbia," inability of county governments to provide orderly land development and use, and unwillingness or inability of municipalities to provide urban services. Initial and continuing capital expenditure needs are greatest for this type of urbanization, leading, particularly in the Gulf Coast area, to establishment by developers of hundreds of special districts (municipal utility districts) to underwrite costs. Water related services (fresh water supply, fire protection, drainage, sewerage) are financed by bond issues secured against fees and property tax revenues of future residential property.[26]

Debate and reaction

Observers are not uniformly agreed that the effects of urban sprawl are all detrimental. Some writers argue that sprawl is normal and explainable in terms of certain existent objective conditions, including economical means in comparison with more expensive alternative choices. Many citizens appear oblivious to low levels of services and a high degree of inconveniences and may actually opt for the kinds of land development patterns now experienced. Moreover, this "scatterization," as it is called, may provide a certain flexibility in urban development and may encourage adaptation to the changing urban environment.

Some communities, however, have reacted to high costs, inconveniences, and unattractiveness of current development patterns by supporting techniques to preserve open space, encouraging planned communities (including new towns), and attempting to reform the property tax with its wide disparities, tax havens for industry, and tendencies to encourage speculation by underassessment of vacant lands.

Issue of land-use management

Other critics of "scatterization" see the issue as need for land-use management to

Preserve the environment,

Enhance the quality of life, and

Conserve basic resources.

Development outside the incorporated cities' extraterritorial jurisdictions escapes subdivision and other regulations. And since counties have been given no powers to impose controls over haphazard and unregulated developments, part of the design of leapfrog developers is to escape the extraterritorial jurisdiction of the more aggressive cities. Consequently, as agricultural land skyrockets in cost, as land syndication schemes abound, and as sewerage and drainage problems and flooding become more acute, land despoliation, soil erosion, loss of agricultural production, pollution of ground water, and air pollution are common.

In a recent Texas legislative session, three bills drafted by the Texas Advisory Commission on Intergovernmental Relations (TACIR) would have

Provided subdivision regulation in unincorporated areas,

Extended city construction standards into extraterritorial sections, and

Given counties, after local referenda, land-use management authority.

These bills were roundly defeated.[27]

Chances appear even slimmer for a comprehensive statewide land-use and management policy (as opposed to placing authority in local elites), although policy studies are being carried out with regard to coastal management. Even in its vital coastal resources, critical decisions lie, by and large, in private hands, while state government continues to take a disintegrated "problem-specific approach to coastal management,"[28] rather than a general or broad tact. See Figure 8–1 for illustration of the piecemeal approach to some of the areas of public interest involved in preservation and protection of estuary and other resources.

Instructive in understanding failures to protect the state's vital interests is the reaction of the incoming Dolph Briscoe administration to an ambitious land-use study under federal funding and encouragement and authorized by the Preston Smith regime, 1969–1973. Submitted to Briscoe in May 1973, the report was released to the public only after considerable pressure brought by environmentalists, reporters, and other groups and with a disclaimer that the study was not intended to be a statement of policy or advocacy.[29] A basic hostility to programs which alter or modify the power of private decision-makers continues to exist.

In a policy area which holds so much potential for better environmental conditions, adequate water resources, lower land and housing costs, equitable property taxation, and adequate recreational facilities, state land-use controls are condemned as socialistic. In the Texas traditionalistic-individualistic (TI) political culture, the viewpoint is commonly expressed that land should be subject only to the conditions of a laissez-faire market system.[30] Economic growth and development take first priority over all other policy goals, given the state of political underdevelopment and values of governing elites.

"Too many governments"

Combined with problems of limited regulatory authority in county and municipal governments and absence of state land-use policies is the problem of fragmented governmental authority, which is expressed by "too many governments." Demography (mobility of populations, population size, and population density) has outstripped historic governmental boundaries (254 counties overlaid by an uneven veneer of incorporated cities). Forty years ago only 18 Texas cities contained more than 20,000 persons each, and the largest city, Houston, had a population of only 292,352 persons. Texas in 1940 was 59 percent rural and population density was only 22 persons per square mile. Relatively dense population was contained within municipal boundaries, and modern suburbia was unknown in Texas.

In urban sprawl, population flows across governmental boundaries, making it difficult to exact single government solutions and resulting in

FIGURE 8–1

Examples of coastal areas regulated by Texas agencies

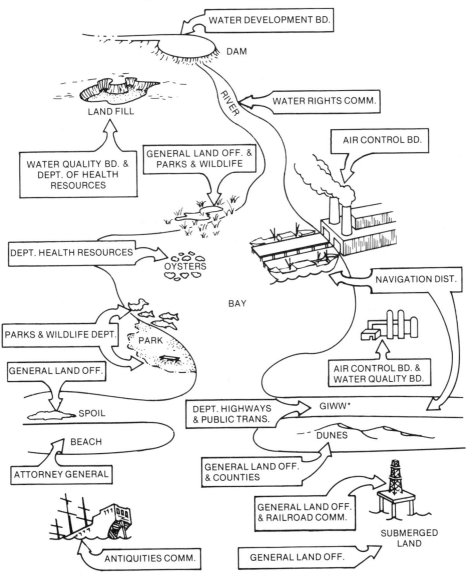

* GIWW = Gulf Intercoastal Waterway.

Source: General Land Office of Texas, *Texas Coastal Management Program: Executive Summary,* Report to the Governor and the 65th Legislature (Austin: General Land Office, November 1976), p. 17.

creation of still more incorporated cities and development water districts, where no municipalities exist, to supply essential, but limited, urban-type services.

Today, widespread diffusion of households, industries, and commercial centers engulf a large number of local jurisdictions. Social, economic, and political lines are not coincident with historic governmental boundaries. Within Texas' regional metropolitan complexes lie 1,400 different governments. See Table 8–2. The ills of urban life have overrun jurisdictional lines of cities, counties, and districts, flooding ever outward with increasing population sprawl into the suburbs and rural, unincorporated areas and absorbing blocks of Texas counties (see Figure 1–5, Chapter 1).

Lawyers speak of "neighborhood effects" of increased population density. Private acts become public nuisances. Some individuals burn their garbage. Other individuals bear the pollution, and costs are increased for all, including demands for collective action. But a dilemma occurs. No single political authority exists which can bridge governmental boundaries to arbitrate complaints of citizens in different jurisdictions.

Problems engendered by population density emphasize the need for greater governmental mediation, arbitration, services, and controls. It is certain that metropolitan area urban problems will have to be faced within the confines of the jungle of existent local governments. For it is true that nearly everywhere governmental consolidation is unpopular.[31] In this chapter and the next we will see that of the various approaches to the integration of public authority, only a few have been employed in Texas, including consolidation of some services among different local governments (such as hospitalization in Harris County), annexation of adjoining unincorporated territory and exercise of extraterritorial jurisdiction by cities over outlying areas (two major approaches by Texas municipalities), and establishment of areawide planning agencies, the councils of governments.

Some observers judge that governmental fragmentation may serve perceived citizen needs of local control and citizen participation and provide means to circumvent state restraints on existent local governments. In Texas, for example, special district governments proliferate to handle specific services and to bypass restrictive legal provisions which limit local governmental activities and taxing powers. Many commentators assert, also, that the structural or institutional approach to urban problems is an oversimplificaion and misdirection—that the serious maladies affecting mankind are unlikely to be affected by tinkering with governmental organization. Nevertheless, uncontrolled sprawl, with its social, economic, and racial restraints and implications, does raise

TABLE 8-2
Local governments in Texas standard metropolitan statistical
areas (SMSAs)

SMSA	Number of local governments
Abilene	15
Amarillo	15
Austin	26
Beaumont-Port Arthur-Orange	54
Brownsville-Harlingen-San Benito	64
Bryan-College Station	7
Corpus Christi	63
Dallas-Fort Worth	288
El Paso	20
Galveston-Texas City	39
Houston	304
Killeen-Temple	57
Laredo	12
Longview	34
Lubbock	21
McAllen-Pharr-Edinburg	66
Midland	4
Odessa	6
San Angelo	12
San Antonio	69
Sherman-Denison	45
Texarkana	32*
Tyler	19
Waco	45
Wichita Falls	31
Total	1,348
Average	54

* Local governments in Bowie County, Texas only.

Source: *1972 Census of Governments,* vol. 1: *Governmental Organization* (Washington, D.C.: U.S. Government Printing Office, 1973,
pp. 230–42.

questions of great social importance, namely: The ability of government
to deliver basic services to its urban and suburban populations, and the
significance for government of creation and retention of many governmental units, some of which appear to be permanently under the influence of special economic and political elites.

RURAL PROBLEMS

Texans are rural in outlook, reflecting their recent rural backgrounds
and traditions and the continuing importance of agribusiness in the
state's economy.[32] Surveyed as to their preferences of places to live, 64
percent of Texans stated they prefer to live in open country or in small

towns and cities. On the other hand, reflecting the ambivalence which plagues many Americans, 70 percent expressed a desire to live near a metropolis.[33]

Rural population and rural-urban economic imbalance

As we saw in Chapter 1, the proportion of rural to total population has declined sharply during the last 40 years to about one fifth. The farm component has experienced an even greater slippage, amounting in 1976 to only 3.9 percent of the nation's population and about 4.2 percent in Texas.[34]

In absolute numbers, also, rural farm population is declining. But rural population as a whole (farm and nonfarm) has remained steady at about 50 million in the nation and about 2.4 million persons in Texas. This latter figure is larger than the total population of each of 25 of the United States.

Higher birthrates and reduced agricultural employment send youthful, relatively unskilled rural migrants with limited occupational experience into our teeming cities and suburbs, there to add to urban problems. Left in small towns and on farms in 146 of 254 Texas counties is a shrinking population disproportionately composed of older, less mobile, less skilled persons who are faced with declining private and public economic resources and opportunities. In income levels, educational facilities, health care and services, housing, and poverty, the rural sector in every instance is in a more disadvantaged position than the urban sector.[35] The incidence of poverty in 1970 among rural farm Texans was 20.2 percent, while it was 27.1 percent among rural persons not on farms. On the other hand, among urban residents of all racial and ethnic groups the poverty level was 17 percent.[36]

This disparity between living conditions in rural communities and in urbanized areas is cited in both state and national statutes as the "rural-urban (economic) imbalance." Lack of understanding of rural problems and failure to provide coverage of some classes of social legislation to 2.4 million Texans on farms and in small businesses has been common. With so much publicity for urban problems, it has been difficult to attract attention to the plight of the rural.[37]

Ethnicity of rural economic problems

The incidence of poverty among rural Texans is particularly high among minority and ethnic groups—three times that for the general population. But even among whites, including the Spanish-speaking Hispanic groups, poverty is 50 percent more prevalent in the rural sector than in the urban, although in absolute numbers, 600,000 more poverty stricken whites reside in urban centers than in rural sections.

Least urbanized of minority ethnic and racial groups are Mexican-Americans. Depressed areas of the state, outside of East Texas, generally follow the configuration of counties with highest percentages of Spanish surnames. See Figure 8–2 for Texas counties with 30 to 39.9 percent and 40 percent and above of their people in poverty, and compare with figures in Chapter 2, which show Texas counties of high ethnic concentration. Compare also with Figure 1–5, and note that these distressed blocks of counties lie outside all but three of the 25 standard metropolitan statistical areas (SMSAs) in Texas (Laredo, McAllen-Pharr-Edinburg, and Brownsville-Harlingen-San Benito). Only 18

FIGURE 8–2
Texas counties with poverty levels of 30 percent and above

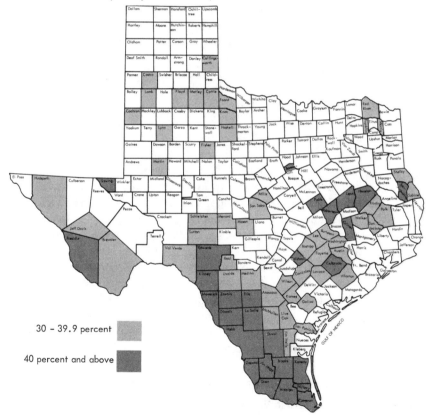

30 – 39.9 percent

40 percent and above

Source: Good Neighbor Commission of Texas, *Texas Migrant Labor: A Special Report* (Austin: Good Neighbor Commission, 1977), p. 83.

Texas cities of 10,000 or over population lie within these poverty-stricken areas.[38]

Texas migrant farm-labor force

Within the large Spanish-language rural population is an even more deprived subgroup, Texas migrant laborers. Hispanics comprise 95 percent of the largest state-based farmworkers force in the nation, which includes an estimated 85,600 households and 496,000 farmworkers and their dependents.[39] These prodigals occasionally or habitually leave their places of residence in Texas and return periodically after temporary or seasonal farm employment, either out-of-state, within-state, or a combination of the two.

Migrant workers and their dependents and associates begin their trek for work in early spring and move from harvest to harvest out of a way of life and from economic necessity. See Figure 8–3 for their basic migratory patterns, destinations, and dates of departure and return. Poorly skilled, often illiterate, suffering misery and hardship, farmworkers face mechanization of agriculture and declining job opportunities, inflationary costs in things they purchase, hostility, suspicion, low levels of social services, and other conditions which make their plight self-perpetuating in large measure. "Adding to their socioeconomic dilemma in the fact that farmworkers are generally excluded from some federal and state laws concerning fair labor practices, minimum wage laws, and collective bargaining."[40] A socioeconomic profile reveals a picture of substandard housing, insufficient health care, low educational attainment, functional illiteracy among a majority, few marketable skills, and little facility in the use of the English language.

Concentrated in identifiable substate regions in Texas, the enormity of the educational, health, housing, employment, transportation, in-transit services, and resident social services problems of migrant farmworkers begs intergovernmental planning, cooperation, and services.[41] An encouraging start has been made by establishment of the Office of Migrant Affairs in the governor's office to apprise state and local officials of needs and to plan and channel alleviative programs. But the plight of migrants presents only one set of ills in rural areas which governments in Texas would do well to face together.

REGIONAL APPROACH TO AREA PROBLEMS:
COUNCILS OF GOVERNMENTS

Besides the need for intergovernmental cooperation in attacking the many faceted ills of particularly disadvantaged area-based target groups, such as migrant workers or the elderly, a need for areawide solutions to

FIGURE 8–3
Texas migrant farmworkers: Annual migratory patterns

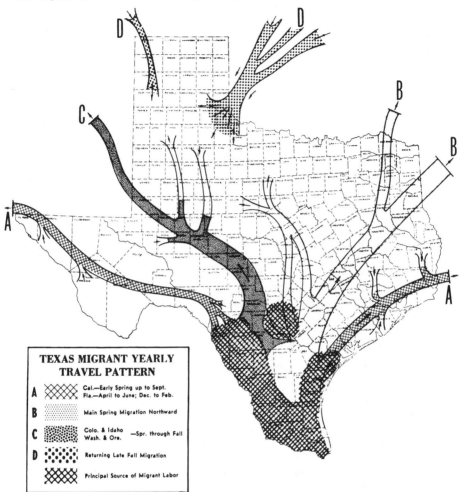

Source: Good Neighbor Commission of Texas, *Texas Migrant Labor* (Austin: Good Neighbor Commission, 1977), p. 15.

problems which beset whole populations, such as in air and water pollution, mass transit, and land use, has been felt but little realized. Two basic bars to areawide solutions is fragmentation of governmental authority in the small jurisdictions of cities, counties, and special district governments and the unpopularity of the consolidation movement.

A limited alternative to consolidation of local governments, or part or all their services, is creation of substate regional planning agencies. Federal statutes during the Johnson administration, 1963–69, required that receipt of federal program or project aid to local governments, particularly in the SMSAs, be preceded and justified by a review of need by a substate regional planning agency. Twenty-four planning regions and agencies were established in Texas in 1966 and have gained wide support among general purpose local governments and allied local interests. Most of Texas counties and nearly 80 percent of municipalities hold membership. Further, it has been mandated that the boundaries of all other of the state's policy development and implementation areas, including especially the regions established by state administrative agencies, be redrawn to conform with the boundaries of the 24 planning regions.

The planning agencies within the 24 planning regions are called councils of governments (COGs). See Figure 8–4. COGs are locally created, state-sponsored, voluntary confederations of local general-purpose governments, special-purpose district governments (such as school district and municipal utility-district governments), and political subdivisions, such as special housing authorities and universities. Being voluntary organizations, they are not consolidations in any form. Hence, they pose little threat to the autonomy and independence of local governments or their programmatic priorities since their basic purpose is comprehensive planning for areawide development of both public and private facilities.

COG structure and activities

Although organization, operations, and procedures rest on local by-laws made by cooperating governments, a high degree of uniformity prevails among Texas COGs. Structures consist of three basic elements:

- A general assembly of delegate representatives of member local governments,

- A small executive committee or board of directors composed of selected member delegates of the general assembly, and

- A full-time staff, headed by an executive director to implement planning and other operations.

Representation in the general assemblies is essentially confederate, that is, equal for each represented government, but weighted slightly in favor of the more populous county and municipal governments. Further, all assemblies contain affiliate members who serve as liaison of major local interests and civic groups. But two thirds of voting members of general assemblies must be, by state law, elected local government officials.

FIGURE 8–4

Texas planning regions and councils of governments (COGs)

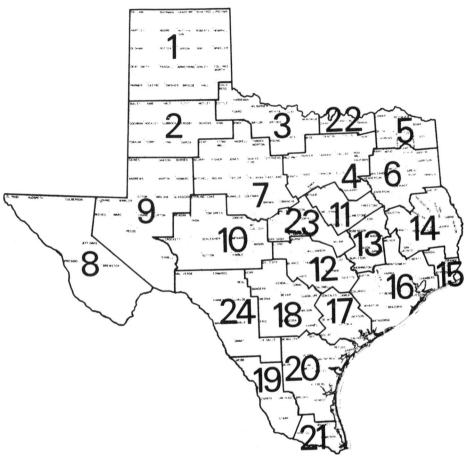

Region number	Regional council		
1	Panhandle Regional Planning Commission	13	Brazos Valley Development Council
2	South Plains Association of Governments	14	Deep East Texas Council of Governments
3	Nortex Regional Planning Commission	15	South East Texas Regional Planning Commission
4	North Central Texas Council of Governments	16	Houston-Galveston Area Council
5	Ark-Tex Council of Governments	17	Golden Crescent Council of Governments
6	East Texas Council of Governments	18	Alamo Area Council of Governments
7	West Central Texas Council of Governments	19	South Texas Development Council
8	West Texas Council of Governments	20	Coastal Bend Council of Governments
9	Permian Basin Regional Planning Commission	21	Lower Rio Grande Valley Development Council
10	Concho Valley Council of Governments	22	Texoma Regional Planning Commission
11	Heart of Texas Council of Governments	23	Central Texas Council of Governments
12	Capital Area Planning Council	24	Middle Rio Grande Development Council

Source: *Handbook of Governments in Texas* (Austin: Texas Advisory Commission on Intergovernmental Relations, 1973, updated), p. V–8.

General assemblies meet infrequently, for bylaws commonly confer upon the smaller executive committees authority to frame assembly agenda, prepare and supervise COG budgets, establish and oversee work programs, execute contracts, authorize staff positions and employment, and review and comment on federal projects requests of local governments. Many of the details of these and other operations are left to the staff officialdom personnel. More than one half of staff time is devoted to three classes of activities:

Areawide planning,

Grantmanship (applications for federal grants), and

Technical and other services to local governments.

Essential to staff activities is the quality of ongoing relationships with member governmental personnel and officials of national, state, and local governments. Executive directors nationwide see significant impact of COGs in zoning and land use, development of water and sewer systems, planning of physical facilities, use of open space and conservation, and aid in criminal justice and law enforcement, while council members and other local officials mention highest impact of COGs in economic development and solid waste disposal.[42]

Finance and oversight of COGs

Regional councils of government have no taxing authority. Income is from

Federal grants,

State grant appropriations,

Membership dues and, on occasion,

Help from nongovernmental sources, and

In-kind staffing and other services from local, state, and federal agencies.

The national government's share of funding, including both pass-through moneys (through the office of the Governor and other state agencies) and grants directly to COGs, has risen to more than 90 percent of the annual total. See Figure 8–5. Total federal moneys in 1976 amounted to nearly $80 million. State grant appropriations, amounting to $1.8 million in 1976, represent the smallest of the regular sources of COG funding, but state funds are allocated in an undesignated fashion to enable COGs to capture larger federal grants. This approach also allows each regional council to tailor plans to local programmatic needs and priorities.

The Office of the Governor, to which the state COG funds are appropriated in a lump sum, has worked out administrative guidelines and procedures for allocations of money and oversight. Authority for these administrative functions comes from statutory designation of the governor as chief planning officer of Texas and from statutory statements of COG eligibility rules for planning assistance grants. The Office of the Governor is able to exercise extensive control over COG goals, priorities, programs, work schedules, and budgets. The major administrative vehicle is the "preapplication conference," essentially an annual work

FIGURE 8–5
Funding of Texas councils of governments (COGs) by source (in percentages), 1968–1976

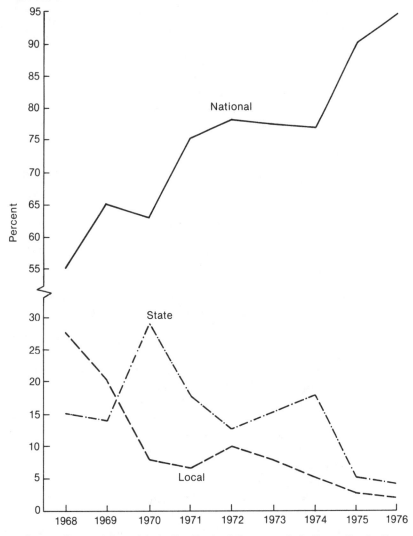

Source: Prepared from data in *Handbook of Governments in Texas* (Austin: Texas Advisory Commission on Intergovernmental Relations, 1973, updated), V–7.

session, during which a COGs' prospective program is outlined and explained to the funding governments and agencies. After the preapplication conference, the COG is sent a follow-up "management letter" which summarizes conference proceedings and which contains conditions which staff personnel of the Office of the Governor feel are warranted as prerequisites for obtaining state and federal funds.[43]

Future of councils of governments

Suffering from lack of taxation and police powers, local jealousies, and little public awareness of operations and impact, COGs continue, however, to receive approbation of officials at all levels of government and the leadership support of the governor. They also received new statutory authority—to deliver services to a limited number of target groups in pilot programs, cooperate on an interstate and international basis, hold strong review and comment positions on local government federal assistance applications, receive notification from state and national governments when their agencies contemplate major facility construction, and review plans for private facilities construction which have regional significance for any level of government. The councils are a viable response to areawide governance problems, providing regional policy capacity which is beyond the scope of authority of the numerous existent local governments.[44]

STATE RESPONSES TO AREA PROBLEMS

In this section are sketched the responses and approaches of Texas state government to the problems and needs of urban and rural Taxas.

Policy planning and leadership, technical services, and intergovernmental cooperation

Policy planning and leadership in major programmatic areas, including coordination of the planning activities of area councils of governments, are supplied by the various divisions of the Office of the Governor, principally by the Office of Budget and Planning.[45] Information on which to base planning is provided by data collection and research in the governor's staff offices and the Department of Community Affairs, by evaluation studies of the Texas Advisory Commission on Intergovernmental Relations, and by information on current programmatic needs garnered by interagency planning councils.

Chaired ordinarily by the governor, each state interagency planning council is representative of the numerous state agencies which are involved in specific policy areas. Interagency councils disseminate information to local governments and coordinate state programs at local levels, thus promoting functional or programmatic consolidation in both the highly disintegrated Texas state administrative structure, which we saw in Chapter 6, and in the complex of numerous local governments, which is described in the next chapter.

Additional planning bodies exist in the Office of the Governor, namely, the Office of Criminal Justice Planning, the Office of Migrant Affairs, the Energy Office, and the Committee on Aging. The Committee on Aging, for example, plans, coordinates, and evaluates programs directed to a specific target group, the aged. Liaison of the agency with state and local cooperating agencies is maintained through an interagency advisory board and with the public through a citizens' advisory council—a common political device for input, support, and leadership for implementation of local programs by state government. Communities are encouraged to establish local committees and staffs to carry services to older Texans. Aided by a base of federal grants provided by the Older Americans Act of 1965, local committees implement such programs as health services, meals on wheels, transportation, telephone reassurance, retired volunteers, and informational and educational services to senior citizens. The Committee on Aging utilizes county extension offices to help the local committees conduct programs in nutrition, recreation, agricultural information, and homemaking. Local committees now exist in all except a few of Texas' 254 counties.

The major conduit of gubernatorial leadership and of technical assistance and federal funds to local government activities in economic development, drug abuse, urban redevelopment, manpower training, youth services, and child development is the Texas Department of Community Affairs. See Figure 8–6, which outlines the department's organization and functions. Technical assistance is available to municipalities, county governments, and special-purpose local governments in problems of local finance, personnel, employment, housing, land use, planning, grant applications, and delivery of services. The department also encourages interlocal and state-local cooperation through intergovernmental contracts for exchange of services through creation of interlocal agencies to perform common functions and services. Not extensively utilized as yet, these devices provide the potential for another type of functional or programmatic consolidation in Texas, this time at the local level.

Another service-center state agency, but serving a particular economic sector clientele group, is the Industrial Commission of Texas. Responsible for attracting, locating, and promoting industry in Texas, this agency conducts national media advertising (see Figure 8–7), aids industrial expansion, encourages minority business ownership, collects economic data on Texas counties and municipalities, assists community leadership in economic development matters, and runs job training programs.

FIGURE 8–6
Texas Department of Community Affairs: Organization and functions

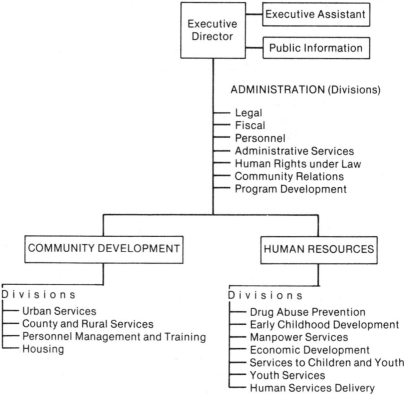

Source: Prepared from information in Texas Department of Community Affairs, *Annual Report* (Austin: Texas Department of Community Affairs, 1976).

A particularly interesting direct subsidy program to private industry is industrial start-up training, titled Profitrain, from the words *profit* and *training*. Classes are held in state technical schools or colleges with the company's own supervisory personnel hired by the Industrial Commission as instructors. Curricula and recruiting and screening of trainees are developed and performed under company guidance and approval, and the company hires only those persons it chooses. "Profitrain programs provided for existing industries have an additional incentive: wages for on-the-job trainees federally subsidized under the Comprehensive Employment and Training Act."[46] Savings to industries are calculated by the Texas Industrial Commission at $800 to $2,000 for each employee trained. (See Chapter 1 for dominant attitudes toward economic development.)

FIGURE 8-7
Texas Industrial Commission advertising

When the old corporate tax bite eats away profits,

Imagine how much you could boost your bottom line figure if you paid no state income tax, corporate or personal. And your unemployment insurance tax was only $22.82 instead of the $86.01 national average.

And there's more. Like sales taxes at retail only. And ad valorem taxes

ILLINOIS 6.6%

TEXAS 0%

PENNSYLVANIA 12.0%

NEW YORK 11.6%

lower than most industrial states. Plus an absence of new tax increases since 1971. And none scheduled through 1978. Making the modest franchise tax your only corporate assessment. Need more inducements? Give us a call or mail the coupon. We think you'll like the way Texas does business.

cut out for Texas.

Please send a corporate tax scale, by states, to:

Name_____ Title_____

Company _____ Address_____

City_____ State_____ Zip_____

⭐ **TEXAS INDUSTRIAL COMMISSION**

Mail to: Texas Industrial Commission, James H. Harwell, Executive Director, Capital Station/Box 12728, Austin, Texas 78711. Phone (512) 475-4331

1177ERT

The Industrial Commission ran ads in major publications such as: *Business Week, Dun's Review, Newsweek,* and *The Wall Street Journal.*

Source: Legislative Budget Board, *Fiscal Size Up: Texas State Services,* 1978–79 Biennium (Austin: Legislative Budget Office, undated).

State agencies' area-organized services and programs

Many, but not all, of Texas state government agencies utilize regional or district schemes for providing services and implementing programs at the local level. These arrangements vary widely. Some state agencies, for example, maintain district offices with no designated areal and clientele boundaries. Other agencies differ in the degree to which regional operations are a vital part of agency activities and programs. Further, state agency area-oriented services and programs are of two classes:

Traditional and long-standing services Examples of this type are local systems of law enforcement and judiciary. These and long-standing regional systems of highway construction and maintenance, employment services and unemployment compensation, agricultural services, and public welfare programs, which date from the New Deal, serve large, statewide clienteles and are well integrated with total agency operations. See Figure 8–8 for illustration of substate administrative regions of the Texas Employment Commission.

More recent area-oriented services and programs These are the result of federal grants dating back to the 1960s which came as a result of project requests sponsored by groups poorly represented then by conservative Democratic forces in control of state government. Demands for these services were not being met in Texas, for legislative majorities perceived no need for most of them.[47]

Offered in the broad category of social services principally to specialized groups, these more recent state regional arrangements and services include the following:

FIGURE 8–8
Texas Employment Commission districts and district offices

Source: *Annual Report,* Texas Employment Commission, 1977, p. 15.

Public health regions for providing comprehensive public health services to local citizens directly and in cooperation with local health departments;

Community mental health and mental retardation centers organized with the assistance of regional directors and other personnel of the regions of the Texas Department of Mental Health and Mental Retardation to provide family counseling, day care, specialized services for alcoholics and drug addicted, children's services, programs for the elderly, and assistance in juvenile problems;

District and satellite offices in the regions of the Texas Rehabilitation Commission to provide vocational and other forms of rehabilitation to the various classes of handicapped persons;

District and local offices of the Texas Employment Commission to provide programs of urban and rural manpower development and training;

Regional and local offices of the Texas Department of Public Welfare to deliver medical assistance, food stamps, and other types of social and community services (discussed in Chapter 10);

Multicounty districts and local offices of the Texas Agricultural Extension Service to supply assorted information and to furnish community development programs to both rural and urban residents;

Regions of the Texas Department of Water Resources to assist cities and industries with their water treatment procedures and facilities (see agency organization, p. 180) and;

Regions of the Texas Air Control Board to develop air pollution abatement standards and plans and to regulate and enforce its rules and regulations.

Many of these programs, until recently, have been only minimally adopted and funded; hence, service tends to be spotty and poorly integrated with other, traditional programs in the old agencies to which they were attached. Indeed, local option provisions are often provided in state enabling statutes, by which local elites and majorities can refuse participation or which require sizable local contributions which local elites are reluctant to give.

Rural problems have only recently received attention, and program implementation seems particularly poor in rural areas as compared with the range of services offered in urbanized and metropolitan areas. But advances are being made. For example, the Department of Health, through development of its regional public health services program since 1969, is providing services to over one half of the 20 percent of the Texas population which is resident in the 178 counties not served by organized local health departments.[48] Other "people-related" programs include manpower training and development, job placement assistance, youth programs, and agricultural information, homemaking, and health services to the aged. Still, by and large, rural areas suffer from a policy of benign neglect.

Part of the problem of neglect is the sheer size of Texas and the number of rural Texans to be served. Other aspects of the problem include the impact of certain emphases of the national government, including insistence upon promotion of industrialization of the rural sector. The object of the latter bias is to provide an industrial and public institutional infrastructure to stem the tide of out-migration from rural to urban areas caused by mechanization of American agriculture. Joining this strategem, the 62d Texas Legislature in 1971 passed the Rural Industrial Development Act, which authorizes investment loans to local industrial development agencies. Two years later, to strengthen state direction and leadership, the legislature established and funded the Rural Business Development Division of the Texas Industrial Commission and enlarged the membership of the Commission to include three residents of Texas' rural areas. Also created was the Division of Community Services of the Texas Department of Community Affairs to work with local officials to obtain federal loans for community facilities and business development in the small towns and rural areas. Professor Niles Hansen argues that the strategy cannot attract enough (light) industry to rural areas to provide people with jobs where they live and is more concerned with physical conditions than with the people left behind. He proposes instead an alternative strategy of federal and state subsidies in rural education, health, and training, and a relocation policy.[49]

Direct state payments to local governments

Unlike the fiscal practices in 45 other American states, Texas grants no general local government support. The lion's share (96.2 percent) of state intergovernmental payments goes to local school districts for education. Other state-aided local-government functions are highways, health services, and hospitals. As stated by the state director of the Texas Municipal League, speaking for the general-purpose local governments (cities and counties), "State government in Texas provides very little assistance to local governments. Usually the state either does things itself or acts as a funnel for federal funds."[50]

Failure to provide intergovernmental payments is reflected, of course, in the state tax structure.[51] The Texas Research League has estimated that to raise Texas' percentage of local aid to the *percentage* level of only the poorest performing states would require an additional $1.6 billion.[52] But additional revenues for these funds could be raised rather painlessly, given the state's *low* state tax status. And tax relief from the local property tax is hardly required when it is seen that Texas' per capita tax burden (per $1,000 of personal income) is below the average of the other United States. In the context of relatively high resources, low tax burden, patterns in the other states, and the growing needs of the people for local urban and rural services, the policy of Texas state government of no sizeable collections of revenues for transfer to its municipalities and county governments has to be counted as a major oversight and policy failure.

State response: Emphasis upon structure

Most of the attention of state governments to their substate regional problems has occurred since 1965 and at the instance of the national government. The total of state area-oriented activities throughout the country is large. In Texas, the emphasis has been on structural paraphernalia more than on programmatic innovation. In this chapter we have seen the establishment of numerous needed structural or organizational features, as follows:

System of area councils of governments (COGs),

Designation of the governor as chief planning officer,

Enlargement of the governor's professional staff,

Creation of the Department of Community Affairs,

Delegation of interlocal contractual authority,

Creation of the Texas Advisory Commission on Intergovernmental Relations,

Establishment of interagency planning councils, and

Expanded arrangements for technical services to local governments.

The urban action policy declared in 1971 by which Texas state agencies were directed to center their actions upon

Preserving the environment,

Improving individual opportunities,

Enhancing community development, and

Strengthening local governments

has been only partially implemented and realized. And while the Texas legislature has passed basic urban legislation in six major policy areas,

Air pollution,

Sewerage treatment and disposal,

Mass transportation,

Area councils of governments,

Multipurpose special districts, and

Urban renewal,

Texas was ranked as moderately inactive among 46 states which reported urban policy initiatives.[53]

More aggressive legislative activity in the following policy areas is suggested if Texas state government is to meet its obligations with respect to a myriad of area problems in both its urban and rural regions:

Medical services,

Migrant labor,

Enforcement of minimum wage legislation,

Land use and management,

Environment,

Resource management, including coastal,

Consumer protection,

Housing and construction standards,

Housing subsidies,

Subdivision development standards,

Property tax equalization,

Equitable distribution of aid to school districts,

Transportation,

Land sales controls and information,

Antidiscrimination practices,

Penal reform,

Minority hiring and promotion practices,

Manpower development and training,

Labor law reforms,

Protection of basic civil liberties,

Public service careers,

Welfare reform,

Equal rights protections for women,

Child welfare and care agencies, and

Vocational education.

In addition, it has been suggested that the powers and authority of county and municipal governments be enlarged to enable these local jurisdictions to serve their citizens in cooperation with the efforts of state and national governments.

Policy development out of phase with environmental challenges

Heinz Eulau's and Kenneth Prewitt's characterization of some cities as having policy development out of phase with environmental challenges seems particularly descriptive also of the Texas political system.[54] In Texas, government policy initiatives stagnate in a traditionalistic set of political and governmental traditions and institutions.[55] Resistance against necessary and acceptable levels of innovative change seems to govern policymaking in government, while development, modernization, progress, growth, and productivity are hallmarks for private institutional development and private policymaking. In social affairs, "modern lifestyles" and change are embraced wholeheartedly by the citizenry, while citizens as voters and consumers of government services cling to outdated, restrictive constitutional provisions, a part-time legislature, and inadequate programs.

A few dominant private economic organizational complexes in Texas appear to team up with the legislative leadership and other officials to assure retention of traditional policy outcomes, despite the challenges for change. The great mass of Texas citizens, not having been activated to meaningful and effective participation in the input structure, political change lags far behind massive changes in social, economic, and demographic environments. Placating a variety of specialized pressures proves not to be conducive to policymaking in terms of the state's objective needs.

CONCLUSIONS

Our examination of governmental relations among metropolitan and rural units permits the following conclusions:

1. Public authority in Texas is fragmented into innumerable units of government, and urban sprawl has reduced the manageability of metropolitan governments. These developments vitiate the capacity of local government to deliver basic governmental services, and leave the local governmental system open to control by vested economic and political elites.

2. Problems of poverty are especially dramatic in Texas' rural areas, and rural poverty is especially sharp among minority Texans. In addition, enormous governmental problems are raised by the large, rural, migrant labor force in the state.

3. With major initiatives and money flowing from the federal government, substate planning regions and area councils of government (COGs) are now operating to provide regional approaches to areawide planning of urban and rural services.

4. Texas government delivers traditional services rather well to local areas. Newer social services, even though encouraged by the national government for more than a decade, are spotty and not well integrated into the existing machinery for implementation for either rural or urban populations.

5. The emphasis of Texas state government, with no general program of state aid to cities and county governments, is on the creation of a variety of administrative arrangements, not on innovative programs and delivery of needed services.

CHAPTER NINE

Local governments

Americans have been obsessed with the idea of a
relationship between structure and effectiveness
of government.

CHARLES R. ADRIAN*

Of the parents who have many children, it is commonly said, "They
surely must love children—they have so many." Commenting on Texas'
4,000 local governments, someone might conclude, "Texans surely must
love local governments—they have so many." Often our attributed reasons are wide of the mark, or true in some cases, not in others. The number and functions of local governments are rooted in broad historical,
social, economic, and demographic trends. The most numerous, the
classes of water district governments, are a product of urban and economic development of the last three decades and of ego investment
and business entrepreneurship. Urges for civic participation, local self-
government, a new start, and professional efficiency all combine with
the pressures of rising population and profit-making. Water districts, as
we shall see in the last portion of this chapter, are public bodies established at the initiative and for the use of private development corporations
in order that new homes with basic urban services may be provided in
urban and suburban neighborhoods.

Texas' 254 counties are basic, traditional, and deeply rooted in the
Constitution. Established from Texas' independence, county government was the only general or multipurpose local government for most
Texans until fairly recent times. Today, even with modern communications and transportation and with other classes of local governments,
counties are still basic. Every Texan has a county government which furnishes essential services. Later, school district governments emerged,
and they are also complete in their coverage of all persons and all areas

---

* *State and Local Governments,* 4th ed. (New York: McGraw-Hill Book Co., 1976), p. 164.

and parts of the state. School district governments, of course, are limited, special-purpose local governments. A consolidation movement has greatly decreased the number in the last three decades.

Here and there a second class of general or multipurpose local governments was instituted in limited areas of denser population more dependent upon trade and commerce—the class of towns, villages, and cities, which the Census Bureau simply classifies as municipalities. With great growth and shifts in state population, cities and city life-styles have come to be dominant. More than 9 million Texans now live in the 25 SMSA core cities of more than 50,000 population each and in their satellite cities and suburbs. Still more municipalities are created every year as urbanization continues apace.

Finally, in the 20th century there developed a diverse set of other special district governments, with the several types of water districts the most numerous. This is the age of special districts in Texas. Their rate of increase in the five year period, 1972–77 was 20 percent, and they now constitute four of every ten governments in Texas.

Thus, Texas local governments consist of four Census Bureau types: municipal governments, county governments, school district governments, and other special purpose governments. See Table 9–1 for the number in Texas and in all the states of each class of local governments, and the direction of change. Note that in New England, the Middle Atlantic States, most of the West, and in some Border States another class exists, the towns and townships, which are not indigenous to Texas.

TABLE 9–1
Classes and number of local governments, Texas and the United States, 1972 and 1977

	Number in Texas		Number in 50 states	
Classes	1972	1977	1972	1977
Municipal governments	981	1,066	18,517	18,856
County governments	254	254	3,044	3,042
School district governments	1,174	1,138	15,781	15,260
Other special district governments*	1,215	1,455	23,885	26,140
Townships (including New England towns)	—	—	16,991	16,822
Totals	3,624	3,913	78,269	80,171

* See types, with numbers, in Table 9–8. The U.S. Census Bureau under-reports the number of other special district governments in Texas.

Source: U.S. Bureau of the Census, *Census of Governments, 1972.* Vol. 1, *Governmental Organization* (Washington, D.C.: U.S. Government Printing Office, 1973) and *Census of Governments, 1977,* Preliminary Report No. 1, "Governmental Units in 1977" (Washington, D.C.: U.S. Department of Commerce, 1977).

This chapter is an extension of the preceding chapter. Local governmental structures, activities, functions, and policy responses are viewed in the dual regional context of urban Texas and rural Texas. Thus is considered for each class of local governments its approaches to the solution of regional problems, particularly in metropolitan areas.[1]

MUNICIPALITIES

Municipal governments in Texas are classified as cities, villages, and towns, but distinctions are few and often muddled. A more meaningful classification is that of home-rule cities and general law cities. Municipalities with a population larger than 5,000 persons may choose to become home-rule cities through drafting and approving their own municipal charters, while cities of 200 to 5,000 inhabitants must operate under the general statutes and are known as general law cities.

Although the legal distinctions between the two classes of cities are not great in practice, home-rule municipalities are said to enjoy greater flexibility in governmental forms, taxation, annexation, and extraterritoriality and more autonomy in selection of services for their people. Whether these differences hold up in the case of any particular city depends, however, upon the wording and effect of numerous special and local statutes which may apply to that municipality and to others in its population group. Many of these special laws hamper the ability of larger home-rule cities to meet increased and changing needs of citizens in our metropolitan areas.

Of significance to all municipalities, regardless of status or size, is that cities have the power to enact local ordinances. This is the authority, which counties do not have, of *rule-initiation* in local matters, consistent with state statutes and the Constitution.

The central tendency is to classify local governments in terms of legal authority of various actors and institutions. All municipal governments have similar institutional parts, including an office of mayor, a multi-member city council or commission, and departments, and some have, in addition, a manager. What we see best by examination of municipal organizations are the formal leadership authority patterns, including who has responsibility for rule-initiation, execution, implementation, and interpretation. See Figure 9–1.

While legal arrangements suggest something of dominant values, electoral structures, ethnic makeup of the community, degree of conflict in politics, policy emphases, and policy performance,[2] politics and processes in wide variety may be obscured or omitted by an examination of formal authority and structures. In a study of four Houston metropolitan area suburban communities, all with similar charter arrangements, it was found that the actual division of authority and responsibility among council members, mayor, and manager varies considerably among these

FIGURE 9–1

Forms of municipal governments

Council-manager:

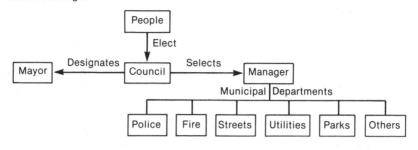

Mayor-manager:

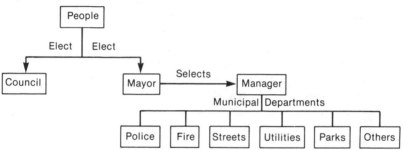

Mayor-council:

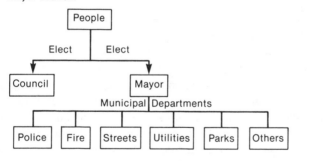

Commission:

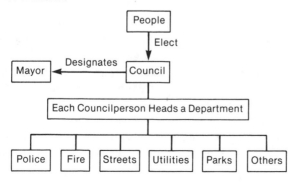

cities. Of more effect in fixing the division of authority and functions are (1) how much concern council members have about the personal traits of their city manager and (2) past manager-council relations.[3]

Council-manager form

Dominant among the state's larger, home-rule cities is the council-manager plan. This form separates the functions of rule-initiation and rule-implementation or administration, placing the former in an elected city council (or commission, as it may be termed) and the latter function in a city manager. The manager is a specially trained, outside expert in municipal affairs who serves at the will of the council. In the pure model, the manager appoints and removes department heads, has responsibility for operations of municipal administrative agencies (such as the parks, police, fire, and public works departments), and supervises preparation and execution of the budget. In actual practice, many variations exist in the initiatives and powers of the manager.

At any rate, the effectiveness of the manager depends upon the support of the city council, for the manager's job depends upon pleasing the council majority. Interestingly enough, as we shall see below, the council-manager system is usually combined with a system of election of city council members which produces councilpersons with markedly homogeneous socioeconomic characteristics and interests, thereby decreasing the potential for political conflict inside the council and in council-constituency relations.

Nevertheless, the manager must appear to build no effective independent power base, and he or she certainly is not permitted to mobilize political groups and activate their membership.[4] But, depending upon relations with the council, expectations of other political actors, and goals of the community, the manager can be more than an expert housekeeper. Policy innovation and leadership roles can emanate from a competent and aggressive manager in running the affairs of the city. If they do not, the city government may not have a strong, single, visible focus of political power since in the pure form the mayor is only a ceremonial figurehead.[5]

Two dominant structural features, nonpartisan elections and at-large selection of council members, mark election of city councils under the council-manager plan in Texas and elsewhere.

Nonpartisan elections In nonpartisan elections, no formal party nominating procedure, such as a party caucus, convention, or direct primary, is required, and the ballot does not carry party affiliations of candidates. As at result, recruitment processes for producing candidates for city councils in Texas are even more obscure than recruitment and nomination processes for legislative, county, district, state, and federal candidates. Probably, *self-recruitment* is the dominant pattern, as it is for legislative candidacies, although the formal and informal activities of oligarchies of business people, citizens groups, charter associations, good government leagues, interest groups, party factions, cliques of organizers, and even political parties probably determine in large measure the amount of campaign resources (money, endorsements, workers, and word-of-mouth appeals) which are available to each of the individual candidates for the city councils.[6]

At-large representation   Two traditional constituency systems exist for city council members, representation from wards and representation of all the city at large, with the latter overwhelmingly predominant. While the at-large system has come under heavy legal attack, it is not illegal except under a special set of circumstances which produce dilution of minority voting strength.[7] Hence, at-large election of city councilpersons, including mayors, will continue to dominate the selection process.[8]

In the ward system, each member of the council is elected from a separate, designated geographical area within the municipality, instead of being elected by a vote of all of the qualified voters of the city, as in the at-large system. The ward system is used in only 13 of Texas' home-rule cities, and in 9 of these municipalities, the arrangement is modified by requiring some city council members to be elected at large. In Houston, for example, the mayor and three councilpersons are elected at large, while five other members are elected from wards.[9]

In the at-large system, all candidates for the council are required to be elected by the voters of the entire city. Both the traditional at-large method and a variant, the place system, are used in Texas. In the traditional system, of the candidates standing for election, candidates who receive the most votes for the number of council seats are elected. Each voter casts as many votes as the number of places to be filled on the council. In the place variation, each of the seats on the city council is assigned a number, as Place 1, Place 2, Place 3. Various candidates stand for election for each of the places. The voter casts a vote for one candidate for each place. For each place, the candidate receiving the highest number of votes is elected, providing he or she has a majority of all votes cast for all candidates running for that place on the city council. (The two candidates who receive the highest number of votes in the first election face each other in the runoff contest.)

A modified place variation requires that some or all candidates be resident of designated geographical areas of the city.

Ideology and institutional forms   These structural forms dominant in Texas' home-rule cities,

Council-manager form,

Nonpartisan elections, and

At-large representation of councilpersons,

are commonly associated with the success of what is known as the municipal reform movement. This movement developed over the last century to fight city machines and bosses, reduce the influence of ethnic politics on local government, separate politics from administration, and install "sound business-like principles, carried out by an expert, trained manager." The nonpartisan ballot was promoted as useful to curb party machines and to assure no party politics in the cities. To eliminate ward politics, patronage rewards, party politics, and the necessity of conflict resolution mechanisms among ethnic groups, the at-large electoral system was recommended.

Of the influence of the values of the municipal reform movement in Texas, history records "a complete conquest of ideology over municipal institutions."[10] Evidence of its success in Texas is seen in the use of the mayor-council form only in Houston among Texas' large cities.[11] By state legislation Houston must use the nonpartisan ballot. Also contrary to its antireform tradition, Houston has the combination at-large and ward system for representation of councilpersons. This system was adopted by popular referendum in 1955, but black leaders now feel that they were "sold a bill of goods" in endorsing the combination at-large and ward representational arrangement.[12] Only in Houston has been found the underlying political characteristics—overt ethnic politics, that is, integration and participation of blacks and Hispanics in electoral politics—which are associated elsewhere in the United States with the mayor-council type of city government. Houston blacks, in comparison with blacks in Dallas, for example, are better organized and have a voting turnout in recent elections which is 15 percentage points higher than that of blacks in Dallas.[13]

The style of politics in Texas' other large cities (with their reform institutions) features

Token representation of minority ethnic and racial groups on city councils,

Nonsocialization and nonintegration of these same groups into electoral politics,

Nonexpression of cultural and class differences in representative government, and

Control of city government by white, Anglo-Saxon, Protestant business oligarchies underpinned by good government leagues or citizens groups.

These characteristics are markedly different from those found in the nation's largest municipalities.

Mayor-manager form

A variation of the council-manager type, the mayor-manager form, is used in several cities, notably New York, Philadelphia, San Francisco, and New Orleans, to fill the vacuum of formal political leadership in municipal affairs. The plan gives an elective mayor authority to be the chief political, ceremonial, and administrative officer. A manager, the chief lieutenant in rule-implementation, is appointed by the mayor and is responsible to him or her rather than to the council.[14] The council and the mayor share in rule-initiation, as is common in the stronger type of the mayor-council form and in some variants of the council-manager plan, such as in Dallas.

Mayor-council form

The mayor-council structure is used in most of Texas' small cities. These cities, towns, and villages constitute, of course, most of Texas' 1,066 municipalities. Even in the larger of the small cities, we see the mayor commonly weakened by restrictions of various kinds. Thus, most Texas cities are said to have the weak mayor-council form.

Weak-mayor subtype   In this variant, the mayor is weak in both rule-initiation and rule-implementation. By weak, we mean the absence of one or more of the following legal prerogatives:

Authority of rule-initiation

Veto over council ordinances

Appointment and removal of city department heads

Budget preparation and execution.

In the absence of these powers, a mayor has difficulty exerting much leadership, even if he or she has long tenure, great resources, and the respect of the community. But in many small incorporated communities,

Collegial type government, of mayor as just another councilperson,

Low budgets,

Low tax rates on property, and

Many volunteer services, or services for fees,

fit both political and economic needs and realities.

Strong-mayor subtype   By contrast with the above, the mayor has a strong, independent power base and resources as well as grants of charter powers, including the veto, budgeting, council leadership, executive appointments and removals, planning, and executive supervision of city services.

Commission form

In use in Texas by scarcely 100 general law cities and only a few home-rule municipalities, this form combines rule-initiation and rule-implementation in the same persons. Each one of the elected city commissioners serves also as the head of a city administrative department. The commission form, like the weak mayor-council subtype and the council-manager form, suffers from lack of effective political leadership since one of the coequal commissioners commonly performs the ceremonial duties which are usually accorded a mayor.[15]

Approaches to area problems

Municipal annexation Texas, along with other states, has experienced since 1945 renewed use of municipal annexation as a device for planned development and orderly and relatively inexpensive extension of municipal services to growing population centers. While in most states annexations have been modest, in the Lone Star state, as we saw in the last chapter, sizable, even spectacular, land additions to metropolitan area cities have taken place. Of the 19 American cities in the 100,000 and over population range which are leaders in the annexation movement since 1950 (each city gaining 100 or more square miles), five are Texas municipalities.[16]

Although legislation in 1963 slowed the pace of annexation in Texas, current public policy clearly favors a highly liberalized annexation prerogative for Texas cities. The larger the population, the larger the physical growth. Houston's territory, for example, now exceeds 500 square miles, an increase of more than 300 percent since 1950. Underlying the annexation movement during the past three decades is simply the existence of a large amount of raw land (undeveloped and unannexed) adjacent to large municipalities. Houston and other large cities were largely not hemmed in by other municipalities, as were many cities in the earlier established metropolitan complexes in the East. Given this basis, the Texas pattern of large-scale annexation was produced by numerous factors. Foremost is perhaps the spirit of urban economic development uninhibited by the exercise of substantial regulatory authority in unincorporated areas. Neither state nor county governments have effective land-use controls. Urban county governments are kept without authority to provide common municipal-type services, a void filled by annexation and resting, before a community is annexed, on special district governments. As we shall see in the last major section of this chapter, an integral element in the strategy of annexation is provided by state policy allowing ease of establishment (and later annexation) of urban water district governments. Water districts supply minimal essential urban services while fixing in law great economic incentives for profitable speculation.

Annexation has served to neutralize the economic impact on cities of "white flight" from central cities to the suburbs. After sufficient development of property values in homes and businesses in the urban fringe area, the community is annexed. But a look at service levels shows that it is precisely in this urban fringe, lying just outside the dominant municipality, where, even after annexation, urban services are deficient, water and air pollution grow unabated, and transportation problems are the greatest.

Extraterritoriality Texas has a "most imaginative approach" to annexation because the Municipal Annexation Act of 1963 allows, in effect, "a city to combine its annexation powers with the exercise of extraterritorial powers."[17] This statute bestows on large cities five miles of extraterritorial jurisdiction and annexation without popular referendum up to 10 percent of its territory annually.[18] "Buffer zones" in surrounding unincorporated contiguous areas range from one half mile for cities of less than 1,500 population to five miles around municipalities of 100,000 or more people. Within this jurisdiction, a city may require of a developer a plat of any subdivision and insist upon conformity with city ordinances and regulations governing alleys, streets, parks, utility easements, placements, and standards. Extraterritoriality also allows cities to provide water to adjacent areas and to enact quarantine and sanitary regulations, jointly with county governments, to a distance of ten miles.[19] Further, no other city can annex within a city's jurisdiction, and municipalities whose jurisdiction overlaps into a central city's area cannot annex without that city's permission. Houston's options were preserved, for example, when city officials in 1963 extended the city limits along ten-foot strips stretching up to 40 miles. See Figure 9–2.

Municipal revenues and expenditures

Several significant points can be made about municipal revenues in Texas. (See Table 9–2, which compares revenue sources of various cities in Texas of different population sizes and which presents the revenue picture for all U.S. municipalities.)

1. For all Texas cities, the sales tax is very important, producing 20–26.1 percent of their total revenue needs.
2. Revenue patterns among Texas cities of different population size are remarkably similar.
3. But the largest of Texas cities of 50,000 or more population have greater reliance on property taxes than the smaller cities.

FIGURE 9–2
Strip annexation in Houston

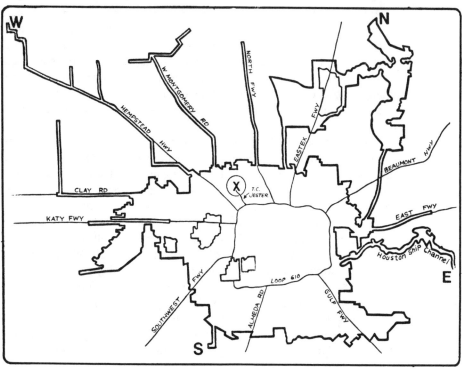

Note: Width of the annexed strips is not to scale. X marks the spot of the geographic center of the City of Houston.

Source: *The Houston Post,* January 30, 1977, p. 1D. Copyright 1977 *The Houston Post.* Reprinted by permission.

4. Conversely, Texas' smaller cities experience a somewhat greater reliance on fees and service charges than the largest cities.

5. Texas cities cannot rely on state aid, which for U.S. cities constitutes one fourth of their total revenues! Texas municipalities receive only 1.5 percent of total revenues from state government, while receiving as large a share of federal funds as the U.S. average. Texas cities, large and small, realize 40 percent of their funds from the property tax, nearly 20 percent from sales taxes, and 17 percent from various charges.[20]

Looking at expenditure patterns, we see that Texas municipalities spend nearly four times the total spending of the 254 Texas counties and at about one third the amount of the state budget. And spending priorities of Texas municipalities and counties are quite similar, with the exception

TABLE 9–2

Finances of selected Texas cities compared with all U.S. cities: Types of revenues as percent of total revenues, 1975–1976

Types of revenues	All U.S. cities	Tyler (pop. 61,434)	Amarillo (pop. 138,743)	Dallas (pop. 812,797)	Houston (pop. 1,326,809)
Intergovernmental					
From state	24.9	0.5	2.3	1.7	1.3
From federal	13.4	11.5	10.5	16.2	15.8
From local	1.8	0.0	1.7	0.8	1.5
Totals	40.1	12.0	14.5	18.7	18.6
Own sources					
Property taxes	25.6	30.6	32.7	41.0	35.6
Sales taxes	9.3	26.1	21.0	18.5	20.0
Other taxes	7.3	.6	1.2	1.1	1.2
Charges	11.1	19.3	19.7	10.9	14.3
Miscellaneous* ...	6.6	11.3	10.9	9.6	10.3
Totals	59.9	87.9	85.5	81.1	81.4

* Includes interest earnings, special assessments, sales of property, and "other and unallocable."

Source: U.S. Bureau of the Census, *City Government Finances in 1975–76*, Series GF76 No. 4 (Washington, D.C.: U.S. Government Printing Office, 1977), Tables 1 and 5.

that Texas cities are not called upon to perform varied financial administration and general control functions for state government (such as tax collections) that the counties perform as administrative arms of the state.[21] Certain essential characteristics of Texas municipal spending emerge:

1. Given low municipal expenditures, a certain amount of functional and financial centralization exists in state government. For example, what welfare expenditures are made in Texas are centralized at the state level.

2. Given low municipal and state expenditure levels, the range of municipal programs is relatively small, producing neglect of some programs and services by governments in Texas.

3. Texas municipalities, given the high level of urbanization and patterns of urban sprawl (discussed in Chapter 8), have particularly large and distinctive transportation needs. Roads and highways outlays are nearly double percentages found in all U.S. cities. Also, a much larger proportion is spent on airport construction, maintenance, and administration.

4. Texas municipalities have negligible expenses in education, while educational outlays account for one sixth of expenditures of all U.S. cities.

5. Texas cities have not embarked on general assistance and other types of welfare programs, the average expenditures for all U.S. cities being 85 times that in Texas cities!

The last three characteristics are illustrated by figures in Table 9–3.

COUNTIES

Legal position

Duality County government in Texas is both an administrative arm of state government and 254 local governmental units endowed with local responsibilities. As an administrative extension of the state, the county is charged with such duties as

Enforcing state laws,

Financing and servicing local courts and some state courts,

Administering and collecting certain state revenues, and

Implementing state rules in a variety of policy areas.

In their local responsibilities, Texas counties have traditionally

Built roads and bridges,

Maintained jails and detention homes,

Built and maintained court houses,

Kept records,

TABLE 9–3
Spending by function, U.S. and Texas municipalities

General expenditure category	Percentage United States	Percentage Texas
Education	16.3	0.7
Police protection	11.1	13.7
Sanitation and sewerage	9.3	14.9
Public welfare	8.5	0.1
Highways	7.8	13.0
Hospital and health	7.7	4.3
Fire protection	6.2	9.4
Parks and recreation	4.4	9.4
Housing and urban renewal	4.2	2.0
Airports	1.5	5.9
All other*	23.1	26.7

* Includes water transport and terminals, parking facilities, libraries, financial administration, general control, public buildings, and interest on general debt.

Source: U.S. Department of Commerce, Bureau of the Census, *1972 Census of Governments,* vol. 4, no. 4, *Finances of Municipalities and Township Governments* (Washington, D.C.: U.S. Government Printing Office, 1974), Table 12, pp. 27–28. Prepared with the assistance of Larry Gaskamp.

Established a local system of criminal justice, and

Provided some fire and health protection.

Primary emphasis has been placed on serving the needs of citizens resident outside incorporated municipalities, where county government served, until a few decades ago, as virtually the only government for many Texans.

Devolution   Even today, benign neglect by state government, plus traditional attitudes with respect to local self-government, tend to give county government a large measure of autonomy. As a result of failure of state government to exercise administrative control over state functions performed by county officials, a substantial devolution of state authority has resulted, but not a broad, specific delegation of powers to these local units of government.

Discretion   County governments can largely determine the manner in which state-imposed services are financed and administered. Further, they may decide which, if any, of numerous state-authorized optional programs will be undertaken and to what degree they shall be performed.[22] Policy discretion is enhanced, of course, by political factors, such as local election of county officials on the long ballot. State laws are applied in the light of county officials' own judgment and locally prevailing sentiments, legal conditions, and norms. But Texas counties do not have the power of local ordinance, as the cities do. Until authorized via constitutional or statutory change, counties will perform only those services set by state law. Metropolitan counties will find it increasingly difficult to govern without both additional authority and flexibility in governmental structures.

Structure of county government: Commission form

The structure of county government is so firmly set in the Constitution and statutes that no fundamental change has occurred since 1876.[23] Identical basic forms exist in all 254 counties. Known as the plural executive, or commission, structure, county government is characterized by a number of independently elected county officers and lack of clear focus of executive leadership. See Figure 9–3.

The following elective officials and boards are provided in the Constitution: judge, commissioners, justices of the peace, constables, clerk, tax assessor-collector, treasurer, sheriff, surveyor, attorney, inspector of hides and animals, county commissioners court, board of (tax) equalization, and board of elections. In addition, the statutes provide for a county superintendent and county school board. Various other appointed officers may exist, including an auditor, health officer, and agricultural and home demonstration agents.

FIGURE 9–3

County government in Texas

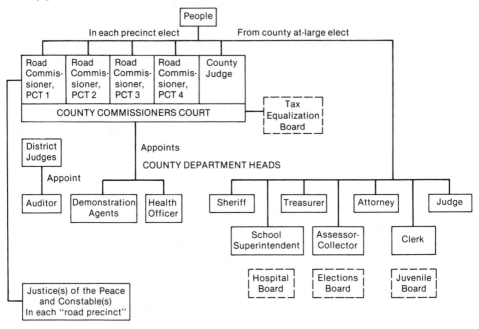

County commissioners court

Centralized services and duties To the extent that county services are not assigned to specific county officers, the performance of centralized services is supplied by the county commission. The policymaking organ of county government, the commissioners court is a multimember, five-person body comprised of the county judge and four road commissioners, who individually have additional important duties. Policymaking is largely confined to determining the extent of financial support and mode of administration of state-imposed programs, the court deciding which of the optional services shall be funded and carried out and setting salaries of county officials. The secretary of the commissioners court, the county clerk, furnishes a record of the financial condition of the county, and all officers who handle county funds regularly report to the clerk the collection and disposition of all moneys.

Besides adopting the budget of county government, the court has significant discretional financial authority also in

Deciding at what level to tax (to the constitutional limit) and whether to submit propositions for approval to levy additional special purpose taxes and

Sitting annually as a board of tax equalization to equalize taxes and to certify the tax valuations.

Thus, in its financial authority, the body can affect, but not direct, performance of the duties of each of the independently elected county department heads.

Additional authority of the county commissioners court includes

Letting contracts for equipment, supplies, construction, and other purposes,

Appointing nonelective officers and exercising direct control over administration of their duties, and

Filling vacancies in any of the constitutional offices.

Election and terms of judge and commissioners   Members of the commissioners court are popularly elected in partisan elections for four-year terms. The county judge, the presiding officer of the group, is selected from the county at-large, while each of the four commissioners is elected from a separate precinct (not to be confused with the more numerous voting precincts in each county). Boundary lines of commissioners precincts are determined by the court itself, subject to the "one-person, one-vote" rule.[24] With equal population precincts, in the largely urban counties county government need no longer be regarded as rural government. Nevertheless, in the face of inflexible governmental structures and shallow powers, the rewards of control of county government may be primarily symbolic. But the symbolic payoffs of urban ethnic and racial representation on county commissioners courts and hope of more sympathetic consideration of urban, suburban, and metropolitan problems of county populations may be considerable.

Actual election of all but a small minority of county officials takes place in the open Democratic primaries. Very few Republican candidates challenge the Democratic courthouses, even in the face of a large number of Central Texas German and West Texas Panhandle traditional Republican counties, burgeoning Republicanism in metropolitan areas, and superior strength of Republican electoral activities and monetary resources in many areas. Harris and Dallas counties elected Republican county judges in 1974. But social, economic, and political sanctions, combined with the practical political fact that lack of Republican control at the state level until 1979 provided no patronage rewards for unsuccessful Republican candidates, continue to inhibit second-party candidacies.[25] Even in the Democratic primaries, one study showed that 24 percent of judges and 20 percent of county commissioners had never faced opposition, and about one-fifth of these officials had first been appointed to office (by the commissioners court and the county judge, respectively).[26] Average tenure runs to about 10 years.

County judge

In addition to his role as weak county executive—as presiding officer of the commissioners court—the county judge combines judicial, political, administrative, and management duties in other roles. Thus, the office mixes discretion and implementation, as well as interpretation or adjudicatory functions.

Judicial role A prime duty of the county judge in most counties is service in a judicial capacity as judge of the county court. Over the years, many judges have been relieved of some or all their judicial duties by creation of one or more county courts-at-law. The legislature is expected to continue this practice, leaving judges more time to act as county executives.

Political role In most Texas counties, the county judge is the leader of the dominant Democratic party faction, or the spokesperson of the county's political leadership. With the sheriff and clerk, he or she is a member of the county elections board, a formal position of some consequence in county politics. In some counties the judge is challenged for political leadership, most often by the sheriff.

Administrative role In "wet" counties where beer and wine sales are permitted, county judges hold application hearings for permits, after which they issue licenses to applicants found in conformity with state laws. In counties which have abolished the county school superintendent's position or which have fewer than 3,000 school children, or which have in excess of 30,000 population but no common school districts, the county judge acts as ex officio county school superintendent. With other county officers, judges may serve on administrative boards, such as the juvenile or hospital board.

Management role In most counties, the county judge is chief budget officer. Budget preparation, presentation to the commissioners court, and a vote on adoption give the judge considerable influence over priorities, tax levels, services, and operations of county departments and offices. However, in counties of 225,000 and more population, the budget, and postauditing as well, are placed in the hands of an auditor appointed by the county's resident district judges. Conflict generated between the commissioners court and the auditor by this 1939 bracket statute is regularly transferred to the state legislative arena and to the state's chief legal officer. Scores of opinions of the attorney general have been generated in Harris County alone, where, for example, the auditor resisted establishment of the office of executive assistant to the county commission. In another skirmish, the commission substituted, again through special legislation, the county's chief probation officer as the budgeting officer of the probation department.[27]

Other county officers

Justices of the peace and constables Each county is divided into four or more (to a total of eight) precincts for criminal justice purposes. One or more justice courts are established in each county. A justice of the peace presides over the justice court and small claims court. He or she also serves as coroner in most Texas counties and as a magistrate for arraigning prisoners, fixing bails, and holding preliminary hearings. A constable assists the court in serving writs, processes, and warrants and as executive officer of the justice court.

Sheriff The county peace officer, the sheriff serves county and district courts in the same ways that constables service justice and small claims courts. In addition, sheriffs are custodians of prisoners and run county jails. They are also tax assessor-collectors in about 40 counties of fewer than 10,000 people.

Attorney County attorneys represent the state in criminal prosecutions and the county in civil suits, mainly in delinquent tax collections, and serve the commissioners court as legal advisor. Twice a year, when a district judge visits each county which is not the site of a district court, the county attorney also acts as the district attorney, prosecuting criminal cases and handling civil litigation in the district court sessions.

Clerk Secretary of the county commissioners court, the clerk combines other administrative duties with judicial functions. As clerk of the county court, he or she attends sessions, records proceedings, keeps the docket, files records of impending cases, and files completed court records, acting also in these capacities in small population counties in the district court.

The county clerk maintains numerous other records, such as deeds, marriage records, contracts, bonds, and voting records, and in counties without an auditor keeps finance ledgers of county financial transactions and reports quarterly summaries to the commissioners court. Finally, the clerk is a county elections official, serving as a member of the county elections board, conducting absentee balloting, notifying and instructing election judges and clerks, receiving and subsequently properly disposing of all ballots, and certifying and transmitting election returns to the Texas Secretary of State.

Tax assessor-collector Charged with assessing and collecting county and state ad valorem taxes, the tax assessor-collector also sells automobile license plates, registers titles of automobiles, collects state sales taxes on automobile transfers, and registers voters for national, state, and local elections. By statute passed in the 65th Legislature, the county commissioners court may transfer voter registration duties to the clerk or to a separately created appointive office of county elections administrator.[28]

Treasurer   Custodian of county funds, the treasurer receives moneys from various county offices, provides for depositories, and authorizes, under direction of the commissioners court, expenditures of county funds.

Health officer   Commissioners courts are required to appoint health officers to enforce state regulations with respect to jails, care of prisoners, health of indigents, quarantines, and general health care facilities operated. Some counties appoint a private physician to the post with the apparent intention of meeting only minimum requirements, while others establish a full-time physician and staff to offer a range of health care and preventive health services, including county hospital services.

Agricultural and home demonstration agents   Under supervision and salary augmentation by Texas A&M University, agricultural and home demonstration agents, appointed by the county commission, offer ambitious programs in most Texas counties, including lecturers, workshops, advice to individuals, free publications, assistance in plant and animal disease control, food preparation, and other projects and needs.

County expenditures and revenues

Financial outlays of the 254 county governments in Texas amount to only a little more than 10 percent of total state-local expenditures, an imbalance which reflects

Financial centralization of some services in higher government levels,

Lack of responsibility of counties for public education,

Neglect of some programs, particularly in urban areas, and

Utilization of county governments by state government for financial administration and general control services. Counties serve as tax collection and assessment agencies, bear a significant portion of state costs in law enforcement and judicial functions, and in numerous other ways bear financial administration and general control costs. Texas' expenditure level of 20.9 percent in this category is two and one half times the average among U.S. counties.

Two thirds of Texas county spending is in three areas: financial administration and general control, hospitals, and roads and highways. See Figure 9–4, which also contrasts spending patterns and levels in Texas with all U.S. counties. In three public service areas—welfare, education, and roads—spending by Texas counties is in marked contrast with the

FIGURE 9–4
County government spending by function, United States and Texas

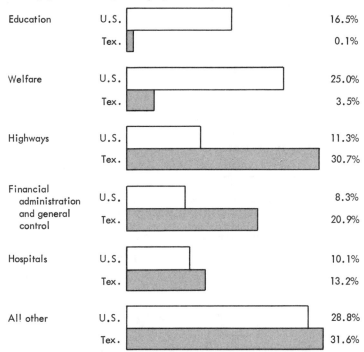

Education	U.S.	16.5%
	Tex.	0.1%
Welfare	U.S.	25.0%
	Tex.	3.5%
Highways	U.S.	11.3%
	Tex.	30.7%
Financial administration and general control	U.S.	8.3%
	Tex.	20.9%
Hospitals	U.S.	10.1%
	Tex.	13.2%
All other	U.S.	28.8%
	Tex.	31.6%

Source: U.S. Department of Commerce, Bureau of the Census, *1972 Census of Governments,* vol. 4, no. 3, *Finances of County Governments* (Washington, D.C.: U.S. Government Printing Office, 1974), Table 7, p. 17. Prepared with the help of Larry Gaskamp.

average spent among all 3,042 U.S. county governments. Public welfare outlays, representing one fourth of expenses among U.S. counties, claims only 3.5 percent of Texas county budgets. Education, claiming outlays of 16.5 percent among U.S. counties, is the responsibility in Texas of state and school district governments. Texas expenditure levels of 30.7 percent on roads and highways, as against only 11.3 percent among all U.S. counties reflect topographical features, distances, values, and lack of centralization of the function in Texas.

For all their services to state government, Texas counties realize only 7 percent of their revenue from that level, as contrasted with 40 percent received, on the average, by all U.S. counties from their state authorities. While all Texas local governments are heavily dependent upon the ad valorem or property tax, county governments are the most dependent, after the classes of urban water districts, on revenues from taxes laid on

TABLE 9–4

Sources of county revenues, Texas and United States

Sources	Texas counties	U.S. counties
Intergovernmental		
From federal	10.5	7.9
From state	6.6	37.3
Totals	17.1	45.2
Own sources		
Property taxes	48.9	31.4
Other taxes	5.2	6.9
Charges	28.8†	11.8
Miscellaneous*		4.8
Totals	82.9	54.9

* Includes interest earnings, special assessments, sales of property, and "other and unallocable."

† Source does not give separate figures.

Source: U.S. Department of Commerce, Bureau of Census, *County Government Finances in 1975–76,* Series GF76–No. 8 (Washington, D.C.: U.S. Government Printing Office, 1977), Table 5 and *Governmental Finances in 1975–76,* Series GF76–No. 5 (Washington, D.C.: U.S. Government Printing Office, 1977), Table 16.

the value of real property. Texas counties derive nearly 50 percent of their moneys from this source, as contrasted with 31.4 percent for all U.S. counties. These sources, and others, contrasted with figures for all American counties, are depicted in Table 9–4.

FEDERAL AID TO TEXAS LOCAL GOVERNMENTS

We have seen the proportion of federal funds in the revenue structures of both municipalities and county governments.[29] Only the largest of Texas cities receive a considerably greater share of their revenues from federal grants (of both kinds, categorical and revenue sharing) than do county governments. Overall, about one half of all federal moneys to Texas multipurpose local governments is in the form of revenue sharing grants, which can be spent in any program category, at the option of local officials.

Use of revenue sharing funds

Top priorities of Texas cities and counties in revenue sharing funds are almost identical, with cities spending 49 percent of these grants for transportation and public safety and counties allocating 46 percent in these two categories. For municipalities, the third priority area is environ-

TABLE 9–5
Use of revenue sharing funds by Texas local governments, 1975

	Percent of funds used by	
Programmatic categories	Cities	Counties
Transportation	28	23
Public safety	21	23
Environmental protection*	14	3
General government	11	22
Recreation	10	5
Health	6	7
Housing/community development	3	†
Social services for aged/poor‡	2	3
Libraries	2	3
Financial administration	2	10
Other	1	1

* Mainly for construction of waste water treatment plants, flood control improvements, and maintenance of sanitary land fill sites.

† Less than 1 percent.

‡ A priority expenditure category in 1975, but not in current revenue sharing legislation for Texas counties and municipalities, which spent only $4.5 million of their total funds ($212.2 million) in this area.

Source: Texas Comptroller of Public Accounts, "Financial Statement," Issue 76–12 (August 1976).

mental protection, mainly construction projects. Other allocations were for general government expense, recreational facilities, and health care. Counties, experiencing escalating costs as general administrative arms of the state, spent one third of their sharing funds in general control and administration, with small amounts in recreational facilities and health care. See Table 9–5. Most of the moneys are being used to support more traditional programs within categorical areas listed in Table 9–5, not to generate new programs for different users of local public services.

City-county programmatic differences

As we saw in the earlier treatments of urban Texas and local finance, city and county programmatic differences in Texas reflect two essential considerations, one based on a legal distinction, the other inherent in basic environmental conditions:

Greater legal responsibility of county governments to serve as administrative arms of state government.

Greater pressures on cities to allocate resources to federal priority areas and in problem areas peculiar to the urban environment, as in pollution abatement, environmental protection, mass transportation, law enforcement, and housing.

National tax actions favorable to local governments

Besides increased amounts of categorical grants and extension of general revenue sharing legislation through 1980 (with prospects that it will be renewed after that), three other legal changes significantly affect the financial condition of local governments, namely:[30]

1. Counter-cyclical assistance, a program of temporary antirecession aid for local governments in areas of high unemployment, affecting to 1977 365 cities and counties in Texas.
2. Payments in lieu of taxes, a program designed to make up tax losses attributable to federal ownership of land, with 43 Texas counties estimated to share about $2 million initially as offsets on about 2.4 million acres of federally controlled lands.
3. Unemployment compensation insurance coverage for approximately one-half million employees of all types of Texas local governments.

SYSTEM OF LOCAL PROPERTY TAXATION

The tax on property by value remains for local governments their major revenue source. Although different classes of local governments are not equally dependent upon property tax revenues, tax collections from this source amount to $3 billion annually in Texas and provide more than 86 percent of all locally collected tax revenues for Texas local governments.

"Equal and uniform" on "all property"

Two notable characteristics of the Texas property tax are contained in the first two sentences of Article VIII, section 1 of the Texas Constitution:

> Taxation shall be equal and uniform. All property in this State, whether owned by natural persons or corporations, other than municipal, shall be taxed in proportion to its value, which shall be ascertained as may be provided by law. . . .

Problems of administration, charges of inequitable taxation, court challenges, and burdens imposed on low income groups all stem in part from these twin constitutional prescriptions.

Besides the administrative problems in locating and assessing intangible personal property—stocks, bank accounts, bonds, and other paper wealth—we see an ingrained reluctance of local tax assessment officials to tax many categories of tangible personal property. As a result, the proportion of revenues derived from collections against the value of *real* property (land and improvements thereon) is about four times collections against *personal* property.[31] Commonly, automobiles, household goods, and other personal, tangible property are exempted in practice, contrary to the clear prescription of the Texas Constitution.

Decentralized and fragmented administration

No constitutional provision prohibits some form of centralization or uniform valuations and assessments among 1,500 different local tax assessor-collectors. But repeated movements over the past decade to achieve these conditions have met with failure. Many tax offices are too small to permit staffing for expert administration of the tax. Even though the same piece of real property may be subject to a large number of overlapping taxing jurisdictions (state, county, school district, municipal, junior college district, conservation district, hospital district, and perhaps others), all located in the same county, few central tax offices exist in Texas counties. And inequality and lack of uniformity in tax rates, valuations, and tax bills persist among the various taxing authorities.

Failure to assess property at market value

Besides the practice of preferring assessment of real property over personal property, tangible and intangible, local tax assessors-collectors also fail to assess at full market value.[32] While Texas law presumes that *value* means market value for tax purposes, in practice the assessment ratio (the percentage of the market value at which property is assessed) averages 52 percent of market value in cities and school districts, 16 percent in county governments, and 21 percent in hospital and junior college districts.[33] The widest variations exist, perhaps, in the state's 254 counties, where the highest assessment ratio is 35.6 percent and the lowest county assessment ratio is 2.6 percent, with a statewide average of only 15.6 percent. See Table 9–6. With property (mainly real property) valued at $36.4 billion on the tax rolls, Texas counties raised in

TABLE 9–6
County assessment ratios for property taxation

Assessment ratios*	Number of counties
35.6% (the highest)	1 (Reeves County)
32.0%–18.8%	35
18.6%–7.7%	182
15.6% (average among all 254 counties)	
7.6%–3.0%	35
2.6% (the lowest)	1 (Real County)

* The percentage of the market value at which property is placed on the county tax rolls for taxation purposes is the assessment ratio.

Source: Prepared from data in Texas Research League, "TRL Analyzes" (May 1978), pp. 2–3.

1975 $388 million of revenues, using an average tax rate per $100 valuation of only $1.07. If property taxes in Texas are inequitably and illegally applied, they are not high, on the average. Figure 9–5 shows a sectional pattern of high assessment ratio counties and low assessment ratio counties in Texas. Highest valuations of property in relation to market values occur in extreme South and West Texas and in scattered counties in the Panhandle-High Plains region and along the Gulf Coast. Low assessment ratio counties lie mainly in Central to Southeast Texas, with a few located in the South Plains-Panhandle area.

The assessment ratio, of course, has a relation to the overall revenue needs of local governments, for the total value of the property tax rolls, as determined by the tax assessor-collector, is multiplied by the tax rate

FIGURE 9–5

Sectional pattern of high and low assessment ratios of property, in use by Texas county governments

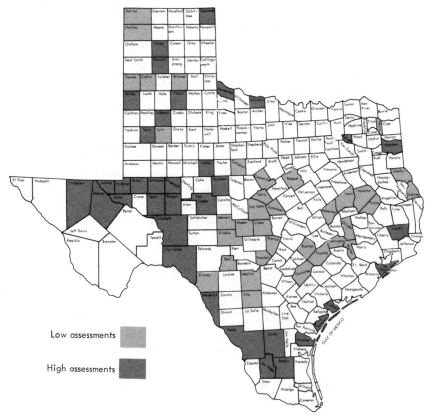

Low assessments

High assessments

Source: Prepared from data in Texas Research League, "TRL Analyzes" (May 1978), pp. 2–3.

per $100 of valuation to produce the needed amount of property tax revenues. A wide range of fairly high legal tax rate limits (if the governments valued property at market value) are imposed on the various classes of local governments by the Constitution and statutes.

Beyond inequities inherent in nonuniform assessment ratios and the practice of taxing mainly real property, many patently slipshod, haphazard, and illegal actions are said to be common all over the state, such as applying different tax rates to locally owned and nonlocally owned property, making little effort to reappraise and keep assessments current on old property (while placing newer construction on the rolls at a high percentage of market value), never seeking out taxable property (with the result that some property is not on the tax rolls), and making few efforts at tax equalization and review as required by law.[34] The property tax is also regressive. The burden for nonelderly poor families with low incomes is four times that of all U.S. families, as a proportion of incomes.[35] Various methods exist, but are not used in Texas, to base the tax more on ability to pay.

Challenges to the property tax

Tax equity, not tax freezes, is the gist of concerns in Texas. Legal challenges have been launched in several school districts against the index for allocation of state funds to school districts, on the grounds that

The index of state aid, as figured mainly on real property, does not reflect true property values

The index discriminates against rural school districts, in that intangible properties in urban districts are not on tax rolls

If intangible property values were used to calculate state aid to large metropolitan school districts, drastically less money would come, creating, at least temporarily, financial crisis. Additionally, no amount of administrative reforms would save the property tax for school districts unless the allocation formula were revised or unless districts actually taxed intangibles. Courts have already issued warnings of this result. Yet, the special session of the legislature in 1978 failed to address these questions in a direct manner. Larger state and federal grants to Texas school districts are in prospect.

SCHOOL DISTRICTS

School district governments are special-purpose entities established under state law and standards[36] with responsibility for educational programs which are compulsory for children ages 5–16. While elective school boards (of 5 or 7 members) determine local curricula, design and build facilities, determine programs of transportation, set local budgets, establish tax rates, assess property,[37] act as equalization boards, and employ teachers, administrators, and staff, state law and administrative policy fix basic curricula, accreditation of school programs, certification of teachers, minimum-pay schedules of teachers, retirements and benefits, and other conditions and standards. In addition, the state government maintains a massive aid program to local schools, with local districts, on the average, raising (from property taxation) only about one half of their revenues.[38] Thus, Texas has a relatively centralized state educational system. Responsible for state standards and oversight of local school programs is the Texas Education Agency.

School district governments in Texas are of two basic types: (1) independent school districts under the management of a local school board, and (2) common school districts whose operations under a local board are supervised by the county board of school trustees. Only about 10 percent of all school districts are of the latter class.

As seen in Table 9–7, large population districts maintain more than one campus so that school campuses in Texas are five times as numerous as local school-district governments. Also, in most of Texas' 254 counties will be more than one school district, but 21 countywide districts do exist. And about one third of all districts are known as "county-line" districts because their geographic boundaries lie across county lines.

With great consolidation of school districts, large geographic areas, large operations, increasing amounts of money coming from state and federal governments, and continuing trends in state policy centralization, combined with little conflict over educational goals, most school opera-

TABLE 9–7
Texas public school districts and campuses, 1976–1977

School districts, types of	Number
Independent school districts	1,011
Common school districts	113
Total	1,124
Countywide districts	21
County-line districts	396
Within county districts	707
Total	1,124
Campuses	
High school campuses	1,232
Junior high campuses	898
Elementary school campuses	3,265
Total	5,395

Source: *Handbook of Governments in Texas* (Austin: Texas Advisory Commission on Intergovernmental Relations, 1973, updated), IV–3.

tions are quite similar throughout Texas. Essential differences turn on money spent per school child among the various rich and poor districts and the consequent enrichment programs found in the more affluent districts. School districts are stratified on the basis of socioeconomic levels, particularly in urban and suburban areas, but school politics in Texas are amazingly nonconflictual on both state and local levels.

NONSCHOOL SPECIAL DISTRICTS

Seldom appreciated about "other special-district governments" is that these numerous organized entities represent considerable variation from the more standardized forms of our general-purpose local governments and of our familiar school district governments. They offer an interesting variegated pattern of forms and structures—single-purpose and multipurpose districts, authorities, boards, and other units. A wide variety of services in both rural and urban areas are provided. In geographic size, they vary from whole sections of the state to small districts nestled in our smallest towns and cities. And they have varying degrees of fiscal and administrative independence from counties and cities and from state government agencies.

One mark of autonomy or independence from other governments is a fixed and separate revenue source. Marks of administrative independence include determining their own budgets, incurring indebtedness, and running their own affairs. Ordinarily, special districts are governed by specially elected or appointed multimember boards or commissions (as in school districts). If a governing body is appointed, to be counted by the U.S. Census Bureau as a special-purpose local government, the board must be able to act with a large measure of autonomy and the district must provide services which are essentially different from the functions performed by the government of the appointing officials.

Using these criteria, municipal housing authorities (in spite of the name "authorities") are counted as special district governments, even though their membership is appointive, their creation results from city council resolution in pursuance of a federal statute, and their income is largely from federal grants initially and rents and charges later. Autonomy extends to deciding types and location of public housing, issuing bonds for construction and purchase of housing units, appointing the local housing manager, and fixing rentals and other charges. See Table 9–8 for the basic types and subtypes of other special district governments and trends in their development in Texas since 1940.[39] Not counted are another class of dependent subordinate agencies of local and state governments. These units often, but not always are called *special authorities.* An example on the state level is the Texas Turnpike Authority, established by special act, administered by a board composed of the state

TABLE 9–8

Classification and number of active special-district governments

	Number			
Types of special districts	1940	1959	1974	1977
Water districts	284	524	940	929
[a]Municipal utility districts (MUDs)	0	0	287	365
[b]Water control and improvement districts (WCIDs), including master districts and municipal districts	41	266	382	314[c]
[d]Levee improvement districts	84	44	38	42
Supply districts	23	41	46	41
Improvement districts	33	43	23	25
Drainage districts	63	56	35	49
[e]Conservation and reclamation districts, including underground water districts	8	23	88	47
Navigation districts	10	19	20	26
River authorities	22	21	21	20
Housing and redevelopment authorities ...	0	121	288	306
Soil conservation districts	46	174	192	197
Hospital districts	0	6	86	112
Rural fire prevention districts	0	1	6	10
Airport authorities	0	0	3	f
Noxious weed control districts	0	3	2	f
Totals	330	829	1517	1554

[a] MUDs are created pursuant to the Texas Constitution, Art. 16, Sec. 59 and may provide hydroelectric power and "other useful water purposes," reclamation of lands and forests, "preservation and conservation of all natural resources," water development and purity, water pollution abatement, sewerage and other liquid and solid waste collection and treatment, parks and recreational facilities, and water for other beneficial uses.

[b] WCIDs can have all authority of MUDs except providing parks and recreational facilities and water for other beneficial uses if they are created pursuant to the Texas Constitution, Art. 16, Sec. 59. If created pursuant to another provision, Art. 3, Sec. 52, WCIDs are authorized to engage in flood control, navigation, irrigation, drainage, and fresh water supply activities. Thus, the WCID type may subsume other classes of water districts.

[c] Conversion and dissolution: Conversion to MUDs accounts for decreases in some categories since 1974. One hundred two water districts, most of them outside Harris County and the Gulf Coast area, were dissolved 1974–1977, probably because of depressed housing starts in those years.

[d] Some levee improvement districts have all the services and functions associated with WCIDs.

[e] Conservation and reclamation districts are either water improvement, drainage, or levee improvement districts organized under provisions of the Canales Act of 1918 to take advantage of more liberal taxation and debt authority. See *V.T.C.A., Water Code,* Sec. 55.021 and Woodworth G. Thrombley, *Special Districts and Authorities in Texas* (Austin: Institute of Public Affairs, University of Texas, 1959), p. 76.

[f] Not given in source.

Source: 1940 data from Texas Bureau of Municipal Research, University of Texas, *Units of Local Government in Texas* (Austin: Bureau of Municipal Research, 1941), p. 71; 1959 data adapted from Thrombley, *Special Districts,* p. 7; figures for active water districts for 1972 from Texas Water Rights Commission, *Thirty-first Report* (Austin: Texas Water Rights Commission, 1975), A–99; other data for 1974 from U.S. Bureau of the Census, *1972 Census of Governments,* vol. 1, *Governmental Organization* (Washington, D.C.: U.S. Government Printing Office, 1973), pp. 449–51, which under-reports active water districts by at least 207, and perhaps under-reports in other types as well; 1977 data from Texas Water Rights Commission, *Thirty-third Report* (Austin: Texas Water Rights Commission, 1977), A–56 and U.S. Bureau of the Census, *Census of Governments, 1977,* Preliminary Report No. 1, "Governmental Units in 1977" (Washington, D.C.: U.S. Department of Commerce, 1977).

highway and public transportation commissioners and other members appointed by the governor, and empowered to collect tolls and to issue revenue bonds for tollroad improvements. Admittedly, the line between a subordinate agency, or special authority, and a special-district government is a thin one.[40]

Types of districts and services performed

As seen in Table 9–8, Texas has seven classes of other special purpose governments. Of the total governments, more than 60 percent are water districts of all kinds, while most of the remainder are housing and urban renewal authorities, soil and water conservation districts (counted separately from water districts by the Census Bureau), and hospital districts.[41] Three categories—airport authorities, noxious-weed-control districts, and rural fire prevention districts[42]—contain few organized governments.

Texas statutes authorize at least 16 classes of water districts and authorities,[43] of which one class (water control and preservation districts) is dormant and not mentioned in the *Water Code,* two classes (water supply districts and water power control districts) are "master districts" created to serve, coordinate the operations, and pool the resources of other water districts, and another (soil and water conservation districts) is separately classified and listed by the Census Bureau. An old class, once appearing in the statutes, was included in the *Water Code* by statute in 1977.[44] For reporting purposes, the Texas Water Commission collapses the remaining 11 types of water districts into 9 classes. See Table 9–8 for the 9 classes.

About two thirds of nonschool special districts in Texas are single-purpose entities. Hospital districts, for example, provide medical care services through operation of hospital and other facilities. On the other hand, municipal utility districts (MUDs) and water control and improvement districts (WCIDs), or their equivalent, and some levee improvement districts are multipurpose districts. Although in practice they commonly supply fresh water, provide sewer services, and construct drainage facilities, they are authorized to perform other water-connected activities (flood control, irrigation, reclamation, and navigation) plus additional functions only remotely related to water-related services. Subsidiary service authorizations include firefighting facilities, natural resources, solid waste collection and disposal, pollution abatement, and recreational facilities.[45] These multipurpose Texas districts are urban districts. Nearly 80 percent are in Texas SMSAs, with four fifths of these concentrated in the Gulf Coast area. For a visual presentation of the most extreme example of governmental disintegration in urbanized areas, see Figure 9–6, which depicts 222 water districts in Harris County even in 1971.

FIGURE 9–6
Harris County water districts 1971

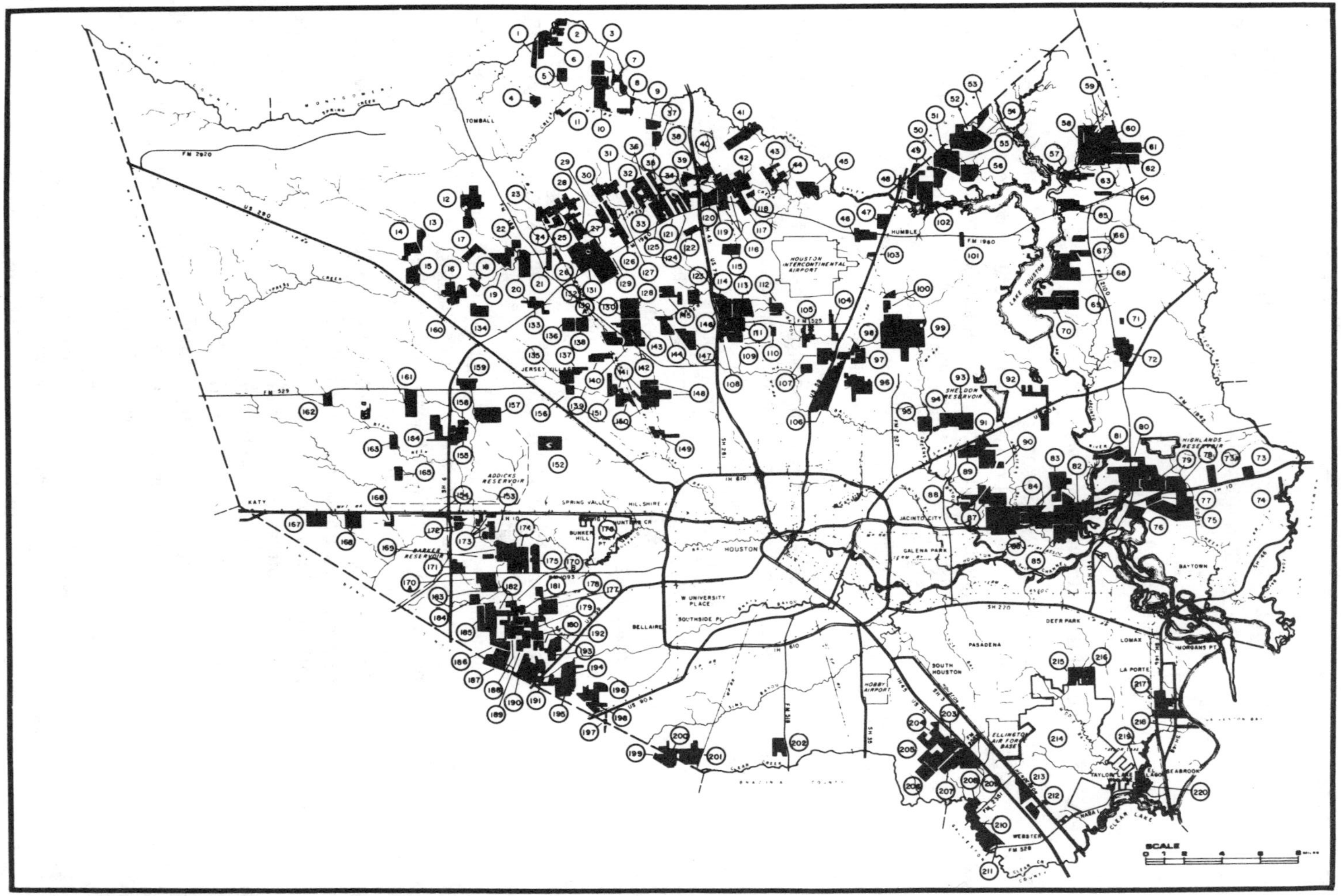

Source: Houston-Galveston Area Council, *Regional Atlas, 1972* Houston, Tex.: Houston-Galveston Area Council, 1972), p. 27.

Special district governments

Selection   In Texas, the nonwater and nonschool special district governing bodies are commonly appointed by other local officials (of the general-purpose governments). Boards of rural fire prevention districts, for example, are appointed by county commissioners courts. On the other hand, the governing bodies of most water districts are selected by direct election of resident qualified voters, with vacancies appointed by remaining members.

Governing body and officers   The governing body is commonly titled "board of directors" and has three to nine members with two-year staggered terms. Receiving only expenses or a nominal sum for services rendered, board members elect among their membership a president, vice president, and secretary of the board. In the case of large water districts with broad authority, full-time staff personnel are selected by the board, including a district engineer and general manager, who may also have tax assessment-collection duties.

Employees   Most special district governments in Texas (but not including school districts) are "hip-pocket" operations, without a staffed headquarters office. In the case of MUDs, most WCIDs, and some levee districts, the government employees are so intermingled initially with the developer's personnel that district government activities appear to be (and, in practice, are) private operations.

Of special districts reporting to the Census Bureau, more than one half had no full-time employees. But one in six had 1 to 20 personnel and one in 20 had more than 20 full-time employees each. Most districts with a large number of personnel are, of course, hospital districts.[46]

Creation and establishment of water districts

Water districts may be created by legislative act, by city ordinance, or by valid order of the Texas Water Commission or a county commissioners court. Of the districts in existence in 1978 (after a great deal of dissolution activity, 1974–1977), only 2 were created by city ordinance and the remainder almost equally by action of the other three creating entities. See Figure 9–7.

Great activity in creation of water districts has come in the past 25 years, with an average of more than 40 new governments per year. In the decade down to 1971, legislative action was dominant over the orders of the Texas Water Rights Commission (TWRC). These new governments were "development districts" created at the initiative and under control of private developers. At the height of the trend in 1971, 114 water district governments, mostly MUDs, were created by legislative statutes.[47]

FIGURE 9–7

Water districts in 1978 by creating entities

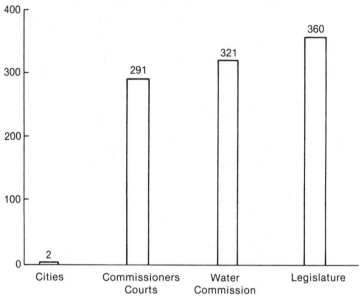

Source: Texas Water Rights Commission, *Thirty-third Report* (Austin: Texas Water Rights Commission, 1978), Table 11, A–55.

See Figure 9–8, which shows the number of districts created by the legislature and by order of the TWRC, 1952–77 and the heightened water district activity, 1967–1975. Figure 9–8 implies much also about underlying environmental conditions in the Gulf Coast area of Texas and of "development politics" in Austin. The combined graphs constitute an index of economic activity in Texas during these years. But the MUD device was used most extensively in the Houston area. Only two Texas counties, Harris and Montgomery (adjacent to Harris), each have more than 40 development water districts. Only two others, Fort Bend (adjacent to Harris) and Cameron (in the Southmost part of Texas) have from 21–30 districts each. Ten other counties contain 11–20 districts each, and only three of these (Dallas, Bexar, and Travis) are not in the Gulf Coast area.

The increase in TWRC creating activity after 1971 coincides with

Clear statutory authority in the *Water Code* (1971) to create MUDs

Outcry against influence peddling (during the Sharpstown scandals in 1971) expressed in reform legislation giving TWRC more oversight authority against the avalanche of special bills creating MUDs

FIGURE 9–8

Water districts created by the legislature and the Texas Water Rights Commission, 1953–1977

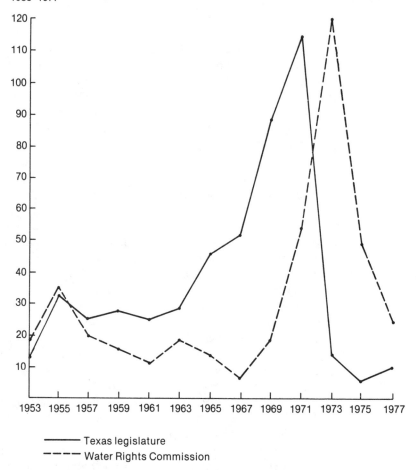

Texas legislature

Water Rights Commission

Source: Prepared from legislative data in *V.A.T.S., Water Auxiliary Laws,* 1977 Pamphlet, Table III, pp. 56–74. Agency data in Texas Water Rights Commission, *Twenty-first Report* through *Thirty-third Report.* September 1, 1952 through August 31, 1977 (Austin: Texas Water Rights Commission, 1952–1977). (From 1962 to 1965 the Texas Water Rights Commission was the Texas Water Commission; before that, back to 1913, it was known as the Texas Board of Water Engineers. In 1977, the Legislature reorganized the water agencies of the state as the Texas Department of Water Resources. A subsidiary board, known as the Texas Water Commission, replaced the Texas Water Rights Commission.) Note that from 1961 to 1971, the Texas Water (Rights) Commission was empowered to create only water control and improvement districts (WCIDs) and underground conservation districts (UDCs). See Texas Water Commission, *Twenty-sixth Report* (Austin: Texas Water Commission, 1965), p. 92.

Proposal of a constitutional amendment, ratified in November 1973, that makes it more difficult to create by legislative statute water districts in clear violation of the constitutional provision against local and special legislation.

Lessened creating activity after 1973 is a reaction to depressed conditions in the construction and housing industries and to a TWRC rule of 1974 which requires that developers must be able to absorb 30 percent of the costs of drainage, water, and sewer installations. This makes water district development ventures less profitable, for formerly these costs could be paid for from borrowed funds guaranteed by future property taxation. But with an estimated 70,000 persons per year streaming into the immediate Harris county area, the water district device is still advantageous to developers.

Creation and establishment of water districts by order of the TWRC or by a county commissioners court is a much more complicated process than creation by legislative statute or by city ordinance. Steps include petition, notice of hearing and publication, hearing before the TWRC or the commissioners court, order to establish, nomination of temporary directors of the board of directors, and a confirmation election by resident voters to establish the district, approve the directors, and vote bonds and bonded indebtedness for construction of the water-related projects by the water district government.

In district confirmation elections, legal provisions usually permit no filing of alternative candidates for board positions, but write-in blanks are provided. Hence, only a write-in campaign can be launched against the directors, who are nominated by the development corporation, in the case of MUDs and WCIDs and their equivalent. But there is no inclination for a write-in campaign. The acreage in which the district government is to be established has few residents (and, hence, are called "bald prairie" districts) when the establishment vote occurs. Tied to the developer, they dutifully troop to the polls for the avowed purpose of approving all referenda items in order to make the area desirable for future purchasers of lots and homes. Of 59 water district elections held in the Houston area in 1972, in only 5 elections did more than 10 persons vote, and in only one of these did the issue fail to carry. In the remaining 54 elections, only a total of 224 residents voted the total bonded indebtedness of $216 million. Thus, an average of four persons per election voted nearly a million dollars each of bonded indebtedness, and not a single vote was cast against any bond issue.[48] Since 1973, contrary to former practice, new purchasers of property within the newly created districts must receive legal notice of the existence of the taxing district, indebtedness, and tax rate.

Functions of special districts

Special district governments provide the student with a distinctive opportunity to view the effects upon local government of environmental conditions peculiar to Texas. These local governments are said to be functional to Texas, that is, they reflect

The pressures of urbanization and population shifts,

A favorable economic climate,

The political acumen of developers and other political actors,

A shortage of surface fresh water to meet the twin challenges of citizen needs and economic and industrial expansion,

Legal restraints on county governments,

The political cultural tenet which sees government as a marketplace of opportunity for "individual initiative," and

Philosophical attitudes attuned to the virtues of grassroots politics and local self-government and control.

The following are some of the more obvious functional aspects of special districts:

A way to provide services without altering the existing system of local governments. Special districts represent a simple structural device to provide piecemeal, and relatively easily and quickly, a group of services. Structural flexibility is a prime characteristic. Districts can be small or large, single or multipurpose, comprised of only a portion of an existent local governmental geographic area or coterminous with that area, and easily converted to new services, or dissolved. In some metropolitan areas, poor planning and development of water resources lead builders and developers to utilize water district governments for fresh water supply and sewerage disposal and drainage needs.

A way to overcome fiscal legal restraints on general purpose local governments. The special district device is used as a financing mechanism to escape fiscal limitations. In Harris county, for example, city and county officials cooperated to support establishment of a separate hospital district to divest themselves of a financial burden and to use freed resources for other essential needs. Texas statutes offer special district governments greater fiscal discretion, such as in charging fees, receiving federal and state project grants, and, in the case of MUDs and WCIDs, no limitations on tax rate and indebtedness.

A way to attract community leadership and technical expertise. Organizational and fiscal strength of special districts is said to attract community leadership and expert staff, with services performed efficiently and competently, if not expeditiously. These proclaimed virtues jibe well with the values of affluent, white, Anglo Protestants and others who escape to suburbia and who receive many of the district services. Especially the water district arrangement fulfils citizen aspirations for a new, fresh start amidst local self-government and citizen participation. For the affluent, the flight to suburbia is rendered virtually painless. The developer has seen to installation of streets, curbs, gutters, a drainage system, a sewerage system, a water reservoir, parks, golf courses, other recreational facilities, green belts, police and fire protection, and the construction of new homes with the latest features. Other developers move in nearby with new and gleaming (all-white, upper socioeconomic) schools, shopping centers, filling stations, service establishments, and churches.

A way to provide development by use of "private governments."[49] Passage of numerous "reform bills" has not altered the nature of the water district scheme—a device to facilitate development through control of government for private business ends for a profit. Water districts are public bodies established at the initiative of developers, who manipulate the projects for private gain. Original directors of the government are nominated by the developers. Friends of the development corporation are the voters in confirmation and bond elections, and they share in the profits. Huge debts and service charges are left to the residents when the developers move out. Commonly, the burden is so great that municipal annexation and assumption of the debt is an expectation if residents are ever to be assured lower tax bills and a complete system of urban services.

As we have seen, the water district development device is dependent largely upon physical and other environmental conditions in the Gulf Coast area—population insurge, critical water shortage, abundant supply of relatively cheap land, few incorporated municipalities in a relatively large land area, and absence after 1968 of a real estate price disclosure statute. These conditions spawned an entire generation of young men in the real estate, brokerage, mortgage, investment, banking, consultant, planning, and development fields. Land syndication schemes, along with kickbacks and other corruption, are quite common.[50] At the height of passage of local and special water district legislation, 1969–1972, when 223 special districts were established in this fashion, influence peddling in the state legislature was widespread.

Benefits and costs of development districts

Apologists argue that water district development operations meet the needs of citizens and of industry in the midst of great population increases and economic expansion. Houston city officials contend that the system presents desirable growth patterns, allowing creation of basic urban services, build-up of population, and a tax base in suburban areas without financially obligating the city. Once growth conditions reach a certain plateau, the city annexes the water district,[51] assumes its indebtedness, and extends additional municipal services.

Critics point to poor and expensive services, costs in terms of the environment, and the problems in urban sprawl. They contend that in purely monetary terms, developers and land speculators and their allies make too large profits and drive up costs of land and housing while despoiling the environment. In the early ventures, interest to maturity of bonded indebtedness, plus interest during construction of water district facilities, legal fees, administrative costs, engineering services, and costs of acquisition of utility easements (which developers purchased from themselves), frequently absorbed from one third to more than two fifths of the money voted in initial bond elections. For the first three development years, interest was paid on the bonds by the bond money itself (in effect, a balloon note). Developers still may be able to sell their lots and exit without paying any taxes to the district government which they have created. In the meantime, while developers are taking risks, they have spent money that is not theirs and that they have no legal obligation to repay (on the construction of the government installations—water, sewer, and drainage). The 1974 TWRC rule that developers bear up to 30 percent of these costs will have the effect, critics claim, of driving up costs to consumers of lots and homes and government services. The TWRC has been given stricter controls over creation of districts and powers of construction supervision. The Commission must approve the economic feasibility of a development venture, including the proposed bonded indebtedness for the government projects. And it sets building standards and inspects during construction of the sewer, water, and drainage facilities.

Because of expense, only the affluent can flee to the developments. When annexation does come, the people back in the city must help assume the indebtedness which they cannot afford and did not participate in creating. Further criticisms directed to "undemocratic aspects" of water district operations have been met, in some measure, by reform legislation to assure more public information and greater participation in water district governance. But creation is still at the initiative of developers and on their terms. Neither the device nor its use has been changed in essential respect by "reform" legislation.

NEW INTERGOVERNMENTAL DIMENSIONS

An important fragmented, polycentric structural dimension has been added to the governmental mosaic in Texas' metropolitan areas. Besides special districts, this dimension includes (as we saw in Chapter 8) the existence of 24 federally encouraged substate planning regions, with their area councils of governments (COGs).

Beyond consolidation of local governments

Although fragmentation of public authority continues, consolidation of local governments in metropolitan areas is not the essential issue any more. Emphasis has shifted to (1) strengthening existent local governments in their service capacities and (2) coordinating programmatic governmental efforts on a regional basis. The question is what form metropolitan governance will take. Texas COGs should be able to establish—provided they receive continued support from the Office of the Governor—more and more opportunities for intergovernmental communication, planning, technical assistance, and coordination of programs (if not delivery of services) at the local levels.

Urban services in an unincorporated context

The state's voters may be persuaded to give metropolitan county governments more potential for providing urban services in unincorporated areas. In the meantime, expansion of services of municipal utility districts may contribute much. Potentially, MUDs can exercise many urban services, but MUDs commonly fail to increase their activities because of high taxes and service charges resulting from heavy bonded indebtedness. Further, incorporated cities under Texas' liberal annexation statutes hold out prospects of annexation, assumption of debts, and delivery of the additional urban services. Clearly, services of MUDs would increase if annexation rates were slowed for any reason, or if initial costs of MUDs were reduced.

New confederal relationships

A complex of intergovernmental relationships already exists at the substate level, but so far only a low-level of cooperation and coordination has been achieved. Probably, most of the potential interrelationship mechanisms have not been worked out among cities, counties, special districts, councils of governments, state government agencies, the Office of the Governor, and agencies of the national government. As local governments achieve more professionalization and as they take on delivery of more services, local specialists will come to share program objectives, goals, habits, aspirations, and outlooks of other specialists at other governmental levels, resulting in easier and more harmonious interaction among local governments in regional coordination and policymaking. Along with specialists, generalists in state and local governments seem to be becoming a little more concerned, under the incessant pressures of the national government, with strengthening local governments in Texas and arming councils of governments with authority for some degree of areawide governance.

CONCLUSIONS

Local government is abundant in Texas. In this chapter we have taken stock of Texas municipalities and counties, we have explored local government financing by focusing upon federal aid and local property taxation, and we have examined the profusion of school and special districts on the Texas scene. Our exploration of Texas local government permits these conclusions:

1. Urbanization and changes in metropolitan political problems have produced demands for governmental reforms, the most prevalent of which is the council-manager form of government. Council-manager government for Texas cities emphasizes professional management and nonpartisan elections. This governmental form reflects the values and policy preferences of the reform movement, which has been successful in Texas' mid-sized and largest cities. Among the state's largest cities, only Houston retains the mayor-council form of local government.

2. Texas has developed an imaginative approach to urban growth, combining liberal annexation authority with powers of extraterritoriality. Moreover, particularly in Harris County and in the Gulf Coast region, cities permit unbridled use of development districts, using municipal utility districts (MUDs) to provide water, sewer, and drainage services.

3. The state's local governments are heavily dependent upon the property tax for revenues because Texas has no program for general state financial aid to its local units except for state aid to school districts. The system of local property taxation is fraught with inequities. The 1,500 assessors follow varied administrative practices, tangible personal property is not always taxed, intangibles like stocks, bonds, and bank accounts are hardly taxed at all, and property taxes are low because property is underassessed.

4. Texas cities and counties exhibit both similarities and differences in their governing. Their spending priorities are similar, stressing transportaton, criminal justice, and health and hospitals. But the two governmental units bear different obligations; so cities need to finance sewerage and sanitation costs, and counties, because of their performance of

certain state functions, have expenses for financial administration and general control. City government has tended to take the council-manager form, but commission government is characteristic of Texas counties.

5. Special purpose local governments, taking the form of single-purpose districts, provide a method for providing many public services. The most numerous of these is the school district. The system of education in Texas is highly centralized. Half of the resources and the major policy guidelines for the educational system come from the legislature and the Texas Education agency. The abundance of other special districts reflects the frailties of municipalities and counties in providing services. But these districts also satisfy economic development goals, the psychological and social needs of citizens, and the myths of local control and self-government. One kind of special district, the water district, is especially significant in Texas, resulting from a distinctive set of environmental conditions peculiar to the state and to a few other high development areas in the nation.

CHAPTER TEN

Public finance, public programs, and politics of the budgetary process

Never before has the Legislature been asked to accomplish a tax relief program of the magnitude to be placed before you. . . . The Texas tax situation is not like California's.

GOVERNOR DOLPH BRISCOE*

In this final chapter we appropriately deal with who gets what, who pays, and how spending and allocation decisions in the state budget document are arrived at. First, we look briefly at the various taxes and other state government revenue sources[1] and at their productivity and administration. Extraction of money and other resources from citizens can be for purposes other than raising revenues to pay directly for governmental services and regulation. We consider briefly the nonrevenue uses and impact of taxation. Then we survey the spectrum of state programs and the major functional areas in which government makes expenditures. Finally, we describe the politics of budgetmaking. The budget is a summary policy statement of governmental economic resource allocations. In following the budget to adoption, we see in microcosm the entire political process and review the chief characteristics of the Texas political system.

STATE TAX STRUCTURE

Sales taxes account for the largest portion of the total revenues of Texas state government, and federal grants constitute the second largest revenue source. A small part of the state's revenues is derived from *nontax* sources, including moneys from

Royalties, sales, and rentals;

Interest and dividends;

Permits and fees;

---

* Message to the called session of the legislature, July 10, 1978, in which he asked for drastic limitations on the legislature's ability to pass tax measures.

Licenses, including automobile registration; and
Borrowed funds.

Development of the tax structure

The Texas Constitution, Art. VIII, Sec. 1 explicitly mentions four types of taxes which the legislature is authorized to levy

Poll taxes,

Occupation taxes,

Property taxes, and

Income taxes on both natural persons and corporations.

Section 17 of the same article allows "other subjects or objects to be taxed."

With regard to the four constitutional categories, Texas political leaders seem to have an ingrained aversion to enactment of either type of income tax. The poll tax became associated closely with voter qualifications and is illegal for that purpose. Consequently, the state tax structure until modern times fell into a mold of two categories: (1) property and (2) occupation taxes.

Until 50 years ago the base of the state tax structure, the property tax has declined to one percent of total state revenues, and it is for a dedicated purpose. Occupation taxes, while still important, have also declined to little more than one fifth of state revenues. Occupation taxes are levies on occupations as much for regulation as for revenues. Persons having firms or businesses engaged in the taxed occupations must register with the state and pay fees to defray registration costs and issuance of permits. The occupation taxes are then levied in one of four ways

On gross receipts (sales or premiums) of public utility corporations, liquor stores, and insurance companies;

As flat fees, on a score or more of occupations, including bedding manufacturers, antifreeze distributors, and automobile service clubs;

On production of oil, gas, sulphur, carbon black, and cement; or

On capital assets and surplus in the state, or on the assessed value of all properties, of corporations doing business in the state. Numerous exemptions (insurance, transportation, banking, and certain nonprofit corporations) and low rates (for utilities and corporations which pay local property taxes on intangible assets) pose questions of discrimination and produce a small amount of revenues.

The production (severance) tax on the price per million cubic feet of natural gas is the largest source of revenue in the class of occupation taxes.

Property and occupation taxes were always, to some extent, in jeopardy, since the intangible assets tax on railroads, severance tax on crude oil production, and many of the other occupation taxes (for their regulatory aspects) were bitterly attacked in the Texas and federal courts on the grounds of constitutionality.

Later, when taxes were selectively placed on the retail sales of certain products and commodities, these sales levies were labeled occupation taxes to avoid a possible constitutional confrontation with conservative judges who might read Article VIII as excluding any tax other than poll, property, income, or *occupation*. Another motivation for naming a tax an occupation tax is that one fourth of the proceeds are earmarked for a dedicated purpose, the public schools. Notably, the general sales tax of 1961 is officially entitled, Limited Excise, Sales, and Use Tax. While it replaced numerous excise taxes on specific articles and commodities, *selective* sales, use, and excise levies still remain on motor vehicles, gasoline and special fuels, tobacco products, alcoholic beverages, hotel occupancy, and admissions to places of amusement. Note here the distinctions in the meaning of the terms, *sales, use,* and *excise,* and why the three can be lumped together.

A *sales* tax is figured as a percentage of the retail or selling price of a tangible commodity, such as a dress or a suit of clothes, and it is added to the price. In Texas, the state rate is four percent of the price, plus one percent, which is collected along with the state's levy, in the cities which have adopted this tax by popular referendum. Many items, such as food items, are exempt.

A *use* tax is a levy applied to a sales tax item which was purchased elsewhere and brought into the state, for example, an automobile. Thus, the use tax prevents a person from escaping sales tax liability.

An *excise* tax, although paid on first sale of a commodity or merchandize, is not figured and added as a percentage of the retail sale price. For example, the state gasoline tax of five cents per gallon is included in the sales price, and the amount is excised, or cut off, as the government's portion.

Tax revenues today

As seen in Figure 10–1, the sales taxes (general, selective, and use) and a small amount of gross receipts taxes on occupations constitute more than one half of all tax revenues of state government. The second most lucrative class of taxes is the production or severance tax on natural gas and crude oil, which produces more than one fifth of tax revenue. The remainder (about one fourth of the total) comes from motor fuel ex-

FIGURE 10–1

Tax revenues, Texas and all states

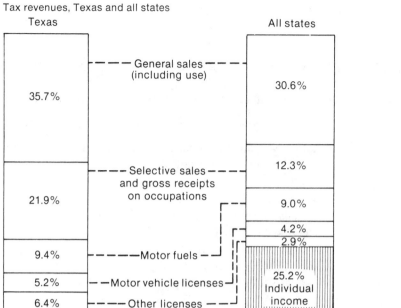

Source: U.S. Bureau of the Census, *State Tax Collections in 1977*, Ser. GF–77 No. 1 (Washington, D.C.: U.S. Government Printing Office, 1977), Tables 6 and 10, pp. 10 and 33.

cise taxes and licenses of all kinds, mainly on occupations and businesses.[2]

Tax administration

Like administration in other areas, tax administration is disintegrated. Texas has a large number of taxation statutes, a variety of collection procedures, and numerous tax collectors. Although the comptroller of public accounts is the tax commissioner of the state, administering many of the different taxation laws and collecting about 70 percent of tax revenues at the state level, several other officers administer other taxes and collect significant amounts of revenue, including the secretary of state (corporate organization and qualification fees), the state treasurer (cigarette and tobacco taxes and alcoholic beverages taxes, except on beer), members of the State Board of Insurance (insurance tax), and county tax assessors-collectors (motor vehicle registration fees and sales or use taxes, plus the state's small ad valorem tax).

INTERGOVERNMENTAL DIMENSION OF REVENUES AND EXPENDITURES

Collections and expenditures among Texas governments[3]

Several tendencies exist in intergovernmental transfers

State government collects 55.2 percent of all state-local taxes but expends only 43.4 percent of all state-local revenues (including federal aid).

General support by state government of county and municipal governments is 0.5 percent, as compared with an average of 10.5 percent among the United States.

Most of the state government intergovernmental transfers (96.2 percent) go to school districts for education, as compared with 59 percent to education among all the United States.

Federal grants to state government

Federal intergovernmental aid to both state and local governments has experienced rapid growth—from $7 billion in 1960 (representing 20 percent of federal domestic spending) to $86 billion in 1979 (more than one fourth of federal domestic outlays). Approximately 27 of every 100 dollars spent by Texas state government come from the national government. Total federal aid to Texas state and local governments in 1979 was nearly $3 billion, with about 80 percent channeled to or through state government.

Welfare, health, and other social services programs receive nearly one half of all federal categorical[4] aid to state government, the remainder being divided about evenly among education, highways, and all other programs. See Figure 10-2. Note also that each major program is not supported equally by federal funds. Federal aid constitutes nearly 70 percent of money budgeted in welfare (welfare is highly centralized, with local governments supporting only 2.5 percent of the burden), while in highways Texas receives 42.3 percent of funding by federal aid. Education, the most expensive of state programs, receives an infusion of only 11.3 percent, a fact which leads education lobbyists back annually to the national government with pleas to increase spending in that program area.

The federal government also makes noncategorical grants, called revenue sharing funds, to state and local governments. These moneys, which can be spent in any program area at the option of the recipient

FIGURE 10–2
Federal grants by program category: Percentage of total federal funds to
Texas; amount by program category; and percentage of total spending for
program category

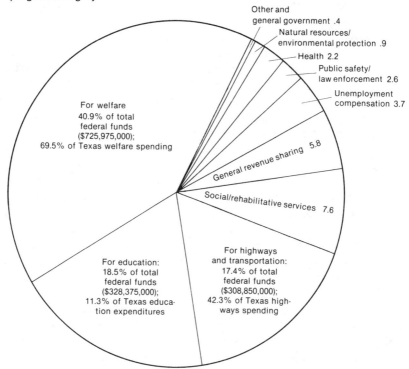

Other and
general government .4

Natural resources/
environmental protection .9

Health 2.2

Public safety/
law enforcement 2.6

Unemployment
compensation 3.7

General revenue sharing 5.8

Social/rehabilitative services 7.6

For welfare
40.9% of total
federal funds
($725,975,000);
69.5% of Texas welfare spending

For education:
18.5% of total
federal funds
($328,375,000);
11.3% of Texas educa-
tion expenditures

For highways
and transportation:
17.4% of total
federal funds
($308,850,000);
42.3% of Texas high-
ways spending

Source: Texas Comptroller's Office, *1976 Annual Financial Report* (Austin: Comptroller
of Public Accounts, November 1, 1976), Vol. 1, pp. 9, 12, 16.

government, amount to 8 percent of all federal state-local transfers. As
seen in Table 10–2, about 6 percent of state grant funds is from revenue
sharing. Two thirds of these nondesignated moneys are used in a single
state area, education, where categorical funding is shortest. Few new
program areas have been created by state governments, and a third of
the states, including Texas, have been able to avert tax increases. In
Texas, which has a large percentage of revenues dedicated to specific
program areas, regular receipt of nondesignated funds from the federal
government lends increased flexibility in budgeting.

REVENUE DEDICATION

In treating the state's tax structure, the Legislative Budget Board lists
a total of 39 separate taxes. Revenues produced from only eight of these
levies flow directly into the state's General Revenue Fund, from which

the legislature has a free hand in spending. Moneys from each of the other 31 tax categories are channeled into one or more of the 273 *special funds* maintained in the Texas treasury. Revenues in these special funds are *dedicated,* or earmarked, for specific purposes and programs.[5] For example, all or part of the moneys from the gasoline tax, vehicle registration, federal categorical grants for highways, special sales tax levies on some items, and miscellaneous taxes, permits, and fees flow into the State Highway Fund for the designated purposes of construction, maintenance, policing, and safety of Texas roads and highways.[6]

In fiscal 1979, the General Revenue Fund, with general revenue sharing moneys, contained only 35 percent of all state revenues. The percentage of total state revenues which is earmarked for specific purposes and programs has not changed significantly through the years since 1967 when the figure was 72 percent and exceeded by only five states.[7] Further, 191 of the 274 special funds have originated within the last two decades. Revenue dedication presents serious legislative and administrative disabilities, a bar to comprehensive budgeting, offering little opportunity to balance program needs and to elect priorities.

The probable main reason for the practice of earmarking is the higher than usual opposition in Texas to governmental taxing and spending, with emphasis placed, therefore, on keeping governmental costs and services to a minimum.[8] In this context, legislators have had to offer politically feasible, acceptable, and justifiable uses for each tax and expenditure increase. Hence the large assortment of user fees, occupation taxes dedicated to education and highways, and the general practice of earmarking for most all programs. Note in Table 10–1 the pattern of dedicated funds for support of the various departments and classes of agencies, as outlined in the general appropriations measure.

The Texas Constitution of 1876 institutionalizes the aversion to positive government. As we saw in Chapter 1, two thirds of the numerous constitutional amendments involve financial changes, usually additional restrictions on government finance. Of the finance article in the proposed revised constitution of 1976, George D. Braden judged that it alone was almost worth the entire revision effort.[9] But by landslide proportions, the Texas electorate embraced the century-old bundle of financial restraints.

NONREVENUE USES AND IMPACT OF TAXATION

Taxation commonly is exercised, of course, for purposes other than generating revenues. A large number of socially useful purposes and exemptions are imbedded in any tax structure. To people who disagree with these purposes, exemptions may appear as tax loopholes, havens, or privileges which are seen as unnecessarily driving up their own taxes.

TABLE 10–1
Use of dedicated funds, 1979

| Departments and classes of agencies | General revenue fund | Dedicated funds | | All moneys appropriated |
		Amount	Percent	
Judiciary	$ 21,279,157	$ 881,072	4.0	$ 22,160,228
Public health, hospitals, and youth institutions	534,078,779	1,349,390,314	71.6	1,883,469,091
Executive and administrative departments and agencies	541,097,500	1,566,646,772	74.3	2,107,744,272
Education	1,620,517,720	2,176,120,033	57.3	3,796,637,753*
Legislature	29,336,083		0.0	29,336,083
Totals	$2,746,309,238	$5,093,038,191	65.0	$7,839,347,429

* Nearly $600,000 additional appropriations were made for fiscal year 1979 in a special called session on July 15, 1977.

Source: Texas Legislature, House of Representatives, *Supplement to House Journal,* Text of Conference Committee Report, H. B. 510, Sixty-Fifth Legislature, Regular Session, 1977, p. vii.

Constant attempts are made by all groups to legislate or secure administrative tax advantages for themselves or disadvantages for others. Common regulatory and administrative uses of taxation, with examples, are as follows:

1. *Regulation of products and occupations.* In taxation of occupations, levies are used for regulating conditions under which certain products—fireworks, cement, herbicides—are sold. Prohibitively large taxes can drive products off the market. Occupation fees are designed to maintain a rein on people who engage in certain professions and occupations, such as veterinarians, real estate brokers, morticians, and barbers, thus aiding the occupations to maintain professional standards and policing morals and health.

2. *Enforcement of general public policies.* Through the franchise tax and other fees paid to do business, the attorney general, by threat of proceedings for revocation of the right, has a weapon for enforcement of general public policies, such as antimonopoly statutes, fair trade practices, and pollution abatement regulations as well as the taxation statutes themselves.

3. *Tax collection and administration.* In another tax administrative use, retail sales outlets are rebated portions of their collections as an incentive to defray clerical, reporting, and other expenses incident to tax collection. And a documentary stamp tax on the transfer of real

estate could provide tax assessors with current market values to aid them in uniform property valuation for equity in property taxation.

4. *Benefits through tax exemptions.* A positive boon to individuals, businesses, and other groups is the policy of the state not to use certain taxes at all, or to selectively exempt individuals or groups from taxation. Taxes which Texas does not have include

a tax on income of individuals

a tax on income of corporations

a documentary stamp tax on property sales

a stock transfer tax

a gift tax to prevent individuals from dissipating their estates, thus shielding heirs from the inheritance tax

a severance tax on other natural resources than natural gas, crude oil, natural gas distillates, cement, and sulphur

Tax policy and industrial development

Since World War II, the relatively poorer states have embarked on positive fiscal policies, in league with broad social and economic forces, to attract industrial development and business growth. Taxation policies in particular, as we saw in Chapter 1, have reflected a desire to produce a "good business climate" and industrial plant relocations. Table 10–2 is a list prepared by the Office of the Comptroller of Public Accounts, the state's chief tax collection agency, to illustrate "Texas' position with regard to the most significant taxes affecting business."[10] To the list could be added at least two others

Wide differentials in the property tax within each metropolitan area, amounting to industrial tax havens, and

A policy of selective reduction of taxes which fall upon business.

TABLE 10–2
Texas' position on the most significant taxes affecting business

Tax	Texas' position
Corporate Income tax	No tax imposed
Personal income tax	No tax imposed
Sales and use tax	State rate of 4% equal to U.S. average
Property taxes	Low. $50 per capita below U.S. average
Motor fuels taxes	Lowest rate in nation
Unemployment insurance tax	Lowest average rate in nation

Source: Bob Bullock, "Texas Means Business," Comptroller of Public Accounts, State of Texas, December 1977, p. 2.

In following the selective reduction route, Texas in recent years has[11]

Eliminated the chain store tax,

Enacted a "freeport law" to exempt property in interstate transit from the property tax,

Exempted state and national banks from the corporation franchise tax, and

Reduced the franchise tax rates.

But unlike numerous other states, Texas state government has not given property tax exemptions to new industry or exempted business purchases from sales taxation.

Many of the taxation policies of the United States and localities can be understood primarily in terms of the fact that the states see themselves in competition for the favors of business and industry. The strategy of lower business taxation, whether it attracts industry or not, has worked quite well to decrease, on the average, the share of business taxes in the United States.[12]

That tax reductions in order to attract industry has been a false issue is seen in various reports that a variety of economic and social forces, including labor and material cost advantages in the Southwest, have been the main reasons for industrial dispersion in the United States. Further, among states within a given region, no direct relationship appears to exist between industrial growth and tax differentials, "due largely to the fact that states are careful not to get 'too far out of line' with their immediate neighbors."[13] On the other hand, within-state advantages do accrue to those local governments with low property taxes. Failure of local tax assessors in Texas to attempt to effect more uniform valuation of property may reflect as much policy *choice* as administrative difficulties in obtaining reliable market information. "Inefficient" administration of local ad valorem taxes may be the most important tax benefit to business and industry, including agribusiness.[14]

Nevertheless, state government officials may also have overestimated the importance of tax considerations in attracting business and industry. Studies indicate that the quality of government services, particularly in education, has received increased attention as a factor in industrial location decision-making. If so, many of the states in which "industrial fever" runs highest will be caught on the horns of a dilemma: how to keep a "good business climate" without letting public service standards deteriorate as to discourage business. Texas acts on the following policy:

> selective decreases in business taxes in order not to excite a consumer tax revolt, along with raising general sales tax rates, enlarging the list of items on which sales taxes fall, and increasing the rates of cigarette, liquor, and other consumer levies.

The pattern of post-World War II tax policies, so far, has met with little political opposition here.[15]

Tax policy as a redistributive tool

Taxes can also be redistributive, that is, have the effect of taking wealth from some groups and redistributing it to others indirectly in the form of educational, medical, health, housing, and other services, or by direct payments. But redistribution can work also in the opposite, regressive direction, by high tax rates on the relatively poor or on middle income groups, thus leaving large capital assets, tangible and intangible, in the hands of the affluent. Many years ago, the authors of a popular textbook on Texas government and politics termed Texas "a haven for the wealthy."[16] Evidence indicates that today's programs and tax policies are regressive. Progressive redistribution is an important determinant for low-income groups of the quality of life in our society.

In a calculation of the net redistributive impact of state revenues and expenditures combined for the three lowest income classes in each state, Texas was ranked 47th most regressive among 48 states for which data were available.[17] And in regressive impact of state-local taxation only, Texas ranks 46th among the 50 states.[18] A tax is said to be *regressive* if the *percentage* of income paid in taxes rises as incomes decrease. It should be noted that all states except two (Oregon and New York) have regressive state-local taxation, falling at a higher percentage on lower income groups. Figure 10–3 illustrates the regressivity of state-local tax burden in Houston.

A question associated with regressivity is the portion of state-local taxation assumed by business establishments and corporations. Another related question is tax equity among all taxpayers in the same class. How evenly do taxes initially fall on households and various segments of the economy, including business corporations? Do some corporations bear most of the burden for business? As we saw in Chapter 9, inequities of the highest magnitude, contrary to clearly stated constitutional prescriptions, exist in the administration of the property tax.

Thus, we see that taxation policies are not only decisions about raising revenues. Taxation policies have social and economic impacts and consequences for all Texans. Generally, Texas' tax policies constitute an economic determination by government to[19]

Reward material acquisitiveness,

Promote accumulation of capital in the private sector,

Keep total governmental expenditures relatively low,

Promote plant location and expansion, and

Depress redistributive effects of state and local spending.

FIGURE 10–3
State-local tax burden as a percent of family income in Houston, Texas, by income levels

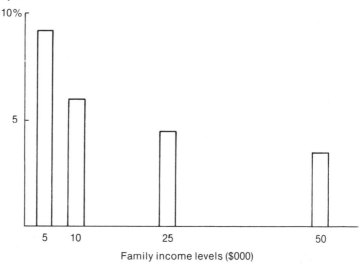

Family income levels ($000)

Source: Prepared from data in Stephen E. Lile, "Family Tax Burden Differences Among the States," *State Government,* XLVIV, no. 1 (Winter 1976), Tables 5, 16.

PUBLIC PROGRAMS

State expenditure pattern

For more than 40 years, about 80 cents of the state-level appropriations dollar in Texas have been spent in three program areas: education, welfare, and highways. While the proportion has remained unchanged, three significant developments have occurred:

1. Public welfare and highways expenditures have exchanged places, with welfare assuming within the past decade the second largest amount, behind public education.

2. The total of spending in each category has risen immensely, from $158 million in 1938 to $8.4 billion in 1979 (an amount 53 times that spent 40 years ago!).

3. State-local finance has become the leading "growth" sector of the American economy, the rate of increase in recent years far exceeding rates in other segments of the economy. Figure 10–4 places in perspective the growth of Texas state government, 1968–1979, with adjustments for population growth and inflation.

FIGURE 10–4

Trends in Texas state expenditures

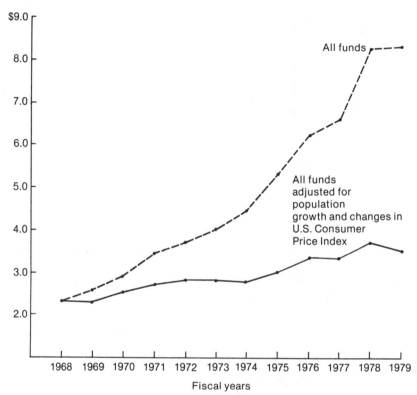

Fiscal year ending August 31	Texas state expenditures (all funds)	State expenditure adjusted for population and price increases
1968	$2,339,869,601	$2,339,869,601
1969	2,514,507,766	2,347,374,688
1970	2,954,745,796	2,554,903,412
1971	3,436,834,379	2,780,835,326
1972	3,790,834,698	2,911,994,698
1973	4,019,409,512	2,899,170,162
1974	4,426,663,249	2,854,622,589
1975	5,377,326,615	3,084,921,470
1976	6,203,503,772	3,276,037,057
1977	6,606,979,385	3,226,221,683
1978	8,392,019,470	3,778,997,374
1979	8,412,832,391	3,533,022,170

Source: Legislative Budget Board, *Fiscal Size Up: Texas State Services, 1978–79 Biennium* (Austin: Legislative Budget Office, 1978), p. 2.

Education

Education for many years has accounted for almost one half of the total annual spending by Texas state government. See Figure 10–5 for the distribution of state expenditures among major policy areas in the 1978–79 biennium. Table 10–3 shows how educational funds are distributed among secondary and elementary education, universities, medical schools, teacher retirement systems, junior colleges, and other educational programs.

The huge amount appropriated annually, more than $4 billion in 1979, is matched almost equally from local school district sources, principally from property tax collections. An additional sum, representing approximately 11 percent of the total allocated by state and local governments, is received as grants from the national government.

Although huge intergovernmental revenues are thus used to aid local educational efforts, the quality of public elementary and secondary education in Texas depends largely upon factors related to the local dis-

FIGURE 10–5
Spending by function

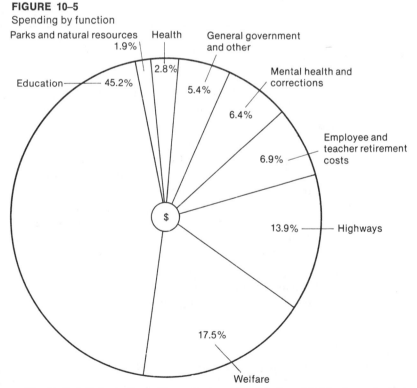

Source: Bob Bullock, *Texas Means Business!* Comptroller of Public Accounts, State of Texas, December 1977, p. 12.

TABLE 10–3

Distribution of education appropriations

Public school education including S.B. 1 and schools for the blind and deaf	$5,145,503,428 61%
24 senior universities and system offices	1,410,977,580 17%
8 upper-level universities and centers	93,652,282 1%
Medical schools, health science centers	515,465,119 6%
Teacher retirement systems	646,486,430 8%
47 junior colleges, academic and vocational-technical programs, including industrial start-up and adult education programs	458,303,613 5%
Coordinating board, three museums, Engineering extension service, and rural medical education board	94,172,863 1%
Marine Academy and Texas State Technical Institute	53,113,386 1%
	$8,417,674,701

Source: Legislative Budget Board, *Fiscal Size Up: Texas State Services, 1978–79 Biennium* (Austin: Legislative Budget Office, 1978), p. 31.

tricts' varied financial pictures. Within the state, huge differences still exist among districts in the per pupil value of taxable property and in expenditures per pupil. Also, depending upon community values and the press of noneducational demands, differences in lesser degree mark the willingness of local school authorities to tax for educational programs. As pointed out in the Rodriquez case,[20] districts with the smallest tax base frequently make the largest tax effort, and, even with state and federal aid, they still fall far below what is spent on the average and what is considered a minimum expenditure level for quality education. Although the legislature since 1973 has provided each biennium a massive infusion of additional moneys, equalization of educational opportunity among school districts is still a distant dream and probably unachievable without property tax equalization in the school districts and a larger share of funding by state and national governments.

Public welfare

Public welfare costs absorb about 18 cents of every state expenditure dollar; yet, Texas bears only about 33 percent (less than $500 millions in 1979), the rest being received from the federal government. See Table 10–4. For the range of expensive federal income maintenance services and their costs, including costs of grants to the states in this area, see Table 10–5. The national government has always held major responsibility under the Social Security Act of 1935 for social insurance funding and administration. Commonly called social security, included in the Act are income security insurance programs for old age retirement, dis-

TABLE 10–4
Welfare expenditures by source and program in Texas[1]

	Federal	State	Total
AFDC program	$ 99,855,614	$ 37,950,447	$ 137,806,061[2]
Medical assistance programs	416,192,985	236,572,704	652,765,689
Administration and service	198,316,226	86,808,607	285,124,833[3]
Cuban refugee assistance	148,235	0	143,235
Repatriated U.S. citizens program	9,232	0	9,232
Indochinese assistance	978,205	0	978,205
Adult category adjustments	-99,414	-20,607	-120,021[4]
Total	$715,396,083	$361,311,151	$1,076,707,234

[1] Does not include value of commodities or bonus Food Stamps.
[2] Includes $4,443,134.10 for Foster Care.
[3] Includes delivery of services and eligibility determination for assistance and services.
[4] Negative amounts are adjustments in aged, blind, and disabled programs (cancellations, refunds, lost warrants).
Source: Texas State Department of Public Welfare, *Annual Report 76* (Austin: State Board of Public Welfare, 1976), p. 30.

TABLE 10–5
Types and costs of federal income maintenance programs

		Costs	
Programs		Billions of dollars	Percent of federal budget
Income security		148.0	29.6
retirement and			
disability insurance	108.4		
unemployment compensation	11.8		
public assistance	27.8		
Health care services		45.1	9.0
Veterans benefits and services		19.3	3.9
(income security, education, training, rehabilitation, hospitalization and medical, housing, and other benefits)			
Training and employment services		13.3	2.7
Social services		5.1	1.0
Consumer and occupational health and safety		.9	0.2
Totals		231.7	37.4

Source: *The United States Budget in Brief,* Fiscal Year 1979 (Washington, D.C.: U.S. Office of Management and Budget, 1978), Table 3.

ability, Medicare, and survivors of workers. The states, on the other hand, were charged with unemployment compensation and employment service programs (administered in Texas by the Texas Employment Commission) and the public assistance programs to the needy, administered by the Texas Department of Public Welfare.

In 1974, the public assistance programs for needy adults (old aged, blind, disabled) were transferred to the federal government, Texas retaining responsibility for the public assistance programs of

Medical assistance (MEDICAID), including nursing home care for needy elderly, disabled, and blind, and

Aid to families with dependent children (AFDC), plus child protection against abuse, day care, and family planning programs.

See Figure 10–6 for the number of recipients for the various public assistance programs in Texas, 1968–77.

Medical assistance (MEDICAID) MEDICAID is the more expensive of the two major welfare programs, taking about 60 percent of the total spent by the Department of Public Welfare. Persons eligible include needy dependent children, disabled, blind, and aged (including aged in nursing homes). MEDICAID pays for doctors' services, prescribed drugs, laboratory fees, radiation therapy, nursing home care, hospital care, eyeglasses, family planning, institutional care, screening of the general health of children, and other services. For most of the services, except nursing home and public institutional care, the state buys insurance premiums from Blue Cross-Blue Shield, and the payments are made by the health insurance company for a profit. In the case of nursing home care, each nursing home must have a contract with the Department of Public Welfare, a license from the State Department of Health, and be approved for one to three different levels of services and payments. MEDICAID may also pay for care in an extended care facility after a person leaves a hospital but does not enter a nursing home. Figure 10–7 attempts to show schematically the different services and costs under MEDICAID.[21]

Aid to families with dependent children (AFDC) Among the classes of welfare recipients, Texas retained the care of families with dependent children when in 1974 assistance to the other categories was nationalized (and termed the Supplemental Security Income (SSI) programs). In the nationalized programs (to the adult aged, blind, and disabled), benefit payments were

Raised significantly,

Made uniform among the states, and

Tied to cost of living.

FIGURE 10–6

Welfare recipients by category in Texas (in thousands)

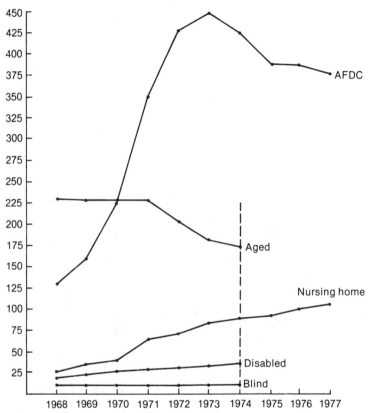

Note: Texas retains costs of MEDICAID (medical aid to the needy) for all of these classes.

Adult public assistance programs (aged, blind, disabled) assumed by the national government and called Supplemental Security Income (SSI) programs.

Source: "Selected Trends in Texas State Government Expenditures, Workloads, and Employees," A report to the Joint Advisory Committee on Governmental Operations, Legislative Budget Board (November 1975), 17.

And eligibility for benefits was:

Made uniform among the states and

Applied in a nondiscriminatory fashion.

In AFDC, on the other hand, benefits are

Relatively low,

Different in different states, and

334

FIGURE 10–7
Medical assistance program expenditures

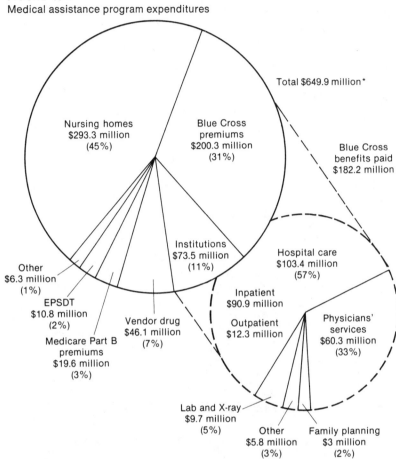

Total $649.9 million*

Nursing homes
$293.3 million
(45%)

Blue Cross
premiums
$200.3 million
(31%)

Blue Cross
benefits paid
$182.2 million

Other
$6.3 million
(1%)

Institutions
$73.5 million
(11%)

Hospital care
$103.4 million
(57%)

EPSDT
$10.8 million
(2%)

Inpatient
$90.9 million

Medicare Part B
premiums
$19.6 million
(3%)

Vendor drug
$46.1 million
(7%)

Outpatient
$12.3 million

Physicians'
services
$60.3 million
(33%)

Lab and X-ray
$9.7 million
(5%)

Other
$5.8 million
(3%)

Family planning
$3 million
(2%)

* Does not include $41.0 million in costs for estimated encumbrances.

Source: Texas State Department of Public Welfare, *Statistical Summary for 76* (Austin:
State Board of Public Welfare, 1976), p. 53.

In some states, such as Texas, lagging by two decades the economic
needs of recipients.

Further, eligibility standards:

Are not uniform among the states and

May be applied in a capriciously discriminatory fashion.

And, with the exception of MEDICAID, AFDC is the largest (but not the
most expensive), most controversial of the various categories of public
assistance. Because of myths and perpetrated falsehoods, it is the whip-

ping boy in the welfare family. Cynics like to argue that the states retained AFDC so that recipients could be duly "punished" for alleged laziness, unwillingness to work, brazen sexual immorality, and drain on the public treasury.

In Texas, AFDC rolls and total costs are kept small by

Extremely low monthly benefits and

Barriers to eligibility.

As seen in Table 10–6, Texas ranks 45th among the states in the average monthly payment to *families* with dependent children. Figured *per person,* Texas ranks 48th, above only Alabama and Mississippi.[22] Although payments were raised slightly by the 65th Legislature in 1977, the benefits are still less than 100 percent of an amount needed in 1969 to meet the barest human needs. Yet, myths are common in Texas that the poor are well off and that they are able-bodied males who will not work. In fact, the group of approximately 400,000 persons are largely children and their divorced, widowed, or abandoned mothers.

The number drawing AFDC payments is only 3.3 percent of the current population. Yet, one third of Texas children are in poverty. And in

TABLE 10–6
Average monthly payments to families with dependent children

New York	$392.25	South Dakota	196.65
Hawaii	340.22	Ohio	196.57
Wisconsin	319.95	Delaware	194.93
Alaska	289.29	Colorado	193.99
Massachusetts	284.38	Virginia	192.47
Michigan	284.07	Wyoming	187.07
Pennsylvania	282.69	Maine	183.01
New Jersey	274.53	Kentucky	173.06
Iowa	266.91	West Virginia	171.47
Illinois	265.96	Montana	169.69
Connecticut	261.78	Indiana	167.70
Vermont	261.36	Maryland	166.02
California	260.84	Nevada	159.11
Minnesota	255.88	North Carolina	155.41
Oregon	248.86	Arizona	142.45
North Dakota	247.18	Missouri	140.11
Idaho	243.82	New Mexico	138.59
Rhode Island	240.30	Louisiana	121.04
Washington	237.53	Florida	120.53
Washington, D.C.	232.14	Arkansas	118.10
United States	230.38	TEXAS	105.42
New Hampshire	223.54	Tennessee	103.30
Utah	221.62	Alabama	99.58
Kansas	218.37	Georgia	95.75
Nebraska	203.16	South Carolina	85.50
Oklahoma	202.00	Mississippi	48.19

Source: Texas State Department of Public Welfare, *Statistical Summary for 1976* (Austin: State Board of Public Welfare, 1976), p. 54.

families headed by women, the poverty rate is three times the rate of families headed by men.[23] In all, 15.2 percent of Texans are in poverty, about 600,000 of whom are school-age children.[24] Children under 18 years of age who, normally, have lost the financial support of at least one parent and who are citizens living in Texas with a parent or close relative are eligible. A monetary allowance is also given the "caretakers" of children. Eligible families qualify also for some other Department of Welfare programs, including food stamps[25] and social and medical services.

That many children are not signed up for AFDC is indicated not only by levels of poverty but also by Texas' rank of 43rd among the states in the number of AFDC recipients per 1,000 of the population. No one is able to rush to the welfare rolls in Texas. Reasons given for denial of AFDC applications reflect difficulties in meeting qualifications because of large case loads and other administrative problems. See Table 10–7. Adminis-

TABLE 10–7
AFDC applications denied by reason, fiscal year 1976

Reason	Number	Percent	Number	Percent
Administrative follow-up problems			31,042	56.5
Applicant failed to keep appointment	13,871	25.2		
Refusal of applicant to furnish information or follow agreed plan	8,066	14.7		
Voluntary withdrawal of application	5,193	9.4		
Location of applicant unknown	2,483	4.5		
Unable to establish continued absence of father	751	1.4		
Conflicting information on management	365	0.7		
Refusal to obtain medical information	313	0.6		
Adequate or excess earnings			17,853	32.5
Earnings of parent or person acting in parent's place	9,182	16.7		
Receipt of benefit, pension, or social security	4,519	8.3		
Support from absent parent	2,089	3.8		
Absent parent returned home	1,068	1.9		
Income from sources not listed elsewhere	656	1.2		
Excess resources	167	0.3		
Marriage of parent	125	0.2		
Child has spouse relatives assuming responsibility	47	0.1		
Other reasons			6,068	11.0
Does not meet other eligibility requirement	1,899	3.5		
Parent not incapacitated	1,614	2.9		
Age, residence or citizenship	1,563	2.8		
Child admitted to institution	8	0.0		
Other reasons	984	1.8		

Source: Texas State Department of Public Welfare, *Statistical Summary for 1976* (Austin: State Board of Welfare, 1976), Table 11, p. 14.

trative follow-up problems barred possible eligibility and benefits in 56.3 percent of the 55,000 applications denied in 1976. One fourth was denied because "applicant failed to keep appointment." Adequate or excess earnings under the Department's formula accounted for only one third of all reasons given for denial.

Future of state welfare programs   National assumption of elements of the public welfare and health systems will continue in the years to come. Enlarged federal grants for current programs, plus enactment of a national health program, will relieve Texas and other state governments eventually of a large share, if not all, of current programs in public welfare. None too soon. Texas is the only state with a constitutional limit on welfare spending. With under-financing of AFDC, bars to eligibility, heavy administrative work loads, low benefits, and perpetrated welfare myths, it is very difficult in Texas to sustain a viable welfare program, even with federal grants for welfare at or near the 70 percent level.

Highways

About 14 cents of the expenditure dollar goes to construction and maintenance of highways, administration and research, equipment, and highway patrol and safety. Acquisition of rights-of-ways and construc-

FIGURE 10–8

Expenditure items by percentage, State Department of Highways and Public Transportation

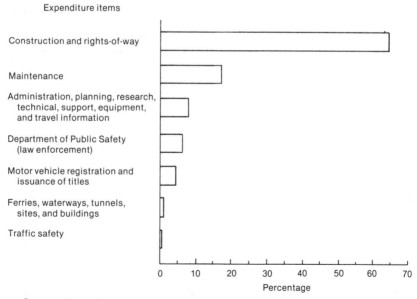

Source: Texas State Department of Highways and Public Transportation, *Thirtieth Biennial Report* (Austin: State Department of Highways and Public Transportation, 1976), p. 9.

tion costs take about two thirds of the annual highway dollar. See Figure 10–8.

Dedicated moneys in the state highway fund go to the support of the State Department of Highways and Public Transportation and the Department of Public Safety. As depicted in Figure 10–9, besides the motor fuel excise tax, earmarked revenues include also vehicle registration fees, title fees, and sales taxes on motor lubricants. Thus, about 98 percent of all moneys spent are from dedicated funds.

Highway needs are expected to increase. The state maintains about 70,000 miles of highways of various classes in both rural and urban Texas. See Table 10–8. In addition to passenger car and trucking needs, demands for mass transit systems around and between Texas' major metropolitan centers, even if some rail systems are utilized, will greatly strain transportation resources in the 1980s and 1990s.

POLITICS OF THE BUDGETARY PROCESS

A budget is "a representation in monetary terms of governmental activity."[26] A major policy statement, it

FIGURE 10–9

Major revenue sources by percentage of total, State Department of Highways and Public Transportation

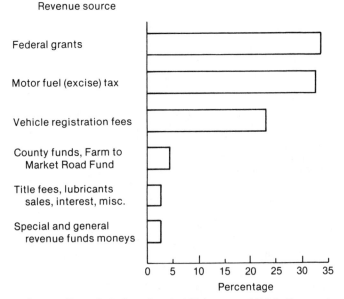

Source: Texas State Department of Highways and Public Transportation, *Thirtieth Biennial Report* (Austin: State Department of Highways and Public Transportation, 1976), p. 9.

TABLE 10–8
Urban-rural mileage, classes of state highways and roads

	Mileage	
Class	Urban	Rural
Multilane primary, U.S. and state	2,525.55 miles	2,252.53 miles
Two-lane primary, U.S. and state	4,337.91	16,856.15
Multilane secondary—farm to market roads	220.80	39.08
Two-lane secondary—farm to market roads	9,588.80	30,369.56
Controlled access, all systems	2,106.77	1,376.02
Totals	18,779.83	50,893.34

Source: Texas State Department of Highways and Public Transportation, *Thirtieth Biennial Report* (Austin: State Department of Highways and Public Transportation, 1976), p. 90.

1. Records preferences, priorities, and goals of the political community, and

2. Authoritatively allocates scarce resources for the entire society.

A discussion of the politics of the budget is a fitting conclusion for a textbook about Texas government and politics, for the budgetary process is the center of the universe of political activities with major interests vying to have their preferences recorded as the goals of the entire political community. As a microcosm of the political process, the budgetary process provides an opportunity to review the interactions of primary Texas political actors in their institutional settings and to note again functional consequences of these organizational patterns of behavior, including their impact upon public policy.

Budget priorities and the processes by which they are established:

Record the preferences of the winners of political struggles;

Reflect prime values of the political culture;

Show us other forces at work in the Texas environment, such as economic resources, scarcity of water, and problems generated by social change;

Demonstrate the filtering effect of governmental structures, including the various political arenas, the rules, and political conditions under which political combat is staged;

Illuminate distinctive features of the Texas political system; and

Because each budgetary decision establishes a precedent and because these decisions tend to be incremental and cumulative over time, establish a pattern of decisions which affect the allocation of scarce resources and benefits not just for a year or two but for generations to come.

The budgetary process consists of four phases or stages, each of which is discussed below under separate major headings. To begin with, several matters should be noted:

1. The governor is given only a very weak form of budgetary execution, Phase 3.
2. In Texas, unlike in most of the states and in the national government where budgeting is considered an executive function, the budgetary phases are managed by the *legislative* branch.
3. In Texas, the budget is not really adopted (Phase 1) until legislative hearings are held and demands of major economic interests are brokered.[27] The budget is finally adopted when the appropriations bill is in the House-Senate conference committee, where priorities finally emerge and all parts of the biennial spending plan are finally welded together. Thus, Phase 1 and Phase 2 telescope together because, as we shall see, of distinctive political conditions.
4. Texas has a biennial budget, although annual budgeting is not prohibited.

Phase 1—Budget preparation

Two budget agencies Texas is in the anomalous position of having two budget agencies

Legislative Budget Board and
Budget and Planning Office, Office of the Governor.

But budget preparation is the special preserve of the legislative leadership and its staff through the Legislative Budget Board, a ten-member joint legislative committee composed of the legislative presiding officers, chairpersons of appropriations and finance committees, and other members appointed by the leadership.[28] The two central budget offices formally duplicate budget preparation processes

Preparation of budget forms and instructions,
Receipt of detailed programmatic requests from budget officers of the various administrative agencies,
Agency justification of requests at budget agency hearings,
Review of agency requests, and
Compilation of the budget document for submission to the legislature in January of each biennium,

but it is the Legislative Budget Board which recommends a unified plan of spending. What emanates from the Office of the Governor, Budget and Planning Office, is a *revenue plan* for funding state programs, including any proposéd revenue measures, that is, what amounts to an *expenditure ceiling* for state government. Although the governor is designated by statute as chief budget officer of Texas, this role has never been realized in practice, either in the budget preparation phase or the adoption phase.[29]

It should be mentioned that the governor has the item veto by which the final budget adoption processes in the legislature can be influenced, including nailing down the chief executive's spending ceilings. With detailed program requests reflected in more specific items in the appropriations bills, the governor may enjoy revival of item veto authority. The chief executive may also exert through a greatly enlarged staff (with its data reservoir, expertise in planning programs, and potential for policy review) influence and authority in the budget preparation phase. Figure 10–10 attempts to show the various actors and their interrelationships in the budgetary process.

Zero-base budgeting In 1973, zero-base budgeting was adopted in Texas. Zero-base budgeting entails a study and justification of all programs from base zero, departing theoretically, at least, from the incremental budgetary pattern in which last year's spending plan becomes accepted and legitimate as the base for building this year's budget.[30] To carry out the zero-base concept in budget preparation, the administrative agencies are required to submit funding requests which list all current and proposed programs in order of priority and in detailed "decision packages." Zero-base budgeting does not alter budget phases or the distinctive nature of the budgetary political process in Texas. It is a management tool for more thorough, rational budget preparation based on current and anticipated needs.

The "skeleton budget" What is submitted to the legislature at the beginning of a regular session every two years is only a "skeleton budget," a budgetary framework which is used by the legislative leadership as a *working document*. This means, as stated above, that the budget preparation stage (Phase 1) continues in the legislative fiscal committees (Phase 2). Indeed, the state spending plan is never finally prepared and fashioned until the conference committee completes the budget document in semisecrecy, usually only hours before the end of the session. Only then is the budget preparation stage (Phase 1) complete. Phase 2 becomes, at that late point in time, a vote of the legislature to adopt the appropriations measure on a "take it or leave it" basis.

The budgetary preparation process in the legislature grew so extreme and grotesque by the 62nd Legislature in 1971 that it led to the Sharpstown scandals and a strong and sweeping reform movement. The Texas Research League, powerful business research organization, its fiscal responsibility values violated by legislative budget preparation processes, complained of the existence of "200 spending surprises" in the 1972–73

biennial appropriations bill when it emerged from the conference committee.[31]

The place of the conference committee The House-Senate joint conference committee is the place where all deals are finally consummated.
Hence, the practice of delaying consideration of the appropriations measure until the last few days of the session is a pragmatic necessity to

FIGURE 10–10
Actors in the budget process

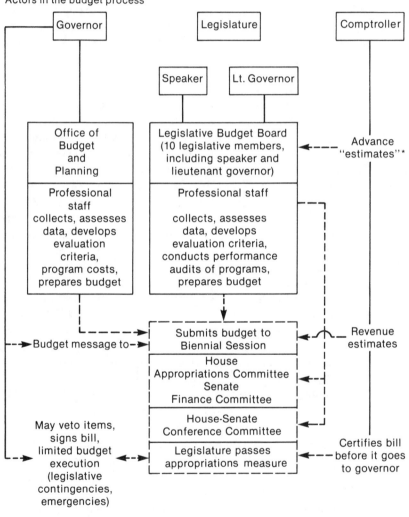

——————— Full time

– – – – Nonpermanent, occasional, periodic relationships

* Has same relationship with Governor's Office of Budget and Planning.

maximize leadership authority and support so that it can remain effective in the fiscal payoffs and in the exchanges involving passage or nonpassage of other proposed legislation.[32] For example, in the system of exchanges in the House, the chairperson of the House Appropriations Committee supports a safe, conservative Democrat for speaker, secures his or her own pivotal position in the next legislature on the Appropriations Committee, projects himself or herself as the kingpin into the next speaker's race, and receives additional promises from the heir apparent leader and back-up candidates of the appointment of compliant majorities on appropriations and other key standing committees. Thereby, a network of power arrangements, inside and outside the legislature, are established for the leadership in other policy matters.

The Texas political system, thus, has become very stable, producing ideological affinity among the legislative leadership, the governor, and the attorney general. By this extensive network of influence inside and outside the legislature and by an unusually large block of personal prerogatives lodged in the speakership and lieutenant governorship is management and control exercised in the Texas legislature in making budgetary and other public policy.

Localism and group politics   This appropriations process rather accurately reflects traditional legislative behavior since it is congruent with power arrangements in the Texas legislature. As we saw in Chapter 4, the legislative system lacks institutional arrangements for building strong, legitimate bases of political authority. Individualistic and personalistic politics, marked by an intense spirit of localism, produce fragmented bases of authority in which interest groups become unchallenged aggregators of political influence—both at election time and in the legislative assemblies. As a result, in the budgetary process, "The Texas appropriation system virtually excludes the majority of the legislators from the decision-making process and prohibits any meaningful public debate over spending issues."[33]

The appropriations process affects, as we have seen, not just the important matters of procedure and process but all policy outputs of the Texas political system. Thus, it can be faulted on far more serious grounds than being inefficient or unsound, or for violating the budget preparation authority of the Legislative Budget Board, or for producing $400 million additional, unplanned expenditures. The legislature has never come to grips with the twin democratic requisites of

1.   Vesting power in responsive institutional arrangements for

2.   Dispersing responsible decision-making authority.

As we saw in Chapter 4, formal powers are concentrated in the hands of presiding officers, lawmaking authority is in the "Speaker's team" and a "Senate directorate," and no broad-based party caucuses exist for leadership selection and management of the statute-making processes. The causes of this state of affairs are much more complex and the remedies much more remote than the realm of the budgetary process.

Phase 2—Budget adoption

Budget adoption is formally the legislative phase of the budgetary process. Legislative Budget Board staff shift to act as expert staffs of the House Appropriations Committee,[34] the Senate Finance Committee, and, ultimately, the conference committee. The LBB staff personnel follow the "skeleton budget" until finally the state's master plan of spending is worked out in conference committee. In such a system, the integrity of the original budget plan is not defended, and long-range positive policy goals are difficult, if not impossible, to make. Administrators in charge of the spending agencies work with their boards and with the legislative leadership to frame a budget which reflects the low-taxing, low-spending values of the dominant coalition of interest groups. Little meaningful debate over spending issues occurs because of the short time and the lid on government spending and taxing. The expert staff of the Legislative Budget Board, instead of managing the proceedings, is reduced to a scheduler of committee business and a collator of the various bargains to fashion a final version of the state budget. The budget is adopted, as we have seen, on a "take it or leave it" basis when it emerges from the conference committee.

Under zero-base budgeting and other reforms, involving a larger, more expert staff, priority ranking of detailed programmatic requests from the agencies, price tags attached to all legislation proposing new programs, performance auditing, and policy analysis, the budget system is neater, more systematic, and efficient, but it is by no means sure that the budget plan prepared and submitted to the legislature will be more than skeletal. Dispersal of decision-making authority cannot be effected in the Texas legislative subsystem because of lack of authority in any institution to counter the power of the dominant interest system.

Role of the comptroller of public accounts The "pay-as-you-go" limited debt provision of 1942 gives the comptroller direct and continuing effect in the appropriations process in budget-making. To each legislative session, the comptroller submits estimates of anticipated revenues for the next biennium. All state spending must fall within those figures unless the legislature is willing to enact new tax legislation or declare an emergency and pass excessive spending bills by four-fifths majorities. The comptroller's willingness to increase the estimates during the crucial final negotiations in conference committee greatly facilitates bargaining and brokering necessary commonly to produce an acceptable spending bill. Before the appropriations measure goes to the governor, the comptroller must certify that enough revenues are in prospect to cover spending obligations.

The comptroller has to be cautious because tax collection statutes schedule receipt of a large portion of state tax revenues during the last two months of the fiscal year. For the second year of the biennium, the comptroller is attempting to make correct estimates nearly three years in advance of collections. Past comptrollers used the estimates as a conservative check on spending, underestimating tax growth rates and ruling that taxes *earned* but not collected until after the end of a fiscal year could not be counted in the year earned. Comptroller Bob Bullock has not exercised such fiscally conservative restraints.

Phase 3—Budget execution

Texas has not provided true budget execution. This authority would

Assure that the state's immediate budgetary policy is followed by the operating agencies and

Allow flexibility in spending for long-range programmatic purposes.

Budget execution normally entails the following:

1. Quarterly spending allotments to each agency, based upon submission and approval of agency operating budgets;
2. Allocation of more money or withholding moneys from agencies, under carefully prescribed conditions, when administration spending priorities change; and
3. Approval of transfers of funds among categories of spending and among agencies.

Given the other types of authority already exercised by the Legislative Budget Board, it would seem practical and consistent to place budget execution authority and processes in that body's staff. But in 1951 when the legislature wrote into the general appropriations bill special provisions requiring the Board to give prior approval of expenditures from designated appropriations, the Texas attorney general held that the riders were an unconstitutional invasion of executive prerogatives.[35]

For many years, however, the legislature has authorized three types of gubernatorial action to ease the uncertainties inherent in a two-year spending period. The governor

1. Aids agencies with inadequate operating moneys from appropriated contingency funds,
2. Spends appropriated moneys for defined classes of emergencies, and
3. Has prior approval authority before some agencies can spend money. There must be a finding of fact by the governor that preexisting legis-

lative conditions have been met or have come about for spending. The decision of the governor, together with findings of fact, are filed with the comptroller of public accounts and the Legislative Budget Board.

All attempts at broader authority have been thwarted—by tradition, countervailing action of actors in the disintegrated administrative system (especially by the attorney general and the comptroller of public accounts), strict interpretation of both executive and legislative authority, restraints of the 1876 Constitution, and forces outside state government. Opposition has been voiced in terms of defense of

The disintegrated administrative system and

The spirit of localism in a disintegrated legislative system.

Opponents argue that budget execution authority would take away every discretionary authority of the state's boards and commissions and that the governor could coerce legislators by threatening to cut funds appropriated to institutions in their districts.

Phase 4—Policy review

Flying in the face of traditional features of the political system, Texas has established fiscal policy review to attempt to judge state agency performance in terms of

1. Service levels,
2. Objectives of policies and programs, and
3. Results, including impact of programs on target groups and consequences of these programs for society.

By use of proper methods, old programs can be altered and new services created to adjust state programmatic objectives and efforts. Texas expects to achieve policy review in part by use of the zero-base concept of identification of program objectives, supported by needs statements, and by requiring the Legislative Budget Board to establish a system of performance audits and evaluation criteria designed to provide comprehensive and continuing review of programs and operations of each state agency.

In the performance auditing program in Texas, the staff of the Legislative Budget Board states explicitly each agency's statutory responsibilities and analyzes the operational efficiency and program performance in terms of unit-cost measurement, workload efficiency data, and program output standards. The Board makes a performance report to the legislature upon the advent of each regular session.[36]

Such an operation greatly enhances the expertise and data base of the budgetary staffs. Greater cooperation can be expected between the Legislative Budget Board and the Office of Budget and Planning of the governor. Both staffs engage in data collection and information and assessment of program costs and program alternatives. Inputs also are made from the Department of Community Affairs, which gathers information on a variety of state problems and logs attempts by administrative agencies to handle their assigned tasks.[37] These matters should find reflection in the budget through altered programs and financing. A budget based upon program performance should lend greater rationality to budget-making, providing thereby greater efficiency in terms of costs and quicker attention to new and changing policy problems and needs.

The future

The Texas budgetary process is still one of the few legislatively dominated systems in the United States. Recent changes may alter but slightly

1. The relation between the legislature and the budget staffs and
2. The weak position of the governor in the budgetary system.

Staffs will become more important. They will leave a professional impact. Hence, leadership and interest groups will have to pay more attention to ensuring the loyalty of the staff to regime values, including how to make a budget and what is important in a budget. And in the Office of the Governor, strong planning facilities are being developed separately from the legislatively managed budget preparation processes. If the prerogatives of staff do not continue to yield to the spirit of localism and interest group politics in the legislature and the realities of disintegration in the executive branch, the Governor's Office of Budget and Planning can be expected to exert a considerable degree of influence in the planning processes of state government. If so, the governor will accrue more budgetary authority, including that which continues to flow from responsibility for the state's revenue plan.

Getting the legislative committees to defer to the "skeleton budget" as authoritative and to persuade them to abstain from adding to the document and restructuring it in line with individual and local demands has always been difficult. Members are dependent upon moneys for local projects and institutions, and administrators value access to the budget preparation stage. In the end, these disintegrative influences have to be curbed by the leadership. And their effective control and management of the system supply the pledges of support for the political leadership of Texas, even in administrative and judicial branches, and sustains their own positions to act as brokers to meet the demands of the pressure group system.

Newer formal budgetary processes must accommodate traditionally dispersed and disintegrated bases of authority, processes and rules which feature decision-making in the hands of a few, and the spirit of localism and pressure politics. The budgetary system will continue to operate in a traditional manner. Political scientists, as well as practitioners of politics in Austin, know full well that traditional political behavior is seldom changed by adjustments of the political system. Broader forces at play in the political environment, most notably the political culture, will have to be altered before the behavior of political actors, inside government and outside government, is altered in any marked degree. These forces often move very slowly.

CONCLUSIONS

In this chapter we have considered the way in which money is raised for public purposes in Texas, the way it is spent, and the processes involved in state budgeting. Here are the main conclusions we can offer from this analysis:

1. The major source of revenue for Texas state government is the sales tax, a tax which is generally considered to be regressive in the sense that, because all people pay at the same rate, higher income people pay a lower proportion of their incomes in sales taxes than lower income people pay. About 58 percent of all Texas state tax revenues come from sales taxes, and this does not count revenues from the excise tax on motor fuels. But federal categorical grants and revenue sharing funds contribute importantly to Texas revenues, making up a full 27 percent of all the state's annual spending.

2. Taxation is intended to fulfill a variety of purposes which are thought to be socially useful, and in doing so tax benefits accrue to some persons and corporations and not to others. In Texas, as well as in many other states, fiscal policies, including tax policies, support economic development, giving incentives and assistance to businesses for plant relocations and for other purposes.

3. Most states levy regressive taxes, but many offset this by progressive expenditure policies—providing assistance and services to low-income groups. In regard both to taxes and services, Texas ranks among the five most regressive states, although its citizens enjoy one of the lowest per capita tax burdens in the land. Thus, Texas is a low tax, low spending state with a relatively small range of poorly supported services.

4. Three major policy areas—education, welfare, and highways—account for about 80 percent of the state's budget. As in all states, the federal government provides the funds to pay for most welfare and other

income maintenance programs. The major state program least aided from federal funds is education.

5.   While the legislature plays a central role in budgetary allocations, its capacity to affect state spending is limited by the fact that fully 65 percent of all Texas revenues are earmarked. This means that tax receipts flow into various special funds which are, by law, dedicated to spending only for specific purposes. Within the range of its discretion, the legislature has a larger role to play in budgeting in Texas than in most other states. Although the governor has the power of the item veto, which he can use to enforce spending limitations, his budgetary role vis-a-vis the legislature is relatively nonconflictual. Within agreed-upon spending ceilings, the state budget is hammered out in the legislature through interaction between spokesmen for the dominant interest groups and the legislative leadership.

Notes

CHAPTER ONE

1. As quoted in the *Houston Post,* September 18, 1972, p. 3B, in reaction to Harvey Katz, *Shadow on the Alamo: New Heroes Fight Old Corruption in Texas Politics* (Garden City, N.Y.: Doubleday & Co., Inc., 1972).

2. Daniel J. Elazer, *American Federalism: A View From the States,* 2d ed. (New York: Thomas Y. Crowell Co., 1972), p. 20n.

3. Because the public policy literature is small and sketchy and policy theory is not well developed, what we conclude is suggestive rather than complete or definitive in any way.

4. See Lucian Pye, "Culture and Political Science: Problems in the Evaluation of the Concept of Political Culture," *Social Science Quarterly,* 53, no. 2 (September 1972): 285–96; Samuel C. Patterson, "The Political Cultures of the American States," *Journal of Politics,* 30, no. 1 (February 1968): 187–209; and Robert L. Savage, "Patterns of Multilinear Evolutions in the American States," *Publius,* 3, no. 1 (Spring 1973): 75–108.

5. Elazar, *American Federalism,* pp. 93–114.

6. For the salience of cultural determinants of state political system characteristics, see Charles A. Johnson, "Political Culture in the American States: Elazar's Formulation Examined," *American Journal of Political Science,* 20, no. 3 (August 1976): 491–509; John D. Hutcheson, Jr. and George A. Taylor, "Religious Variables, Political System Characteristics, and Policy Outputs," *American Journal of Political Science,* 17, no. 2 (May 1973): 414–21; and the literature cited in the last, 415.

7. James Conaway, *The Texans* (New York: Alfred A. Knopf, 1976), p. 5.

8. Ibid., p. 257.

9. V. O. Key, Jr., *Southern Politics in State and Nation* (New York: Vintage Books, 1949), pp. 298–316. See also Malcolm E. Jewell and David M. Olson, *American State Political Parties and Elections* (Homewood, Ill.: The Dorsey Press, 1978).

10. Oddly, as the late Professor O. Douglas Weeks observed, traditionalistic political structures, habits, and processes with a "southern flavor" have survived in Texas even with the modernization of our social and economic institutions. O. Douglas Weeks, "Texas: Land of Conservative Expansiveness," in *The Changing Politics of the South,* William C. Havard, ed. (Baton Rouge: Louisiana State University Press, 1972), p. 203.

11. Key, *Southern Politics,* chap. 12, "Texas: A Politics of Economics," pp. 254–76.

12. See J. Morgan Kousser, *The Shaping of Southern Politics: Suffrage Restriction and the Establishment of the One-Party South, 1880–1910* (New Haven: Yale University Press, 1974) and Roscoe C. Martin, *The People's Party in Texas* (Austin: University of Texas Press, 1933). For a theory of a class base of U.S. politics and participation, see Sidney Verba and Norman H. Nie, *Participation in America: Political Democracy and Social Equality* (New York: Harper & Row, Pubs., 1972), esp. chap. 20.

13. Numan V. Bartley and Hugh D. Graham, *Southern Politics and the Second Reconstruction* (Baltimore: Johns Hopkins University Press, 1975), pp. 161–62.

14. See Chandler Davidson, *Biracial Politics: Conflict and Coalition in the Metropolitan South* (Baton Rouge: Louisiana State University Press, 1972), pp. 52–82.

15. See Bernard L. Weinstein, "Why the Business Climate in Texas Is Rated No. 1," *Texas Business,* 1, no. 1 (July 1976): 27–30, 62. For treatment of this policy emphasis of the southern states, including presentation of rational, underlying reasons for southern development politics, see Ira Sharkansky, *The United States: A Study of a Developing Country* (New York: David McKay Co., 1975).

16. Bob Bullock, *Texas Means Business!* Comptroller of Public Accounts, State of Texas, December 1977, p. 10.

17. A struggle over "right to work," a prohibition against contracts which require employees to be or to become union members as a condition of employment, was featured in the failure of the constitutional convention of 1974.

18. Bullock, *Texas Means Business!* p. 9.

19. For expansion of this thesis, see Chapters 2 and 3.

20. See Clifton McCleskey, *The Government and Politics of Texas,* 3d ed. (Boston: Little, Brown & Co., 1969), p. 115.

21. Numan V. Bartley and Hugh Davis Graham, "Whatever Happened to the Solid South?" *New South,* 27, no. 4 (Fall 1972): 34.

22. See John R. Todd and Kay Dickenson Ellis, "Analyzing Factional Patterns in State Politics: Texas, 1944–1972," *Social Science Quarterly,* 55, no. 3 (December 1974): 718–31.

23. For a particularly good summary discussion of participation and its costs, see Larry L. Wade,

The Elements of Public Policy (Columbus: Charles E. Merrill Pub. Co., 1972), chap. 7.

24. See Dan Nimmo and William E. Oden, *The Texas Political System* (Englewood Cliffs: Prentice-Hall, Inc., 1971), pp. 104–5.

25. Robert S. Erikson and Norman R. Luttbeg, *American Public Opinion: Its Origins, Content and Impact* (New York: John Wiley & Sons, 1973), pp. 310–22 demonstrate that a state such as Texas with a dominant ideology and non-competitive parties may achieve "policy congruency," that is, policy compatible with public opinion.

26. See Jack L. Walker, "The Diffusion of Innovations Among the American States," *American Political Science Review,* 63, no. 3 (September 1969): 880–99 and Robert L. Savage, "Policy Innovativeness as a Trait of American States," *Journal of Politics,* 40, no. 1 (February 1978): 212–19.

27. See Texas Office of Economic Opportunity, Texas Department of Community Affairs, *Poverty in Texas 1973* (Austin: Department of Community Affairs, 1974).

28. Note the sentiments in November 1963 of a former Texas congressman, former college regents president, former general counsel of Southwestern Bell Telephone, and state district judge amidst an unsuccessful effort by popular referendum to eliminate the poll tax: "Every pinko and every red in the country has always favored elimination of poll taxes. They would go further and eliminate all voting regulations and restrictions. Their efforts are obvious. The poll tax has been some defense, at least, against mass fraud, mass hysteria, mass ignorance, and mass indifference in the voters." Quoted in Dick Smith, "Texas and the Poll Tax," *Southwestern Social Science Quarterly,* 45, no. 2 (September 1964): 171.

29. Paul Wehrle, "The Texas Election Code: Some Proposals for Change," in *TexaStats '72,* Douglas S. Harlan, ed. (Austin: Lyndon B. Johnson School of Public Affairs, University of Texas, 1974), p. xix.

30. Karl W. Deutsch, *Politics and Government: How People Decide Their Fate,* 2d ed. (Boston: Houghton Mifflin Co., 1974), p. 238.

31. Kenneth Newton, "Feeble Governments and Private Power: Urban Politics and Policies in the United States," in *The New Urban Politics,* Louis H. Masotti and Robert L. Lineberry, eds. (Cambridge: Ballinger Pub. Co., 1976), p. 40.

32. Fred Bonavita, "Hill Encouraged by Professor's Poll on Governor's Race," *Houston Post,* November 4, 1978, p. 6A.

33. For detailed information of the state's physical properties and economic development, see the biennial editions of the *Texas Almanac and State Industrial Guide* (Dallas: A. H. Belo Corp.) and *Atlas of Texas* (Austin: Bureau of Business Research, The University of Texas at Austin, 1976).

34. See John Graves, "Texas: You Ain't Seen Nothing Yet," in *The Water Hustlers,* Robert H. Boyle, John Graves, and T. H. Watkins, eds. (San Francisco: Sierra Club, 1971) for a conservationist's account of the politics of the water plan, narrowly defeated in a statewide referendum.

35. See "An Assessment of Surface Water Supplies of Arkansas, With Computations of Surplus Supplies and a Conceptual Plan for Import to Texas," by Stephens Consultant Services, Inc., Little Rock, Arkansas, prepared under contract for the Texas Water Development Board, December 1976.

36. See Timothy K. Barnekov and Daniel Rich, "Privatism and Urban Development: An Analysis of the Organized Influence of Local Business Elites," *Urban Affairs Quarterly,* 12, no. 4 (June 1977): 431–60.

37. Glenn H. Ivy, "An Organizational Structure for Gubernatorial Leadership in Texas State Government" (Ph.D. diss., University of Texas, 1970), p. 125.

38. For data which justify Census Bureau treatment of Texas SMSAs as economic and social regions, see David L. Huff and Diana R. DeAre, *Principal Interaction Fields of Texas Metropolitan Centers,* Urban and Regional Studies No. 1 (Austin: Bureau of Business Research, University of Texas, 1974).

39. See Chapter 8.

40. Texas Office of Economic Opportunity, *Poverty in Texas 1973,* foreword. From 1960 to 1970, 146 of Texas' 254 counties experienced a net loss of population.

41. See the maps and discussion in Chapter 2 of the distribution of ethnic minorities in Texas metropolitan and rural areas.

42. Janice C. May, *Amending the Texas Constitution* (Austin: Texas Advisory Commission on Intergovernmental Relations, 1972), pp. 12–13.

43. Ibid., p. 1.

44. Nimmo and Oden, *The Texas Political System,* p. 35.

45. Janice C. May, "The Texas Voter Registration System," *Public Affairs Comment,* 16, no. 4 (July 1970): 1.

46. See Earl Black, *Southern Governors and Civil Rights: Racial Segregation As a Campaign Issue in the Second Reconstruction* (Cambridge: Harvard University Press, 1976).

47. Lewis A. Froman, "Some Effects of Interest Group Strength in State Politics," *American Political Science Review,* 15, no. 4 (December 1966): 954–62.

48. May, *Amending the Texas Constitution.*

49. Ibid., p. 20.

50. Ibid.

51. This finding is substantiated in Gilbert A. Smith, "Amending the Texas Constitution: 1948–1968" (Master's thesis, Sam Houston State University, 1969).

52. John E. Bebout, "Perspectives on Preparing for Constitutional Revision," *National Civic Review*, 62, no. 2 (February 1973): 70.

53. Quoted in the *Houston Chronicle*, October 15, 1975, p. 1, sec. 1.

54. Darrell Hancock, "Charter Voting Not Attack on Reform," *Houston Post*, November 9, 1975, p. 10B.

55. The following session of the legislature, in 1975, pulled together a draft of a revised constitution and submitted the document in eight separate propositions to the voters. All were rejected by landslide proportions.

56. John E. Bebout, "The Meaning of the Vote on the Proposed Texas Constitution, 1975," *Public Affairs Comment*, 24, no. 2 (February 1978): 8.

57. See ibid., and the sources cited therein.

CHAPTER TWO

1. The author is well aware of the lack of agreement on appropriate terms to be used in describing each of the minorities, even among the groups themselves. In this chapter *Mexican-American* and *chicano* are used interchangeably. The term *Non-Anglo* will be used to designate the combination of Mexican-American and black or Negro populations; the term *Anglo* is used as a residual category designating the remainder of the population.

2. These and similar data in this chapter are from the U.S. Census Bureau, *1970 Census of Population, General Social Characteristics: Texas* (Washington, D.C.: U.S. Government Printing Office, 1972).

3. The 6,000 (1835) figure is from Juan N. Almonte (translated by Carlos E. Casteñeda). "Statistical Report on Texas, 1835," *Southwestern Historical Quarterly*, 28 (January 1925): 229, as quoted in S. Dale McLemore, "The Origins of Mexican-American Subordination in Texas," *Southwestern Social Science Quarterly*, 53, no. 4 (March 1973): 665. The 30,000 figure is from Vernon M. Briggs, *Chicanos and Rural Poverty* (Baltimore, Md.: Johns Hopkins Press, 1973), p. 10. A good discussion of early Spanish-speaking/Anglo relations is found in McLemore, "Origins of Mexican-American Subordination." The March 1973 issue of the *Southwestern Social Science Quarterly* is devoted entirely to chicanos and includes valuable materials relevant to understanding the situation of black Texans as well.

   Rodolfo Acuña, *Occupied America: The Chicano's Struggle Toward Liberation* (San Francisco: Canfield Press, 1972), p. 11 uses figures for 1830 of 20,000 Anglos and 2,000 slaves. On page 16 he notes that there were "5,000 or so" Mexicans in the province at that time (1835), an often-used figure in other histories. Chapter 2 of Acuña's book is an excellent counter to the traditional Anglo views concerning Anglo-Mexican political and social relations.

   The unsolved problem of "defining" the Mexican-American and counting heads of same continues to confound observers. See José Hernández, Leo Estrada, and David Alvirez, "Census Data and the Problem of Conceptually Defining the Mexican-American Population," in *Southwestern Social Science Quarterly*, 53, no. 4 (March 1973): 671, 687. I find the 1970 definition more satisfying than prior reports, although it includes a small percentage of Spanish-speakers and/or surnamed who are not Mexican-Americans. At the same time there remains no effective way of accounting for the apparently substantial numbers of illegal migrants moving into the state.

4. Texas Office of Economic Opportunity, Texas Department of Community Affairs, *Poverty in Texas* (Austin: Department of Community Affairs, 1972).

5. See the section, "Ethnicity of Rural Economic Problems," chap. 8, pp. 254–56.

6. Texas Office of Economic Opportunity, Texas Department of Community Affairs, *Poverty in Texas 1973* (Austin: Department of Community Affairs, 1974).

7. College and university enrollment data are provided by the Coordinating Board, Texas College and Universities and by the U.S. Department of Health, Education, and Welfare, "Racial and Ethnic Enrollment from Institutions of Higher Education, Fall, 1970," OCR–72–8 (Washington, D.C.: U.S. Government Printing Office, 1972).

8. See Acuña, *Occupied America*, chap. 2, esp. pp. 42–46, where he discusses the largely successful efforts of King, Kennedy, Stillman, Bolden, and a number of other "robber-barons," in his terms, in mostly illegally taking land from Mexican-Americans in Texas.

9. *Rodriguez* v. *San Antonio Independent School District*, 93 S. Ct. 1278 (1973).

10. Chandler Davidson and Charles M. Gaitz, "Ethnic Attitudes as a Basis for Minority Cooperation in a Southwestern Metropolis," in *Social Science Quarterly*, 53, no. 4 (March 1973): 738–48, esp. pp. 740–41.

11. Other studies include Leo Grebler, Joan W. Moore, and Ralph Guzman, *The Mexican-American People: The Nation's Second Largest Minority* (New York: Free Press, 1970), which specifically cites data from San Antonio and Los Angeles; Robin Williams, *Strangers Next Door* (Englewood Cliffs, N.J.: Prentice-Hall, 1964), which uses Bakersfield, California data; Angus Campbell, *White Attitudes Toward Black People* (Ann Arbor: Institute for Social Research, The University of Michigan, 1971); Andrew M. Greeley and Paul B. Sheatsley, "Attitudes Toward Racial Integration," *Scientific American*, 225 (December 1971): 13–19.

12. Frank L. Baird, "An Anglo View of Mexican-Americans," *Public Service* (Lubbock: Center

for Public Service, Texas Tech University), 1, no. 2 (February 1974).

13. *Brown* v. *Board of Education of Topeka, Kansas,* 347 U.S. 483 (1954).

14. *Nixon* v. *Herndon,* 273 U.S. 563 (1927) knocked down the state law excluding blacks from the Democratic primary; *Nixon* v. *Condon,* 286 U.S. 73 (1932) overthrew a state law allowing party leaders to exclude blacks. *Smith* v. *Allwright,* 321 U.S. 640 (1944), was a direct attack on the white primary. The last major case was *Terry* v. *Adams,* 345 U.S. 461 (1953). Note that all these decisions, from 1927 to 1953, had Texas origins and required U.S. Supreme Court action to overturn Texas court decisions.

15. *United States* v. *Texas,* 252 F. Supp. 234 (W.D. Tex.), 384 U.S. 155.

16. See Dan Nimmo and Clifton McCleskey, "Impact of the Poll Tax on Voter Participation: The Houston Metropolitan Area in 1966," *Journal of Politics,* 31 (August 1969): 682–99; Allen M. Shinn, Jr., "A Note on Voter Registration and Turnout in Texas, 1960–1970," *Journal of Politics,* 33 (November 1971): 1120–29; Stanley Kelley, Jr., Richard E. Ayres, and William G. Bowen, "Registration and Voting: Putting First Things First," *American Political Science Review,* 61 (June 1967): 359–73.

17. Clifton McCleskey and Dan Nimmo, "Differences Between Potential, Registered and Actual Voters: The Houston Metropolitan Area in 1964," *Social Science Quarterly,* 49 (June 1968): 103–14.

18. Shinn, "Note on Voter Registration and Turnout in Texas," p. 1122.

19. Reported in Clifton McCleskey and Bruce Merrill, "Mexican-American Political Behavior in Texas," *Social Science Quarterly,* 53, no. 4 (March 1973): 785–93.

20. Prairie View students alleged that the college president was receiving kickbacks from teachers, to cite only one of several incidents reported to investigators.

21. A good discussion of the Black Caucus, from which much of the above is taken, is found in Jack Keever, "Sole Brothers," *Texas Monthly,* January 1975, pp. 21–27. Interestingly, although there is a caucus among chicano legislators, in fact, ideological, social, and personal differences among the Mexican-American legislators are sharp and open, denying any really significant bloc action.

CHAPTER THREE

1. See Dan Nimmo and William E. Oden, *Texas Political System* (Englewood Cliffs, N.J.: Prentice-Hall, 1971), pp. 54–61.

2. V. O. Key, Jr., *Southern Politics in State and Nation* (New York: Random House, 1949), p. 254.

3. This writer met his former state representative in the lobby of the capitol in 1973 and discovered that he had just quit his House seat to become the chief lobbyist for the Texas Real Estate Association. Realtors have a powerful lobby in virtually every state legislature.

4. According to Terry Goodman, who heads the Secretary of State's lobby enforcement division, in 1978, no other state had more than 400 registered lobbyists.

5. This general order of precedence from governor down to freshman House member was offered by two lobbyists for nationwide pharmaceutical firms over coffee at the Polonaise restaurant overlooking the capitol during the 1975 session. They knew exactly when a half dozen southern state legislatures intended to take up bills affecting their special interests and had already scheduled their visits to coincide. I observed them pick up the tab for several Texas legislators.

6. Conversation with the author on February 24, 1978.

7. See two articles by Lee Jones in the *San Antonio Express* of June 29 and 30, 1978: "Game of Golf Is a Key Time to Hit the Ball" and "Many Powerful Names Pop Up as Strongest Lobby." Jones concluded that the Texas State Teachers Association (TSTA) might well be considered the most influential lobby of 1978.

8. *Texas Government Newsletter,* April 24, 1978; see also "Money Power Funneled Through Political Groups," by Jon Ford in the July 16, 1978 *Austin American Statesman,* p. C1. The PACs were brought into the open in Texas by the 1973 law requiring them to disclose political contributions. Formerly, only the candidates themselves had to report contributions and outlays.

9. See an article by Mark Browning in the *Corpus Christi Caller-Times,* September 26, 1976.

10. When this writer queried former Senator John Tower on the subject he was told, "There isn't a single Texas Congressman who isn't for deregulation except for Eckhardt" (Bob Eckhardt, liberal Democrat from Houston).

11. The provisions of the law must be reaffirmed by Congress every five years. See the 1970 and the 1975 amendments to the Voting Rights Act of 1965.

12. *Dunn* v. *Blumstein,* 405 U.S. 330 (1972).

13. *United States* v. *Texas,* 384 U.S. 155 (1966).

14. See *TexaStats '72,* county and precinct election returns compiled and edited by Douglas S. Harlan.

15. Ibid., p. xvii.

16. See James R. Soukup, et al., *Party and Factional Division in Texas* (Austin: University of Texas Press, 1964), pp. 36–40.

17. As reported in *Texas Observer,* May 12, 1962, p. 1.

18. In June 1975 the Mexican-American Legal Defense and Education Fund (MALDEF) filed a suit in federal district court challenging the

validity of the state requirement that voters sign their ballot stubs (as a violation of the secrecy of the ballot which, it claims, has led to voter intimidation in South Texas). Two years later, the state ended the signature requirement without fanfare.

19. Since 1879, over 350 amendments have been submitted to the electorate; 43 percent of these have been submitted since 1953. In a 15 year period, between 1963–78, 114 amendments and a revised constitution (the one rejected in 1975) were submitted. See Jay G. Stanford, "Constitutional Revision in Texas: A New Chapter," *Public Affairs Comment,* 20, no. 2 (February 1974), p. 1; also see, *Texas Government Newsletter,* November 14, 1977.

20. Robert S. Erikson and Norman R. Luttbeg, *American Public Opinion* (New York: John Wiley & Sons, 1973).

21. Article 13.43b.

22. For a close examination of both the permanent and temporary features of the Democratic party, see "Rules of the Democratic Party of Texas" filed in the Office of the Secretary of State in 1972 and 1976.

23. Unlike the Democrats, the Republicans, who are more ideologically cohesive, have traditionally avoided using the unit rule at their conventions.

24. As the majority party the Democrats are more generous with their allotments. In 1976, there were 130 delegates from Texas at the National Democratic Convention, while the Republicans sent 100 representatives to their convention.

25. A procedural notation at this point seems appropriate. Democratic party rules for *all* party conventions specify the following: (1) proxy voting in caucuses, committees, or on the floor is prohibited; (2) minority reports are prepared and presented to the convention if supported by vote of 10 percent of the delegates; and (3) a petition signed by 20 percent of the delegates will automatically place a specified item of business on the convention's agenda.

26. In much the same way, one could argue that the *liberal* party, composed of both Democrats and Republicans, is the one party of Massachusetts.

27. Much of the research data used in this section is taken from a perceptive work on Texas parties by James Hugh Broussard entitled, "The 1961 Special Senate Election: A Turning Point in Texas Political History" (Honors Thesis, Harvard University, 1963).

28. He is no relation to Ralph Yarborough, nor to Don Yarbrough, who was nominated and elected to the State Supreme Court because of this apparent confusion in the minds of the voters.

29. For a more detailed discussion of ethnic group politics, see Chapter 2.

CHAPTER FOUR

1. Willie Morris, *North Toward Home* (Boston: Houghton Mifflin Co., 1967), pp. 203–24.

2. Sherrill has held a variety of newspaper jobs, including the Washington editorship of *Nation,* and has written a large number of articles and books, including a textbook, *Why They Call It Politics: A Guide to America's Government,* 2d ed. (New York: Harcourt Brace, 1974).

3. Morris, *North Toward Home,* p. 206.

4. Ibid., p. 204.

5. Ibid, p. 215.

6. Samuel C. Patterson, "American State Legislatures and Public Policy," in *Politics in the American States: A Comparative Analysis,* 3d ed., Herbert Jacob and Kenneth N. Vines, eds. (Boston: Little, Brown and Co., 1976), p. 140.

7. As a result, the governor's veto is in practice an absolute negative. See Fred Gantt, Jr., "The Governor's Veto in Texas: An Absolute Negative?" *Public Affairs Comment,* 15, no. 2 (March 1969).

8. For comparative information about staff roles, trends in staffing, and staff contributions, see James J. Heaphey and Alan P. Balutis, eds. *Legislative Staffing: A Comparative Perspective* (New York: John Wiley & Sons, 1975). See also Council of State Governments, *American State Legislatures: Their Structures and Procedures,* rev. (Lexington, Ky.: Council of State Governments, 1977).

9. Two additional legislative agencies are the Legislative Redistricting Board and the Commission on Uniform State Laws (composed of members of the State Bar), which works with an annual National Conference of Commissioners to recommend to the legislature enactment of uniform draft bills and to the courts and the Bar uniform judicial interpretation of the uniform statutes already enacted by the Texas Legislature.

10. The Texas Legislative Council, like many such councils in the American states, has shifted during the past decade from interim research to management activities and other assignments. See John A. Worthley and Edgar G. Crane, "Organizational Dimensions of State Legislatures," *Midwest Review of Public Administration,* 10, no. 1 (March 1976): 20–21.

11. The work of the Sunset Advisory Commission is discussed in Chapter 6, pp. 186–88.

12. Activities of the auditor and Legislative Budget Board are discussed in Chapters 6 and 10.

13. Data are from Texas Legislative Council, *Employment in State Government,* Reports 60–4 and 64–1 (Austin: Texas Legislative Council, January 1969 and January 1977) and *Handbook of Governments in Texas* (Austin: Texas Advisory Commission on Intergovernmental Relations, 1973, updated).

14. Alabama, Louisiana, Mississippi, and Nebraska. Council of State Governments, *American State Legislatures,* Table 2.5, pp. 24–25.

356

15. See the discussion of the politics of the budgetary process in Chapter 10, pp. 338–48.

16. The system is described in Glenn H. Ivy, "Organizational Structure for Gubernatorial Leadership" (Ph.D. diss., University of Texas, 1970), pp. 145–46 and Harvey Katz, *Shadow On the Alamo* (Garden City, N.Y.: Doubleday & Co., 1971), pp. 147–50.

17. For linkages between the House leadership selection system and the governor's patronage and executive branch officials, see Chapter 6, pp. 193–95.

18. Ben Barnes, "The Speaker's Office: Seat of Power," in *Governing Texas: Documents & Readings*, 3d ed., Fred Gantt, Irving O. Dawson, and Luther G. Hagard, Jr., eds. (New York: Thomas Y. Crowell Co., 1974), p. 138.

19. Unlike in the House, the president pro tempore of the Senate is not a member of the leadership team. The award goes ordinarily to a senior senator—usually of any ideological bent, faction, or party—who has not had the honor.

20. Lieutenant Governor William Pettus Hobby, Jr., while he was not a senator, is hardly an outsider. The son of a lieutenant governor and governor, he served several sessions as Senate parliamentarian under Ben Ramsey, 1951–61.

21. On an index strictly of formal authority, the Texas Senate leader ranks eighth in strength among the states' Senate leaders, while the House speaker ranks twelfth. Eugene Declercq, "Inter-House Differences in American State Legislatures," *Journal of Politics*, 39, no. 3 (August 1977): 779.

22. J. William Davis, *There Shall Also Be a Lieutenant Governor* (Austin: Institute of Public Affairs, 1967). pp. 66–67. Shivers' biographers agree. See Sam Kinch and Stuart Long, *Allan Shivers* (Austin: Shoal Creek Pubs., 1973), p. 49. See a contemporary description of Shivers' domination of the Senate: Hart Stilwell, "Texas: Owned by Oil and Interlocking Directorates," in *Our Sovereign State*, ed. Robert S. Allen (New York: Vanguard Press, 1949), pp. 329–30.

23. Actually, Senator Oscar Mauzy of Dallas has been able to muster only four to six votes for alternative, power-shifting leadership arrangements, including a strict seniority system, committee nominations by party caucus, strict adherence to the Senate Calendar, and requirement of only a simple majority to re-refer a bill to a standing committee other than the one to which the bill was consigned originally by the lieutenant governor.

24. Alan Rosenthal, *Legislative Performance in the States: Explorations of Committee Behavior* (New York: The Free Press, 1974), p. 42.

25. Declercq, "Inter-House Differences in American State Legislatures," pp. 778–79.

26. Rosenthal, *Legislative Performance,* p. 31.

27. See below, "Abuse of local and consent calendars."

28. Rules for each house, plus the joint rules, are printed in the early pages of the House and Senate *Journals* of regular sessions. A looseleaf, updated *Texas Legislative Manual* is maintained by the Texas Legislative Council. It contains current versions of the rules, interpretations, journal sources of rulings, Congressional precedents, and editorial notes and comments. See also Stanley K. Young, *Texas Legislative Handbook* (Austin: Texas Legislative Council, n.d.), a useful manual on the legislative process.

29. Texas Legislative Council, *Accomplishments of the 65th Legislature, Regular Session: A Summary* (Austin: Texas Legislative Council, 1977), p. 1.

30. Kinch and Long, *Allan Shivers*, p. 46. See also Davis, *There Shall Also Be a Lieutenant Governor*, pp. 63–69, 76–77.

31. For the classic study of the mass of special and local legislation, see Texas Legislative Council, *Laws Based on Population* (Austin: Texas Legislative Council, 1962).

32. See James L. Weatherby, Jr., "The Role of the 'Free' Conference Committee in the Texas Budgetary Process, 1962–1973," *Public Affairs Comment,* 21, no. 2 (February 1975).

33. See "Politics of the Budgetary Process" in Chapter 10 for functional consequences of the "free" conference committee in the Texas political system.

34. See the *Houston Post,* June 3, 1975, p. 1A.

35. This salary is granted in both years of the two-year legislature, even when the legislature fails to meet in even-numbered years.

36. Most of the data in this section and the next on members of the Texas House of Representatives are taken from John W. Holcombe, "The Legislative Perceptions of Texas State Representatives: The Sixty-second Legislature," (Ph.D. diss., Claremont Graduate School, 1972).

37. And only one third of Texas chief executives and United States senators in this century have served in the legislature. Joseph A. Schlesinger, *Ambition and Politics: Political Careers in the United States* (Chicago: Rand McNally & Co., 1966). Law enforcement positions have provided the common apprenticeship for these two offices in Texas and some other states. Where this is true, Schlesinger says, we find the salience of one-partyism, factionalism, regionalism, localism, high expenditures, and personality in statewide nomination and election contests.

38. For patterns which still hold, see David M. Olson, *Legislative Primary Elections in Austin, Texas, 1962* (Austin: Institute of Public Affairs, University of Texas, 1963).

39. Only ten respondents in a recent legislative session attributed their political recruitment to political parties. Four additional legislators were sponsored by interest groups, and several mentioned recruitment by friends.

40. See the discussion in Chapter 3 and Figure 3–1.

41. A settled feature of representation in multi-member policymaking bodies (except for the United States Senate) is that legislators represent equal numbers of people (the famous "one person, one vote" ruling of *Baker* v. *Carr*, 1962). Some variation from strict population equality is permitted for state legislatures. For example, the 1971 House redistricting plan of the Texas Legislative Redistricting Board was upheld, although the total variation from the mean population size between largest and smallest districts amounted to nearly 10 percent. *White* v. *Regester*, 93 S.Ct. 2332 (1972).

42. See *Graves* v. *Barnes*, 343 F. Supp. 704 (1972).

43. See John C. Wahlke, Heinz Eulau, William Buchanan, and LeRoy C. Ferguson, *The Legislative System: Explorations in Legislative Behavior* (New York: John Wiley & Sons, 1962) and Charles G. Bell and Charles M. Price, *The First Term: A Study of Legislative Socialization* (Beverly Hills, Calif.: Sage Pubs., Inc., 1975).

44. See Caleb Perry Patterson, Sam B. McAlister, and George C. Hester, *State and Local Government in Texas* (New York: Macmillan Co., 1945), pp. 61–62.

45. Donald S. Lutz and Richard W. Murray, "Coalition Formation in the Texas Legislature: Issues, Payoffs, and Winning Coalition Size," *Western Political Quarterly*, 28, no. 2 (June 1975): 296–315.

46. See Lance T. LeLoup, "Policy, Party, and Voting in U.S. State Legislatures: A Test of the Content-Process Linkage," *Legislative Studies Quarterly*, 1, no. 2 (May 1976): 225.

47. Heinz Eulau and Kenneth Prewitt, "Eco-Policy Environment and Political Processes in 76 Cities of a Metropolitan Region," *Publius*, 5, no. 1 (Winter 1975): 94–95, found missing democratic linkages between city councilpersons and their electorates where councilpersons adopted the trustee orientation.

48. Alonzo W. Jamison, "The Education of a Legislator," in Gantt, Dawson, and Hagard, *Governing Texas*, p. 146.

49. See Peter Bachrach and Morton Baratz, "Two Faces of Power," *American Political Science Review*, 56, no. 4 (December 1962): 947–52.

50. Michael Parenti, "Power and Pluralism: A View From the Bottom," *Journal of Politics*, 32, no. 3 (August 1970): 529.

51. Holcombe, "Legislative Perceptions of Texas State Representatives," pp. 64–65.

52. Bryan D. Jones, "Why the Legislature Is the Way It Is," in Richard H. Kraemer and Philip W. Barnes, eds. *Texas Readings in Politics, Government, and Public Policy* (San Francisco: Chandler Pub. Co., 1971), p. 140.

53. Quoted in the *Texas Observer*, 69, no. 12 (June 17, 1977), p. 11.

54. See the discussion of interest groups and lobbying activities in Chapter 3, pp. 75–79.

55. See Harmon Zeigler and Michael Baer, *Lobbying: Interaction and Influence in American State Legislatures* (Belmont, Calif.: Wadsworth Pub. Co., 1969).

56. "Right thinking" is a euphemism for *conservative* and is a code or symbol well understood among politically knowledgeable Texans. In the 1978 gubernatorial contest, for example, John Hill used the slogan, "John Hill—Right for Texas."

57. In the House in the 62nd Legislature, 21 percent of respondents flatly refused to name, in confidence, specific organizations considered to be powerful in their districts.

58. A ranking probably reflects for that session the relative division of benefits and of preferences of legislative leadership and the governor. Or it may be an index of preeminent issues for that session and a list of groups which need to be consulted in the various issue areas.

59. But see J. C. "Zeke" Zbranek, "Why the Establishment Controls the Legislature," *Texas Observer*, 55, no. 11 (June 12, 1964): 1–2.

60. For treatment of these and other reform measures, see Texas Legislative Council, *Reform Legislation: Text, Analysis, and Forms* (Austin: Texas Legislative Council, 1973). See also Charles Deaton, ed., *A Financial Profile of Texas' Top 200 Elected Officials* (Austin: Texas Government Newsletter, 1975).

61. See Chapter 6, "The Governor in State Administration," pp. 188–93.

62. Eric M. Uslaner and Ronald E. Weber, "Changes in Legislator Attitudes Toward Gubernatorial Power," *State and Local Government Review*, 9, p. no. 2 (May 1977): 42–43.

63. See Beryl E. Pettus, "A Study of the Advisory Opinions of the Texas Attorney General, 1960–1969" (Ph.D. diss., Texas Tech University, 1970) and "Functions of the Opinions of the Texas Attorney General in the State Legislative Process," in Eugene W. Jones, Joe E. Ericson, Lyle C. Brown, and Robert S. Trotter, Jr., *Practicing Texas Politics*, 2d ed. (Boston: Houghton Mifflin Co., 1974), pp. 185–90.

64. See current editions of the *Texas State Directory*.

65. For a profile of the Austin press corps, plus an assessment of press performance in reporting state government activities, see Hoyt Purvis and Rick Gentry, "News Media Coverage of Texas Government: The State Capital Press Corps," *Public Affairs Comment*, 22, no. 2 (February 1976).

CHAPTER FIVE

1. While Southern sympathies predominated, the attitudes of Texans toward secession varied. The majority had been born in Southern states but others had migrated from Missouri and the nonslave states north of the Ohio. In addition, about 15 percent of the population was composed of foreign-born whites opposed to slavery. Seymour V. Conner, *Texas, A History* (Northbrook, Ill.: AHM Publishing Co., 1971), p. 189.

2. The state severance tax, almost all of which comes from gas and oil production, provides almost 20 percent of the state's annual revenue. It is an important reason why Texas is one of only eight states which has not been forced to adopt a state income tax.

3. Since no state has a black majority, there is not a black governor in the United States. The best known black politician in Texas is former U.S. Representative Barbara Jordon of Houston, who was so widely respected for her service in the Texas Senate that she was made governor for a day in 1973 as a mark of honor.

4. La Raza Unida ran its most attractive candidate ever for statewide office in 1972 and 1974 when Ramsey Muñiz polled about 6 percent of the votes for governor. In December 1973, party chief Jose Angel Gutierrez told this writer that his party aimed at becoming the balance of power in state elections. But the party was badly damaged when its senatorial candidate was indicted for possession of heroin and Muñiz pleaded guilty to massive sales of marijuana.

5. Houston was a slaveholder but fervently opposed secession. He lost the governor's race in 1857 but won in 1859 on the union issue. In 1860 he sought the presidential nomination of the Constitutional Union party but lost to Tennessee's John Bell. To the end, Houston considered secession as folly. Conner, *Texas, A History*, p. 190.

6. James Stephen Hogg did indeed name a daughter Ima, but contrary to popular opinion did not have a second girl named Ura, nor a third named Wera as was incorrectly reported on January 19, 1974, by CBS news commentator Hughes Rudd on a nationwide telecast.

7. The Texas Railroad Commission is composed of three popularly elected members. In recent years, the commission has ruled so favorably toward oil and gas interests that an advertisement commending the commission's activities which appeared in the *San Antonio Light* during the 1972 election was paid for by a grateful oil industry.

8. For a good review of Texas politics through World War I, see Key, *Southern Politics*, especially Chapter 12.

9. For a detailed account of the background of the impeachment, which involved funds for the University of Texas, see Wilbourn E. Benton, *Texas, Its Government and Politics* (Engle-wood Cliffs, N.J.: Prentice-Hall, 1961), pp. 250–60. Impeachable offenses are not clearly defined in either the Texas or United States Constitutions, and this lack of clear definition became a matter of political controversy during the move to impeach President Nixon in 1974.

10. The *Houston Chronicle's* George Kuempel put Briscoe's banking and ranching holdings at $40 million. Land extending over seven South Texas counties exceeds 300,000 acres and at $100 per acre would be worth $30 million, yet was assessed for tax purposes at only $3.27 million. Dave McNeeley of the *News* reported Governor Briscoe had paid $113,000 in county and school taxes on 284,000 acres in 1972—which is only 40 cents per acre. *Texas Government Newsletter,* July 23, 1973. For further information see the *Austin American Statesman,* June 21, 1973, p. 1. The news media estimated Hill's 1978 personal wealth to be a more modest $1.5 million.

11. The most publicized accomplishment of Briscoe's first year in office was the closing of a venerable house of prostitution known as the "chicken ranch," which had quietly flourished over a century. The governor reacted in response to criticism by Houston TV commentator Marvin Zindler. Fayette County Sheriff T. J. Flournoy vainly protested, citing proprietress Edna Milton's many donations to local charities, but 1973 saw an end to Texas's worst kept secret. *Austin American Statesman,* August 1, 1973, p. 1.

12. U.S. Congress, *Congressional Directory,* 93d Cong., 2d sess., 1974, p. 41. At $85,000 per year the governor of New York is the highest paid. After Texas comes Illinois at $50,000 and California at $49,000.

13. This is a national trend. When Texas changed to a four-year gubernatorial term, there were only seven states left with two-year limitations.

14. Recall was a product of turn-of-the-century progressivism and has been adopted by only about a dozen, mostly western, states starting with Oregon in 1908. The only governor ever removed by popular recall was North Dakota's Governor Frazier in 1921. He subsequently won election to the U.S. Senate. For a full discussion see Austin MacDonald, *American State Government and Administration* (New York: Thomas Y. Crowell Co., 1961), pp. 362–68.

15. See Proposed Constitution of the State of Texas, Office of the Secretary of State, 1976, Proposition 1, Article 4, p. 6.

16. Naturally, there is no proscription of a woman holding the office. Ma Ferguson was Texas' sole woman governor, and Sissy Farenthold made a strong bid for the Democratic nomination in 1972 and 1974. Being of the liberal wing of the party, however, she was unsuccessful. The most recent female state governor was elected in 1974 and re-elected in 1978—Connecticut's Ellen Grasso.

17. It is customary practice for both the governor and lieutenant governor to "leave" the state for one day of each regular session, thereby permitting the senate's president pro tempore the honor of being governor for a day. That was the circumstance under which Houston's Barbara Jordan was honored as governor. The senate selects its president pro tempore each year, normally choosing the senior senator.

18. In the 1969 regular session Governor Preston Smith vetoed one bill. After adjournment he vetoed 54. See Gantt, "Governor's Veto in Texas." For a full examination of the governor's office see Gantt, *Chief Executive in Texas* (Austin: The University of Texas Press, 1964).

19. The constitutional provisions of the veto are contained in Article 4, Section 14 of the Constitution of 1876. The governor of Texas has always been provided with a veto, but the item veto on appropriation dates from 1876.

20. Article 12, Section 9, Texas Constitution.

21. In 1972, a special session was called to deal with welfare problems. In 1974 the legislature sat in special session as a constitutional revision committee. In 1976 the senate was convened and convicted the impeached state judge O. P. Carrillo. In 1978 the legislature was called for tax reform.

22. For a discussion of the special session, see Fred Gantt, Jr., "Special Legislative Sessions in Texas: The Governor's Bane or Blessing?" *Public Affairs Comment* (Austin: Institute of Public Affairs, University of Texas, November 1970).

23. By 1971, the majority of state legislatures had gone to regular annual sessions. The defeated constitutional revision would have provided for a regular session of 90 days in even-numbered years to supplement the 140 day regular sessions in the odd-numbered years.

24. Texas Legislature, *House Journal*, 63d Leg. Reg. Sess. January 17, 1973, p. 136.

25. In briefly discussing his experience as Texas state representative, 1949–58, Governor Briscoe referred to the difficulty of meeting the state's responsibility to deal with current state problems:

". . . We faced problems so severe that even some of our concerns today become less awesome when I think about those earlier times.

"I believe it can be said that Texas grew up during those postwar years. We began to understand a new concept of state government—that we had clearly defined responsibilities which had been neglected and all but abdicated to the federal government for a generation.

"We awoke to the fact that mental health . . . a decent prison system . . . juvenile delinquency . . . bad roads . . . aged citizens and . . . decent schools for our children were our concern." Ibid., 142–43.

26. In 1978, Joe Christie resigned as insurance commissioner to begin an unsuccessful bid for the U.S. Senate. When Governor Briscoe replaced him with Guy Yantis, a poorly regarded administrator, Senator Lloyd Doggett of Austin, Yantis' home district, exercised the power of senatorial courtesy to deny Yantis confirmation in the August special session.

27. The governor's staff is now over 400. For an account of how it grew from four in 1920 to 300 in 1950, see Gantt, *The Chief Executive in Texas,* pp. 92ff.

28. See *Kentucky* v. *Dennison,* 24 Howard 66 (1861).

29. This is true even though the governor since 1931 has been referred to in the statutes as the chief budget officer of the state and has been required since 1951 to present a budget document to the legislature. As a matter of fact, the Legislative Budget Board prepares the line-by-line appropriations measures, the staff of that body acting during the legislative sessions as the professional staff of the House and Senate appropriations committees.

30. In 1978, Governor Briscoe's renomination campaign was jarred when it was revealed that the Governor's Office of Migrant Affairs (GOMA) had hundreds of employees consuming grant money in a grossly inefficient manner. Opponent John Hill was quick to charge Briscoe with maladministration. The press reported a "GOMA-gate" of hidden employees far beyond the numbers Briscoe reported for his staff. The agency's job-training costs were five times the national average.

31. Although Briscoe could not stop Senator Edward Kennedy from sending federal assistance to Crystal City, Texas, when that municipality refused to pay its utility bills, in 1978, he was able to veto a proposed collectivist land scheme which seemed inspired by a visit by Raza Unida's Jose Angel Gutierrez to Cuba.

32. Democrats have held every Texas governorship for a century to 1979.

33. The last Texas governor of a truly liberal hue was James Allred, a product of the depression years.

34. In the aftermath of the Sharpstown bank scandal in 1972, Dolph Briscoe defeated Republican Henry Grover by only a plurality: Briscoe (Democrat) 47.8 percent, Grover (Republican) 45 percent, Muñiz (La Raza Unida) 6.2 percent.

35. In 1972, Briscoe had to overcome the effects of the Sharpstown bank scandal which had seriously damaged the state Democratic party. Additionally, La Raza Unida candidate Muñiz drew more than 6 percent of the popular vote —most of which would otherwise have gone to the Democratic candidate. Although Jose Angel Gutierrez told this writer that the Democrats had tampered with late reporting boxes from the southwestern parts of the state, no official complaint was ever filed in support of such a charge.

In 1978, Muñiz pleaded guilty to conspiracy in massive marijuana importations from Mexico and received a five-year sentence. This was a body blow to La Raza Unida.

36. In 1974, Grover told this writer that personal financial considerations deterred him from running in 1974. In January of that year in advising reporter Jon Ford that he had at last wiped out his 1972 campaign debt, he complained, "I have done it with nothing but opposition from the Republican hierarchy. . . . I don't think Senator Tower would like a primary fight since he has never had one." *Austin American Statesman,* January 24, 1974, p. 7.

37. Technicalities in Briscoe's fund raising for the 1972 campaign haunted Governor Briscoe as late as 1975, as rival Democrat Sissy Farenthold pressed for details concerning the $15,000 cash donation made by Clinton Manges to Governor Briscoe in 1972. For a discussion of enforcement of the Texas campaign finance reporting laws, see Sam Kinch's article in the *Dallas Morning News,* November 16, 1974.

38. When the election of Thomas Jefferson was complicated by the fact that his party's vice presidential hopeful received the same number of electoral votes in 1800, and Aaron Burr did not have the grace to accept the spirit in which the voting was done, the resulting 12th Amendment resolved this uncertainty. Since then, the national party executive candidates run for the office of president and vice president respectively.

39. Lt. Governor Ben Barnes assigned the famous banking bill, which was meant to accommodate the Sharpstown bank's highly questionable objectives, to the Roads and Bridge Committee. This fact was not unnoticed. The odds-on favorite to succeed Preston Smith as governor up to that time, Barnes was subsequently badly defeated in his run for the governorship.

40. Until 1974, the lieutenant governor appointed every member of every committee, but those powers were slightly reduced in the aftermath of the Sharpstown bank scandal.

41. When the Texas Senate sits as a Committee of the Whole the lieutenant governor may vote on all questions, but no legislation can be passed by this committee.

42. The Texas lieutenant governor is far more powerful than his counterpart in virtually any other state, but is one of the poorest paid (at $7,200 per annum plus expenses). "Many Lieutenant Governors Demanding Larger Roles," an AP release from Atlanta to the *Austin American,* April 20, 1974.

43. Constitution, Article 4, Section 1. Jacksonian democracy spawned the multiple executive along with the spoils system. Texas did not adopt the plural executive until the constitution of 1869.

44. Single executives head the offices of governor, lieutenant governor, secretary of state, comptroller, treasurer, land commissioner, attorney general, plus the commissioners of agriculture and of labor statistics and the adjutant general. Almost all the other agencies have plural heads organized as boards or commissions.

45. In 1974, when the Texas legislature sat as a constitutional convention, it made only mild efforts to strengthen the governor's hand—and none of those steps was entertained when it appeared that they would have to be at the expense of the legislature's powers. For example, they thought it might be well to reduce the governor's veto powers and limit him to two terms. Not even the Texas Constitutional Revision Commission which made its report to that legislature dared to support any changes in the multiple elected executive, and it was left as it was constituted in 1876. *A New Constitution for Texas* prepared by the Texas Constitutional Revision Commission (Austin, 1973), Art. 4, Sec. 1.

CHAPTER SIX

1. Murray Edelman, *Political Language: Words That Succeed and Policies That Fail* (New York: Academic Press, 1977), p. 77.

2. Steven M. Neuse, "Texas State Administrators: A Partial Profile," *Public Affairs Comment,* 23, no. 3 (May 1977).

3. Note the existence also of a second, full-time commission of three members, the Texas Water Commission. It serves as the judicial arm of the Department of Water Resources, resolving conflicts over water rights, fixing water rates, issuing water use and waste permits, and approving the establishment of the water districts which are discussed as separate units of local government in Chapter 9.

4. For the pattern in other states, see Council of State Governments, *Central Management in the States* (Lexington, Ky.: Council of State Governments, 1970).

5. As we shall see in Chapter 10, these operations in practice place unusual restraints on spending and service levels in Texas.

6. See these operations in a later section of this chapter, "The Office of the Governor."

7. See "Politics of the budgetary process" in Chapter 10 for a detailed account of how the comptroller's estimates fit into the overall budgetary process.

8. See Beryl E. Pettus, "A Study of the Advisory Opinions of the Texas Attorney General, 1960–1969" (Ph.D. diss., Texas Tech University, 1970) and James G. Dickson, Jr., *Law and Politics: The Office of Attorney General in Texas* (Austin: Sterling Swift Pub. Co., 1976).

9. See Legislative Budget Board, *Performance Report to the Sixty-Fourth Legislature* and *Performance Report to the Sixty-Fifth Legislature* (Austin: Legislative Budget Board, 1975 and 1977).

10. For an outline of responsibilities of Texas state agencies, see *Handbook of Governments in Texas* (Austin: Texas Advisory Commission on Intergovernmental Relations, 1973, updated).

11. As reported in the *Houston Post,* February 21, 1978, p. 5A.

12. Ibid. The same pattern of industry control and inattention to consumer complaints was found in the agency which is charged with regulation of administrators of nursing homes. See *Houston Post,* June 24, 1978, p. 20A.

13. As reported in ibid., April 23, 1978, p. 14A.

14. An integrated administrative structure featuring a strong governor is found in only about one fourth of the United States. See Council of State Governments, *Cabinets in State Government* (Lexington, Ky.: Council of State Governments, 1969).

15. For this descriptive term, I am indebted to the late Stuart Long, editor of the *Austin Report* and perceptive observer of the Texas political scene.

16. As reported in the *Houston Post,* May 26, 1974, p. 20C.

17. See Earl Black, *Southern Governors and Civil Rights: Racial Segregation As a Campaign Issue in the Second Reconstruction* (Cambridge: Harvard University Press, 1976).

18. See Texas Research League, *Texas' State Government Organization* (Austin: Texas Research League, 1975), part I, pp. 68–69.

19. Texas is ranked as having a "high patronage potential." Ronald E. Weber, "Competitive and Organizational Dimensions of American State Party Systems," Paper prepared for annual meeting of the Northeastern Political Science Associations, 1969, pp. 1, 15–16, cited in Malcolm E. Jewell and David M. Olson, *American State Political Parties and Elections* (Homewood, Ill.: The Dorsey Press, 1978), p. 80.

20. See "TRL Analyses—Developments in Texas State and Local Government" (Austin: Texas Research League, 1973), pp. 3–4 and Glenn H. Ivy, "An Organizational Structure for Gubernatorial Leadership in Texas State Government" (Ph.D. diss., University of Texas, 1970), pp. 115–119.

21. Cooption, the renewal of a body or group by action of its own membership or group, takes the form in Texas of gubernatorial appointments to elective executive and judicial posts of the governor's personal and political allies, commonly conservatives. For discussion of cooption by elites as a device for building regime stability, see Charles A. McCoy and Alan Wolfe, *Political Analysis: An Unorthodox Approach* (New York: Thomas Y. Crowell Co., 1972), pp. 104–110.

22. Bancroft C. Henderson and T. C. Sinclair, *The Selection of Judges in Texas: An Exploratory Study* (Houston: Public Affairs Research Center, University of Houston, 1965).

23. Ibid., p. 25. See also Chase Untermeyer, "Most District Judges Here First Appointed by Governor," *Houston Chronicle,* August 18, 1974, sec. 4, p. 6.

24. See the *Texas Register,* 2, nos. 12–45 (February 11 through June 7, 1977).

25. For accounts of the relationships of specific interest groups with the Texas boards and commissions which are charged with their regulation, see Eugene W. Jones, Joe E. Ericson, Lyle C. Brown, and Robert S. Trotter, Jr., *Practicing Texas Politics,* 2d ed. (Boston: Houghton Mifflin Co., 1974), "Politics of Administration," pp. 213–15.

26. Dan Nimmo and William E. Oden, *The Texas Political System* (Englewood Cliffs, N.J.: Prentice Hall, Inc., 1971), p. 85.

27. Glenn H. Ivy, "An Organizational Structure for Gubernatorial Leadership in Texas State Government" (Ph.D. diss., University of Texas, 1970), p. 118n. For one of the most recent studies of the Texas Research League, see the series of critic John Muir in the *Texas Observer,* beginning with 66, no. 14 (August 9, 1974).

28. See the discussion of the pluralist elite in Nimmo and Oden, *The Texas Political System,* esp. pp. 158–59.

29. For the history of staffing of the Texas governorship, see Fred Gantt, Jr., *The Chief Executive in Texas: A Study in Gubernatorial Leadership* (Austin: University of Texas Press, 1964), pp. 93–107.

30. See below the discussion of the activities of the Department under the heading, "Control of federal programs." See also Chapter 8.

31. Activities of these substate regional councils of governments are discussed in detail in Chapter 8.

32. See Lorna A. Monti, "Social Indicators, Prices, and Politics: Uses of Planning and Evaluation Data in Texas State Government," *Texas Business Review,* 48, no. 6 (June 1974): 132–36.

33. For explanation of the model and its uses, see Herbert W. Grubb and William G. Lesso, "The Input-Output Model for the State of Texas," *Texas Business Review,* 48, no. 1 (January 1974): 4–10.

34. Thad Beyle and J. Oliver Williams, *The American Governor in Behavioral Perspective* (New York: Harper & Row, 1972), pp. 3–4.

35. See Ivy, "Organizational Structure for Gubernatorial Leadership," p. 240.

36. Actual staff levels of executives are often difficult to determine because of such practices as "borrowing" of operating agency personnel and "contracting out" staff work to private or quasi-private organizations and consultants.

37. See Lester Seligman, "Leadership, Political Aspects" in *International Encyclopedia of the Social Sciences* (New York: Macmillan Co. and Free Press, 1977), vol. 9, pp. 107–13, esp. p. 109.

38. For factors which everywhere tend to govern size and specialization of gubernatorial staffing, see Beyle and Williams, *The American Governor,* p. 105 and Martha Wagner Weinberg, *Managing the State* (Cambridge: The MIT Press, 1977), esp. pp. 58–67.

39. See the various annual editions of the *Congressional Almanac* from 1966 to 1969 for accounts of ultimately successful attempts, led by Governor John Connally, to give state governors a veto over project grants to local groups.

40. See Wagner, *Managing the State,* esp. p. 209.

41. James Conaway, *The Texans* (New York: Alfred A. Knopf, 1976), p. 257.

42. See Earl Black, "Southern Governors and Political Change: Campaign Stances on Racial Segregation and Economic Development, 1950–1969," *Journal of Politics,* 33, no. 3 (August 1971): 703–34, updated in his *Southern Governors and Civil Rights, Appendix A. See also Ira Sharkansky, *The United States: A Study of a Developing Country* (New York: David McKay Co., Inc., 1975).

43. Many studies find a high correlation between a state's wealth and its spending levels. See Thomas R. Dye, *Understanding Public Policy,* 3d ed. (Englewood Cliffs, N.J.: Prentice-Hall, Inc., 1976), chap. 13.

44. Teachers in public and special schools, professors in state colleges and universities, and nonacademic employees of the higher educational institutions have their own classification and salary schedules different from the plan established in the current appropriations bill.

45. The attorney general ruled that the classification plan does not apply to employees of the Finance Commission, Banking Department, Savings and Loan Department, and Texas State Board of Plumbing Examiners. Texas Research League, *Quality Texas Government* (Austin: Office of the Governor, 1972), p. 36.

46. Operation of the state's personnel system is described in Texas Research League, *An Inventory of Texas' Basic State Personnel Statutes* (Austin: Office of the Governor, 1977).

47. Texas Research League, *Quality Texas Government,* p. 42.

48. Texas Research League, *An Inventory of Texas' Basic Personnel Statutes,* p. 9.

49. See Ray Marshall and Robert W. Glover, *Compensation of Texas State Employees* (Austin: Texas Public Employees Association, 1972), pp. 39–40.

50. Bureau of the Census, *Public Employment in 1976.*

51. Marshall and Glover, *Compensation,* pp. 31–33, 41.

52. For overview of legal and environmental forces in Texas affecting public employee-employer relations, see I. B. Helburn, *Public Employer-Employee Relations in Texas: Contemporary and Emerging Developments* (Austin, Institute of Public Affairs, University of Texas, 1971), pp. 1–15.

53. Chester A. Newland, "Public Employee Strikes: Administrative Change and Political Protest," *Public Affairs Comment,* 14, no. 3 (May 1968): 2.

54. For the severity of the law, see V.A.C.S., Art. 5154c.

55. I. B. Helburn, "Public Employee Organization: Texas Breakthroughs Amid National Change," *Public Affairs Comment,* 20, no. 1 (November 1973): 4.

56. See Charles J. Morris, "Everything You Always Wanted to Know About Public Employee Bargaining in Texas—But Were Afraid to Ask," *Houston Law Review,* 13, no. 2 (January 1976): 291–323.

57. Reported by Fred Bonavita, "State Employee Group Official Out," *Houston Post,* December 10, 1977, p. 26A.

58. The original authorization, a rider in the appropriations bill, was ruled unconstitutional by Attorney General John Hill, *Opinion H–351* (1974), on the ground that general legislation must be by separate statute.

59. Texas Legislative Council, *Employment in State Government,* Staff Reports 60–4, 62–1, 63–1, and 64–1 (Austin: Texas Legislative Council, January 1969, 1973, 1975, and 1977).

60. Total black employees in 1968 in state government numbered 2,905; total with Spanish surnames numbered 4,585. Texas Legislative Council, *Employment in State Government,* 1969.

61. Except for 98 "other" males (American Indian, Asian American, and other).

CHAPTER SEVEN

1. Truman McMahon, "Court System 'Hotly Debated'," *Austin American Statesman,* May 10, 1973, p. 88.

2. *Avery* v. *Midland County,* 390 U.S. 474 (1968).

3. The chief justice's Task Force for Court Improvement called for the abolishment of justice of the peace courts. Such a move was defeated at the constitutional convention in 1974, primarily because of the lobbying efforts of the justices. See "Proposed Judiciary Article of the Texas Constitution" (St. Paul, Minn.: West Publishing Co., 1970), p. x.

4. Except for judges on the courts of civil appeals, all other judges including county commissioners are considered magistrates under Texas law.

5. State law requires that in the aforementioned counties the commissioners court appoint medical examiners as coroners.

6. House Bill No. 168 (62d Leg.); House Bill No. 81 (63d Leg.). The Texas Justice of the Peace Training Center is located at Southwest Texas State University in San Marcos.

7. By law, county courts, as well as district courts and criminal district courts, are designated as juvenile courts of original jurisdiction in cases in which a determination is made as to whether the child is delinquent. If a determination is to be made as to whether a child is dependent or neglected, the jurisdiction rests with the district courts. In large urban areas, the legislature has created domestic relations courts to resolve cases involving juveniles as well as divorce, child custody, and other domestic matters.

8. *Measuring Court Performance: A Summary of a Report by the Texas Research League* (Austin: Texas Research League, 1972), p. 4.

9. "Measuring Court Performance: A Report on the Data Collection Process of Texas Civil Judicial Council," (Austin: Texas Research League, 1972), Appendix M-2; see also, *Texas Government Newsletter*, Charles Deaton, ed., Austin, Texas (November 1, 1976).

10. For a detailed description of these agencies, see *Guide To Texas State Agencies*, pp. 206–210.

11. Article IV, Section 26 (1876).

12. In February 1978, the new SCJC censured a county judge in Liberty for official misconduct.

13. Official Style and Drafting Committee Report, "The Judiciary Article V, Final Third Reading," (unpublished). Also, see George D. Braden, *Citizens' Guide to the Proposed New Texas Constitution* (Austin: Sterling Swift Publishing Co., 1975), pp. 91–93.

14. Article 1408.

15. *Pointer* v. *Texas*, 380 U.S. 400 (1965).

16. Texas Code of Criminal Procedure, Article 711 (1925). These statutory provisions were repealed by implication by Article 36.09 of the Texas Code of Criminal Procedure of 1965, which became effective after the defendant's trial.

17. *Washington* v. *Texas*, 388 U.S. 14 (1967).

18. Ibid., pp. 22–23.

19. Amended in 1918 to provide that "when the witness resides out of the state and the offense charged is a violation of any of the antitrust laws of this state, the defendant and the state shall have the right to produce and have the evidence admitted by deposition; under such rules and laws as the Legislature may hereafter provide."

20. Actually the term *civil* is a misnomer since its Latin root *(civilis)* pertains to citizenship or "of the citizen." These liberties are more properly called *personal* or *individual* rights.

21. This narrow interpretation had been handed down by the Court in *Barron* v. *Baltimore*, 7 Peters 243 (1833); however, prior to *Gitlow*, the Court had intimated that there may be occasions in which a state denial of a "fundamental" or "essential" liberty might be violative of the due process clause of the 14th Amendment. See *Hurtado* v. *California*, 110 U.S. 516 (1884) and *Twining* v. *New Jersey*, 211 U.S. 78 (1908).

22. Unfortunately there are a number of other significant decisions in which the U.S. Supreme Court has held that Texas had abridged the 14th Amendment by infringing upon the free exercise of religion—*Jamison* v. *Texas*, 318 U.S. 413 (1943); *Largent* v. *Texas*, 318 U.S. 418 (1943); *Tucker* v. *Texas*, 326 U.S. 517 (1946); freedom of speech and press—*Gelling* v. *Texas*, 343 U.S. 960 (1952); *Interstate Circuit* v. *Dallas*, 390 U.S. 676 (1968); the prohibition against unreasonable searches and seizures—*Aguilar* v. *Texas*, 378 U.S. 108 (1964); *Stanford* v. *Texas*, 379 U.S. 476 (1965); by employing the use of coerced confessions—*Ward* v. *Texas*, 316 U.S. 547 (1942); and by systematic racial exclusion in the selection of grand and petit juries—*Smith* v. *Texas*, 311 U.S. 128 (1940); *Hill* v. *Texas*, 316 U.S. 400 (1942); *Atkins* v. *Texas*, 325 U.S. 398 (1945); *Cassell* v. *Texas*, 339 U.S. 282 (1950) and *Hernandez* v. *Texas*, 347 U.S. 475 (1954).

23. *Congressional Quarterly*, Weekly Report, May 23, 1969, p. 798.

24. See, for example, *Harris* v. *New York*, 401 U.S. 222 (1971) and *United States* v. *Calandra*, 414 U.S. 338 (1974).

25. *Justice at the Crossroads: Court improvement in Texas* (Austin: Chief Justice's Task Force for Court Improvement, 1972); Herbert Jacob, *Urban Justice: Law and Order in American Cities* (Englewood Cliffs, N.J.: Prentice-Hall, 1973).

26. In contrast, an average of 765 cases were filed with judges in rural counties. Only 55 percent of the district courts are in the 16 metropolitan counties, and yet they disposed of 79 percent of the total number of cases filed in 1971. See "Measuring Court Performance."

27. *Justice at the Crossroads*, p. 6.

28. Ibid., pp. 9–10 [Emphasis added.]

29. It would do well to recall that the report was completed prior to the Supreme Court's decision which invalidated the death penalty, as it was then imposed, as a "cruel and unusual punishment" in violation of the Eighth and Fourteenth Amendments in *Furman* v. *Georgia*, 408 U.S. 238 (1972). Ibid., p. 10.

30. See Criminal Justice Council, *Criminal Justice Plan for Texas* (Austin: Criminal Justice Council, 1971), Appendix C.

31. "A Proposed New Penal Code for Texas," *Texas Bar Journal*, 35, no. 11 (December 22, 1972): 1,112.

32. *Furman* v. *Georgia* (decided with *Branch* v. *Texas*), 408 U.S. 238 (1972). Near the end of the 1974 term, however, the Supreme Court of the United States announced a postponement on considering the validity of newly written laws imposing capital punishment.

33. The most important element in determining the reasonableness of a search is the sufficiency of probable cause. While a mere hunch or suspicion on the part of the officer does not constitute probable cause, the officer need not have the kind of proof necessary to convict. To experienced law enforcement personnel, probable cause consists of "the practical considerations of everyday life on which reasonable and prudent men, not legal technicians, act." See *Draper* v. *United States, 358* U.S. 307 (1959).

34. The right of counsel including court-appointed attorneys for indigents must be extended to all offenses—petty, misdemeanor, or felony—which involve any form of imprisonment. *Angersinger* v. *Hamlin,* 407 U.S. 25 (1972).

35. *Harris* v. *New York,* 401 U.S. 222 (1971). In order to squeeze through the loophole provided by the latter case, the 1977 legislature enacted an anticrime law which allows the use of oral confessions during a trial to impugn the testimony of a defendant.

36. Apparently there is *not* total public indifference to this problem in Texas. Raymond Frank became sheriff of Austin after defeating longtime incumbent T. O. Lang in the June 3, 1972 Democratic primary run off. Frank's major campaign issue was the deterioration of Travis county jails, with particular emphasis on the lack of a subsistence diet and the high incidence of homosexual attacks on younger inmates.

37. As reported in the *Austin American Statesman,* February 13, 1973, p. 36.

38. Central (Sugarland): Clemens (Brazoria); Coffield (Tennessee Colony); Darrington (Sandy Point); Diagnostic, Ellis, Goree, Huntsville and Wynne (Huntsville); Eastham (Weldon); Ferguson (Midway); Jester (Richmond); Ramsey (Rosharon); and Retrieve (Angleton).

39. *Guide to Texas State Agencies,* p. 103.

40. See *Criminal Justice Plan for Texas,* I, pp. 45–46.

41. In 1975, the Joint Committee on Prison Reform issued a report recommending that the Texas Department of Corrections change from relying on large, rural prisons to community-based correctional programs. It has been estimated that 40 percent of the state's 17,000 inmates could be safely placed in such programs.

42. The term, from the Attica, New York prison revolt, has come to symbolize neglect of criminal justice problems.

43. *In re Gault,* 387 U.S. 1 (1967).

44. *In re Winship,* 397 U.S. 358 (1970).

45. *Juvenile Delinquency and Youth Crime,* Task Force on Delinquency, The President's Commission on Law Enforcement and Administration of Justice, 1967, p. 25.

46. See *Guide To Texas State Agencies,* pp. 105–106.

47. Texas Youth Council, *Texas Juvenile Court*

Statistics for 1970 (Austin: Texas Youth Council, 1971), pp. 2–3.

48. See Lisa A. Richette, *The Throwaway Children* (Philadelphia: J. B. Lippincott Company, 1964).

49. The Texas Research League, *A Local Approach to Delinquency Prevention: Youth Services and Resource Bureau* (San Angelo, Tex.: Texas Research League, 1971), p. 1.

50. Ibid., pp. 6–7.

51. Ibid., pp. 20–21.

52. Although it became a victim of the end-of-session logjam in the House, the Texas Senate approved a plan in 1975 setting up a statewide alcoholic rehabilitation program under the Texas Commission on Alcoholism which would have abolished the crime of public intoxication and would have required commitment to an approved treatment facility.

CHAPTER EIGHT

1. This introductory section draws heavily from two excellent edited works, Louis H. Masotti and Robert L. Lineberry, eds., *The New Urban Politics* (Cambridge, Mass.: Ballinger Pub. Co., 1976) and Willis D. Hawley and Michael Lipsky, eds., *Theoretical Perspectives on Urban Politics* (Englewood Cliffs, N.J.: Prentice-Hall, Inc., 1976).

2. See discussion of "Council-manager form" in Chapter 9, pp. 278–280.

3. Williams Lyons, "Reform and Response in American Cities: Structure and Policy Reconsidered," *Social Science Quarterly,* 59, no. 1 (June 1978): 130.

4. See Robert Lineberry and Edmund Fowler, "Reformism and Public Policies in American Cities," *American Political Science Review,* 61, no. 3 (September 1967): 701–717 and Thomas R. Dye, *Understanding Public Policy,* 2d ed. (Englewood Cliffs: Prentice-Hall, Inc., 1975), Chap. 8.

5. Ira Katznelson, "Class Capacity and Social Cohesion in American Cities," in *The New Urban Politics,* Masotti and Lineberry, eds., p. 28.

6. Ibid.

7. Theodore J. Lowi, "Machine Politics—Old and New," *The Public Interest,* No. 13 (Fall 1967): 83–92.

8. Masotti and Lineberry, *The New Urban Politics,* p. 12.

9. Michael Lipsky, "Toward a Theory of Street-Level Bureaucracy," in *Theoretical Perspectives on Urban Politics,* Hawley and Lipsky, eds., 196–213.

10. Bryan D. Jones, "Distributional Considerations in Models of Government Service Provision," *Urban Affairs Quarterly,* 12, no. 3 (March 1977): 291–312.

11. Kenneth Mladenka, "Rules, Service Equality and Distributional Decisions," *Social Science Quarterly,* 59, no. 1 (June 1978): 200.

12. Patterns of uneven service allocations result also from other reasons, such as differences in clientele demand, preferential treatment, internal organizational rules of the implementing agencies, failure to qualify all persons in the target group, and for congeries of other political system factors and environmental forces.

13. Michael Lipsky, "Toward a Theory of Street-Level Bureaucracy," in *Theoretical Perspectives on Urban Politics,* Hawley and Lipsky, eds., p. 209.

14. See John E. Jackson, ed., *Public Needs and Private Behavior in Metropolitan Areas* (Cambridge, Mass.: Ballinger Pub. Co., 1975).

15. See Stephen K. Mayo, "Local Public Goods and Residential Location: An Empirical Test of the Tiebout Hypothesis," ibid., pp. 31–65.

16. See David Harvey, "Social Processes, Spatial Form and the Redistribution of Real Income in an Urban System," in *Regional Forecasting,* Michael Chisholm, Allan E. Frey, and Peter Haggett, eds., Colston Papers No. 22 (Hamden, Conn.: Archon Books, 1971), pp. 267–300.

17. Masotti and Lineberry, *The New Urban Politics,* p. 11.

18. Katznelson, "Class Capacity and Social Cohesion in American Cities," pp. 19–35. Randall B. Ripley and Grace A. Franklin, *Congress, the Bureaucracy and Public Policy* (Homewood, Ill.: The Dorsey Press, 1976) make the point also that distributional solutions have the utility of greater political feasibility (than regulatory or redistributional policies) as well as creation of a sense of equity based on eventually operating in practice to restore the balance in any temporary imbalance in benefits.

19. Quoted in Katznelson, "Class Capacity and Social Cohesion in American Cities," p. 32.

20. See Ripley and Franklin, *Congress, the Bureaucracy and Public Policy,* esp. chap. 4.

21. Masotti and Lineberry, *The New Urban Politics,* p. 11.

22. John P. Kotter and Paul R. Lawrence, *Mayors in Action: Five Approaches to Urban Governance* (New York: John Wiley & Sons, 1974).

23. Ibid., p. 232.

24. Ibid., p. 243.

25. U.S. Advisory Commission on Intergovernmental Relations, *Urban and Rural America: Policies for Future Growth* (Washington, D.C.: U.S. Government Printing Office, 1968), p. 12. See "The Costs of Sprawl: Environmental and Economic Costs of Alternative Residential Development Patterns at the Urban Fringe," Prepared for the Council on Environmental Quality, Department of Housing and Urban Development, and Environmental Protection Agency by Real Estate Research Corporation (Washington, D.C.: U.S. Government Printing Office, April 1974).

26. See the discussion of special districts in Chapter 9, pp. 301–311.

27. For innovative measures enacted in other states, see Nelson Rosenbaum, *Land Use and the Legislatures: The Politics of State Innovation* (Washington, D.C.: The Urban Institute, 1976).

28. General Land Office of Texas, *Texas Coastal Management Program: Executive Summary* (Austin: General Land Office, November 1976), p. 14.

29. Texas Office of the Governor, *Texas Land Use,* 9 vols., developed by Research and Planning Associates, Ron Jones, Project Director (Austin: Office of the Governor, 1973), vol. 9, letter of transmittal, p. 1.

30. See essays in James D. Mertes and David E. Sullivan, eds., *Land Use Planning and Management in Unincorporated Areas* (Lubbock: School of Law and Department of Park Administration and Horticulture, Texas Tech University, 1973).

31. For reasons why city dwellers and suburbanites are disinclined to approve governmental reorganization, even in the face of poor public services, see Amos H. Hawley and Basil G. Zimmer, *The Metropolitan Community: Its People and Government* (Beverly Hills, Calif.: Sage Publications, 1970).

32. See *Texas Almanac and State Industrial Guide* (Dallas: A. H. Belo Corp., biennial editions).

33. Texas Rural Development Commission, *Building Rural Texas* (Austin: Texas Rural Development Commission, 1973), p. 10.

34. See Table 1–4 for the absolute numbers and percentages of Texans in the various census classifications in 1970.

35. For a still relevant survey of conditions in these policy areas, see Texas Rural Development Commission, *Building Rural Texas.*

36. Derived from U.S. Bureau of the Census, *1970 Census of Population,* vol. 1: *Characteristics of Population,* part 45: *Texas,* section 1 (Washington, D.C.: U.S. Government Printing Office, May 1973), Table 58. For differentials in housing conditions in Texas by ethnic group and by urban and rural places, see Office of the Governor and Texas Department of Community Affairs, *Texas Housing Report: Results of Comprehensive Survey of Texas Housing Conditions and Occupant Attitudes* (Austin: Department of Community Affairs, 1972), pp. 16–19. See also Texas Advisory Commission on Intergovernmental Relations, *Public Housing in Texas: Past, Present and Prospective* (Austin: Texas Advisory Commission on Intergovernmental Relations, 1974).

37. For state responses and approaches to rural needs, see "State agencies' area-organized services and programs" later in Chapter 9.

38. For a map showing population distribution in Texas, including incorporated places scaled to population, see *Atlas of Texas* (Austin:

Bureau of Business Research, The University of Texas at Austin, 1976), p. 60.

39. Good Neighbor Commission of Texas, *Texas Migrant Labor*, A Special Report to the Governor and Legislature (Austin: Good Neighbor Commission, 1977), p. 18.

40. Ibid., p. 21.

41. For the plight of farmworker families who reside in unincorporated colonies of South Texas, see Lyndon B. Johnson School of Public Affairs, *Colonias in the Lower Rio Grande Valley of South Texas: A Summary Report,* Policy Research Project Report No. 18 (Austin: Lyndon B. Johnson School of Public Affairs, The University of Texas at Austin, 1977).

42. U.S. Advisory Commission on Intergovernmental Relations, *Substate Regionalism and the Federal System,* vol. 1, *Regional Decision Making: New Strategies for Substate Districts* (Washington, D.C.: U.S. Government Printing Office, 1973), pp. 92, 99–101.

43. Office of the Governor, *Guide: Performance Effectiveness Program for Texas Regional Councils* (Austin: Office of the Governor, 1973), pp. 5–8.

44. See Melvin B. Mogulof, "Federally Encouraged Multijurisdictional Agencies," *Urban Affairs Quarterly,* 9, no. 1 (September 1973): 119–23.

45. See discussion of organization and operations of the Office of the Governor in Chapter 6, pp. 195–200.

46. "Texas Facts: The Book on Profitable Plant Locations" (Austin: Texas Industrial Commission, March 1976).

47. For an overview of this development, which affected many of the more traditionalistic and individualistic states, see Earl M. Baker, Bernadette A. Stevens, Stephen E. Schecter, and Harlan A. Wright, *Federal Grants, the National Interest and State Response: A Review of Theory and Research* (Philadelphia: Center for the Study of Federalism, Temple University, 1974).

48. See Texas Legislative Budget Board, *Fiscal Size-Up: Texas State Services, 1978–79* (Austin: Legislative Budget Board, 1978) and annual reports of agencies mentioned herein.

49. See Niles M. Hansen, *Rural Poverty and the Urban Crisis: A Strategy for Regional Development* (Bloomington: Indiana University Press, 1970), esp. pp. 222–38.

50. Quoted in the *Houston Post,* January 19, 1975, p. 8B.

51. See discussion of the state's tax structure in Chapter 10, pp. 316–320.

52. Texas Research League, "Property Tax Relief: The Illusion and the Reality," *TRL Bulletin on Texas State Finance,* Bulletin No. 4 (March 22, 1977), p. 2.

53. Michael C. LeMay, "The States and Urban Areas: A Comparative Assessment," *National Civic Review,* 61, no. 11 (December 1972): 548.

54. Heinz Eulau and Kenneth Prewitt, "Eco-Policy Environment and Political Processes in 76 Cities of a Metropolitan Region," *Publius,* 5, no. 1 (Winter 1975): 88–92.

55. See discussion of political culture in Chapter 1, pp. 6–16.

CHAPTER NINE

1. For a survey of structures, politics, and policies of local governments from a national perspective, see George E. Berkley and Douglas M. Fox, *80,000 Governments: The Politics of Subnational America* (Boston: Allyn and Bacon, Inc., 1978).

2. See Thomas R. Dye, *Understanding Public Policy,* 2d ed. (Englewood Cliffs, N.J.: Prentice-Hall, Inc., 1975), pp. 188–92.

3. Alan L. Saltzstein, "City Managers and City Councils: Perceptions of the Division of Authority," *The Western Political Quarterly,* 27, no. 2 (June 1974): 275–88.

4. See Ronald O. Loveridge, *City Managers in Legislative Politics* (New York: Bobbs-Merrill Co., 1971).

5. For the impact of mayoral leadership in council-manager government (in Dallas), see Bruce Kovner, "The Resignation of Elgin Crull," in *Urban Government: A Reader in Administration and Politics,* rev. ed., Edward C. Banfield, ed. (New York: Free Press, 1969), pp. 316–21. For a very useful study of recent mayors of Texas' two largest cities, Houston and Dallas, see John P. Kotter and Paul R. Lawrence, *Mayors in Action: Five Approaches to Urban Governance* (New York: John Wiley & Sons, 1974).

6. See Richard D. Feld and Donald S. Lutz, "Recruitment to the Houston City Council," *Journal of Politics,* 34, no. 3 (August 1972): 924–33.

7. See Ronald G. Claunch and Leon C. Hallman, "Ward Elections in Texas Cities," *The Municipal Matrix,* 10, no. 1 (March 1978).

8. See Robert J. Macdonald, "Council-Manager Governments and Electoral Reform: Adaptation or Demise?" *Public Affairs Comment,* 23, no. 2 (February 1977).

9. See Philip W. Barnes, "Alternative Methods of Electing City Councils in Texas Home Rule Cities," *Public Affairs Comment,* 16, no. 3 (May 1970).

10. Barnes, "Alternative Methods of Electing City Councils," 1.

11. Actually, a number of council-manager cities (notably Dallas, San Antonio, and Austin) depart from the pure model by featuring direct election (instead of indirect selection by the council) of the mayor. Thus, these cities provide the structure of political leadership which is lacking in the usual council-manager arrangement.

12. Jorjanna Price, "Blacks 'Sold Bill of Goods': At-Large System Attacked," *Houston Post,* November 9, 1976, p. 18A.

13. Richard Murray and Arnold Vedlitz, "Race, Socioeconomic Status, and Voting Participation in Large Southern Cities," *Journal of Politics,* 39, no. 3 (November 1977): 1071n. Given this differential in voting among blacks of similar socioeconomic status in the same state, the authors speculate that voting participation among blacks is related more to local political organization than socioeconomic status.

14. See Leonard E. Goodall, *The American Metropolis* (Columbus: Charles E. Merrill Pub. Co., 1968), pp. 43–45.

15. The commission plan as outlined in the Texas statutes for adoption of home-rule cities is not actually the commission form since no provision exists to assign departments to members of the city council or commission. Carefully written home-rule charters may provide, however, for the commission plan.

16. John C. Bollens and Henry J. Schmandt, *The Metropolis: Its People, Politics, and Economic Life,* 3d ed. (New York: Harper & Row, Pubs., 1975), pp. 242–43.

17. John J. Harrigan, *Political Change in the Metropolis* (Boston: Little, Brown and Co., 1976), pp. 218–19.

18. See Stuart A. MacCorkle, *Municipal Annexation in Texas* (Austin: Institute of Public Affairs, University of Texas, 1965).

19. Wilbourn E. Benton, *Texas: Its Government and Politics,* 3d ed. (Englewood Cliffs, N.J.: Prentice-Hall, Inc., 1972), pp. 269–71.

20. U.S. Department of Commerce, Bureau of the Census, *1972 Census of Governments,* vol. 4, no. 4, *Finances of Municipalities and Township Governments* (Washington, D.C.: U.S. Government Printing Office, 1974), Table 9, p. 21.

21. See Figure 9–4 in Chapter 9.

22. For example, counties may establish, if they so decide, the office of county fire marshall and furnish firefighting personnel and equipment and inspection personnel. See Minor B. Crager, *Legal Aspects of Fire Prevention and Control in Texas* (Austin: Institute of Public Affairs, University of Texas, 1969), p. 34.

23. See Robert E. Norwood, *Texas County Government: Let the People Choose* (Austin: Texas Research League, 1970).

24. *Avery* v. *Midland County,* 88 S.Ct. 1114 (1968). See Minor B. Crager, "County Reapportionment in Texas," *Public Affairs Comment,* 17, no. 2 (March 1971).

25. Edwin S. Davis, "Texas County Judges and Commissioners: A Personal, Political and Attitudinal Profile" (Ph.D. diss., Texas Tech University, 1972), pp. 86–88.

26. Ibid.

27. See *Ops. Tex. Atty. Gen.* M–678 (1970) and M–1056 (1972).

28. *V.A.C.S., Election Code,* Art. 5.09a.

29. Compare Tables 9–2 and 9–4.

30. *Intergovernmental Notes,* no. 77–1 (Texas Advisory Commission on Intergovernmental Relations, January 1977), pp. 4–7.

31. Texas Research League, *The Texas Property Tax: Background for Revision* (Austin: Texas Advisory Commission on Intergovernmental Relations, 1973), p. 16.

32. Since repeal of the federal documentary stamp tax in 1968, Texas is one of a small number of states which has not passed legislation requiring that amounts involved in exchange of real property be divulged. Thus, no official or other reliable data on property values exist, rendering very difficult valuations of the class of property (real) which is taxed in Texas. As would be expected, data from real estate brokerage firms are also unavailable. Robert L. Lineberry, *Equality and Urban Policy: The Distribution of Municipal Public Services* (Beverly Hills, Calif.: Sage Pubs., 1977), p. 92, reports that in San Antonio local real estate multiple listing services "secreted their own data from tax authorities."

33. Texas Research League, *The Texas Property Tax,* p. 33 and "TRL Analyzes" (May 1978), pp. 2–3.

34. John A. Grounowski, "The Texas Property Tax: Ills and remedies," in proceedings of *The 63rd Texas Legislature Pre-Session Conference* (Austin: Lyndon B. Johnson School of Public Affairs, University of Texas at Austin, 1973), pp. 88–92.

35. U.S. Advisory Commission on Intergovernmental Relations, *Financing Schools and Property Tax Relief: A State Responsibility* (Washington, D.C.: U.S. Government Printing Office, 1973), p. 19.

36. The voluminous *Texas Education Code* governs school district creation, annexation, consolidation, and abolition.

37. Tax assessment and collection may depend in some local areas upon county assessment ratios and rates and collection.

38. See discussion of state education financial policy in Chapter 10, pp. 329–330.

39. Not tabulated are 45 "inactive" water districts that have legal existence but have never been organized to perform their water-related services. See Texas Water Rights Commission, *Thirty-third Report* (Austin: Texas Water Rights Commission, 1977), Table 12, p. A–56.

40. See John C. Bollens, *Special District Governments in the United States* (Berkeley: University of California Press, 1957), pp. 228–46 and *Handbook of Governments in Texas* (Austin: Texas Advisory Commission on Intergovernmental Relations, 1973, updated), "Special Districts and Authorities."

41. For discussion of establishment, governance, financing, and services of hospital districts and hospital authorities in Texas, see Texas Advisory Commission on Intergovernmental Relations, *Government and Personal Health,* vol. 2, *Responsibilities of Local and Regional Texas Government* (Austin: Texas Advisory Commission on Intergovernmental Relations, 1975), pp. 21–35.

42. For an excellent treatment of constitutional authorization, statutory authority, and governments of rural fire prevention districts, see Minor B. Crager, *Legal Aspects of Fire Prevention Control in Texas* (Austin: Institute of Public Affairs, University of Texas, 1969), pp. 37–38.

43. See *V.T.C.A., Water Code,* and *V.A.C.S.,* Art. 165a–4, Sec. 4 (1939).

44. *V.T.C.A., Water Code,* chap. 58.

45. See *Ops. Tex. Atty. Gen.* H–491 (1975).

46. U.S. Census Bureau, *1972 Census of Governments,* vol. 1, *Governmental Organization* (Washington, D.C.: U.S. Government Printing Office), Table 15.

47. The device of local or special legislation has a long and interesting history. See Texas Legislative Council, *Laws Based on Population,* Report No. 57–3 (Austin: Texas Legislative Council, 1962). For a muckraking account of the worst excesses of the local or special water district legislation scheme, see Harvey Katz, *Shadow On the Alamo: New Heroes Fight Old Corruption in Texas Politics* (Garden City, N.Y.: Doubleday & Co., Inc., 1972). chap. 9, "The Water District Conspiracies," pp. 160–73.

   Special legislation creating municipal utility districts (MUDs) by that name go back at least to the 59th Legislature in 1965. The title first appears in the general statutes in the *Water Code,* which was effective August 30, 1971. A special class of local legislation relating to water districts are statutes which validate all proceedings and actions ever taken in the creation and activities of MUDs and other types of water districts. These bills validate all proceedings of boards of directors, all bond elections, all annexations, and other activities, even if such actions and proceedings were illegal at the time taken. See, for example, *Vernon's Annotated Session Laws,* 62nd Leg., Reg. Sess., chap. 66, p. 701.

48. *The Houston Post,* January 21, 1973, p. 9A.

49. Candidate Frances Tarleton ("Sissy") Farenthold popularized the theme of privately controlled Texas governments (at all levels) in her bid for the gubernatorial nomination in 1972. Her candidacy was a reaction to water district, banking, and leadership corruption scandals, known collectively as the Sharpstown scandals.

50. See Amos Burton, "Dealing Dirt," *Texas Monthly,* 3, no. 6 (June 1975): 40–44.

51. See discussion of municipal annexation policy, earlier in Chapter 9.

CHAPTER TEN

1. An interesting and significant intergovernmental dimension of public revenues is that state government and each of the various classes of local governments depend substantially and in varying degrees upon different types of taxation. Local government revenues, including discussion of the property tax, are covered in Chapter 9, pp. 283–86; 292–99.

2. For historical and current statutory and administrative information about each Texas tax, including rates, new laws, tables of cases of litigation, and a tax calendar of payment and reporting schedules, see Commerce Clearing House, *State Tax Reporter,* 2 vols. (Chicago: Commerce Clearing House, 1967), looseleaf and current. An equally good service is provided by *Prentice-Hall State and Local Taxes, Texas* (Englewood Cliffs, N.J.: Prentice-Hall, Inc., 1969), looseleaf and current.

3. See *The Book of the States* (Lexington Ky.: Council of State Governments, biennial editions).

4. By categorical aid is meant aid to specific programs, like welfare, highways, correctional, and education.

5. See Legislative Budget Board, *Revenue Dedication, Special Funds, and Priority Allocation Practices,* 2 vols. (Austin: Legislative Budget Board, 1974), vol. 1, foreword.

6. For the specific funds which feed each of the agencies of state government, see the appropriations bills.

7. James W. Fesler, *The 50 States and Their Local Governments* (New York: Alfred A. Knopf, 1967), p. 397.

8. See Chapter 1, Table 1–2.

9. George D. Braden, *Citizens' Guide to the Proposed New Constitution* (Austin and Houston: Sterling Swift Pub. Co. and Institute of Urban Studies, University of Houston, 1975), p. 44.

10. Bob Bullock, *Texas Means Business!* Comptroller of Public Accounts, State of Texas, December 1977, p. 2.

11. Commerce Clearing House, *State Tax Reporter, Texas.*

12. See U.S. Advisory Commission on Intergovernmental Relations, *State-Local Taxation and Industrial Location* and *State-Local Finances: Significant Features and Suggested Legislation* (Washington, D.C.: U.S. Government Printing Office, 1972).

13. Ibid., pp. 78–79.

14. See discussion of the property tax in Chapter 9, pp. 296–99.

15. But see A. R. Schwartz and Oscar H. Mauzy, *A Consumer Viewpoint on State Taxation: An*

Analysis of Alternative Tax Proposals for the 62nd Legislature, 2d ed. (Austin: Texas Senate, March 31, 1971).

16. Caleb Perry Patterson, Sam B. McAlister, and George C. Hester, *State and Local Government in Texas* (New York: Macmillan Co., 1945), p. 191.

17. Bernard H. Booms and James R. Halldorson, "The Politics of Redistribution: A Reformulation," *American Political Science Review,* 67, no. 3 (September 1973): 924–33. See also Brian R. Fry and Richard F. Winters, "The Politics of Redistribution," *American Political Science Review,* 64, no. 2 (June 1970): 508–22 and Donald Phares, *State Local Tax Equity: An Empirical Analysis of the Fifty States* (Lexington. Mass.: D. C. Heath & Co., 1973), p. 78.

18. Stephen E. Lile, "Family Tax Burden Differences Among the States," *State Government,* 49, no. 1 (Winter 1976): 9–17.

19. See Dan Nimmo and William E. Oden, *The Texas Political System* (Englewood Cliffs, N.J.: Prentice-Hall, Inc., 1971), p. 141.

20. *Rodriguez* v. *San Antonio Independent School District,* 93 S. Ct. 1278 (1973).

21. In addition, the Texas Department of Health and the Department of Mental Health and Mental Retardation spend approximately $460,000 annually for medical and health services, including maternal and child health care, medical and dental screening, communicable disease control, community health services, and treatment and training of the mentally impaired.

22. Sar A. Levitan, *Programs in Aid to the Poor,* 3d ed. (Baltimore: The Johns Hopkins University Press, 1976), p. 30.

23. Texas Department of Community Affairs, Office of Economic Opportunity, *Poverty in Texas 1973* (Austin: Department of Community Affairs, 1974), pp. 31, 93.

24. As reported in the *Houston Post,* June 23, 1978, p. 15A.

25. With 13 percent of the work force below the poverty level, it is estimated that one fourth of all Texans may be eligible for food stamps. To receive food assistance, persons need not be drawing either AFDC benefits or federal assistance under the SSI programs. Although food assistance is relief, it is not a program of general relief as is found in most states. Texas does not have a general relief program.

26. Aaron Wildavsky, *The Politics of the Budgetary Process,* 2d ed. (Boston: Little, Brown & Co., 1974), p. 4.

27. The system of leadership brokerage of demands of a dominant coalition of economic interest is discussed in detail in Chapters 4 and 6, pp. 193–95.

28. An account of motives in the establishment of the legislatively managed Texas budget system is given in Vernon A. McGee, "A Legislative Approach to State Budgeting," *State Government,* 26, no. 8 (August 1953): 200–5.

29. Indeed, the governor's budget document has not often even been introduced in the legislature, and it has received little attention except in those occasional years when the chief executive has been able to develop broad public support for the recommendations.

30. See Peter A. Pyhrr, *Zero-Base Budgeting: A Practical Management Tool for Evaluating Expenses* (New York: John Wiley & Sons, 1973).

31. See James L. Weatherby, Jr., "The Role of the 'Free' Conference Committee in the Texas Budgetary Process, 1962–1973," *Public Affairs Comment,* 21, no. 2 (February 1975).

32. This entire process for creating a network of influence tied to the appropriations process is described in Glenn H. Ivy, "An Organizational structure for Gubernatorial Leadership," pp. 145–46 and in lurid detail in Katz, *Shadow On the Alamo,* pp. 147–50.

33. "How State Spending Grows During the Appropriation Process," *TRL Analyzes,* January 1972, p. 2.

34. Under the Speaker's rules of 1975, each substantive committee, rather than the House Appropriations Committee, reviews spending figures proposed for agencies under its oversight. In the legislative session of 1977, the cumulative spending additions of House committees added $400 millions more than the figure in the "skeleton budget." The strategy of positing spending decisions in the substantive committees of course strengthens the forces of localism and disintegration and makes the conference committee budget-making activities seem inevitable.

35. *Ops. Atty. Gen. Tex.* V–1254 (1951).

36. For initial reports, see Legislative Budget Board, *Performance Report to the Sixty-fourth Legislature* and *Performance Report to the Sixty-fifth Legislature* (Austin: Legislative Budget Board, 1975 and 1977).

37. See Allen Schick, *Budget Innovation in the States* (Washington, D.C.: Brookings Institution, 1971), pp. 213–14 for a discussion of advantages of a separate gubernatorial planning system which can be harnessed to a legislatively managed budget system, as in Texas, without the necessity of reshaping radically traditional budgetary processes. See also Ivy, "Organizational Structure for Gubernatorial Leadership."

Bibliography

CHAPTER ONE

Atlas of Texas. Austin: Bureau of Business Research, The University of Texas at Austin, 1976.

Conaway, James. *The Texans.* New York: Alfred A. Knopf, 1976.

Easton, David. *A Systems Analysis of Political Life.* New York: John Wiley & Sons, 1965.

Elazar, Daniel J. *American Federalism: A View From the States,* 2d ed. New York: Thomas Y. Crowell Co., 1972.

Elazar, Daniel J., and **Joseph Zikmund, II,** eds. *The Ecology of American Political Culture: Readings.* New York: Thomas Y. Crowell Co., 1975.

Katz, Harvey. *Shadow on the Alamo: New Heroes Fight Old Corruption in Texas Politics.* Garden City, N.Y.: Doubleday & Co., Inc., 1972.

Key, V. O., Jr. *Southern Politics in State and Nation.* New York: Vintage Books, 1949.

May, Janice C. *Amending the Texas Constitution.* Austin: Texas Advisory Commission on Intergovernmental Relations, 1972.

Pye, Lucian. "Culture and Political Science: Problems in the Evaluation of the Concept of Political Culture," *Social Science Quarterly,* 53, no. 2 (September 1972): 285–96.

Sharkansky, Ira. *The United States: A Study of a Developing County.* New York: David McKay Co., 1975.

Texas Almanac and State Industrial Guide. Dallas: A. H. Belo Corp., annually.

Todd, John R., and **Kay Dickenson Ellis.** "Analyzing Factional Patterns in State Politics: Texas, 1944–1972." *Social Science Quarterly,* 55, no. 3 (December 1974): 718–31.

Vernon's Annotated Constitution of the State of Texas. 3 vol. Kansas City: Vernon Law Book Co., 1955, updated.

Weinstein, Bernard L. "Why the Business Climate in Texas Is Rated No. 1." *Texas Business,* 1, no. 1 (July 1976): 27–30, 62.

CHAPTER TWO

Acuña, Rodolfo. *Occupied America: The Chicano's Struggle Toward Liberation.* San Francisco: Canfield Press, 1972.

Baird, Frank L. "An Anglo View of Mexican-Americans." *Public Service* (Lubbock: Center for Public Service, Texas Tech University), 1, no. 2 (February 1974).

Bonjean, Charles M. "The Chicano Experience in the United States." *Social Science Quarterly,* 53, no. 4 (March 1973): 652–942.

Campbell, Angus. *White Attitudes Toward Black People.* Ann Arbor: Institute for Social Research, The University of Michigan, 1971.

Kelley, Stanley, Jr., Richard E. Ayres, and **William G. Bowen.** "Registration and Voting: Putting First Things First." *American Political Science Review,* 61, no. 2 (June 1967): 359–73.

Nimmo, Dan, and **Clifton McCleskey.** "Impact of the Poll Tax On Voter Participation: The Houston Metropolitan Area in 1966." *Journal of Politics,* 31, no. 3 (August 1969): 682–99.

Texas Office of Economic Opportunity, Texas Department of Community Affairs. *Poverty in Texas.* Austin: Department of Community Affairs, 1972.

———. *Poverty in Texas 1973.* Austin: Department of Community Affairs, 1974.

CHAPTER THREE

Jacob, Herbert, and **Kenneth Vines,** eds. *Politics in American States,* 3d ed. Boston: Little, Brown, 1976.

Jones, Lee. "Game of Golf is a Key Time to Hit the Ball" (June 29, 1978), "Many Powerful Names Pop Up as Strongest Lobby." (June 30, 1978) in *The San Antonio Express.*

Key, V. O., Jr. *Southern Politics.* New York: Alfred A. Knopf, 1949.

Plano, Jack C. and **Milton Greenberg.** *The American Political Dictionary,* 4th ed. Hinsdale, Illinois: The Dryden Press, 1976.

CHAPTER FOUR

Council of State Governments. *American State Legislatures: Their Structures and Procedures,* rev. Lexington, Ky.: Council of State Governments, 1977.

Davis, J. William. *There Shall Also Be a Lieutenant Governor.* Austin: Institute of Public Affairs, University of Texas, 1969.

Declercq, Eugene. "Inter-House Differences in American State Legislatures." *Journal of Politics,* 39, no. 3 (August 1977): 774–85.

Holcombe, John W. "The Legislative Perceptions of Texas State Representatives: The Sixty-second Legislature." Ph.D. diss., Claremont Graduate School, 1972.

Jamison, Alonzo W. "The Education of a Legislator," in *Governing Texas: Documents and Readings,* 3d ed., Fred Gantt, Jr., Irving O. Dawson, and Luther G. Hagard, Jr., eds. New York: Thomas Y. Crowell, Co., 1974, pp. 141–47.

Lutz, Donald S., and **Richard W. Murray.** "Coalition Formation in the Texas Legislature: Issues, Payoffs, and Winning Coalition Size." *Western Political Quarterly,* 28, no. 2 (June 1975): 296–315.

Patterson, Samuel C. "American State Legislatures and Public Policy," in *Politics in the American States: A Comparative Analysis,* 3d ed., Herbert Jacob and Kenneth N. Vines, eds. Boston: Little, Brown and Co., 1976, pp. 139–95.

Purvis, Hoyt and **Rick Gentry.** "News Media Coverage of Texas Government: The State Capital Press Corps." *Public Affairs Comment,* 22, no. 2 (February 1976).

Texas Legislative Council. *Accomplishments of the Legislature.* Austin: Texas Legislative Council, biennially.

Texas Legislative Manual. Austin: Texas Legislative Council, 1971. looseleaf and updated.

Texas State Directory. Austin: Texas State Directory, biennial editions.

Rosenthal, Alan. *Legislative Performance in the States: Explorations of Committee Behavior.* New York: The Free Press, 1974.

Young, Stanley K. *Texas Legislative Handbook.* Austin: Texas Legislative Council, n. d.

Zeigler, Harmon, and **Michael Baer.** *Lobbying: Interaction and Influence in American State Legislatures.* Belmont, Calif.: Wadsworth Pub. Co., 1969.

CHAPTER FIVE

Benton, Wilbourn E. *Texas: Its Government and Politics.* 4th ed. (Chapter 8, "The Governor" and Chapter 9, "The Role of the Governor"). Englewood Cliffs, N.J.: Prentice-Hall, 1977.

Conner, Seymour V. *Texas: A History.* Northbrook, Ill.: AHM Publishing Co., 1971.

Gantt, Fred, Jr. *The Chief Executive in Texas.* Austin: The University of Texas Press, 1964.

Key, V. O., Jr. *Southern Politics.* New York: Alfred A. Knopf, 1950.

"Special Legislative Sessions in Texas: The Governor's Bane or Blessing?" *Public Affairs Comment.* Austin: Institute of Public Affairs, University of Texas, 16, no. 6 (November 1970).

Deaton, Charles, ed. *Texas Government Newsletter.* Austin: Deaton Press (1976–1978).

CHAPTER SIX

Beyle, Thad, and **J. Oliver Williams.** *The American Governor in Behavioral Perspective.* New York: Harper & Row, Pubs., 1972.

Dickson, James G., Jr. *Law and Politics: The Office of Attorney General in Texas.* Austin: Sterling Swift Pub. Co., 1976.

Gantt, Fred, Jr. *The Chief Executive in Texas: A Study in Gubernatorial Leadership.* Austin: University of Texas Press, 1964.

Handbook of Governments in Texas. Austin: Texas Advisory Commission on Intergovernmental Relations, 1973, updated.

Henderson, Bancroft C., and **T. C. Sinclair.** *The Selection of Judges in Texas: An Exploratory Study.* Houston: Public Affairs Research Center, University of Houston, 1965.

Ivy, Glenn H. "An Organizational Structure for Gubernatorial Leadership in Texas State Government." Ph.D. diss., University of Texas, 1970.

Morris, Charles J. "Everything You Always Wanted to Know About Public Employee Bargaining in Texas—But Were Afraid to Ask," *Houston Law Review,* 13, no. 2 (January 1976): 291–323.

Neuse, Steven M. "Texas State Administrators: A Partial Profile." *Public Affairs Comment,* 23, no. 2 (May 1977).

Nimmo, Dan, and **William E. Oden.** *The Texas Political System.* Englewood Cliffs: Prentice-Hall, Inc., 1971.

Public Employment. Washington, D.C.: Bureau of the Census, U.S. Government Printing Office, annually.

Texas Legislative Council. *Employment in State Government.* Staff Reports 60–4, 62–1, 63–1, and 64–1. Austin: Texas Legislative Council, January 1969, 1973, 1975, and 1977.

Texas Register. Austin: Office of the Secretary of State, weekly.

Texas Research League. *An Inventory of Texas' Basic State Personnel Statutes.* Austin: Office of the Governor, 1977.

Weinberg, Martha Wagner. *Managing the State.* Cambridge: The MIT Press, 1977.

CHAPTER SEVEN

"An Analysis of Juvenile Justice in Texas," a study conducted by the Lyndon B. Johnson School of Public Affairs, unpublished, 1976.

Bland, Randall W. *Constitutional Law in the United States: A Systematic Inquiry into the Change and Relevance of Supreme Court Decisions.* Minneapolis: Burgess Publishing Company, 1976.

Deaton, Charles, ed. *Texas Government Newsletter.* Austin: Deaton Press (1976–1978).

Richette, Lisa A. *The Throwaway Children.* Philadelphia: J. P. Lippincott Company, 1964.

CHAPTER EIGHT

Chance, Truett Lamar. "The Relation of Selected City Government Services to Socioeconomic Characteristics of Census Tracts in San Antonio, Texas." Unpub. Ph.D. diss., University of Texas, 1970.

Good Neighbor Commission of Texas. *Texas Migrant Labor: A Special Report.* Austin: Good Neighbor Commission, 1977.

Hawley, Willis D., and **Michael Lipsky,** eds. *Theoretical Perspectives on Urban Politics.* Englewood Cliffs, N.J.: Prentice-Hall, Inc., 1976.

Jackson, John E., ed. *Public Needs and Private Behavior in Metropolitan Areas.* Cambridge, Mass.: Ballinger Pub. Co., 1975.

Kotter, John P., and **Paul R. Lawrence.** *Mayors in Action: Five Approaches to Urban Governance.* New York: John Wiley & Sons, 1974.

Lineberry, Robert L. *Equality and Urban Policy: The Distribution of Municipal Public Services.* Beverly Hills, Calif.: Sage Pubs., Inc., 1977.

———. "The Impact of Municipal Reformism: A Symposium." *Social Science Quarterly,* 59, no. 1 (June 1978): 117–77.

Masotti, Louis H. and **Robert L. Lineberry,** eds. *The New Urban Politics.* Cambridge, Mass.: Ballinger Pub. Co., 1976.

Mladenka, Kenneth. "The Distribution of Urban Public Services." Unpub. Ph.D. diss., Rice University, 1975.

Ripley, Randall B. and **Grace A. Franklin.** *Congress, the Bureaucracy and Public Policy.* Homewood, Ill.: The Dorsey Press, 1976.

Texas Department of Community Affairs. *Annual Report.* Austin: Department of Community Affairs, annually.

Texas Rural Development Commission. *Building Rural Texas.* Austin: Rural Development Commission, 1973.

Texas Urban Development Commission. *Urban Texas: Politics for the Future.* Austin: Urban Development Commission, 1971.

374

CHAPTER NINE

Berkley, George E., and **Douglas M. Fox.** *80,000 Governments: The Politics of Subnational America.* Boston: Allyn and Bacon, Inc., 1978.

Handbook of Governments in Texas. Austin: Texas Advisory Commission on Intergovernmental Relations, 1973, updated.

Kotter, John P., and **Paul R. Lawrence.** *Mayors in Action: Five Approaches to Urban Governance.* New York: John Wiley & Sons, 1974.

Lineberry, Robert L. *Equality and Urban Policy: The Distribution of Municipal Public Services.* Beverly Hills, Calif.: Sage Pubs., 1977.

Loveridge, Ronald O. *City Managers in Legislative Politics.* New York: Bobbs-Merrill Co., 1971.

Municipal Year Book. Washington, D.C.: International City Management Association, annually.

Norwood, Robert E. *Texas County Government: Let the People Choose.* Austin: Texas Research League, 1970.

Texas Advisory Commission on Intergovernmental Relations. *Government and Personal Health.* Vol. 2, *Responsibilities of Local and Regional Texas Government.* Austin: Texas Advisory Commission on Intergovernmental Relations, 1975.

———. *Public Housing in Texas: Past, Present and Prospective.* Austin: Texas Advisory Commission on Intergovernmental Relations, 1974.

Texas Water Commission. *Report.* Austin: Texas Water Commission, biennially.

U.S. Bureau of the Census. *1977 Census of Governments.* Vol. 1, *Governmental Organization.* Washington, D.C.: U.S. Government Printing Office, 1978.

———. *City Government Finances.* Washington, D.C.: U.S. Government Printing Office, annually.

———. *County Government Finances.* Washington, D.C.: U.S. Government Printing Office, annually.

———. *Governmental Finances.* Washington, D.C.: U.S. Government Printing Office, annually.

CHAPTER TEN

Legislative Budget Board. *Fiscal Size–Up: Texas State Services.* Austin: Legislative Budget Office, biennially.

———. *Performance Report to the Sixty-Fourth Legislature.* Austin: Legislative Budget Office, 1977.

———. *Performance Report to the Sixty-Fifth Legislature.* Austin: Legislative Budget Office, 1977.

———. *Revenue Dedication, Special Funds, and Priority Allocation Practices.* 2 vols. Austin: Legislative Budget Office, 1974.

Levitan, Sar A. *Programs in Aid to the Poor,* 3d ed. Baltimore: The Johns Hopkins University Press, 1976.

Prentice-Hall State and Local Taxes, Texas. Englewood Cliffs: Prentice-Hall, Inc., 1969, updated.

Pyhrr, Peter A. *Zero-Base Budgeting: A Practical Management Tool for Evaluating Expenses.* New York: John Wiley & Sons, 1973.

State Tax Reporter. 2 vols. Chicago: Commerce Clearing House, 1967, updated.

Texas Comptroller's Office. *Financial Report.* Austin: Comptroller of Public Accounts, annually.

Texas State Department of Highways and Public Transportation. *Report.* Austin: State Department of Highways and Public Transportation, biennially.

Texas State Department of Public Welfare. *Report.* Austin: State Board of Public Welfare, annually.

Weatherby, James L., Jr. "The Role of the 'Free' Conference Committee in the Texas Budgetary Process, 1962–1973." *Public Affairs Comment,* 21, no. 2 (February 1975).

Index

This book has been set linotype in 9 point Helvetica, leaded 3 points, and 8 point Helvetica, leaded 2 points. Chapter numbers are 24 point and chapter titles are 20 point Avant Book.